EDWARD MEAD JOHNSON

FRANCIS COTES

Complete Edition
with a Critical Essay and a Catalogue

PHAIDON

Phaidon Press Limited, Littlegate House, St. Ebbe's Street, Oxford
First published 1976

Published with the help of a grant from
THE PAUL MELLON CENTRE FOR STUDIES IN BRITISH ART

ISBN 0 7148 1704 X

Printed in Great Britain
Text and monochrome illustrations printed by R. & R. Clark Limited, Edinburgh
Colour plates printed by Well Hall Press Limited, Bromley, Kent

FRANCIS COTES

Paul Sandby (*No.* 95). Oil, 1759. Tate Gallery, London

To Julie, Anne, and Mead

CONTENTS

ACKNOWLEDGEMENTS

I WISH especially to thank Dr. Robert Wark for directing this project as a Ph.D. dissertation; Professor Sir Ellis Waterhouse for making his files and library available, editing the catalogue, and advising upon the text; Mr. Frank Simpson for his invaluable assistance with sales records; the staffs of the Henry E. Huntington Library and Art Gallery, the Witt Library, the Frick Art Reference Library, and the Paul Mellon Centre for Studies in British Art for their interest and help; the owners of works by Cotes for their generosity with information; Dr. I. Grafe for editing; my wife, Julie, Miss Alexandra Leich, and Miss Mollie Luther for typing; and Miss Lizanne Davies for general assistance with the manuscript.

E.M.J.

London, 1976

INTRODUCTION: A CRITICAL ESSAY

WHEN Francis Cotes died in 1770 and his portraits were removed from the limelight of public exhibitions, his fame slowly faded into oblivion. His pictures settled into the depths of country houses or lay hidden in secluded London drawing rooms. It was not until the early twentieth century, when America came into prominence as an art market, that his works began to be widely noticed once again. There was a demand in America for British portraits, and the resulting boom in sales resurrected the reputations of many artists, Cotes among them.

In his case, however, what was brought before the public were a few genuine pictures and several hundred falsely attributed to him. Compared to the portraits of Gainsborough, Ramsay, Raeburn, and Reynolds, those of Cotes were good bargains. Their prices were considerably lower, and they usually had the touch of grandeur and charm that was wanted, but relatively few authentic examples came on to the market. Most were owned by families which could afford to keep them and saw no particular reason to sell them, since the monetary gain was minimal. Thus, the art trade was faced with a large demand for Cotes's portraits and a small genuine supply. The reputable firms accepted this situation, but the more unscrupulous dealers took advantage of it; they classified under the name of 'Cotes' practically any mid-eighteenth-century English portrait of unknown origin. As the chairman of the department of painting in one of the world's leading auction houses confided to the author, 'Let's face it, the name of "Cotes" became a generic term.' This was especially true in America, where portraits were passed off as having been painted by Cotes when they bore not the slightest relation to his style.

In the early 1930's scholars became seriously interested in the artist, but even the most important of these, Carl Winter,[1] was prevented from giving anything more than a brief sketch of his career by the lack of revealing historical documents and the discouraging dispersal of his works. Documents are still at a premium today; there are no sitters' books and relatively few significant letters. Most of the paintings and drawings, however, have been rediscovered with the assistance of the Witt Library, the Henry E. Huntington Library and Art Gallery, the Frick Art Reference Library, dealers, auction houses, and, most of all, through the generosity and interest of private owners.

Francis Cotes was born in London on May 20, 1726.[2] He was descended from an old Leicestershire family, the Coteses of Ayleston and Burbach.[3] During the Civil War, John Cotes, who took up the cause of Charles I, was deprived of his estate near Leicester after the King had been defeated by Cromwell, and fled to Ireland, where he settled in County Roscommon. His descendants retained their English identity and continued to distinguish themselves by their devotion to the Crown. It was not surprising, therefore, that John's grandson, Robert, was appointed mayor of the town of Galway by the English government. Robert was expected to deny to the Catholics in his community any significant political voice.[4] When he failed to advocate this policy, he was brought to trial for treason before the Irish Parliament in 1717. Shortly afterwards he also presented his case before Queen Anne's Council.[5] Both in Ireland and in London he was acquitted, but his political future was ruined, and he chose to remain in London, where he established his branch of the Cotes family.

The historian John Nichols states that Robert first married Anne, daughter of Nathaniel Fowler, of Prescot Street. She died on December 11, 1722, and their infant son, Robert, died in March 1723.[6] Robert's second wife was Elizabeth, daughter of Francis Lynn, whom Nichols describes as 'Secretary to the African Company'.[7] They were living in the Strand in 1726 when their first child, Francis, was born. In the parish register of St. Mary-le-Strand the following inscription records Francis's date of birth and baptism:

> May 20th, 1726. Francis Cotes, son of Robert
> and Elizabeth, Strand. Christened 29th May.[8]

After Francis, another child named Robert was born, but according to Nichols he 'died young'.[9] The next two children were Samuel, born in 1734, who became a famous miniature painter, and Frances Maria (birthdate unknown), who, according to Nichols, 'died in infancy'.[10]

The family moved to Cork Street, Burlington Gardens, in Mayfair. Edward Edwards, writing in 1808, said that Robert 'lived long in Cork Street'.[11] We know that by 1752, Francis, then just beginning his career, was using the Cork Street residence as a kind of gallery from which to sell prints after his own pastel portraits.[12] The urban environment in which Francis grew up had a definite effect on him. Just as Gainsborough developed a close identification with nature by living in the Suffolk countryside, Cotes absorbed the sophistication and sense of fashion that London had to offer.

His father's business in Cork Street was that of an apothecary.[13] The English apothecary in those days had a licence not only to sell drugs, but also to prescribe them. His career was referred to as that of 'Medicine',[14] and although he was never granted the title of doctor, he was held in high esteem.[15]

It is not unlikely that Francis's family background gave him certain attitudes and advantages which influenced him in later years. For example, his desire to obtain royal patronage may have been motivated, to some extent, by his family's long-standing tradition of service to the Crown. In addition, his father's business may have provided him with a form of specialized knowledge which was useful to him as a pastellist. From watching his father concoct medicines he could have derived a general appreciation for chemistry, which would have been particularly helpful to him when he began to make his own pastel crayons. The most important eighteenth-century treatise on the methods of making crayons was written by Cotes's pupil, John Russell, who acknowledged that he was expounding what he had learned from his master.[16] The procedures that Cotes and Russell followed were long and complicated. A thorough understanding of chemicals was necessary in order to achieve the desired shade and consistency of each crayon.

As far as can be determined, around the time of his fifteenth birthday Cotes entered the studio of George Knapton, a highly respected connoisseur and a competent artist.[17] Horace Walpole, a good judge of pictures himself, spoke of Knapton as an expert who possessed a 'thorough knowledge of the hands of good masters'.[18] Frederick, Prince of Wales, sought out the opinions of Knapton before permitting the royal collections to be catalogued.[19] In 1751, after the Prince's death, the Dowager Princess Augusta chose Knapton to do a large portrait of herself and her children, which is now at Marlborough House in London.[20] One of the sitters in this grandiose family picture was the future George III. When he ascended the throne in 1760, he continued to consult Knapton, as his father and mother had done, and in 1765 he appointed him to the important post of Surveyor and Keeper of the King's Pictures.

Knapton also counted among his patrons the Society of the Dilettanti, an exclusive club of wealthy connoisseurs who had been to Italy. They were to play an important part in the development of late eighteenth-century trade by sponsoring the publication of learned works on Greek and Roman art and architecture. The members were attracted to Knapton because he shared their interests. In 1740 he published one of the earliest accounts of the ruins at Herculaneum,[21] and from 1741 to 1749 he painted the portraits of the members of the Society.

Like so many of their countrymen, Knapton and the Dilettanti looked abroad for artistic inspiration, because at the time Britain offered little that could compare with the riches of continental painting and sculpture. Since the death of Van Dyck, portraiture, then the principal form of British art, had been dominated by men with large studios, first Lely, then Kneller, and, in the 1740's, Thomas Hudson and Allan Ramsay. With the exception of Ramsay, the others fell prey to the temptations of mass production. In order to turn out a large number of portraits, the master employed many assistants, especially men skilled in painting drapery. The master worked out a number of set poses and backgrounds that were popular with clients; usually he did the head, and the assistants finished off the drapery and background according to the particular formula chosen. This was a well-organized system for producing large quantities of stereotyped portraits. Those facets of the sitter's personality that did not fit into the stereotype, and stylistic innovations that were not sanctioned by the system, were generally neglected. The result was that British portraiture became repetitious and insular.

The most active source of foreign artistic influence was France. In the 1740's the rococo style had been spread in England by three prominent French artists, Hubert Gravelot, Philippe Mercier, and Louis François Roubiliac. It was then taken up by a significant group of forward-thinking British portraitists, among them William Hogarth, Joseph Highmore, Francis Hayman, and Thomas Gainsborough.[22]

As yet, the classical tradition of Italy was of comparatively little importance for most British painters. Excluding men like Allan Ramsay and George Knapton, it is fair to say that most British portraitists were unaware of the riches Italy had to offer. They were acquainted with the pastel portraits of Rosalba Carriera, which British tourists brought back from Venice, but they had slight knowledge of the classical antiquities in Rome or of the works of High Renaissance and Baroque masters. At this early date the union between the classical tradition and British portraiture had been realized by very few.

Pastel portraits had become very fashionable in the 1740's because it was known that many important people on the Continent had chosen to have their portraits done in pastels.[23] Maurice-Quentin de la Tour was internationally famous as the portraitist of the court of Louis XV, and most of the royal families of Europe had sat to Rosalba. A second factor that contributed to the popularity of pastel portraits was that they could be done rapidly.[24] The pastel medium was suited to capturing the momentary and fleeting aspects of a personality; it thrived on the intimate and informal. People accustomed to regarding portraits as occasions for highly dignified and grand displays were pleased to find a medium that could express the more personal and relaxed side of their nature, the 'moi intime' as the French called it.

George Knapton's pastels were influenced by those of Rosalba. He tended to emulate the soft, gentle qualities found in her portraits (figs. 1, 3). This is understandable since the English had been among Rosalba's earliest and most constant admirers.[25] Among the most famous of English tourists to visit her studio in Venice was Horace Walpole, who collected her works[26] and praised them highly in his writings.[27] Joseph Smith, the British Consul in Venice, was also one of her devoted patrons; in 1762 George III bought Smith's collection, which contained important pictures by Rosalba, including her late self-portrait, now at Windsor Castle.[28]

Knapton's style in oils is best illustrated by his charming portrait of THE HON. JOHN SPENCER AND HIS SON, JOHN, LATER IST EARL SPENCER, WITH THEIR NEGRO SERVANT, CAESAR SHAW (fig. 2). An unsophisticated, direct, almost naïve, observation of his sitters, combined with a rather wooden, stiff way of drawing figures, gives Knapton's work in oils a delightfully primitive air not nearly so noticeable in his pastels (fig. 1).

As soon as Cotes began to do pastel portraits in the late 1740's, it was apparent that, although young and inexperienced, he was extraordinarily talented. The immediate impression one gets from his earliest portraits, such as that of A GENTLEMAN (no. 1, fig. 4), is that he has made the best possible use of what Knapton had to offer, and then gone considerably beyond the capabilities of his master. His figures have the same slightly stiff, static nature as Knapton's. Like most artists of the 1740's, he conceives of the sitter as an harmonious aggregate of clearly distinct parts: the figure is precisely silhouetted against the background rather than being blended in with it, and the details of costume have a flashing, jewel-like individuality of their own. Having absorbed this concept of painting not only from his own provincial English tradition of the 1740's but also from the internationally popular Rococo, Cotes added certain stylistic traits which sprang forth from his own artistic personality. The first of these was an unerringly precise, though at this stage naïve, sense of line. There were, from the very beginning of his career, a sureness, a confidence, and a strength in his drawing that far surpassed anything in Knapton's pastels. One has only to compare the rather weak and flaccid pastel by Knapton of JOHN, IST EARL SPENCER, AND AN UNKNOWN CHILD (fig. 1) with Cotes's portrait of A Gentleman (fig. 4) to see the different viewpoints and talents of each artist. Where Knapton is soft and smooth, Cotes is firm and precise, taking much more inspiration from his master's oil style (fig. 2) than from his pastels (fig. 1). It is also important to note that in pastels Knapton preferred low-keyed colours, usually pale greys, blues, pinks, and browns; whereas in oils he was accustomed to using stronger shades. Unfortunately, the enhancing effect that he might have achieved by means of these more vibrant and vivacious colours was largely diminished by his flat, unimaginative way of laying on his paints, which did not permit any hint of self-expression or bravura in the brush-strokes. Cotes, in his pastels, managed both pale and strong colours with equal mastery, which immediately set him apart from Knapton. In his earliest known pastel, the portrait of A Gentleman (fig. 4), the sitter's coat is a strong, deep blue with a brilliantly rich resonance such as Knapton had never been able to achieve. At the collar and fastenings of the coat is a bright gold emblem in the form of a stag's head. The colouristic contrast Cotes sets up between the gold stag's head and the blue coat is intense and striking, and clearly illustrates his gift, at the earliest point in his career, for arranging high-keyed colours. Possibly one of the most important and intriguing aspects of his colours was their surprising strength. No English pastellist had ever used such bright colours so skilfully, and no eighteenth-century pastellist of any nationality so consistently attained the deep, rich tones of which Cotes was to prove himself capable.

We know from John Russell, Cotes's pupil in later years, that Cotes made his own pastel colours and applied them in a methodical fashion,[29] but whether he actually invented new ways of making and using pastel crayons is a question that is difficult to answer. Apart from Russell's book, *Elements of Painting with Crayons*, published in 1772, eighteenth-century literature on crayon painting in Britain gives only a vague notion of how Cotes's predecessors went about their art, nor, as yet, have chemical analyses of Cotes's own pastel portraits revealed anything of particular significance. It has been impossible, therefore, to determine from such sources how much he may have contributed to the technique of pastel painting. On the other hand, just by looking at his pastels, one can see that his colours have a deep, glowing quality and a brilliance that were new in Britain at the time. It is important for this reason to get an idea, even if a general one, of what he was doing with colour, and, in this respect, Russell in the *Elements of Painting with Crayons* is our best guide. He begins by saying:

> With respect to Crayon Painting, the present age has produced an uncommon instance of excellence in one of our own Countrymen, I mean the late Mr. Francis Cotes, whose Method I propose to explain in the following pages.[30]

Russell then goes on to propound Cotes's 'Method'. The pastellist first selects a strong blue paper, 'the thicker the better',[31] and removes all its lumps and knots by scraping it smooth with a razor. He then sketches in the outline of the figure and its features with a carmine crayon, adds the shadows, and works up the colours to the middle tones. This initial process is an extremely complicated one, because a wide range of colours is applied to different parts of the figure. For the interested reader, Russell gives detailed instructions on the drawing and initial colouring of the nose, eyes, cheeks, neck, hair, and drapery. When this phase has been completed, the artist applies paste to the back of his paper, and sticks the paper on to a stretched linen canvas. Here Russell observes:

> The advantages arising out of pasting the paper on the frame, according to this method, are very great, as the Crayons will adhere much better than any other way, which will enable the Student to finish the Picture with a firmer body of colour, and greater lustre. The late Mr. Cotes found out this method by accident, and esteemed it as a valuable acquisition.[32]

Russell then describes the final task of filling in the remaining details and bringing the colours up to the greatest brilliance possible. On the subject of attaining brilliant colour in this final phase he makes a particularly interesting and pertinent point. Following Cotes's tenets, he notes that brilliance will best be achieved if various layers of colour are permitted to show through or between one another.[33] This kind of interpenetration is especially suitable to pastels and produces depth, resonance, and scintillation in the coloured areas. As we shall see in studying Cotes's pastels more carefully, they offer the very finest examples of the use of this method and of the colouristic qualities it was designed to obtain.

In discussing Cotes's pastels, critics have been fond of linking his name with that of Rosalba Carriera. An anonymous writer for the March 1814 issue of *The Gentleman's Magazine* observed: 'Francis Cotes was called the Rosalba of England—he chiefly painted in crayons, and carried that branch of the art to the last point of excellence.'[34] Even earlier references of this sort come from Cotes himself, Russell, and Horace Walpole. In an essay on pastel painting which Cotes wrote between 1767 and 1770 (cf. Appendix IV), he ranked some of his own portraits, along with some by Rosalba, as among 'the finest examples that are known' of this type of art. Russell echoed Cotes's opinion:

> In what high estimation are the Pictures of Rosalba held? How happy do connoisseurs think themselves when they possess any of her works! If the Crayon pictures left by Mr. Cotes are not held in equal estimation, posterity will not do justice to his merit.[35]

Walpole also placed Cotes's pastels at a level of 'uncommon perfection', and he commented that 'if they yield to Rosalba's in softness, [they] excel hers in vivacity and invention'.[36]

Since Rosalba's portraits were admired and imitated by Cotes's teacher, George Knapton, and held in high regard by prominent English collectors and critics of the day, Cotes could not help but become acquainted with her style. Russell even records an instance in which Cotes restored one of her pictures:

> And, I remember, on a particular occasion, he (Cotes) removed a fine Crayon Picture of Rosalba's, and placed it on another strained cloth, without the least injury, by soaking the canvas with a sponge, till the paste between cloth and paper was sufficiently wet to admit of separation.[37]

Cotes's early portraits were definitely influenced by Rosalba, but he did not, as Knapton did, imitate her personal style. When he began his career in the late 1740's, Rosalba's head and shoulders portraits of ladies who exuded a kind of fey, airy elegance were enormously popular (e.g. fig. 3), and Cotes very wisely set out to work within the genre Rosalba had already established; however, his figures have a slight stiffness, literalness, and naïveté (figs. 5, 6, 7, 8), which contrast with the greater softness, suppleness, and lightness of Rosalba's (fig. 3). His forms are more clearly and precisely defined; there isn't the cosmetic haze, so typical of Rosalba, which dissolves contours and blends together shapes. The way in which the two artists used colour also set them apart. Rosalba was famous for having introduced bright, high-keyed colours into pastel painting, but her principal concern was in intermingling these colours in order to create an overall effect, a soft, misty look, which was flattering to her sitters and much in demand. Cotes, on the other hand, was interested in emphasizing the individual character of his forms and in stressing their differences. Colour for him, therefore, was not a force which integrated as much as it was one that separated. His earliest known portrait of a lady, the pastel of CATHERINE WILSON of 1747 (no. 2, fig. 5), illustrates his approach. He draws attention to parts rather than to the whole. One is made aware of the appearance and tactile qualities of each object he represents, the crisp, pink silk dress, the strange emerald brooch on the sleeve, the brown hair adorned with flowers, the creamy white skin, shining blue eyes, and red lips. There is a definite connection between Cotes's pastel colours and his communication of visual and tactile properties. Critics often speak of his fine sense of line, yet it is mainly colour that carries his message. His masterly use of colour as a means for communicating an empirical sense of objects is what gives his pastels that 'vivacity and invention' of which Walpole speaks, and differentiates them from Rosalba's work.

Considering his aptitude for empirical observation, it may come as a surprise to discover that in his early pastels he sacrificed both realism and character to fashionable stylization. The casual observer might be tempted to see in this evidence of a suppression of Cotes's natural gifts and a cowardly conformity to the dictates of society, but a careful study of his early pastels reveals that they are well-integrated works of art and show a remarkable simplicity and singleness of purpose. Their unifying factor is always the same, an elegance of style; only on very rare occasions did Cotes interest himself in a profoundly poetic or psychologically penetrating interpretation of his subject. Throughout his career he was fascinated by style for its own sake; it was the mirror of fashion rather than the mirror of the soul that attracted him.

The face in his early pastels is usually a good likeness, endowed with dignity and charm. It is pleasant without being too personal, a socially presentable face, not a private one. Its most important aspect, that which gives it life and interest, is its mode of stylization. The stylistic conventions used in his early pastel portraits (e.g. figs. 4, 5) were derived from Knapton, Rosalba, and the Rococo. Knapton's faces (figs. 1, 2) tended to be rather flat with schematically arranged features, like charmingly simple diagrams, which clearly related to individual persons, but were not realistically descriptive of them. Cotes's early pastels were structured in much the same way. He also borrowed Rosalba's practice of heightening the ornamental quality of the face by using intense, bright tones for the eyes and lips. His basic intention in painting the face was to make it the most fitting complement possible to the fashionable and beautifully coloured clothes of the sitter and an integral part of an essentially decorative composition.

In the late 1740's and early 1750's a small, doll-like face dominated by large eyes set far apart was particularly fashionable in portraits, and nearly all the ladies who came to sit to Cotes between 1747 and 1752 wanted to appear this way (figs. 5, 6, 7). Between about 1750 and 1752, even some of his male clients were portrayed in the same manner (fig. 8). Early and mid-eighteenth-century French rococo paintings offer numerous examples of this kind of stylization of the face. A Frenchman, Hubert Gravelot, popularized it in England, along with the rococo style, after his arrival in 1733. His designs for engravings produced while he was in Britain had a profound effect on the development of English art. He is said to have remarked to Basire, the engraver: 'De English may be very clever in deir own opinions, but dey do not draw.'[38] By the time he returned to France in 1746, he had taught the English his way of drawing. Most deeply influenced was a group of artists who expressed a natural affinity for the Rococo. The most eminent painters among them were William Hogarth, Francis Hayman, and Joseph Highmore. Their chief patron was Frederick, Prince of Wales, a man who had a refined artistic temperament and a predilection for all things French. As has already been pointed out, Frederick and Princess Augusta highly esteemed Cotes's teacher, George Knapton, and it was probably through Knapton that Cotes was introduced to the work of the artists in Frederick's circle. When one compares Cotes's pastel portraits done between 1747 and 1752 (figs. 5, 6, 7, 8) with designs by Gravelot (fig. 9) or paintings by artists in Frederick's group (figs. 10, 11), it becomes evident that he developed his use of the small, doll-like face out of the previously established tradition of rococo art in England.

Cotes's assumption of a rococo motif becomes more understandable if one views his early pastel portraits within the broader context of the rococo style itself. Basically, his approach to line, colour, and light was strongly influenced by the rococo aesthetic, which aimed not so much at representing the mass and solidity of objects as at transforming those objects into flat, decorative patterns that could be silhouetted directly against a background. This concept had appeared as the predominant feature in several major styles that preceded the Rococo, but what gave the Rococo its distinctive quality was the particular way in which pattern was treated. Forms were not arranged with geometric precision in a clearly perceived hierarchic order; their arrangement was asymmetrical or competely unpredictable. The important thing was not to create a rational order, but to give the surface of the paper or canvas a brightly coloured, shimmering appearance. Lines were free, light, delicate, and quick-moving, darting this way and that, and the intricate linear patterns so formed were picked out by local colours that were usually bright and vividly contrasting. The coloured areas were generally constructed in layers, with one layer showing through another, a method which made it possible for the artist to create patterns with colours as well as with lines. The outcome was a rapid alternation of light and shadow on the surface, which was characteristic of rococo painting.

In Cotes's pastels of the late 1740's and early 1750's rococo lighting effects, although usually present in portraits of men, are much more prominent in portraits of women, especially in the representation of the drapery. His female clients wanted themselves pictured in their best clothes and in the most fashionable manner, which, in mid-eighteenth-century England, was in the rococo style, and which, like most matters relating to feminine appearance, had been imported from France. The sumptuous fabrics in ladies' dresses and their elaborate construction made them eminently suitable for representation in the rococo manner.

Rococo lighting depended on the structuring of line and colour in certain specific ways. These ways, however, admitted of many different interpretations. Cotes's approach in his early pastel portraits of women (figs. 5, 6, 7) had the simplicity and the naïveté often found in the works of English artists of the 1740's and 1750's, as well as a unique quality of its own. For example, his representation of drapery folds, closely packed together, hard-edged, and slightly solid in appearance, recalls the style of Francis Hayman (fig. 10), and yet it is distinguished by a greater softness and subtlety. Hard-edged folds which look like undercut sculptural forms are by no means unusual in rococo painting. They were used because they produced a surface on which light would make sparkling reflections alternating with little shadows. On the Continent the most common custom was to arrange the drapery elegantly in fairly broad folds; this gave the figure a certain élan and dignity, whereas in English rococo painting, elegance often gave way to a stiff, doll-like charm. The drapery folds tended to be smaller and more closely packed together, and their relationship to sculptural forms was suggested in an amusingly literal way. This delightful primitivism is a quality Cotes inherited from the English rococo tradition.

The influence of the Rococo is also evident in his treatment of light in relation to colour in the representation of drapery in his early pastel portraits of women (figs. 5, 6, 7). The character of his colours has already been examined, but in this particular context it is important to remember Russell's observation that certain effects Cotes achieved depended upon 'one colour showing itself through, or rather between another'.[39] Clearly, he made use of this technique for doing highlights on female drapery. He gave these highlights an open, transparent, web-like structure that perfectly complemented the structure of the layers of colour beneath them, and, therefore, appeared to emanate naturally from the drapery and to project its qualities.

To forge a union between colour and light is exceedingly difficult, especially within the limits of stylistic conventions which present rigorous demands of their own. Like many early eighteenth-century English painters, Cotes had been taught that highlights were white, and should be used to form whitish patterns on top of the drapery. In other words, light was not conceived of as something which absorbed the colours of the surface it touched, but as an independent white substance. Cotes followed the traditional practice of using white highlights to form decorative surface patterns, but what set him apart from his English contemporaries was the mastery with which he applied these highlights. Although they were white, he was able to make them appear to partake of all the colours of the drapery beneath them. This was not achieved by any kind of rubbing or smearing, as was usually the case in the pastels of Knapton, Rosalba, and Russell, but by dusting on the highlights so finely that he could make the grains of white chalk separate wherever he wanted them to, in order to allow the stronger and more dominant colours of the drapery to show through.

In 1751 the sophistication and beauty of Cotes's work in pastels was recognized by his first important clients, the two most famous beauties of their day, Maria and Elizabeth Gunning. The Gunning family was Irish. John Gunning, a squire of modest means from Castlecoote, County Roscommon, had married the Hon. Bridget Bourke, daughter of Theobald, 6th Viscount Mayo. They had four children, Maria, Elizabeth, Catherine, and John, Jr. John Gunning was hopeless at business, so the family depended to a great extent on the financial support provided by Lord Mayo. When Lord Mayo became estranged from the Gunnings and withdrew his support, the family's finances reached a perilous state. As they were being thrown out of their house in Dublin, they were discovered by the actress, George Anne Bellamy, who took pity on them and helped them to get to England.[40] Soon after their arrival, the extraordinary beauty of the two eldest girls attracted considerable attention, and it wasn't long before they were regarded as the most attractive women in England. Maria married the Earl of

Coventry, and Elizabeth the Duke of Hamilton and Brandon, and later the Duke of Argyll. In 1751 Horace Walpole described the two sisters:

> These are the two Irish girls of no fortune who are declared the handsomest women alive. I think their being two, so handsome and both such perfect figures, is their chief excellence, for singly I have seen much handsomer women than either: however, they can't walk in the park, or go to Vauxhall, but such mobs follow them that they are generally driven away.[41]

In the following year Walpole wrote of Elizabeth, then the Duchess of Hamilton and Brandon:

> The world is still mad about the Gunnings: the Duchess of Hamilton was presented on Friday (March 12, 1752). The crowd was so great, that even the noble mob in the Drawing Room clambered upon chairs and tables to look at her. There are mobs at their doors to see them get into their chairs; and people go early to the theatres when it is known they will be there.[42]

How the Gunnings came upon Cotes in London is a mystery. Possibly they had known of his family in Ireland, and were given his name when they came to London. Whatever the case may be, they liked his work, and commissioned numerous pastel portraits from him. He did pastels of each member of the family, John (no. 17), Bridget (no. 12), Maria (no. 19, fig. 6), Elizabeth (nos. 16, 31), Catherine (nos. 15, 33, Supplement no. 7), and John, Jr. (no. 18). The most important of these, as far as Cotes's career was concerned, were the portraits of Maria and Elizabeth (no. 19, fig. 6; no. 16) of 1751, both of which were engraved by James McArdell in 1752. The picture of Elizabeth was also engraved by James Houston. The McArdell engravings were advertised on the front page of *The London Advertiser* for April 6, 1752, and the reader was informed that they could be bought only from Cotes himself at his residence in Cork Street. The trade in these prints was lively, because the public were eager to possess likenesses of the renowned Gunning sisters, and the price was within their reach. Some twenty years earlier Hogarth had taught British artists that prints done after their own paintings provided an excellent form of publicity and generally reaped a financial return which far exceeded the cost of the original works. Cotes had learned this lesson well. The prints made after the portraits of Maria and Elizabeth were of enormous benefit in establishing his reputation in London, and from 1752 onwards he never ceased to take advantage of prints, working throughout the course of his career with nearly every major print-maker in England.

A question that arises out of a study of the early years of Cotes's career is: Did he confine himself to pastel portraits, or did he work in oils as well? His teacher, Knapton, worked in both media, so Cotes probably received some basic training in the use of oil paints, but his first known oil portrait was not painted until 1753. This was the signed and dated portrait of A LADY (no. 47, fig. 12), a disappointing picture, which lacks the confident touch and the liveliness of his pastels, even though he was, in this instance, clearly trying to translate his pastel techniques into oils, and may even have modelled his painting on a pastel he did in the same year (no. 46, fig. 13). This initial attempt at an oil portrait proved something of a failure, and he did not try his hand again at oils until 1757.

Meanwhile, he continued to work as a pastellist, and around 1755 he made some significant alterations in his style. He not only began to concentrate more on the mass and solidity of the figure, but also on the personalities of his sitters. For the first time we see his sitters represented as individuals, rather than as examples of a fashionable, rococo type of stylization. They have their own particular shapes and their own characteristic attitudes.

Actually, this development in Cotes's work was part of a much broader movement in pastel portraiture, which had been initiated on the Continent by the successors of Rosalba Carriera. Around 1746 Rosalba succumbed to blindness and was forced to stop painting. The leadership among pastellists then passed to several other artists, all of whom contributed to the creation of a new trend in pastel portraiture. There was Anton-Raphael Mengs in Dresden, Maurice-Quentin de la Tour and Jean-Baptiste Perronneau in France, and the Swiss, Jean-Etienne Liotard, an itinerant artist, who wandered throughout Europe and the Middle East. These men placed much more emphasis than Rosalba on solidity of form and on individual personality. They led pastel portraiture away from an almost complete dependence on decorative style, and set it on a course towards greater realism.

Cotes was the first English pastellist to absorb their ideas fully. He was introduced to the new fashion by Liotard, who visited England from 1753 to 1755/56. During his English visit Liotard attracted great attention by walking about in bizarre, oriental costumes, and by what was then considered to be the uncompromising realism of his portraits. Walpole remarked in amazement:

> His likenesses were as exact as possible ... he could render nothing but what he saw before him.... Truth prevailed in all his works.[43]

Liotard's utter clarity of vision, his sense for solid form, and his realism are well illustrated by his portrait of LADY MARY FAWKENER (fig. 15). Cotes's reaction to Liotard is evident in his pastels of the middle and late 1750's, like those of ELIZABETH HULSE (no. 56, fig. 14) of 1755, and ROBERT COTES, the artist's father (no. 75, fig. 17), of 1757, in which he treated the faces more realistically than was his previous custom and gave the figures greater weight. The portrait of Robert Cotes is particularly interesting, because it is very similar to certain pastels by Mengs (fig. 16) and La Tour (fig. 19), and shows how closely Cotes identified with the new international trend in pastel portraiture.

Another result of Cotes's identification with this trend, and especially with the work of Liotard, was the introduction of action into his portraits. Generally, the action has to do with some ordinary occupation shown in a domestic or business setting. For example, just as Liotard painted Lady Fawkener drawing a thread from her sewing box, Cotes represented SIR RICHARD HOARE holding pen and paper, pausing for a moment to collect his thoughts before going on with the writing of a letter (no. 76, fig. 21) and TAYLOR WHITE, the Treasurer of the Foundling Hospital, going over the hospital's accounts (no. 86, Pl. 1).

Strangely enough, the fact that Cotes identified with the new trend in pastels made it much easier for him to make contact with recent developments in British oil painting. In the late 1750's the man principally responsible for the dominant fashion in British oil portraiture was Allan Ramsay, who had been deeply influenced by the pastels of La Tour and Perronneau. In 1755 Ramsay stated his admiration for La Tour in a treatise called *Dialogue on Taste*. The characters in the *Dialogue* are Lord Modish and his friend, Colonel Freeman. Lord Modish remarks that the rules for the criticism of the arts are not as widely known as Colonel Freeman would like to think, to which the Colonel replies by suggesting an experiment:

> Your Lordship has only to hide yourself behind the screen in your drawing room and order Mrs. Hannah to bring in one of your tenants' daughters, and I venture to lay a wager that she shall be struck with your picture by La Tour, and no less by the view of your seat by Lambert, and shall, fifty to one, express her approbation by saying they are vastly natural. When she has said this

1 *Taylor White* (No. 86). Pastel, 1758. Thomas Coram Foundation for Children, London

> she has shown that she knew all the proper standards by which her approbation was to be directed as much at least as she would have done if she had got Aristotle by heart, and all his commentators. He has defined those arts as arts of imitation, and his definition, though often obscured and confounded by modern connoisseurs, has never been contradicted in any way.[44]

Ramsay, along with many other eighteenth-century writers, thought that the ultimate test of whether an artist had successfully imitated nature was to subject his work to the scrutiny of the common man, whose mind was conceived of as pure, natural, and uncluttered by the debris of an over-sophisticated education. If the artist presented nature simply and vividly, then the common man was sure to understand it. The theory was that the natural man would respond to natural art. Ramsay considered La Tour's pastel images 'vastly natural', because they were down to earth, direct, and empirical. Despite the fact that they were highly sophisticated portraits of some of the most cultivated people of the age, anyone, including the common man, could react to them on a basic human level.

Ramsay's enchantment with the 'natural' portraits of La Tour and the other continental pastellists of the day became a dominant factor in his own work from the mid-1750's onwards. As early as 1754 he was concentrating less on grand and dramatic pictures and more on the casually elegant and intimate type of image popularized by Rosalba's successors. To bring himself closer to their style, he even used oil paints to imitate the soft, diffuse tints of pastels.

It was in this frame of mind that he wrote the *Dialogue on Taste*, and then departed for Italy, not returning to London until the summer of 1757. He brought back a deeper appreciation of certain elements of classical taste, which he used in combination with the naturalism of La Tour and Perronneau. From a study of seventeenth-century baroque masters, like Domenichino, he had gained a renewed awareness of the quiet serenity, grace, and harmony of forms in classical compositions, as well as a more profound understanding of the use of light and shadow as unifying elements within these compositions. It is this fusion of the naturalism of pastels, particularly French pastels, with aspects of Italian art, which characterized Ramsay's work, and which was the basis for the type of portraiture he popularized upon his return.

His only serious rival in Britain was Joshua Reynolds, who had been in Italy from 1749 to 1752, and had also been deeply affected by the experience. Reynolds had been especially attracted to the Roman classicism of Raphael and Michelangelo. Idealized history painting seemed to him to be the epitome of artistic endeavour, and he dreamed of somehow grafting history painting onto English portraiture. He also saw the traditional academic hierarchy, in which ideal painting was most valued, as a proven means of placing different forms of art in an intelligible order. When he returned to England, he set about elevating portraiture to the level of history painting and laying the ground work for a system of art education that was to dominate the future Royal Academy in the years to come.

The rivalry between Ramsay and Reynolds became intense after Ramsay came back from Italy in 1757. Until about 1762 Ramsay proved to be the stronger. There were two principal reasons for his supremacy. First of all, his aims for British portraiture were not as revolutionary as those of Reynolds, and therefore, were accepted more quickly by the public; secondly, Ramsay was able to secure the powerful patronage of the royal family, and Reynolds was not. Reynolds, being a highly practical man, adapted himself to Ramsay's aesthetic and began painting in the same vein. As a result, the majority of pictures that these two artists produced between 1757 and 1762 were very closely related, with Ramsay often providing the guiding inspiration.

A typical example of Ramsay's work, and one that is characteristic of the period, is the lovely portrait of his wife, MARGARET LINDSAY (fig. 20). Here we see the intimacy and directness of La Tour's images, the soft colouring reminiscent of pastels, a perfect balancing of forms, and a marvellous use of light. The last two attributes deserve special attention, because they gave English oil portraits a distinctive appearance, which was partially assimilated by Cotes. Unlike rococo painting, flat, decorative pattern is here subordinated to form. The solidity of the figure, the vase of flowers, and the window shutter, is of paramount importance, while the patterns formed by the outline of the figure, the lace, and the flowers are of secondary value. The forms themselves are presented clearly and simply; they are large and few in number, and their shapes and weights are brought into a tightly ordered, symmetrical composition that has the carefully balanced precision one finds in classical architecture. Nor is light used as in rococo painting; its primary function is not to make surfaces sparkle or to enrich patterns, but to blend together the forms in the composition. Its particular relevance in portraiture is that it unites the figure with its surroundings, so that the figure becomes very much an integral part of a scene rather than a favoured object silhouetted against an interesting backdrop.

In 1757 Cotes became intensely interested in this style; its effect on him can be seen in the pastel of SIR RICHARD HOARE (fig. 21), where the composition and lighting were influenced by oil paintings of the period; for example, by Ramsay's portrait of Margaret Lindsay (fig. 20). In each picture the simple shape of the figure is boldly contrasted with the architectural shape of a window shutter, and the forms in the foreground and background are brought into a unified, coherent relationship by means of light and shadow. In the pastel of Sir Richard Hoare, however, light and shadow do not reduce the silhouette to the extent that they do in the portrait of Margaret Lindsay. Cotes still insisted on maintaining as much of the ornamental quality of his style as possible. This meant that he had to retain a good deal of the silhouette, and had to draw special attention to decorative details of costume and decor, like the gold trim on the frock coat and waistcoat and the floral pattern on the wallpaper. In other words, in 1757 he combined elements of a style that was fashionable in oil portraiture with his own essentially decorative orientation, which he had developed out of his experience with the Rococo in the late 1740's and early 50's. In making this combination, he brought British pastel and oil portraiture into a close relationship, and set a precedent for the imitation of the appearance of oil portraits in pastels, just as Ramsay had set a precedent for the imitation of the appearance of pastel portraits in oils. From their own vantage points, therefore, Cotes and Ramsay created a common set of stylistic aims which could be shared and interpreted by both pastellists and oil painters.

This closeness between British pastels and oils in the late 1750's was a deciding factor in persuading Cotes to try his hand once again at oil portraiture, because the distance he had to travel between what was fashionable in pastels and in oils was not as great as it had been formerly. The half-lengths and three-quarter lengths that he painted in oils in the late 1750's were closely related to contemporary trends in both pastels and oils, and were considerably better than his portrait of A Lady (fig. 13) of 1753. The most important picture in this series, and one of the finest he ever painted, is the portrait of PAUL SANDBY (no. 95, frontispiece) of 1759, which is very pastel-like in appearance, as he was attempting to follow Ramsay's example of making oil paints create effects generally associated with pastels. The composition and the lighting are of a type that was popular at the time in both media, and they clearly recall earlier precedents, especially Ramsay's oil portrait of Margaret Lindsay (fig. 20) of about 1754, and Cotes's own pastel portrait of Sir Richard Hoare (fig. 21) of 1757.

In 1760 Cotes exhibited his work publicly for the first time at the initial show of the Society of

Artists. To appreciate the atmosphere of the Society's exhibitions it should be recalled that the rooms generally had high ceilings, that the paintings covered most of the wall space, and that sculpture was crammed in wherever possible. To make a work stand out from this chaotic background and to attract the attention of the jostling crowd was a considerable feat in itself. For example, size was obviously an important factor; large paintings and sculptures could at least be easily spotted, and they looked impressive. The choice of subject matter was crucial. Portraiture was the most popular, and portraits of famous people were readily noticed. Virtuosity was also much admired; if an artist demonstrated that he could work with different styles or in different media, he would almost certainly win over the gullible public, who were easily persuaded to prefer one who did many things tolerably well to one who did a single thing magnificently.

The dominant artist in the exhibition rooms for the entire decade was Reynolds. Ramsay did not choose to exhibit publicly, so, in the public arena at least, Reynolds was never seriously challenged. At the 1760 exhibition of the Society of Artists he won great acclaim. He showed a pair of charming bust-length portraits of LADY ELIZABETH KEPPEL and GENERAL KINGSLEY, and, for contrast, a pair of large full-lengths, a dashing military portrait of LORD VERNON in the manner of Van Dyck, and a grand portrait of THE DUCHESS OF HAMILTON AS VENUS (fig. 22). Historically, the most important of these pictures was that of The Duchess of Hamilton. It was the first time Reynolds had used the type of classically inspired draperies that he had invented for grand portraits of ladies. This picture also illustrated the union of history painting and portraiture that he had devised and would try to make fashionable through the Society's annual exhibitions. The Duchess (Elizabeth Gunning) is shown standing, full length, beside a classical relief of the Judgement of Paris, with the doves of Venus perched in the background. The mind of the beholder, stimulated by the classical associations provided, was to rise from the contemplation of the beauty of the Duchess to the contemplation of Ideal Beauty.

In 1760 Cotes exhibited four portraits, two pastels and two oils. The Society's catalogues which relate to Cotes are reproduced here in Appendix III, along with Horace Walpole's notations. Only two of the portraits Cotes showed in 1760 were identified in the catalogue. The first of these was a pastel of SIR EDWARD HULSE, 1ST BT. (no. 77, fig. 18), the Physician-in-Ordinary to Queen Anne, George I, and George II. The picture is a fine example of the greater realism which affected Cotes's pastel portraiture in the late 1750's as a result of his contact with Liotard. The portrait, calculated to show his skill in pastels and to attract attention by means of the sitter's status, was well liked. After the exhibition Cotes had an engraving in mezzotint made after it by James Watson, clearly intended to capitalize on the success in the showroom.

The second picture was an oil described in the catalogue as that of 'a Young Lady in the Character of Emma, or the Nut-Brown Maid'. This was the portrait of ANNE SANDBY (no. 96), born Anne Stogden, the wife of Paul Sandby, which Cotes had done in 1759, possibly as a pendant to his oil painting of her husband (no. 95, frontispiece) of the same year. The portrait of Anne Sandby has been lost, and is only known through the engraving in mezzotint which Edward Fisher made after it and published in 1763 (fig. 23).

Fisher's engraving is worth studying because it reveals how far Cotes was from the sentiments and style of Reynolds's portrait of The Duchess of Hamilton as Venus (fig. 22), the principal picture exhibited in 1760. Anne Sandby was shown in the role of Emma from Matthew Prior's poem, *Henry and Emma*, which was based on one of the most popular themes in rococo literature and art, the triumph of love, the supreme power in the universe, over all other powers.[45] The style of the picture, as far as we can judge from Fisher's engraving, seems also to have been very deeply influenced by rococo precedents. The costume Cotes chose for Mrs. Sandby was a contemporary one, very decolleté to reveal her charms. He posed her in front of a pretty landscape setting, and showed her in the act of hanging on the bough of a tree a wreath made of flowers and her lover's hair. The image conveyed was of an amorous lady of fashion acting out a delightful role; it followed the tradition, previously established by Jean-Marc Nattier at the court of Louis xv, of painting ladies selfconsciously portraying characters from popular poems and plays of the period. After its first publication in 1709, Prior's *Henry and Emma* had enjoyed an intense and prolonged popularity. The second edition, put out in 1718, was translated into Latin in 1748, German in 1753, and French in 1764, and parts of it were set to music by Thomas Arne in 1749, and by Sir Henry Bates Dudley in 1774. A picture like that of Anne Sandby was certain to attract attention and win approval, and one cannot escape the conclusion that Cotes had this in mind when he exhibited it in 1760. As far as its content and style were concerned, however, it was the antithesis of the trend towards classicism and idealized painting that Reynolds was trying to bring to the fore.

An interesting feature of the painting of Anne Sandby is the presence of a landscape background. Landscapes are rare in Cotes's work before 1760. The most notable examples appear in his earliest known double portrait, the pastel of JOHN AND JOSEPH GULSTON (no. 52, fig. 24) of 1755, and his oils of Paul and Anne Sandby (frontispiece and fig. 23) of 1759. He also did a watercolour drawing of a landscape, the VIEW OF PURLEY HALL (no. 71, fig. 25) of 1756, now at the Victoria and Albert Museum.

There is no evidence to suggest that these landscapes were painted by anyone but Cotes; in fact, he seems to have enjoyed painting landscapes as a hobby. The catalogue of the sale of his property after his death, reproduced here in Appendix II, tends to confirm this. The pertinent lots read as follows:

> Lot 33, A view of the Isle of Wight by ditto [Cotes].
> Lot 48, Two views in water colours by F. Cotes.
> Lot 55, A view of Netly Abbey by F. Cotes.
> Lot 56, The west view of ditto by ditto.

As these watercolour drawings, mainly 'views' like that of Purley Hall (fig. 25), were sold by the artist's widow and executors at a public auction, there is little likelihood that they were incorrectly attributed to him in the sale catalogue.

The various works by Cotes from the 1750's that include landscape painting have certain traits in common. The landscape is always carefully designed in a decorative manner. The foreground, middle-ground, and background are marked off by an exact geometric arrangement into clearly distinct areas. The outlines of the forms are exploited for their decorative silhouettes, and the lines are light and delicate, especially in the representation of a feathery foliage. The tree trunks are dainty and elegant and beautifully coloured to accentuate the varying textures of bark and moss. The colours are soft and pastel-like.

An outside influence apparent in Cotes's landscape style comes, appropriately, from Paul Sandby, the master of the type of view illustrated by the watercolour of Purley Hall. Cotes was well-acquainted with the Sandby family, and painted Elizabeth Sandby, Paul's sister-in-law, in 1755 (no. 58), Paul and Anne in 1759 (no. 95, frontispiece; no. 96, fig. 23), and Anne again in 1765 (no. 183, fig. 82).

He probably had ample opportunity to study Paul's work. Comparing Cotes's View of Purley Hall (fig. 25) with Sandby's VIEW OF ROCHESTER (fig. 26), possibly a later drawing than the Cotes but an example of essential qualities Sandby maintained throughout his career, one can see what Cotes probably took from Sandby: the schematic arrangement of the landscape, the feathery foliage, and the way of drawing precise, neat little figures. Sandby's lines, however, are much firmer and stronger than Cotes's, and his colours more definite. Cotes's approach to both line and colour was finer, softer, smoother, in fact, exactly what one would expect of a pastellist.

After the Society of Artists' show of 1760, Cotes's oil paintings of the next three years were strongly influenced by his desire to compete with Reynolds at public exhibitions. Confronted with Reynolds's mastery of a wide range of styles and portrait types, Cotes decided very wisely to limit himself to those kinds of pictures in his rival's repertoire which he could easily master at this stage of his career: pictures of ladies or gentlemen posed in outdoor settings and military portraits, always eliminating idealization and any intellectual content derived from the classical tradition. Within these two broad categories he usually adopted a basic formula that had previously been established by Reynolds. Typical of his work in oils between 1761 and 1763 are his paintings of ELIZABETH ADAMS (no. 103, fig. 28), HENRY PAULET, 6TH DUKE OF BOLTON (no. 109, fig. 30), and LIEUTENANT-COLONEL ALEXANDER CAMPBELL (no. 123, fig. 31). These were based on precedents by Reynolds, such as the portraits of LADY ANSTRUTHER (fig. 27), REAR-ADMIRAL RODNEY (fig. 29), and CAPTAIN AUGUSTUS HERVEY (fig. 32).

Although Cotes followed the fashions set by Reynolds, his interpretation was quite different. Reynolds subordinated line and colour to the creation of an harmonious overall effect; Cotes preferred to isolate particular features and to draw attention to them for their decorative value. This is especially apparent in the way in which he preserved much of the silhouette of the figure so that one could enjoy its elegant outline against the background, in his use of strong, bright, local colours, and in his emphasis upon the intricate details of an elaborate dress, smart uniform, or florid background setting.

The oil portraits Cotes did between 1761 and 1763 are important for an understanding of his work, because during this period he developed a way of painting that depended mainly on a knowledge of the oil medium rather than on his past experience with pastels; he also hoped to give his pictures in oils a stronger appearance, since Reynolds was famous for his bold manner of painting. For inspiration and instruction he evidently turned to his early training in oils as a student, and to the oil paintings of his teacher, George Knapton. He no longer arranged colours so that one layer showed through another, but adopted Knapton's practice of simply putting one layer on top of another, which resulted in clearly defined areas of a single colour that were flat and monotonous in appearance. In order to make his oil paintings more striking he followed the concept that the more paint one applied, the bolder the picture would become. This, in fact, did occur, but, as a result, his colours became denser and harder, and he was forced to sacrifice much of the subtlety and sophistication that characterized his pastels and the best of his early oils, like that of Paul Sandby (no. 95, frontispiece).

Stylistically, he retained many of the rococo features of his previous work, but occasionally these took on a slightly different look. For example, in his oil painting of LADY FORTESCUE (no. 113, fig. 33), one finds the same type of hard-edged drapery folds and whitish highlights that he had used so frequently in his pastels (figs. 6, 7), but their appearance is now quite different. Colours are more sharply defined and separated. This is especially noticeable in his treatment of the highlights, which in the oil painting seem to be separated from the drapery, like a structure imposed on top of it, rather than reflecting from it and blending with it, as in the pastels.

In 1763 or 1764 Cotes began to employ an assistant to help him with the painting of draperies in his oil portraits. His name was Peter Toms, and he remained in Cotes's service until the latter's death in 1770. Toms had little, if any, influence on Cotes's way of painting drapery. By the time he joined Cotes, the master had already formulated the essential elements of his style, and Toms merely imitated these. It is true that Cotes developed his drapery painting between 1763/1764 and 1770, but this development proceeded coherently out of his previous work, and its course was not altered by Toms.

Toms had originally worked for Reynolds as a drapery assistant at Great Newport Street,[46] where Reynolds lived between 1753 and 1760. Edward Edwards mentions one portrait with which Toms assisted:

> Among the pictures which he [Toms] did for Sir Joshua, are some very excellent; and candour must allow, that many of Sir Joshua's best whole-lengths are those to which Toms painted the draperies. Among these was the picture of Lady Elizabeth Keppel, in the dress she wore as bridesmaid to the Queen.[47]

Unfortunately there is no other reference to a painting on which Toms worked, and beyond showing Toms's talent for painting the elaborate court dresses fashionable in the early 1760's, the portrait of ELIZABETH KEPPEL (fig. 34) is not particularly helpful, because Toms subordinated himself completely to the style of Reynolds and left no traces of his own personality.

Of his work for Cotes Edwards relates:

> At the time the late Duke of Northumberland went as Lord Lieutenant to Ireland, Mr. Toms went in his suite to Dublin, in hopes of being employed as a portrait painter: Not meeting with the success he hoped for, he soon returned to London, where he again resumed his profession, and was almost wholly employed by Mr. Cotes.[48]

The 'late Duke of Northumberland' referred to here was the first Duke, Sir Hugh Smithson, who held the post of Lord Lieutenant of Ireland from 1763 to 1765. Judging from Edwards's account, Toms accompanied the Duke to Ireland, but 'soon returned' to London and began working for Cotes. This would have been in 1763, or possibly 1764.

Apart from his employment of an assistant, another indication of Cotes's growing success during these years was his purchase of the lease of 32, Cavendish Square. We have no idea how much Cotes paid for the lease, but it was probably a substantial sum, because Cavendish Square was extremely fashionable, and the house was quite spacious. The lease dates from 1763,[49] and by 1765, no. 32, Cavendish Square was given as Cotes's address in the Society of Artists' catalogue (cf. Appendix III).

After his death, the house was sold at a public auction in February of 1771. In the sale catalogue, reproduced in Appendix II, it was described as 'Large and commodious . . . With an elegant Suite of Five Rooms on the First Floor, and Coach-Houses and Stabling'. There was also a 'Pupil's Room', a 'Painting Room', and a 'Shew Room'. Humphrey Ward stated in 1904 that he had seen the architectural plans for the remodelling of the painting room, which were signed by Cotes,[50] but these plans were not published, nor have they been found. However, whatever the details of the remodelling might have been, the end result was that Cotes possessed a very fine, well-located house, which he had attractively renovated for his own purposes. Its charm and usefulness were later to appeal to two other artists—George Romney, who bought the lease when it was auctioned in 1771, and Sir Martin Archer Shea, who bought it in 1798.

The purchase and remodelling of the house at Cavendish Square must have cost Cotes a great deal, and one would like to know something about his income at the time. Presumably he kept an account with a bank, but the archives of London banks that were in existence in the 1760's have no record of an account in Cotes's name.

His primary source of income was his practice as a portrait painter; his family was not prosperous enough to be of considerable assistance. The most important document relating to his practice would have been his sitters' book, a diary in which appointments were recorded, generally with the names of the sitters, and often with the prices the artist charged. Most British portraitists of the day kept such books, but Cotes's sitters' book has never been discovered, and the information available on Cotes's prices is often vague. Edwards says:

> Mr. Cotes's prices were twenty guineas for a three-quarter, forty for a half-length, and eighty for a whole length. Mr. Toms painted most of his draperies.[51]

Edwards does not state the date for this particular scale of charges, but he does mention the scale in connection with Toms, who was working for Cotes between 1763/64 and 1770. In the very same context Edwards also observes that:

> Mr. Walpole has already given a list of some of his [Cotes's] principal portraits in crayons, to which may be added the whole-length of her Majesty with the Princess Royal in her lap, that he painted in oil in the year 1767. . . .[52]

The 'list' Edwards speaks of appears in Walpole's *Anecdotes*,[53] and consists of six pastel portraits ranging in date from 1763 to 1770. Therefore, when Edwards talks of Cotes's scale of prices, he does so in relation to the period of c. 1763 to 1770.

One of the terms he uses in describing the prices has caused some difficulty in the past;[54] this is the phrase, 'a three-quarter'. Quite clearly, it does not refer to a three-quarter length picture, because the price is less than that quoted for a half-length. In fact, the term 'a three-quarter' or 'a three-quarters' was an eighteenth-century measurement for portraits that were 30 in. by 25 in., or approximately three-quarters the size of a kit-cat, 36 in. by 28 in.[55] This measurement was particularly popular in the 1760's. Its most interesting example appears in Reynolds's price list of 1764: 30 guineas for a head, 35 for a three-quarters, 50 for a kit-cat, 70 for a half length, and 150 for a whole length.[56]

Around 1768 Cotes probably raised his prices above the scale quoted by Edwards. In May of 1768 he sent the Duke of Portland a bill for three pastel portraits (nos. 208, 211, and 212), each of which measured about 25 in. by 19 in. and cost £26 5s 0d.[57] Since a 25 in. by 19 in. picture cost £26 5s 0d, and was smaller than a three-quarter (30 in. by 25 in.), which Edward says cost 20 guineas, one suspects that by 1768 Cotes had increased his prices.

At twenty, forty, and eighty guineas, his prices were between those of Reynolds and Gainsborough, although, even if he did raise them by 1768, it is very unlikely that they ever closely approached those of Reynolds. Nevertheless, Cotes's prices were quite substantial for his day, and indicate that he was enjoying a considerable degree of success.

A key factor that contributed to his prosperity was his growing practice in oils. Although his reputation still rested primarily on his skill as a pastellist, he realized that oil portraits were capable of earning him a great deal more money than pastels. There were two reasons for this. First of all, it was the custom of the day for artists to vary their prices in direct proportion to the size of their pictures. Since pastels were invariably small, Cotes could not charge as much for them as he could for oil portraits, which were usually larger, even though the quality of his pastels generally exceeded that of his oils. Secondly, British society in the 1760's was prospering from the spoils of the newly-won Empire. As a consequence, portraitists in London had a growing number of rich clients intent on expressing their sense of dignity and self-importance in large, formal, and imposing oil portraits. This type of portrait projected an image of grandeur and wealth to their families, friends, and, if the opportunity presented itself, to the public at one of the Society of Artists' yearly exhibitions.

By 1763/1764 Cotes's practice in both pastels and oils was beginning to attract attention and to gain him a good deal of renown. A critic writing for the *Public Advertiser* in May of 1764 said:

> It is with infinite Pleasure one yearly sees this Artist [Cotes] presenting to the World, fresh Instances of his masterly Elegance both in Crayons and in Oils. His portraits may justly vie with those of Reynolds; and greatly to his Honour be it said, that he generally preserves a beautiful Correctness in his Pictures, which the latter Master too often neglects. Those praises which the Public have lately bestowed on Mr. Cotes, will make him, I dare say, aim at still further Excellence in his Profession.[58]

Although Cotes was not yet a serious rival, the comparison between the two artists is pertinent, because Reynolds, more than any other portraitist of the day, understood the feelings of affluence and self-importance most clients wished to express, and his grand style of portraiture was a highly suitable vehicle for capturing and idealizing such emotions. The emotions themselves, as well as Reynolds's increasingly fashionable way of expressing them, were factors with which Cotes was going to have to come to terms.

Reynolds's primary concern since the 1750's had been to promote his own version of a grand style in portraiture. That version, considered in its strictest sense, involved historical associations based mainly on Greek and Roman sources, on the work of Renaissance masters, particularly Raphael and Michelangelo, and on that of the seventeenth-century classicists, especially the Bolognese; and it aimed at elevating the beholder's mind from the particular person portrayed to Truth, Beauty, and Goodness. It took several decades before public acceptance of Reynolds's aim became more or less complete. During this period, from about 1753 to 1770, Reynolds painted certain portraits that were of crucial importance in gradually converting people to his point of view. He introduced his grand style with a full length in oils of COMMODORE AUGUSTUS KEPPEL (fig. 35) of 1753–1754, in which the sitter's pose approximates that of the Apollo Belvedere in reverse. As Professor Ellis Waterhouse has remarked: 'Nothing so easy and so heroic had been produced in England since the days of Van Dyck.'[59] The second important statement of his grand style was his full length of THE DUCHESS OF HAMILTON AS VENUS (fig. 22), which he presented at the first exhibition of the Society of Artists in 1760. Despite the impact that this picture made, most of the public still preferred more casual and intimate portraits, and Reynolds, therefore, chose to go along with this bias in the early 1760's, realizing that for the time being he could do nothing to resist it. By 1763, however, he began to promote his grand style once again. At the Society of Artists' exhibition that year, he presented his appealing yet austere portrait of THE LADIES ELIZABETH AND HENRIETTA MONTAGU (fig. 36). It is a tender and somewhat intimate picture, but idealized so that the two sitters look more like classical deities in a moment of divine repose than mere mortals seated casually in a landscape. The idealization of the faces, the classically inspired drapery, and the geometric arrangement of the composition are typical of Reynolds's grand style.

Cotes's work offers an interesting contrast in 1763/1764. At a moment when Reynolds was trying to push British portraiture along the pathways of his own taste, Cotes was doing his best work by remaining essentially conservative and only following Reynolds's lead in superficial ways. Basically, Cotes was unsympathetic to what Reynolds was promoting, except insofar as he could use elements of Reynolds's style to create the illusion of being up-to-date. When he occasionally tried to approximate Reynolds more closely, his work lost some of its individual character and charm.

The problems Cotes faced in adapting his style to the ideas Reynolds was popularizing around 1763 are evident both in his pastels and his oils from this period. His difficulties can be illustrated by two pastels of unknown ladies at the Huntington Library and Art Gallery in San Marino, California. The earlier of these, a portrait (no. 22, fig. 37) of 1751, is sensual, intimate, and rococo. The sitter gazes straight out at the beholder with a slight smile on her lips. Her hair is arranged in the simple manner fashionable in the early 1750's. She wears a beautiful brown dress adorned with two large pearl and emerald brooches and a cloak of brilliant blue, rose, and gold, which shimmers with tiny reflected lights. The other portrait (no. 119, fig. 38), done in 1763, is idealized, remote, formal, and strongly influenced by the concepts Reynolds was incorporating into his grand portraits of women. Her head is in profile; she has idealized features; her hair is arranged in the more piled-up and imposing style popular in the 1760's, and is embellished with a tiara; her drapery, adorned only with two discreet strands of pearls, is of the classically-inspired type invented by Reynolds. The comparison of these two pastels from different periods reveals not only the change in taste which Reynolds was bringing about by 1763, but also the extent of Cotes's ability to adjust himself to such a change. In the later pastel he captured the fashion Reynolds was promoting in portraiture, but he expressed it blandly and without panache. Most notably absent is the characteristic personality, dignity, and strength of mind Reynolds gave his sitters. Compare, for example, the head of Cotes's unknown lady (fig. 38) with that of Lady Elizabeth or Lady Henrietta Montagu in Reynolds's painting of the same year (fig. 36). It is evident in this pastel that, in order to adapt his work to Reynolds's style, Cotes abandoned his habitual orientation towards the rococo. But the sacrifice was not worth the effort, for although his portrait is attractive, what he achieved fell far short of the models he was trying to approximate, and revealed that he understood something about the form of Reynolds's images, but very little about their content.

The resurgence of Reynolds's grand style around 1763 also affected Cotes's oil portraits of the same period. The exhibition of Reynolds's painting of The Ladies Elizabeth and Henrietta Montagu (fig. 36) at the Society of Artists in 1763 was of special interest to Cotes; consequently, he began to experiment with the compositions Reynolds used for portraits of ladies seated in an outdoor setting. A typical example of such an experiment is his painting of LADY ALSTON (no. 144, fig. 40) of 1764, which is in the fashion of Reynolds's portrait of THE HON. HARRIET BOUVERIE (fig. 39) of the same year. The half or three-quarter length picture in which a lady is shown seated out-of-doors, her head turned to one side, her eyes averted from the beholder, her arm resting on a simple stone pedestal, sometimes her hand raised to her cheek, her features idealized, and her draperies classically inspired, was a standard type developed by Reynolds, and which Cotes was improvising upon in his portrait of Lady Alston (fig. 40).

This painting illustrates how close Cotes came to Reynolds, and yet how far away he remained. It oscillates between the merits of Cotes's past training in the 1740's and the avant-garde fashions in portraiture of the mid-1760's, without ever capturing either effectively. The head in profile, the arm resting on a pedestal, and the style of the draperies are straight from Reynolds, but Cotes combined these features, which call for an idealized and intellectual treatment of the portrait image, with old-fashioned decorative elements of style that look completely out of place and fight against the very nature of the kind of picture he was at pains to imitate. Instead of painting Lady Alston in a pensive mood, with her hand raised to her cheek, as Reynolds would have done, he painted her with one hand raised to her pearl necklace. This shifts the emphasis away from the intellectual to the ornamental. Rather than idealizing her features, he left them as they were, double chin and all, and even turned up the corners of her mouth ever so slightly, to give her lips the suggestion of a smile. Reynolds would have transformed her into a goddess with a serious and dignified expression. Cotes painted her right arm extended and her hand making a conversational gesture, as if she were speaking to someone. This attitude draws attention to the personal and momentary aspects of the image; it fixes the viewer's attention on a particular person in a particular situation, rather than following Reynolds's example of showing her detached from time, so that the mind of the beholder can rise from the temporal to the eternal, from the particular to the universal.

Various combinations were possible between the old-fashioned approach of the 1740's and early 50's and the trends Reynolds was trying to establish in the 1760's, but in order to make an effective image, the portraitist had to put the emphasis firmly on one side or the other. Portraits like that of Lady Alston (fig. 40), in which opposing forces are joined in almost equal strength, are examples of conflict and confusion instead of harmony and integration. Reynolds had been successful in weaving together the intimate and the ideal, because he had firmly placed the ideal in the ascendancy. Cotes, on the other hand, was incapable of making the ideal predominant, nor was he able in 1763 and 1764 to assert his old-fashioned aesthetic strongly enough. Consequently, he stayed away from grand portraiture during this period and devoted most of his energies to pictures in which elements of formality inspired by Reynolds were present, but to such a slight degree that they presented no problem.

When one considers these more conservative pictures, it is apparent that Cotes was able to assert his own aesthetic most effectively in those types of portraits that the public habitually associated with the artistic ideals of the first half of the century. In this category were pastel portraits, which were not thought suitable for the expression of grandeur, formality, or a weighty intellectual content; half and three-quarter length oil portraits of children, which were limited mainly to intimate images; and those quintessentially British half and three-quarter length oil portraits of country squires posed with purposefully casual elegance in landscape settings. None of these pictures had to be composed in terms of the ideal; on the contrary, an awareness of the particular and the intimate was required. Therefore, Cotes found them very much to his liking and suited to his talents.

Among his pastels of the period, the best portraits of women are those of MARIA, DOWAGER COUNTESS OF WALDEGRAVE (no. 143, fig. 41), LAURA KEPPEL (no. 155, fig. 43), and LADY SUSAN FOX-STRANGEWAYS (no. 128, fig. 42). Here he adapted himself only slightly to the fashions that were being established by Reynolds, and, as a result, the quality was much higher than in his oil painting of Lady Alston.

In these portraits the sitters were shown in contemporary dress, which lent itself to a rococo form of representation in pastels, particularly when lace was used as an adornment on the rich and brightly coloured silks and satins. Lace was interesting visually because it broke up the coloured lights reflected from beneath it, and accentuated their sparkling quality. Cotes's method of arranging his pastel colours in layers so that one layer showed through another was ideal for recreating the transparent character of lace and the marvellous light effects it produced.

The Waldegrave, Keppel, and Fox-Strangeways portraits offer fine examples of Cotes's pastel painting of lace around 1763 and 1764. In the pictures of Lady Waldegrave (fig. 41) and Lady Susan Fox-Strangeways (fig. 42), bright colours are juxtaposed. Lady Waldegrave's dress is done in shades of pink, Lady Susan's in pinks and blues. Over these dresses Cotes then painted black lace shawls, whose effect against the colours beneath is quite striking and makes the scintillation of reflected lights exciting and dramatic. The sharp contrast of colours and the movement of the reflected lights could easily have produced a harsh and disorganized appearance in the draperies, but Cotes's skill in the use of the soft, powdery properties of the pastel medium beautifully blended together the various parts of these pictures, so that their appearance is both sophisticated and orderly. The problem he faced when he painted the portrait of Laura Keppel (fig. 43) was rather different. The task was not so much to harmonize sharply contrasting colours as to capture the subtle nuances of soft colours that naturally tended to blend in with one another. Laura Keppel's dress is of a soft green silk shot through with streaks of blue, and over it she wears a cream lace mantle. In contemplating her portrait one sees the remarkable sensitivity and artistry with which Cotes painted these draperies. Passages of rococo crayon painting of this type give his pictures an exquisite character, which is highly pleasing and mirrors the courtly spirit so assiduously cultivated by the ladies he portrayed; their refined sense of pleasure, their sensuous beauty, charm, gaiety, and wit are expressed in the very style of his painting.

Vitality and decorativeness and an unerring sense of form and colour typify Cotes's best pastels of 1763 and 1764. These qualities are present not only in his portraits of women, but in those of men and children as well. The male portraits tend to be much more simple than those of women, primarily because men's clothes were less complex. The eye is not distracted by so many frills and flounces and more readily focuses on the sitter's physiognomy. The costume, composed of a few sharply contrasting colours, as in the portrait of DR. JOHN GREGORY (no. 139, fig. 45), merely serves as a kind of elegant accompaniment for the face, which is shown in a relaxed, casual attitude. Admittedly, Cotes excelled neither in deep psychological penetration nor in abstract intellectualization, but the incisiveness and beauty of his pastel images of men were unsurpassed in Britain in the 1760's.

Cotes's merits as a pastellist did not go unrecognized by his contemporaries. Horace Walpole noted in his Society of Artists' catalogue of 1763 (Appendix III) that Cotes's pastel of WILLIAM O'BRIEN (no. 120, fig. 44) was 'the best picture in the exhibition', even though Reynolds's portrait of The Ladies Elizabeth and Henrietta Montagu (fig. 36) was in the same show. WILLIAM CHAMBERS, the architect, sat to Cotes for a pastel portrait (no. 137, fig. 46) in 1764. He was especially fond of the picture and was probably responsible for having it copied three times (cf. Appendix VI, nos. 5, 6, 33). James Watson, whose engravings after portraits by Reynolds appeared almost yearly at the Society of Artists' exhibitions and served to publicize Reynolds's work, honoured Cotes in 1764 by exhibiting an engraving after the pastel of WILLIAM CAMPBELL SKINNER (no. 153, fig. 47), the five-year-old son of General William Skinner.

It is significant that Watson chose a pastel and one of a child. In the early 1760's Cotes had no serious rivals among pastellists, either native or foreign, who were working in Britain at the time. None of his oil paintings of 1763 and 1764 had engravings made after them in the eighteenth century, but six of his pastels from these years were engraved, four of them by Watson (no. 120, fig. 44; no.

128, fig. 42; no. 141; and no. 153, fig. 47), one by Richard Houston (no. 137, fig. 46), and one by J. Bengo (no. 139, fig. 45). By 1763 Cotes was becoming increasingly popular as a pastel portraitist of children, and for the remainder of his career he made child portraiture one of his specialities. His pastels of children from 1763 and 1764 are particularly sensitive and delicate, and it was at this time that he developed a basic formula for child portraiture which served him both in pastels and in oils. He showed the child with something that related to it personally. Most often this was a plaything like a doll, a handkerchief made to look like a rabbit, a kite, or a cricket bat; then there were favourite pets, usually dogs, and occasionally objects associated with more intellectual interests, like books of mathematical calculations, surveying instruments, and maps.

Arguably the finest of these works is the pastel of SELINA CHAMBERS (no. 136, Pl. II) of 1764, a straightforward picture with no impressive tricks of composition and no hidden intellectual meanings. It is simply a half-length of a child holding a doll, but done with mastery. In this picture Cotes showed his skill as a pastel colourist, beautifully harmonizing flesh tones, the different shades of brown in the eyes and hair, the lively red of the lips, the white and pink of the pearl necklace, and the creams, blues, and greens of the dress, while strongly emphasizing with his colours textures and tactile sensations, such as the softness of the child's skin, the hardness of her pearls, and the slight stiffness of the lace trim on her dress.

In his oil portraits of children of 1763 and 1764 he adopted the same basic formula. The two best examples of this are his paintings of the BARWELL brothers, one in a red coat holding a book of mathematical calculations and leaning against a surveying instrument called an azimuth (no. 146, fig. 48), and the other dressed up in a naval officer's blue coat with a sword at his side and holding a map of the city and harbour of Havana (no. 145, fig. 50). Here, just as in the pastel of Selina Chambers (Pl. II), Cotes caught something of the charm and innocence of his sitters, but he presented them more formally. One is more immediately aware of a self-conscious arrangement of the figure according to a pre-conceived scheme; in fact, the poses of the two brothers, for all their appearance of naturalness, were not only carefully planned, but also conformed to a general pattern that had been used in European portraiture for at least two decades. In half and three-quarter length portraits of the 1740's, 50's, and early 60's, it is quite common, especially in pictures of British sitters, to come across the figure with one arm leaning against an object, the opposite hip thrown out, and the head facing forward or slightly to the side. The effect is one of elegant relaxation. The body is allowed to fall into easy, flowing curves, rather than being held rigid. Among painters influenced by the Rococo, the curved outlines of the body are silhouetted against the background; with a painter like Reynolds, the decorative silhouette is minimized. No matter what the treatment of the outline of the body is, the facial expressions are reflective, reposeful, and somewhat distant, although occasionally, for the sake of immediacy, the slightest suggestion of a smile is permitted to play across the lips.

Many examples could be cited, but the following ones come to mind: Allan Ramsay's portrait of PHILIP, 2ND EARL STANHOPE, of 1749 (fig. 51), Pompeo Battoni's portrait of SIR JOHN ARMYTAGE, 2ND BT., of 1758 (fig. 52), and Reynolds's portrait of EDWARD LASCELLES, IST EARL OF HAREWOOD, of 1762–1764 (fig. 49). All three artists used the type of figure arrangement and treatment of expression found in the Barwell portraits. The most significant differences between these pictures depend on the outline of the figure. Ramsay and Battoni, painting in the 40's and 50's, used shadows to soften the silhouette, yet they made a point of emphasizing its decorative quality. Reynolds, painting in the early 60's and wanting to create a different effect, tended to stress mass rather than decorative outline. Cotes sharply outlined his figures in the Barwell portraits and made much of the decorative silhouette. He had far more in common with Ramsay and Battoni and the traditions of the 40's and 50's than with Reynolds and the painting of the 60's. In relatively small portraits of children, such as those of the Barwell brothers (fig. 48, 50), he could get away with being old-fashioned, and whenever this occurred, he almost always produced paintings of high quality.

Among his oil portraits of 1763 and 1764 is his typical three-quarter length view of a gentleman posed casually in a landscape setting. Cotes did a number of these portraits, particularly for the members of the Burdett family at Ramsbury Manor in Wiltshire. Some pictures in the Burdett series are less successful than others. This is especially noticeable in the four portraits of FRANCIS BURDETT (nos. 147, fig. 54; 148; 149; and 156), which show the sitter in the same pose in front of the same landscape, the differences being in the colours of the frock coat and waistcoat. Burdett evidently ordered these portraits in order to have paintings of himself in different colours all over Ramsbury Manor. Cotes obliged his client, but seems to have become bored with the job, for only in the painting now at the Ferens Art Gallery in Hull (no. 147, fig. 54) does he appear to have taken his customary care; the rest (nos. 148, 149, and 156) are rather shoddy by comparison, and look as if he had only painted the heads and had left the draperies to Peter Toms. Nevertheless, by experimenting with the Burdett pictures Cotes evolved his own interpretation of a standard portrait type. The best paintings which resulted from this experience are two very handsome portraits, one of WILLIAM JONES (no. 159, fig. 55), Francis Burdett's father-in-law, and the other of CHARLES COLMORE (no. 157, fig. 56), both painted c. 1764. Their poses are reminiscent of precedents established by Reynolds in portraits such as that of SIR JOHN ANSTRUTHER (fig. 53) of 1761. Cotes's pictures were distinguished by his old-fashioned style. This is particularly noticeable in his portrait of William Jones (fig. 55), whom he posed against a bright blue sky, wearing a scarlet suit and cream-coloured waistcoat trimmed in gold. There was no attempt to capture the spirituality of Reynolds's work, because Cotes was totally absorbed in making the figure as strikingly decorative as possible. His interpretation has the character of an extremely well done fashion plate, patently superficial but brilliantly conceived. The painting of Charles Colmore (fig. 56) is less obviously decorative and more intimate and relaxed. The sitter looks directly out at the viewer, and his pose has the appearance of being natural instead of planned. Most interesting of all, the landscape behind him is opened up and painted in a delicate manner reminiscent of Cotes's watercolour View of Purley Hall (fig. 25), his pastel of the Gulston brothers (fig. 24), and his oil paintings of Paul and Anne Sandby (frontispiece and fig. 23).

Cotes's work from 1765 to 1770 can best be understood if one considers this time span as a single period without breaking it up into smaller units. First of all, the entire period was marked by his efforts to enhance his reputation as an oil painter. The vast majority of his unsigned and undated works were oils, and among his signed and dated portraits there were at least twice as many oils as pastels. This noticeable increase in the quantity of oil portraits seems to have had the desired effect on the public, if we can judge from the engravings: whereas in 1763 and 1764 most of the portraits engraved were pastels, the proportion for 1765 to 1770 is thirteen oils engraved to only two pastels. In addition, the exhibition catalogues of the Society of Artists from 1765 to 1768 and those of the Royal Academy from 1769 and 1770, show that Cotes exhibited twenty-five oils as against fourteen pastels.

Other generalizations about the period will be examined in detail in relation to the various types of pictures he was producing; however, it will be helpful to note several points briefly. Cotes's attitude to the work of Reynolds and Ramsay was of particular importance, since much of what he did was a personal adaptation to, or revolt against, the trends they were setting at the time. His main difficulty was the one he had had from the very beginning of the 1760's, namely, how to preserve his gifts for rococo decoration, empirical observation, and the making of intimate and charming portrait images, at a moment when the grandeur, formality, and idealization of classicism were very much in vogue. From 1765 to 1770 this problem was particularly acute for Cotes, because Reynolds, who dominated public exhibitions, had brought his grand style to its full-blown form, and Ramsay, the favourite portraitist of George III, was painting the members of the royal family in his own version of the grand manner. Cotes, therefore, had two very strong forces to contend with, one from the public sector and one from the private. It is indeed remarkable that within the short space of five years he did, in fact, meet the challenge in both areas and securely established himself in the exhibition room and in the royal family's circle of painters.

As a rule, he was most successful when he either ignored the fashion for classicism, or, if he could not ignore it, when he adapted it in such a way as to subordinate it to his own taste. The solutions he worked out and his gradual growth towards a mature style can best be understood by studying the pastels and oils that he produced between 1765 and 1770. These are presented here in the following order for purposes of discussion: head and shoulders portraits, larger pictures with a single figure, double portraits, and pictures influenced by these double portraits.

Head and shoulders portraits are often neglected, because they are small, unpretentious, relatively simple, and offer a rather limited scope for expression. The limitations of the format, however, can serve to condense an artist's style, and to extract from it some of its most essential characteristics. This is true of Cotes's portraits. In 1765, for example, he did the little pastel of ADMIRAL AUGUSTUS KEPPEL (no. 168, fig. 57), which he showed at the Society of Artists' exhibition that year. Admiral Keppel was Reynolds's early patron and benefactor and the subject of his historic portrait of 1753/1754, which had revived the grand style in Britain (fig. 35). Cotes had not been unknown to the Keppel family; in fact, he was first discovered as early as 1752 by the HON. GEORGE KEPPEL, who had himself painted in pastels by the artist in that year (no. 35). Thereafter, Cotes received a steady stream of commissions from the family. He did a pastel of LADY ELIZABETH KEPPEL around 1755 (no. 61), one of LIEUTENANT-GENERAL WILLIAM KEPPEL (no. 140) and one of MARIA, DOWAGER COUNTESS OF WALDEGRAVE (no. 143, fig. 41) in 1764, one of LAURA KEPPEL (no. 155, fig. 43) around 1764, and three in 1765, of THE RT. REV. FREDERICK KEPPEL (no. 169), FRANCIS RUSSELL, MARQUESS OF TAVISTOCK (no. 171), and ADMIRAL KEPPEL (no. 168, fig. 57).

The pastel of Admiral Keppel is one of Cotes's most superb works from the mid-1760's. The image is especially sharp, clear, and colourful, and the strength and determination expressed in the face give the picture a psychological dimension unusual in Cotes's portraits.

A typical head and shoulders oil portrait of the period, the picture of JOHN HOBART, 2ND EARL OF BUCKINGHAMSHIRE (no. 193, fig. 58) of 1766 is not as vivid and clear as the portrait of Admiral Keppel, nor does it have an interesting psychological aspect, but it illustrates how, in small oil paintings of this type, Cotes tried to imitate the appearance of his pastels. In the portrait of the Earl of Buckinghamshire he was attempting to capture the delicacy of line and skilful use of bright colours exemplified in the pastel of Admiral Keppel. What is most striking about the Buckinghamshire portrait in comparison with his earlier oil paintings of c. 1762–1764, e.g. fig. 33, is that he applied his paints more thinly and finely, which made it easier for him to exercise control over the image and to reproduce the delicacy of his pastels.

This practice became fairly standard in his head and shoulders portraits after 1766, and enabled him to make some beautiful paintings, like that of FREDERICK IRBY, 2ND BARON BOSTON (no. 278, fig. 59), which for decorativeness and charm almost rivalled his best work in pastels of the period. Boston is shown wearing the blue and gold academic robes of a Fellow-Commoner of St. John's College, Cambridge. The clarity of the image, the brilliance of the colours, and the crispness of the line recall the pastel of Admiral Keppel (fig. 57). Although the painting of Lord Boston is not as refined, it comes close to the quality of pastel prototypes of this sort and is typical of Cotes's work in head and shoulders oil portraits in the late 1760's.

Among his larger pictures, half, three-quarter, and full-lengths, the first group comprises portraits of gentlemen in which there is a single figure, some shown in an interior, others out of doors. One of his earliest full-lengths of this type is the oil portrait of JAMES, 2ND EARL OF FIFE (no. 173, fig. 60), which he exhibited along with the pastel of Admiral Keppel at the Society of Artists in 1765. The portrait of Fife is very disappointing; it exemplifies the difficulties Cotes experienced when trying to paint in the grand and formal manner. There are numerous earlier portraits by Reynolds of a peer in his robes and regalia, standing, one leg crossed over the other and leaning with one arm on the base of a column encircled by heavy drapery. It is instructive to compare Reynolds's portrait of JAMES, 2ND EARL WALDEGRAVE (fig. 61) with Cotes's portrait of James, 2nd Earl of Fife (fig. 60). Reynolds was mainly interested in idealizing the sitter, while Cotes concentrated on a bolder, more decorative approach, but as he did not paint particularly well in oils at this time, he laid on his paints too heavily in an effort to be impressive, which gives the face and the draperies a crude, lifeless appearance. Cotes did not learn easily that boldness was not best achieved by means of heavy, thick layers of paint.

In the oil portraits of gentlemen in an interior setting which he did between 1765 and 1770 he frequently departed from the precedents set by Ramsay and Reynolds and sought ways of painting the sitter in more spontaneous attitudes. This is noticeable in his portrait of RICHARD MYDDELTON (no. 245, fig. 63) of c. 1767–1770, which bears a certain resemblance to his more Reynolds-like painting of SIR ROBERT BURDETT (no. 214, fig. 62) of 1767. The stance is almost the same, the hand resting on the hip, the arm or hand resting on a chair or table, the hat under the arm, and so on, but Burdett looks away, while Myddelton looks out directly towards the viewer and gesticulates as if conversing with someone. The Myddelton portrait is a much more immediate and natural image.

Ramsay and Reynolds were unaccustomed to painting full-lengths with the figure in as casual an attitude as that of SIR GRIFFITH BOYNTON in Cotes's oil portrait of 1769 (no. 279, fig. 64). Boynton's basic pose is found in many other British paintings from the 1760's, but the extent to which Cotes exaggerated it in order to make the image more spontaneous is unusual for the period, and went beyond what either Ramsay or Reynolds would have considered proper for a portrait of a gentleman.

The fairly large size of the picture, $94\frac{1}{2}$ in. × 58 in., and the heavy draperies at the window and over the chair give it an impressiveness and elegance typical for the time, but the rest of the composition is more closely related to the pastel of Sir Richard Hoare (no. 76, fig. 21), done twelve years earlier, than to any picture of the 1760's. In both portraits the figure is placed near a casement, lit by sunlight coming through a window, and posed standing with one hand on the hip and the other hand holding an object of interest. The painting of Boynton is larger and more developed, and the sitter is shown with more objects that relate to him, his desk, a book, an inkstand, a candle, and some letters, one of which is inscribed 'To Sir Griffith Boynton, Bt.'. The smaller pastel of Hoare certainly offers an intimate view of the sitter, but so does the painting of Boynton, for despite its size and aura of grandeur, the pose is quite casual and the setting very personal. In addition, the virtues of Cotes's pastel technique are in evidence in the oil; the beautiful blending of beige, rose, and brown, and the delicacy of line vividly recall his pastels. His painting of Boynton is, therefore, an example of how cleverly and successfully he adapted himself to the vogue for grandeur in the late 60's by incorporating into his oil portraiture elements of style he had previously evolved for his pastels of the late 50's.

What happened with his oil portraits of gentlemen out-of-doors was analogous to what occurred with his paintings of gentlemen in an interior. Initially he encountered a type of picture that was too formal and intellectual for him, but since it had been popularized by Reynolds, he attempted it, only to find that his chances for success were limited. When he painted portraits of a less formal nature, he discovered that the results were far better.

The naval portrait is an important type of outdoor picture that Reynolds made fashionable but Cotes experienced difficulty with and, therefore, painted infrequently. Two naval portraits that are well-known, not because of the artist, but because of the sitters, are those of ADMIRAL SIR EDWARD HAWKE (no. 239, fig. 67), of c. 1767 to 1770, and of CAPTAIN JOHN JERVIS (no. 281, fig. 68), of 1769. In comparing these portraits with Reynolds's earlier paintings of Rear-Admiral Rodney (fig. 29), Captain Hervey (fig. 32), and CAPTAIN HOOD (fig. 65), which helped to make the fashion Cotes was following, it is clear that he underrated the importance of integrating the figure and the background by means of shadows. Reynolds's sitters appear to be involved in a dramatic scene rather than awkwardly posed in front of what looks like a flat stage backdrop with a rocky mound and a seascape painted upon it. Cotes's preference for the decorative silhouette did not work to his advantage in this type of picture, and when his naval portraits are compared to those of Reynolds, they look charming but second-rate.

In a more informal kind of painting, like that of DR. CONNELL (no. 180, fig. 66), of c. 1765, the whole effect is noticeably different and much more successful, despite the fact that the pose is very similar to that of Hood (fig. 65), Hawke (fig. 67), and Jervis (fig. 68). This was because the precedent established by Reynolds in the early 1760's with portraits like that of Sir John Anstruther (fig. 53) did not demand a degree of formality that Cotes could not handle; on the contrary, formality was subordinated to casual elegance, which suited him very well.

Another informal painting of a gentleman outdoors that can be compared with that of Dr. Connell (fig. 66) is the portrait of WILLIAM, 6TH BARON CRAVEN (no. 257, Pl. IV), of 1768. Although the mood is somewhat the same in both pictures, the portrait of Craven is better painted. Like the portraits of Lord Boston (fig. 59) and Sir Griffith Boynton (fig. 64) it is based on Cotes's pastel technique, which frequently influenced his oils from 1767 to 1770. In the picture of Craven the paint is applied more thinly and carefully than in the earlier portrait of Connell: the colours are softer and more subtle, and the whole image is more refined and delicate. Connell is shown with a very bright blue coat and stridently contrasting pink waistcoat, while Craven wears a dark green hunting coat and cream waistcoat. The figure of Craven is beautifully illuminated from above, and, by means of light and shadow, carefully blended into a golden landscape background suffused with the last rays of a setting sun. The achievement of a satisfactory unity between the figure and a landscape background is relatively rare in Cotes's work.

Turning to his oil portraits of children, one finds two basic groups: half or three-quarter length pictures like those of the Barwell brothers (figs. 48, 50) of 1764, and full-length paintings related to portraits of children in the Van Dyck manner by Ramsay and Reynolds.

II *Selina Chambers* (No. 136). Pastel, 1764.
Osterley Park, Osterley, Middlesex

In the first group, the most revealing examples are the portraits of CHARLES COLLYER (no. 195, fig. 70) of 1766, MIDSHIPMAN GEORGE CRANFIELD BERKELEY (no. 277, fig. 71) of 1769, and FRANCES LEE (no. 285, fig. 69) of 1769. All follow the basic ideas for childrens' portraits which Cotes had already developed in 1763 and 1764. Compare, for example, the picture of Midshipman Berkeley (fig. 71) with that of Master Barwell (fig. 48), or that of Frances Lee (fig. 69) with that of Selina Chambers (Pl. II). In each case, the child is posed with a favourite object. The oils are the most formal, but their formality is always subordinated to the innocence and charm of the child. The finest of the oils are the latest two, those of Midshipman Berkeley and Frances Lee, in both of which Cotes achieved a clarity and delicacy derived from his technique as a pastellist.

One of the most delightful fashions in child portraiture in Britain of the 1750's and 60's was that of painting children in costumes of the Van Dyck period and posing them in ways that Van Dyck had used. Typical examples are Ramsay's JOHN, LORD MOUNTSTUART (fig. 73) of 1759 and Reynolds's THOMAS LISTER (fig. 74) of 1764. Although Cotes is not known to have painted full-lengths of children dressed up in Van Dyck costumes, the portraits by Ramsay and Reynolds influenced him, notably in his painting of LEWIS CAGE (no. 255, fig. 72) of 1768. The sitter's basic pose is found fairly frequently in Van Dyck's portraits, but the treatment of the subject is rather unusual. Cage is shown as if he had been playing cricket; his clothes are dishevelled: his waistcoat unbuttoned, his shirt loose, and his stockings hanging down. Casualness of this sort would never have been tolerated by Ramsay or Reynolds, but it was used effectively by Cotes to give intimacy and immediacy to a type of portrait that was by custom more formal and remote.

His greatest success in this manner was the portrait of MASTER SMITH (no. 270, fig. 75), which, like that of Cage, is derived from elements of the Van Dyck tradition, but is distinguished by a charmingly informal interpretation. The picture of Master Smith is especially interesting because of the marvellous play of lights and shadows over the figure and the wonderfully decorative tail of the kite.

Cotes's portraits of ladies in which there is a single figure are best discussed if they are divided into two groups: those pictures in which the figure is seated and those in which it is standing.

At the beginning of the period ranging from 1765 to 1770, he was painting seated figures like that of LADY CUNLIFFE (no. 176, fig. 76). The motif of a lady seated with one arm resting on a pedestal and one hand raised to her cheek in a passive attitude was derived from Reynolds (e.g. fig. 39). Cotes used it in the portrait of Lady Cunliffe, but he eliminated the classically inspired draperies and the idealization of the figure.

After 1765, however, Cotes conformed more closely to the fashions Reynolds was promoting for this kind of picture. His oil paintings of A LADY (no. 259, fig. 77), of 1768, and of LADY BROUGHTON (no. 233, fig. 79), of c. 1767–1770, are very much in the Reynolds mould, but without the spirituality of Reynolds's work. They have the outward form of fashion, and on this level they are quite attractive, but they lack an interesting content. The same is true of his pastel portraits of this type that show Reynolds's influence, such as that of SARAH CHILD (no. 190, fig. 78), of 1766, but in pastels Cotes's technique is so superb, and the image of the sitter so clear and immediate, that one is inclined to overlook any shortcomings.

The best qualities in his pastels of seated ladies from the period of 1765 to 1770 are generally the result of direct observation and convey a sensuous impression of the sitter. For instance, his portrait of Sarah Child (fig. 78), while charming, and certainly admirable from a technical point of view, is neither as lively nor as appealing as his pastel of LADY HOARE (no. 204, fig. 80) of the same period.

The problem he had in joining together the best qualities in his work with the fashion for intellectual painting is especially noticeable in his portraits of ladies in which the figure is shown standing. Most of these pictures done between 1765 and 1770 were reactions of one sort or another to Reynolds's principal type of female portrait of the period.

At the Society of Artists' exhibition of 1765, Reynolds exhibited the painting of LADY SARAH BUNBURY SACRIFICING TO THE THREE GRACES (fig. 81). As Frederick Cummings has explained, this portrait concerns the nature of friendship, and in particular, the friendship between Lady Sarah and Lady Susan Fox-Strangeways, who appears on the right.[60] Lady Sarah is shown sacrificing to an image of the Three Graces, a symbolic representation of Amicitia or friendship. The roses climbing up the pedestal signify sweetness between friends, the nudity of the Three Graces symbolizes the freedom of spirit and absence of deceit between friends, the ever-green myrtle being held out by one of the Graces signifies that friendship continually propagates itself, and the intertwined arms of the Graces refer to the exchange in friendship of like for like, a theme echoed by Lady Susan, who pours out her libation, and Lady Sarah, who casts hers on the sacrificial flames. Cummings also points out that the effigy of the Three Graces was derived from a Hellenistic sculpture, that the figure of Lady Sarah was inspired by Guido Reni, and that the arrangement of the figures is like that of an antique sculptural group.

From 1765 to 1770 this type of portrait of a lady in Reynolds's full-blown grand manner was what people thronged the exhibition rooms to see; therefore, whether he was in sympathy or not, Cotes had to acknowledge it as a powerful force.

The different mentalities of Cotes and Reynolds are well illustrated by a comparison between Cotes's second portrait of ANNE SANDBY AS EMMA (no. 183, fig. 82), possibly in the 1765 exhibition, and Reynolds's Lady Sarah Bunbury Sacrificing to the Three Graces (fig. 81).

Cotes's theme, taken from Prior's *Henry and Emma*, is a famous rococo motif, the triumph of love (see pp. 13f.). In character it is basically sensuous and frivolous, and has none of the highmindedness connected with the notion of Amicitia. Emma's sacrifice, offered to Hymen, the god of marriage, is a wreath made of flowers and her lover's hair; it hardly evokes the elevated thoughts and historical associations that Lady Sarah's and Lady Susan's libations inspire. Emma's surroundings are also totally different. She stands in a woodland setting, which appears to be heavy with lush summer foliage, and is flanked in the foreground by trees which exhibit unexpected irregularities, and even romantic decay. On her left knarled and twisted roots jut out from the base of a tree and into the ground at her feet, and on the right, just behind her, is an old, broken tree trunk, hollow in the centre and rotting away, hardly a beautiful setting in the classical sense. In contrast, Lady Sarah stands in what seems to be the garden of a classical building. She is flanked by the effigy of the Three Graces and a brazier on one side, and on the other by Lady Susan pouring a libation; in the background there is a high, regularly proportioned wall of a building designed in the classical manner. Emma's draperies are the type invented by Reynolds for portraiture, but their classical style is counterbalanced by bits of contemporary dress here and there, such as the silk under-dress, which she very carefully shows by pulling up her gown, and the two jewelled brooches on the sleeves. Lady Sarah's costume is much more simple; it isn't even a wrapping gown, but a sack-like garment tied with a simple band about the waist. There is no adornment of any sort except for the antique pin at the shoulder.

The portrait of Anne Sandby as Emma has certain features which do, in fact, relate it to Reynolds's work of the early 1760's, and these can best be appreciated by comparing it to Cotes's earlier portrait of the sitter, painted in 1759 and known through Edward Fisher's engraving (fig. 23). Then he had painted her in the very same role, but in contemporary costume, and in the background had depicted a delightful landscape, asymmetrically arranged, with a narrow path winding through the trees and fading away into the distance. In the later picture, however, Mrs. Sandby is clothed in classically inspired draperies, and the background is composed of a broad path that runs straight back into the distance along a row of trees arranged evenly and neatly one after the other; midway along this path, to the right, is the dome of a building that looks neo-classical. These concessions to classical taste in the matter of clothing and composition are, of course, quite superficial. They represent Cotes's effort to cast a thin veil of modernity over what really characterizes his portrait, namely, his choice of a rococo theme and his delight in emphasizing ornamental details; therefore, no matter how apparently up-to-date this second portrait of Mrs. Sandby may seem, essentially its style and its content are a far cry from Reynolds's Lady Sarah Bunbury Sacrificing to the Three Graces.

After 1765 Cotes started to develop his own response to the fashion Reynolds had established with the portrait of Lady Sarah, and at the Society of Artists' exhibition of 1767 he showed the results of his endeavour, the large, full-length portrait of THE DUCHESS OF HAMILTON AS VENUS QUEEN OF BEAUTY (no. 219, fig. 83). The great, weighty figure of the Duchess, with elongated hips and thick legs, is shown standing on the steps of a verandah, resting one hand on a pedestal and daintily pulling up her gown with the other. The gown is of the type Reynolds popularized, but its simple classical lines have been almost obliterated by the strong emphasis on the decorative patterns formed by the heavy folds. Something similar has happened with the architecture and the landscape setting. Instead of stressing the pure design of the pedestal, Cotes has drawn attention to the train of the gown, which has fallen over it, and the huge, fat pot that surmounts it. These large, swelling curves indicate a baroque interpretation of the classical tradition. Cummings notes that in the portrait of Lady Sarah the brazier, urn, and furniture are 'in the antique taste,'[61] but in fact, they look more like baroque versions of antique designs. It is not known whether Cotes's inspiration for the curved patterns in his portrait of The Duchess of Hamilton came directly from a study of Reynolds's picture of Lady Sarah Bunbury Sacrificing to the Three Graces (fig. 81), but whatever the source, a baroque quality is undeniable.

A further breaking-down of the classical design is evident in Cotes's treatment of the landscape setting. Instead of a carefully placed bit of classical architecture or an arrangement of trees that suggest a classical landscape beyond, he painted some exotic foliage and a sky suffused with evening light. To the left there is a willow tree, whose long delicate branches form a pretty pattern beind the figure, and to the right are two large sunflowers. The sunflowers turn not towards the sun but towards the figure, signifying that the beauty of the Duchess, like that of Venus, outshines the sun.[62] This is the sum and substance of the intellectual content of the portrait. Cotes has made use of a classical conceit, but in the simplest possible way.

Unfortunately, the portrait of The Duchess of Hamilton betrays a tendency to overpaint. Most disappointing of all is the head, which has a dead, plaster-like quality and does not do justice to one of the great beauties of the day.

From 1767 to the end of his career in 1770 he reproduced the same essentials of style and composition in about eighteen oil paintings of single, standing female figures, with two significant differences. In these pictures he reduced the extent to which he idealized the features, so that his sitters appear more as themselves and less as goddesses, and he dispensed with any subsidiary content whatsoever, thereby reducing the interpretation to one of mere physical appearances.

A representative sampling of these portraits is enough to reveal their basic nature. For purposes of illustration, two typical pictures have been chosen, the full-length of MRS. WILLIAM COLQUHOUN (no. 256, fig. 84) of 1768, and the three-quarter-length of AGNETA YORKE (no. 228, fig. 85) of 1767. The features are only slightly idealized; there is no explicit intellectual content, and the stylistic treatment of the figures, the drapery, the architecture, and the setting recalls the portrait of The Duchess of Hamilton (fig. 83). We find that once again Cotes has emphasized the decorative patterns formed by curved shapes in the poses, in the way the drapery falls, and in the visually most important of the accessories, which usually have a rather pronounced baroque character.

The quality of these paintings varies according to their size and date. The large full-lengths done around 1767/1768, such as the portrait of Mrs. Colquhoun (fig. 84), have those unfortunate aspects of technique that were observed in the picture of The Duchess of Hamilton (fig. 83). The less ambitious three-quarter lengths were more successful, because Cotes's aim was not so much to create a forceful image as a pretty one. A case in point is the portrait of Agneta Yorke (fig. 85). Admittedly, it is unintellectual, and the sitter is shown posing quite self-consciously in what she knows to be a highly fashionable attitude, but the picture is beautifully painted and cleverly composed. The delicacy of the painting, especially of the head and hands, the pristine quality of the entire image, its simplicity, and its carefully balanced order place it among Cotes's best late works.

Possibly the most interesting of his pictures from the period of 1765 to 1770 are the double portraits. As far as we know, he had done only one double portrait before 1765, the pastel of John and Joseph Gulston (fig. 24) of 1755; however, between c. 1767 and the end of his career in 1770 he is known to have painted eight, two pastels (nos. 205, fig. 103, and 206, fig. 104) and six oils (nos. 215, fig. 105; 216, fig. 89; 220, fig. 102; 250, fig. 86; 284, fig. 92; and 287, fig. 94). What gives these pictures their special quality is the lively interaction between the two figures and the unusual thematic material. The style itself varies according to whether the main influences come from Reynolds, Ramsay, or rococo precedents. Despite these borrowings, the portraits are characterized by a refreshingly personal interpretation and, occasionally, by a surprising originality.

The oil painting which most closely approximates Reynolds's ideas for a grand double portrait with two female figures, as exemplified by his Lady Sarah Bunbury (fig. 81), is Cotes's large oil of LADY STANHOPE AND LADY EFFINGHAM AS DIANA AND HER COMPANION (no. 250, fig. 86) of c. 1767–1770. At first glance, it may appear that this approximation to Reynolds's work is much too close and verges on imitation. A more careful study, however, reveals that the similarities between the two pictures, while striking, are also of a rather superficial nature, for essentially Cotes and Reynolds had different aims in mind, and adopted different means to attain them.

The impression one gets on first seeing the portrait of Lady Stanhope and Lady Effingham (fig. 86) is that these women are not goddesses, but very pretty human beings who are having a marvellous time, dressed up in the latest fashion for grand portraiture, while they act out their roles in a play. The story behind the portrait is probably very near to this. Lady Stanhope was born Anne Hussey Delaval; she married Sir William Stanhope, as his third wife, but separated from him in 1763, and returned to her family; subsequently, she took part with her sister, Lady Mexborough, and her friend, the Countess of Effingham, in private theatricals produced by her brother, Sir Francis Blake Delaval. As Professor Ellis Waterhouse has pointed out, this portrait probably has to do with such a play.[63] Reynolds was trying to convey something much more general, the notion that the friendship between Lady Sarah and Lady Susan mirrors the universal idea of perfect friendship. Reynolds wanted to progress from the particular to the general, while Cotes wanted to stay with particular appearances.

Between 1765 and 1770 Reynolds and Cotes also painted a more intimate type of double portrait, which since the 1740's had appeared in the repertoires of many important artists working in Britain. A standing figure was often depicted leaning over the chair of a seated one, and before them was placed some object of special interest to both, such as a letter, a book, a game, or a work of art.

Reynolds's typical interpretation for the 1760's is illustrated by his portrait of the architect JAMES PAINE AND HIS SON (fig. 88) of 1764. James Paine is shown seated, in contemporary dress, and leaning over him is his son, wearing a simple garment with buttons down the front and long, full sleeves. It looks very much like the costume one would expect to see in an Italian Renaissance portrait; in fact, its design probably comes from the Renaissance period. Spread out before Paine is the architectural plan for a neo-classical building, to which he points with a drawing instrument. From this immediate focus of attention, Reynolds leads us, by means of the symbolism of the Renaissance costume of Paine's son, to thoughts of classicism in Renaissance architecture; then, by means of a classical column in the background, to thoughts of Roman and Greek architecture, and finally, to thoughts of ideal proportions. Such elevated motions were never expressed by Cotes.

Three double portraits by him from the period of 1765 to 1770 illustrate his particular attitude in this regard, those of MR. AND MRS. THOMAS CRATHORNE (no. 216, fig. 89) of 1767, A LADY AND A GENTLEMAN (no. 284, fig. 92) of 1769, and MR. AND MRS. WILLIAM EARLE WELBY (no. 287, fig. 94) of 1769. These portraits all deal with love themes, the Crathornes with the recollection of an absent love, A Lady and A Gentleman with a love that threatens, and the Welbys with the triumph of love. In each case, Cotes has treated his theme in a light-hearted, down-to-earth manner, and followed an earlier rococo interpretation.

The first of these double portraits is that of Mr. and Mrs. Crathorne (fig. 89). If there was any single work which gave Cotes ideas for this picture, it was Philippe Mercier's THE LETTER WRITER (fig. 87), which had probably been painted in the 1740's.

In Mercier's painting the background is shallow and plain, with a curtain drawn neatly back on the right. The impression is of a stage backdrop. The man is in a bizarre fancy-dress costume, possibly from the Commedia dell'Arte. He appears to have crept up behind the seated lady, and is peeping curiously over her shoulder to see what she is writing. The lady, who is in contemporary costume, sits at a desk with a quill in her hand, writing a love letter. Her pose is casual and meditative; she rests her head in her hand, lost in thought about what is she going to say next. As she thinks, she looks straight at the viewer, completely unaware that a mysterious man in a strange costume is spying on her. On her desk is a portrait miniature of a gentleman, the person to whom she is writing. The image is dramatic and filled with decorative details.

Cotes's portrait of MR. AND MRS. CRATHORNE (fig. 89) is in some respects like Mercier's The Letter Writer (fig. 87). Just as in Mercier's painting, the background looks like a stage set. In front of this, Cotes also has a standing man and a seated woman. Thomas Crathorne is in fancy-dress, but not in a Commedia dell'Arte costume; he wears a white Van Dyck suit with lace collar and cuffs. Leaning on the back of a chair, on which there is a book, a folder of papers, and some loose papers tied with a ribbon, he gazes over the shoulder of a lady, who is seated in another chair. Her blue wrapping gown is of the type made fashionable by Reynolds; her pearl jewellery and the arrangment of her hair are in keeping with the fashions of the 1760's, but her lace collar and cuffs are from the Van Dyck era. This indicates that she wanted to appear fashionable in 1767, but that she also wished to express some sort of bond with her husband. She holds a drawing pen in one hand, and with the other turns back the pages of her book and points to her drawing. This is what Thomas Crathorne sees; it is a drawing of Cupid, the messenger and servant of Venus, goddess of love.

The theme of the painting, therefore, has to do with Cupid and with love, but what sort of love? We are given three clues, the chair beside Mrs. Crathorne, her pose, and the elements of Van Dyck dress, all of which would remain mysterious if it were not for a single illuminating fact: Thomas Crathorne had died in 1764. This painting, which was dated by Cotes, was done three years later, in 1767; therefore he probably copied the features of Mr. Crathorne from a picture, possibly a miniature in Mrs. Crathorne's possession, and it must have been she who commissioned the portrait several years later. In this light, the clues just mentioned take on meaning. The empty chair at Mrs. Crathorne's side, the one her husband would have sat in, and now only holding a book and some papers, signifies Thomas Crathorne's physical absence. Mrs. Crathorne's pose, looking straight out at the viewer, instead of at the figure next to her, is another device for indicating her husband's physical absence. Finally, there is the Van Dyck costume, which was often used by British eighteenth-century portraitists to convey a freedom from limitation to a particular period, a timelessness. That Thomas Crathorne is dead, in the realm of the timeless, is signified here by his being painted entirely in a Van Dyck costume. His wife, on the other hand, alive in 1767, is dressed in the contemporary fashion, with the exception of the Van Dyck collar and cuffs. These signify the bond of love linking her with her husband, which is of a timeless nature, unaffected by his death.

The rendering of the drapery in this portrait illustrates Cotes's boldest and most expressive manner for the late 1760's, one which he could use at will whenever he wanted a particularly strong and impressive visual effect. The drapery is enlivened by complicated hard-edged folds and a web of highlights (figs. 90, 91) which recall his earlier technique and style in pastels (figs. 6, 7) and their adaptation to oils at the beginning of the decade (fig. 33). As has already been noted, the appearance of these qualities in his oil portraits is neither as refined nor as sophisticated as in his pastels.

The second double portrait in this series is that of A LADY AND A GENTLEMAN (no. 284, fig. 92) of 1769. Its whereabouts were known as early as 1868, when it was in the possession of the Sacred Harmonic Society in London. Having been sold in 1883 to a British collector, it ended up in New York at the Ehrich Galleries in 1920, but in a frightful condition. Figure 92 is a reproduction of an illustration made by the Ehrich Galleries at that time. The whole painting had been darkened by dirt, with large portions remaining obscure. The surface of the canvas appears to have deteriorated, and the top layer of paint looks as if it had worn away in several areas, notably in the lady's drapery, the background drapery, and the right background behind the gentleman. Beside the gentleman, to the right, the paint has run in a peculiar way, and his coat collar has been badly restored. One cannot make any judgements, therefore, about the quality of a portrait that is in such a deplorable state. The situation is further complicated by the fact that around 1930 the canvas was cut in half. What remains today is only the figure of the lady (fig. 93), while the part with the figure of the gentleman has been lost.

But we can still observe the composition, the costumes, and the theme. The theatrical arrangement of the background is similar to the one in Mercier's The Letter Writer (fig. 87) and in Cotes's portrait of Mr. and Mrs. Crathorne (fig. 89). The lady, her hair arranged in a manner that combines seventeenth and eighteenth-century styles, leans on a pedestal and looks pensively at the viewer, a slight smile on her lips. In her right hand she holds a scroll, and points with her finger to the remains of some writing. The gentleman is seated at a desk, on which there are books entitled *Seldeni Opera* and Petyt's *Power of Parliaments*. He turns from his desk, with its legal and political tomes, and offers to the lady a small biscuit statuette of a seated Cupid with one hand raised slyly to his lips. This is one of the well-known copies of Etienne Maurice Falconet's famous marble statuette called 'L'Amour Menaçant', which was made for Madame de Pompadour. It was exhibited in Paris at the Salon of 1757, and is now in the Louvre. The theme of A Lady and A Gentleman (fig. 92) is, therefore, the offering by the gentleman to his lady of a love that sweetly threatens, a delightful, rococo theme.

The final double portrait of this series is that of MR. AND MRS. WILLIAM EARLE WELBY (fig. 94), of 1769, which Cotes showed that year at the first exhibition of the Royal Academy. Reynolds exhibited several female portraits in his grand manner. The contrast with Cotes's painting could not have been more pronounced. The portrait of Mr. and Mrs. Welby was based on the rococo theme, the triumph of love, while Reynolds drew his inspiration from classical sources.

Cotes's double portrait of Mr. and Mrs. Welby conforms with his standard composition for this type of picture. The background is plain and flat, with a curtain to the side. One figure is standing, the other is seated; both are clothed in the dress that was fashionable in 1769. The object of their attention is a chess game, which has progressed to the last move. Mrs. Welby, who has an expression of mischievous delight, is about to win. Mr. Welby gestures as if to say, 'What more can I do?', and with a smile, he succumbs to defeat. To the educated eighteenth-century observer, such a scene would probably not have been taken solely at its face value, but would have been associated immediately with the theme of the triumph of love. The idea was that love is ultimately the most powerful force in the universe, and in the end wins out over all obstacles. In eighteenth-century painting and sculpture this theme is expressed by Love, in a feminine form as either a goddess or a mortal, triumphing over her adversary. We repeatedly see Venus vanquishing Mars, or a woman defeating a man. The double portrait of Mr. and Mrs. Welby was probably painted to evoke associations with this theme.

A discussion of the double portraits from the final period of Cotes's career would not be complete without a study of the two pastels (nos. 205 and 206, figs. 103 and 104) and two oils (nos. 215 and 220, figs. 105 and 102) which he did for the royal family in 1767. The sitters were all ladies, Queen Caroline and her daughter, Princess Charlotte, and the two sisters of George III, Princess Louisa and Queen Caroline Matilda of Denmark. These were extremely important portraits for Cotes because they gave him the opportunity to establish himself with the royal family.

George III intensely disliked Reynolds. There may have been a number of reasons for this, but one of the main ones was that the King did not like Reynolds's politics, and he particularly disapproved of some of Reynolds's friends, like Edmund Burke and Admiral Augustus Keppel, who frustrated his desire to control Parliament through coercion and bribery. Unfortunately, the conflict of interests that developed between the King and Reynolds was never resolved, and as a result, Reynolds remained firmly excluded from the circle of artists regularly sponsored by the royal family.

The King's favourite painter was Allan Ramsay, who had enjoyed this status since the 1750's, when the King was Prince of Wales. At that time Ramsay had already been given the title of Official Painter to the Prince of Wales, and after the Prince's accession to the throne in 1760, Ramsay was appointed one of His Majesty's Painters in Ordinary. He was a quiet, cultivated man of exceptional talent, and delighted his royal patron with his witty conversation and his superb portraits. In return, the King treated him with a certain degree of familiarity and always with great respect. The King, as well as other members of the royal family, kept him busy with commissions for portraits; as a result, he saw no need to compete with Reynolds at the exhibitions of the Society of Artists or those of the Royal Academy. In fact, he did not exhibit his work publicly, nor did he become a member of the Academy.

Cotes was well aware of the desirability of securing royal patronage and of Ramsay's position. Politics did not present a problem for him as it did for Reynolds. He shuttled back and forth between Whig and Tory clients, between those who opposed the King and those who supported him, between the public world of the exhibition room and the group of artists privately patronized by the King. His political views are unknown, but his policy appears to have been to keep politics and business apart, and as far as his relationship with the royal family was concerned, this was a diplomatic attitude.

His royal clients wanted the kind of portraits Ramsay had painted. Cotes interpreted Ramsay's type of picture, but he used his own compositions, chose his own thematic material, and retained all the essential qualities of his own style. The precedents Ramsay established can be illustrated by his portrait of LADY SUSAN FOX-STRANGEWAYS, (fig. 95) of 1761, and by three of his pictures of QUEEN CHARLOTTE, the famous half-length with a fan, of about 1761 (fig. 96), the state portrait of 1761 (fig. 97), and the group portrait of the Queen and her children, begun in 1763 and finished in 1765 (fig. 98). The portrait of Lady Susan Fox-Strangeways (fig. 95) illustrates the type of seated female figure that appealed to the royal ladies who employed Cotes. The three portraits of Queen Charlotte show how exquisitely refined Ramsay made royal ladies look, and how he portrayed them intimately enough to capture their personalities, yet formally enough to preserve their regal dignity.

The royal family's choice of Cotes for the painting of four important double portraits becomes understandable when one realizes that his work and Ramsay's, although different in certain respects, had a great deal in common. Both artists preferred a sensual and relatively unintellectual treatment of classical qualities. They had been strongly influenced by the aesthetic values prevalent in Britain in the 1740's and early 50's and by the work of the leading continental pastellists of that period; as a consequence, they developed from this common source of inspiration an inclination towards pretty, pastel-like effects. These qualities were not only especially well-suited for conveying feminine charms, they also happened to be highly fashionable for court portraiture, having been established in the works of La Tour and Nattier at the most fashionable of all European courts of the day, that of Louis XV. What the royal women particularly liked in the paintings of Ramsay and Cotes, therefore, was the preservation, above all else, of these French trends traditionally associated with court portraiture and their combination with a carefully made selection of classical elements that had become popular by the late 1760's.

Of the double portraits Cotes did for the royal family, that of PRINCESS LOUISA AND QUEEN CAROLINE MATILDA OF DENMARK (no. 220, fig. 102) is the most historically interesting and revealing, as well as being one of the very finest oil paintings he ever did. The two sisters, Louisa (1749–1768) and Caroline Matilda (1751–1775), grew up under the watchful eye of their mother, the Dowager Princess Augusta, who kept them secluded from the world and from society. King Frederick V of Denmark had originally wanted his son, the future Christian VII, to marry Louisa, but because she was sickly, it was feared that children by her would not be healthy; consequently, the King decided on Caroline Matilda. In January of 1765 the betrothal was announced. Caroline Matilda, a child of fourteen, who had never met Christian, and who wanted desperately to stay at home, was bitterly upset by the thought of her coming marriage. In January of 1766, King Frederick died. Christian succeeded to the throne, and on October 1st of that year, he married Caroline Matilda against her wishes at a proxy wedding at Carlton House. The following day, heavy with sadness at having to leave her family, and especially her sister Louisa, she set out for Copenhagen. She was never to return to Britain again. Christian proved to be a weak king and an unfaithful husband. Caroline Matilda's only consolation were the two children that she had by him.

In 1768 Princess Louisa finally succumbed to tuberculosis and lay dying. Christian, jealous of his Queen's popularity with the English, refused to allow her to return to London to be with her sister, but he went there himself on a riotous pleasure trip. This proved too much for Caroline Matilda, and she entered into a love affair with the King's minister, Dr. Johann Struensee. The pair were discovered and put on trial in 1772. They were both found guilty; Struensee was executed, and Caroline Matilda was officially divorced, deprived of her children, and exiled from Denmark. George III, who did not want her to return to England for political reasons, sent her to Celle Castle in Bavaria, which was governed by Queen Charlotte's brother, Prince Ernst of Mecklenburg-Strelitz (no. 272). Here, Queen Caroline Matilda remained until her death in 1775 at the age of twenty-four.[64]

Cotes did two nearly identical head and shoulders pastel portraits of CAROLINE MATILDA in 1766, after her betrothal had been announced and before her departure for Denmark. Fortunately, both have survived and have ended up in highly appropriate places. One pastel (no. 189) is in the museum at Frederiksborg in Denmark, which is fitting, because Caroline Matilda is still thought of with sympathy and affection in Denmark, and the royal palace at Frederiksborg was one of her favourite residences. The other pastel (no. 188, fig. 99) is better-known. It was engraved in the eighteenth century by James Watson and by Richard Brookshaw, and by others in the nineteenth century. Today it is in the collection of one of Caroline Matilda's relations, S. K. H. the Prince of Hanover, Herzog von Braunschweig und Lüneburg, at Celle Castle.

The purpose of commissioning Cotes to do two small pastels of Caroline Matilda, his first royal sitter, was probably to provide her family with intimate portraits of the young princess before she left for Denmark. One of the versions Cotes did, possibly the better-known picture (no. 188, fig. 99), was recorded as being in the Bedchamber at Buckingham House in about 1790–1795, but generally, the provenances of both pastels are obscure, so that it is impossible to relate their histories. It is not unlikely, for example, that Caroline Matilda took one portrait with her to Denmark as a wedding present for Christian, and left the other behind with her family.

What does appear to be fairly certain is that, when Cotes came to do the large oil portrait of PRINCESS LOUISA AND QUEEN CAROLINE MATILDA (fig. 102) in 1767, he used one of his pastel portraits as a guide for painting the features of the Danish Queen, who had left England in the previous year. A comparison between the Celle pastel (fig. 99) and the head of Queen Caroline Matilda in the double portrait leaves little doubt that this is precisely what happened.

In addition to one of the 1766 pastels of Queen Caroline Matilda, which appears to have been used as a preparatory study for the double portrait, there is an interesting half-length oil of PRINCESS LOUISA (no. 227, fig. 100), done around 1767, which Cotes may have used for the same purpose. In this picture and in the double portrait, Louisa's pose, expression, clothes, jewellery, and hair style are the same; however, instead of holding her music book and guitar, as she does in the double portrait, she is shown holding one of her gloves and a fan. The half-length figure of Louisa holding her fan is reminiscent of Ramsay's half-length of QUEEN CHARLOTTE (fig. 96) of about 1761, in which the Queen holds a fan. Cotes may have tried out the glove and fan in the half-length of Princess Louisa, remembering Ramsay's portrait, and then, in the end, replaced them with the music book and guitar.

Finally, there is a pen and wash drawing by Cotes, done around 1767, of TWO LADIES AT MUSIC (no. 225, fig. 101), which also relates to the double portrait of Princess Louisa and Queen Caroline Matilda. He made this quick sketch to experiment with a possible composition for his oil portrait (fig. 102). As a comparison shows, some of the elements of the composition he was trying out in the preparatory drawing were kept in the final double portrait, and some were changed.

In the double portrait, Louisa and Caroline Matilda are shown in elaborate court dresses, posed against a background that suggests a grand interior. On the left is a lectern with music sheets on it, and on the right is an organ. Louisa is seated with a music book on her lap, and holds a guitar. Caroline Matilda, holding some rolled-up music sheets, stands behind Louisa and looks over her shoulder at the lectern. The two sisters appear to be in a music room of one of the royal residences.

One is much more aware of the intimate aspects of the portrait than of its grandeur. Apart from its large size, the regal bearing of the sitters, and the absence of humour, it recalls three smaller and much less formal works previously discussed, the paintings of Mr. and Mrs. Crathorne (fig. 89), A Lady and A Gentleman (fig. 92), and Mr. and Mrs. Welby (fig. 94). Like these pictures, the portrait of Princess Louisa and Queen Caroline Matilda is an example of Cotes's personal interpretation of a standard type of intimate double portrait, an interpretation that owes more to the artistic taste of the first half of the eighteenth century, and particularly to the rococo, than to anything else.

The arrangement of the figures, one standing and the other seated and looking out at the viewer, is a composition often encountered in this type of double portrait. What gives it a special interest is Cotes's interpretation. His figures are not arranged in a tight, compact order, the way, for example, that Ramsay's are in the portrait of QUEEN CHARLOTTE AND HER CHILDREN (fig. 98). Ramsay's figures look like a sculptural group, and their composition echoes the noble architecture behind them. There is a relationship between Cotes's figures and the background, but classical proportions are not involved. The most noticeable feature in the background is the heavy silk curtain that stretches across the top from one side to the other, and draws attention to the heavy silk dresses of both figures. Principally, Cotes is interested in emphasizing the ornamental quality of these dresses, elaborately constructed court gowns. This is an intention that brings him closer in spirit to the Rococo than to the classical revival in portraiture of the late 1760's.

Ramsay's handling of line, colour, and light is directed at creating an overall effect that both unites the figures with the background setting and expresses their purity, simplicity, and serenity. Cotes's style is far different. It emphasizes individual parts rather than the whole. Each form is carefully defined, so that one tends to notice details, the sheets of music, the lectern, the guitar, the amazingly intricate work on the dresses, the jewellery, and finally, the heads, which have the fine, pencilled quality of pastels.

The heads are the two focal points. Normally, in eighteenth-century portraits of women, especially in the rococo ones, the sitters wanted to appear happy, charming, and witty. It is surprising, therefore, to find Cotes, who was so influenced by the Rococo, actually breaking away from that tradition and daring to show an undertone of sadness in a portrait of women, and a royal portrait at that. Louisa and Caroline Matilda do not appear just as pretty ladies; Cotes went so far as to show Louisa with bags and heavy circles under her eyes, and a wistful expression on her face. Caroline Matilda's expression is full of tenderness, but there is also a slight look of sadness in her eyes. Perhaps Cotes wished to show something of her feelings on parting with Princess Louisa, for her hand rests affectionately on the back of her sister's chair. One also wonders whether she had a premonition that Louisa's illness would end in death the following year.

When Cotes came to paint the double portrait in oils of QUEEN CHARLOTTE AND PRINCESS CHARLOTTE of 1767 (no. 215, fig. 105), his working method was probably similar to the one he used in the picture of Princess Louisa and Queen Caroline Matilda (fig. 102) that same year. Two important half-length, oval pastels of QUEEN CHARLOTTE AND PRINCESS CHARLOTTE of 1767, one in the Queen's collection at Buckingham Palace (no. 205, fig. 103), the other in the Duke of Northumberland's collection at Syon House (no. 206, fig. 104), are clearly related to the larger oil, and were almost certainly done as preparatory studies for it.

Walpole made some interesting remarks about the two small pastels and the large oil. After seeing the Buckingham Palace pastel (fig. 103) exhibited at the Society of Artists in 1767, he jotted down in his exhibition catalogue the following comments:

> The Queen fine; the Child, incomparable. The Duchess of Northumberland has the Original, given to her by the Queen. There is a whole length of the same (This is oval) at the Queen's house in the Park and has been engraved. The sleeping Child is equal to Guido. Cotes succeeded much better in crayons than in oils. (Cf. Appendix III)

From this passage we learn that Queen Charlotte had owned both pastels, one was exhibited at the Society of Artists (fig. 103), and the other was given to the Duchess of Northumberland (fig. 104). The Duchess of Northumberland's pastel is called 'The Original', which seems to indicate that it was done before the Buckingham Palace version, and probably before the large oil. The oil is referred to as the 'whole length of the same', and is said to be at 'the Queen's house in the Park', a wonderful way of describing Windsor Castle. The engraving mentioned was by W. Wynne Ryland; it was not published until 1770. The observation that 'the sleeping Child is equal to Guido' may be quite perceptive, because the pose Queen Charlotte adopts, a finger raised to command silence lest anyone wake the sleeping Princess, is found occasionally in Italian Renaissance and Baroque paintings of the Madonna and Child. A direct precedent from the works of Guido Reni has not been found, but one still wonders whether it exists, especially since among Cotes's bequests to his father was the following: 'the Picture of the Virgin and Child in crayons from Guido painted by myself' (Supplement no. 22). Unfortunately this pastel has been lost. Finally, Walpole concludes with an important judgement, that 'Cotes succeeded much better in crayons than in oils'. This generalization will be discussed in detail at the end of this essay. With regard to the two pastels and the oil of Queen Charlotte with Princess Charlotte, it is only partially true. While the Syon House pastel is by far the most successful of the three pictures, the Buckingham Palace pastel is below Cotes's normal standard and inferior to the Windsor oil.

On June 25, 1783, Walpole saw the Buckingham Palace pastel a second time, and wrote down in his *Journal of Visits to Country Seats*, '. . . the Queen gave a Duplicate of this to the late Duchess of Northumberland.'[65] His choice of the word 'Duplicate' tends to be rather confusing. Are we to understand that the Syon House version is just like the Buckingham Palace pastel, or are we to understand that the Syon House version is a second version, made after the Buckingham Palace pastel? If he meant that the Duchess if Northumberland's picture was a second version, then he was contradicting himself, because in his 1767 catalogue he had referred to it as 'The Original'.

What is evident from a study of both pastels is that they are not, in fact, alike. The Syon House version is considerably better, and is much more closely related to the oil portrait at Windsor. Apparently, Cotes first did the Buckingham Palace pastel for Queen Charlotte, which she exhibited; subsequently, she probably commissioned a second version as a gift for the Duchess of Northumberland. This second version would not have been signed or dated, so as to indicate that it was a duplicate. In it, Cotes would have improved the lighting on the head of the Queen, changed her expression, made some changes in her costume, and generally given the entire image a more finished and sophisticated appearance. The improved version was then probably used by him as his principal preparatory study for the oil portrait.

It is helpful to go into some detail so that one can appreciate how different the Buckingham Palace portrait (fig. 103) is from the other two pictures (figs. 104, 105). In the Syon House version and the Windsor oil the lighting on the Queen's face is stronger than in the Buckingham Palace pastel; on the left, her face is more brightly illuminated to bring out the softness and beauty of her complexion, and on the right, there is a shadow that is handled in a more gentle and flattering way. The shape of the Queen's head and the expression on her face are the same in the Syon House version and the Windsor oil, and make her look much more attractive than she does in the Buckingham Palace pastel. Her costume in the Syon House version and the Windsor oil is also the same; the heavy stripes on her sleeve in the Buckingham Palace pastel have been replaced by two series of more delicate stripes, and the flower on her sleeve has been lowered and changed into a different type. The first circle of pearls in her hair in the Buckingham Palace pastel is a single strand, and this has been replaced in the other two pictures by a double strand. While the composition and colours of both pastels are the same, the Queen in blue and gold and the Princess in blue and white silhouetted against a grey background with a red curtain, the Syon House version is much less sketchy and rough; the colour contrasts are softer, the line more controlled, and the whole image smoother and more finished. The Syon House version and the Windsor oil have many more points in common than the Buckingham Palace pastel and the Windsor oil; consequently, it is likely that the Syon House version immediately preceded the final oil portrait.

The final picture, at Windsor (fig. 105), developed out of these preparatory studies, is another example of Cotes's typical interpretation of a standard type of double portrait. What differentiates it, however, from Cotes's other double portraits is a greater degree of rigidity and formality. The figures are like a heavy block of stone, held in place by the geometric grid pattern of the carpet. They seem quite fixed and static. Even the Queen's hand raised to command silence seems frozen in mid-air.

Cotes wanted his picture to be as regal and imposing as a state portrait. In certain respects it is like Ramsay's state portrait of QUEEN CHARLOTTE (fig. 97) of 1761. Ramsay shows the Queen swathed in ermine, standing by her throne and placing a hand on her crown, which rests on the table beside her. This is an image *par excellence* of Charlotte as Queen. In Cotes's portrait, she is not in official costume, nor is she surrounded by so many regalia, but she sits stiffly in her chair as if it were a throne. She wears an elaborately constructed court dress and commands silence with all the authority of a monarch. The queenly aspects of her pose are accentuated in the oil, while the maternal ones are emphasized in the two pastels.

Several very fine single portraits in oils were developed out of Cotes's work on double portraits for the royal family. The most representative is the lovely three-quarter length of LADY BROWNLOW BERTIE (no. 292, fig. 106) of c. 1769. In one way or another, this painting is reminiscent of all the royal double portraits, both pastels and oils. The background with a column and a heavy curtain recalls all of these pictures, particularly the pastels (figs. 103, 104), where the curtain is placed directly behind the sitter's head. The figure of Lady Brownlow Bertie, seated in a large chair with a music book on her lap, was inspired by the figure of Princess Louisa in the double portrait in oils of 1767 (fig. 102). Cotes has focused on ornamental details like the little flower sprigs embroidered on the pink satin dress, and he has drawn special attention to the head and hands, which are delicately painted in a pastel-like manner. This is an extremely effective and beautiful portrait, typical of his best work in oils at the end of his career.

Our knowledge of the nature and development of Cotes's work between 1765 and 1770 must come principally from a stylistic analysis of his portraits, because historical documents relating to him are few and far between. Nevertheless, some documents have been discovered and do, in fact, provide valuable information about him.

We learn from the *Royal Charter and Statutes of the Society of Artists* that at the beginning of 1765 he and nine other members of the Society presented a petitition to George III requesting that their organization be given a royal charter, and that on January 26, 1765, the King consented and appointed Cotes as a director.[66] This was a position of considerable eminence and is indicative of the high regard in which he was held.

The delightfully talkative and witty friend of Dr. Samuel Johnson, Mrs. Hester Thrale, recorded in her diary an amusing and revealing incident which also occurred in 1765:

> I made worse Mischief by half at Cotes the Painter's once where I was very intimate: whose Picture is that said I, and that Lady's pray? who is as eminent for her ugliness methinks, as any-one here for her Beauty—hold for God's Sake says Francis Cotes in a Fright; 'tis my own Wife, it is indeed; & I have been married to her but a fortnight, this was the year 1765.[67]

It is interesting that Mrs. Thrale was a friend of Cotes's, otherwise very little is known about his friendships. He does not appear to have associated with the Reynolds-Johnson circle, nor do any of the famous lady diarists of the day mention him, save for Mrs. Thrale. In this passage she gives us the date of Francis and Sarah's marriage, 1765, and her opinion that in the picture she saw at that memorable dinner party Sarah appeared 'eminent for her Ugliness'. It is not definitely known to which picture she was referring, but one suspects that Mrs. Thrale was being peevish and provocative and really wanted to make 'worse Mischief by half', because the three portraits by Cotes which are considered to be of his wife show her as a pleasantly attractive woman (no. 65, fig. 107; no. 296, fig. 109; no. 297, fig. 108).

In the newspaper correspondence concerning public art exhibitions in 1766, an anonymous correspondent who signed himself 'T. B.' made some interesting observations on the customary practice among the leading artists of the day of employing assistants.

> 'It is,' says T. B., 'extremely customary to employ some brother artists to finish particular parts of their performances. Mr. Lambert, for instance, never painted the figures in his own landscapes; Mr. Hayman's backgrounds have frequently been executed by a variety of hands; and it is well known that Mr. Hudson, Mr. Cotes, and several other painters of the first reputation seldom, if ever, finish an atom more than the face of their portraits, notwithstanding that the drapery of their pictures—which is generally the production of indigent excellence—acquired them such uncommon approbation from the public'[68].

Our knowledge of Cotes's assistant, Peter Toms, is much too limited to be satisfactory. There is no evidence that he ever knew how to work with pastels or that he assisted Cotes in any way with pastel portraits. He was trained as a drapery painter for oil portraits, and, as Edwards noted, 'was almost wholly employed by Mr. Cotes' from 1763/64 to 1770.[69] From 1765 onwards he helped his master to increase the output of oil portraits from the studio. It is not known, however, whether or not Cotes 'seldom, if ever', finished 'an atom more than the face' and left the drapery completely to Toms. The extent of Toms's assistance remains a mystery. The documents presently available throw little light on the problem, and Cotes's portraits are even less revealing. Toms was, as T. B. noted, a drapery painter of 'indigent excellence'; he laboured to reproduce Cotes's style as perfectly as possible. Consequently, one cannot detect whether Toms or Cotes himself was working on the drapery. This is why Toms was so valuable to Cotes. He did not interfere with the quality of the master's work nor with its stylistic development; what he did was to make it possible for Cotes to produce more oil portraits. It was an arrangement which worked extremely well for both men and kept them busy with a steady stream of clients. Edwards related that Cotes's death in 1770 . . .

> . . . terminated the comforts of poor Toms. In consequence of this loss he became melancholy, and sought relief in that medicine which dissipates but for a short time those reflections it cannot eradicate. He terminated his sufferings, by his own hand, about the latter end of the year 1776. . . . His prints, drawings, and painting utensils, were sold by Gerrard, the auctioneer, in January 1777.[70]

Unfortunately, the Gerrard sale catalogue has never been found.

Cotes taught students at the house in Cavendish Square which he had bought and refurbished around 1763. Very little is known of his teaching methods or of his students, all of whom, save for one, John Russell, have faded into oblivion. Russell was Cotes's star pupil and a very close friend, but his religious views and preoccupations with his own salvation and that of others caused his master a good deal of annoyance. In 1766 and 1767 Russell recorded in his diary several incidents which caused disputes with Cotes over religious matters. The only known copy of the diary is in the library of the Victoria and Albert Museum. It is virtually a day-to-day account of Russell's examinations of conscience, his efforts to set down in writing a description of his feelings, faults, and virtues in order to study them, and, thereby, to become more enlightened. He was a distressingly pious person, whose intense interest in God and religion was very much bound up with his worries about himself. Cotes found this especially irritating because it distracted Russell from his work, and often caused disruption and confusion among the other students. Late in 1766 Russell wrote in his diary that his master had been furious, because he had purposely left one of his religious books in the kitchen at Cavendish Square, 'as he (Cotes) said, to corrupt his Servants.'[71] Not long after this incident Cotes decided that Russell should be kept away from evening prayer meetings. Consequently, after class he arranged for Russell to go to Langford's, the auctioneer's in Covent Garden, where there were evening sales. Russell was not at all pleased and commented: 'My master has made me uneasy by appointing me to attend an auction of drawings which is to last these ten evenings.'[72] The preacher Russell went to hear in the evenings was the Rev. William Romaine, whom Cotes had painted in 1758 (no. 87). Romaine was the leader of an Evangelical group within the Church of England which had very strong leanings towards Methodist doctrines. He was also Russell's spiritual mentor, and hardly a day passed that Russell did not visit him or go to hear him preach. Not only did Cotes find Russell's incessant trips to Romaine aggravating. He also disagreed with Romaine's religious views, and in January of 1767 he and his wife finally spoke very sharply to Russell, who noted in his diary:

> I had a religious argument with my Master and Mrs. Cotes at dinner today. I had the name of Blasphemer given me because I defended the doctrine of Election and spoke of the Exceeding Sinfulness of Sin.[73]

In April of 1767 Cotes used his powers as a director of the Society of Artists to get on to the hanging committee for the Society's annual show, which opened that month at Spring Gardens. He was particularly concerned to see that the two most important pictures he was exhibiting, the Buckingham Palace pastel of Queen Charlotte with Princess Charlotte (fig. 103) and the large oil of The Duchess of Hamilton (fig. 83) were hung in the best possible places in the main exhibition room. His manner of securing these places was rather high-handed, and was remembered with distaste some years later by an anonymous writer, who cited it as a contributing factor to the removal from office in 1768 of Cotes and fifteen other directors. Unfortunately for the Society, those removed went on to form the Royal Academy, which completely eclipsed every other organization of artists in Britain. It was with a sense of bitterness, therefore, that the Society, through this anonymous writer, struck back at Cotes and the other former directors in a pamphlet called *The Conduct of the Royal Academicians*, published in 1771. The passage concerning Cotes's hanging of his pictures in 1767 is as follows:

> One of the Committee (Cotes) occupied, as usual, two principal situations, in one of which he hung a picture of her Majesty and in the other that of a lady of quality [the Duchess of Hamilton]. The carpenter, going to place a fine piece of shipping belonging to a celebrated artist in that branch of painting, above that of the Queen, the Director [Cotes] called out with great vehemence, 'You must not hang that picture there.' 'Why?' 'It will hurt my Queen.' Accordingly it was taken to the other end of the room, when the Director called out with more vehemence, 'It must not be hung there.' 'Why, Sir?' 'Because it will kill my Duchess.'[74]

Cotes was particularly intent that his work should be shown off to best advantage at the 1767 exhibition. The royal family had bestowed a special honour on him by allowing him to exhibit the pastel of Queen Charlotte with Princess Charlotte (fig. 103). Moreover, the King and Queen were coming in person to see the show and to acknowledge in public their approval of Cotes's efforts. Never before had George III or Queen Charlotte thought it fitting that any portrait of them be exhibited, nor had they ever accepted the numerous invitations from the Society to see its yearly exhibitions. Ramsay was the royal family's favourite painter, but he was not a member of the Society. From among the Society's members, the King and Queen had chosen Cotes to be the one they would patronize and honour at a public exhibition. This was obviously a slap at Reynolds. In retaliation he refused to show any works at all at the exhibition—an extraordinary decision, the meaning of which was clear to everyone, although nothing was ever said.

The presence of the King and Queen at the private view of the Society's show was duly reported in the press, accompanied by lavish praise for the picture they had come to see displayed. The critic for *The London Chronicle* got so carried away by the occasion that he wrote part of his review in verse:

> How happy Cotes? Thy skill shall shine,
> Unrivall'd in thy class, almost divine;

For royal Charlotte's finish'd form is thine!
How on thy canvas, Cotes, with joy is seen
The tend'rest Mother, and the mildest Queen;
Who can her dignity with meekness blend,
And lose awhile the Empress in a friend. . . .
Now Cotes have done! now close thy talks of fame
In George's sun shine, and in Charlotte's name.[75]

At some time in 1768 Cotes sat for his portrait to the French artist, Pierre Falconet, son of the famous sculptor. In his *Anecdotes*, Edwards describes Falconet's work in London and the occasion on which he drew the portraits of twelve English artists of the day, including Cotes. Edwards says:

> Peter Falconet, a native of Paris, and son of Falconet, the sculptor . . . was for some years in London, and obtained considerable employment. His name stands in the catalogue of the Exhibitions from 1767 to 1773, soon after which he returned to Paris. He practiced sometimes in history, at other times portraits, and also painted ornaments. . . .
>
> On his first arrival in London, he drew the profile portraits of twelve of the principal English artists, in black lead, and a slight tint of colour on the cheeks and draperies. They were afterwards engraved in the dotted manner by Pariset, and published by Ryland, whose portrait is one of the set; they are in circles, with slight borders, of the octave size.[76]

In the British Museum some of Falconet's profile portraits discussed by Edwards have been preserved. Unfortunately the drawing of Cotes is not among them. The only image of the artist that has come to light thus far is D. P. Pariset's engraving after Falconet's drawing (Pl. III), which shows Cotes in his last years as a rather plump, prosperous-looking gentleman.

Although Cotes achieved considerable success at the Society of Artists exhibition of 1767, he did not follow this up by exhibiting a large number of pictures in 1768. The Society's catalogues for 1768 (cf. Appendix III) show that he exhibited only three portraits at the regular spring exhibition and only two at the special exhibition at the end of September, which was put on in honour of King Christian VII of Denmark. He was extremely ill at the time, and also deeply involved in the political intrigues behind a mass defection from the Society of Artists.

On June 11, 1768, John Russell recorded in his diary the first distressing signs of an illness that was to prove fatal for Cotes two years later. In the eighteenth century it was simply called 'the stone,' which meant either kidney or gall stones. The passage in Russell's diary reads as follows: 'Seen Mr Cotes my Late Master to Day, who is very Ill with the stone and this Week intends to go under the severe operation of being cut.'[77] What kind of surgery a patient suffering from kidney or gall stones could have survived without an anaesthetic is difficult to imagine. Cotes did undergo an operation, however, and not only managed to survive, but continued to paint for two more years.

In August, he and fifteen other directors of the Society were dismissed from office. Since the granting of the Society's royal charter in 1765, the original directors had steadfastly refused to give up their positions, but in August a rival faction introduced a by-law into the statutes which finally forced them to resign.

Following this incident, William Chambers, Architect of Works to the King, Benjamin West, and Francis Cotes, both of whom were admired by the royal family, and George Michael Moser began to

F.Cotes.
Effig.ci Pictor.
P. Falconet del 1768.
Sold by P. Falconet Broad Street Carnaby Market, & Ryland & Bryer, Cornhill.

III D. P. Pariset: *Francis Cotes*. Stipple engraving, after a drawing by Pierre Falconet of 1768, published in the latter half of the eighteenth century. British Museum, London

IV *William Craven, 6th Baron Craven* (No. 257). Oil, 1768. Worcester Art Museum, Worcester, Massachusetts

plot secretly for the formation of a new organization, which would enjoy the official patronage of the King. As James Northcote relates:

> The four persons who first planned the institution were Sir William Chambers, Mr. West, Mr. Cotes, and Mr. Moser; these together carried on the project with such profound secrecy, that no one of the incorporated society (Society of Artists) had the least knowledge or idea of its having been seriously thought of.[78]

By November this clandestine little group of artists was ready to present its ideas for the foundation of a royal academy to George III. The Academy's minute books for December 14, 1768, and January 2, 1769, give us the basic outline of what happened.[79] Chambers, the moving force behind the whole project, was selected as the group's spokesman. In a private interview with the King, Chambers proposed the establishment of a royal academy along the lines which he, West, Cotes, and Moser had planned. The King was pleased by the prospect, and probably made up his mind then and there to push Chambers's proposal through the necessary formalities as quickly as possible. Once the interview between the King and Chambers had been concluded, things moved very rapidly. The King instructed Chambers to have the four artists involved draw up and sign a formal petition, called a memorial, requesting in writing that a royal academy be founded. This was done immediately, and submitted to the King on November 28, 1768. The King then instructed Chambers to formulate a plan for the new organization, and in about ten days' time Chambers managed to do so. The King approved it on December 10, 1768, thus bringing the Royal Academy into existence, much to the surprise of the members of the Society of Artists.

In the structuring of the Academy's principal offices and the choice of the persons to fill those offices, the hand of George III can be seen quite plainly. He arranged to keep a firm control over the Academy through its purse. He saw to it that the office of treasurer carried wide powers relating to financial matters, and he appointed his man, Chambers, as Treasurer. Following Chambers's recommendation, he appointed Reynolds as President. Reynolds had not been identified with any particular political faction within the Society of Artists; he had remained above the intrigues that led to the Academy's foundation, and he was obviously the most erudite and capable person to direct the Academy's teaching programme. Since the King and Chambers were in control of the money, they felt they could direct Reynolds's activities. For his efforts, Cotes was awarded a seat on the Academy's governing Council.

Cotes exhibited eighteen portraits at the Royal Academy's first two exhibitions in 1769 and 1770, including two more portraits for the royal family, the pastels of the DUKE OF GLOUCESTER (no. 273, fig. 110) and the DUKE OF CUMBERLAND (no. 298). He was at the peak of his career and enjoyed considerable fame in these last two years, but was still suffering from the disease called 'the stone', which had only been temporarily alleviated by the operation he had had in 1768. Apparently in a fit of desperation, he took an over-strong and toxic potion made from soap, which was supposed to purge his system and somehow dissolve the gall stones or kidney stones. Instead of curing him, it poisoned him to death. He died on July 19, 1770, at Richmond, and was buried at the parish churchyard there.

Russell recorded the following passages in his diary:

> Thurs., July 19, 1770 ... had the sorrowful account of My Late Master Mr. Francis Cotes's

> Death, tho not unexpected, yet the news affected me much that a man full of worldly honour and pride with schemes of Business should be cut off without leaving any Marks of knowing the salvation of Jesus.[80]
>
> Friday, July 20, 1770. Last night I lay a Long time awake being much affected by the Death of Mr. Cotes. This morning I had the painful office to break it to his aged Father and Mother. . . .[81]
> Wed., July 25, 1770. Paid the last piece of respects to poor Mr. Cotes's Remains—went to see him inter'd at Richmond in Surrey. . . . This Towering Cedar level'd with the dust in the 45th year of his Age, 'twas affecting to hear the people say when the Bell sadden'd the air with its melancholy note, Ha, poor, ingenious Mr. Cotes.[82]

The obituary that appeared in *The Gazeteer and New Daily Advertiser* on the day of his burial indicates the reaction of the public to the news of his death.

> On Thursday last died, At Richmond, Francis Cotes, Esq., R.A.S., who had the honour to be nominated one of the principal members, at the first institution, by his present Majesty: a man whose works will best deliver down his name to posterity; whose just reputation as an artist ranked him high in the esteem of every man of taste, though his own preferred the character (he gained, sustained, and left) of an honest man.[83]

Mary Moser, writing to her friend Henry Fuseli in Rome, observed:

> Sir Joshua a few days ago entertained the Council and visitors with callipash and callipee, except poor Cotes, who last week fell a sacrifice to the corroding power of soap-lees, which he hoped would have cured him of the stone. Many a tear will drop on his grave, as he is not more lamented as an artist than a friend to the distressed. (Ma poca polvere sono che nulla sente !)[84]

Cotes was survived by his wife, Sarah, his mother, his father, Robert, and his brother, Samuel, the miniaturist, all of whom were named as beneficiaries in his will, which he had made on June 16, 1769, and which was proved on July 30, 1770. It is kept today at Somerset House. Sarah was named as the chief beneficiary and the sole executrix. Joseph Wilton, the sculptor, and Joseph Forest, an amateur artist and author, were named as trustees, and Peter Toms was among the witnesses. Sarah was left the house in Cavendish Square and its contents, and two interesting bequests were made to the artist's father. In Cotes's own words these were described as follows: 'The picture of the Virgin and Child in crayons from Guido painted by myself' (Supplement 22) and 'the crayon picture of myself, (Appendix v, 44). Both works have been lost.

On the 21st, 22nd, and 23rd of February, 1771, Sarah sold the house in Cavendish Square and its contents, including linens, china, works of art, and books, at a public auction at Langford and Son in Covent Garden. The sale catalogue, now in the Victoria and Albert Museum library, is reproduced in Appendix II. It not only provides valuable information about Cotes's watercolours of landscapes, but also indicates his interest in studying examples of this genre by other artists. In his collection, for example, there were landscapes by his friend, Paul Sandby, by Gainsborough, by the sculptor Joseph Wilton, and by various Italian masters, Panini, Horizonti, Zuccarelli, and Marco Ricci.

The sale catalogue also reveals Cotes's eclectic attitudes in his collection of casts and in his choice of books for his library. He was acquainted with some of the major artistic styles of the period, but there is little indication in the catalogue of which ones he favoured. He had casts taken from antique pieces, from sculptures by the seventeenth-century classicist, François Duquesnoy (called Fiamingo), and from sculptures by John Michael Rysbrack. Classicism was not the only stylistic tradition represented, however. There were casts from sculptures by the mannerist, Giovanni da Bologna, and from two famous rococo works by Jean-Baptiste Pigalle, Mercury and Venus, which Cotes had bought at the sale of the possessions of the sculptor, Louis François Roubiliac, in May of 1762.[85] He did a pastel portrait of Roubiliac at some time between about 1752 and the sculptor's death in 1762 (no. 82). In his library classicism is represented by the Roman writers, Terence, Tacitus, and Horace; by the Italians, Da Vinci and Algarotti, and by Pope and Dryden. Rococo verse is illustrated by Prior's *Henry and Emma*, probably the only work in the library from which Cotes derived thematic material for portraits. Two well-known sources of inspiration for romantic artists were also among his books: Shakespeare's plays and Edmund Burke's *The Sublime and the Beautiful*. In addition, there were other essays, sermons, and poems; the most interesting of these is Locke's *An Essay concerning Human Understanding*, which provided a philosophical basis for Cotes's natural tendency towards an empirical portrait image.

The principal legacy he left to posterity were his portraits. What level of quality did he attain in these? Two eighteenth-century sources are helpful in formulating an opinion, Cotes's own essay on pastel painting, published long after his death in *The European Magazine* for February 1797 (reproduced in Appendix IV), and Walpole's notes in his Society of Artists catalogue of 1767 (cf. Appendix III).

The relevant paragraph of Cotes's essay reads as follows:

> The finest examples that are known in this branch of painting (pastels) are the pictures by the Caval. Mengs in the gallery at Dresden, the Seasons and other beautiful paintings by Rosalba, and certain portraits of Liotard, which are dispersed and to be found all over Europe, as he painted in almost every country; perhaps to these may be added a few of my late master's portraits; and finally, if it will not be deemed too much presumption, my father's portrait (no. 75, fig. 17) and Mr. Knapton's (no. 223), her Majesty with the Princess Royal sleeping (no. 205, fig, 103, no. 206, fig. 104), Mrs. Child (no. 190, fig. 78), Miss Jones (no. 265), Miss Wilton (no. 303). and a few other portraits by myself.

When did Cotes write this essay and what was his intention in doing so? Of the pastel portraits he specifically identifies by name, only four are known today. The picture of Robert Cotes (no. 75, fig. 17) is dated 1757, that of Sarah Child (no. 190, fig. 78) is dated 1766, and the two pastel portraits of Queen Charlotte with Princess Charlotte were done in 1767; therefore the essay must have been written between 1767 and 1770. There is no doubt, from the way it is written, that Cotes was not merely making a few remarks for his own benefit, but had an audience in mind. Why he withheld publication is not known. Whatever his reasons were, this document serves as an important final comment by the artist on his own work.

His essay builds up to the paragraph just quoted, in which he makes his main point, namely, that 'if it will not be deemed too much presumption', certain of his own pastel portraits should be ranked among 'the finest examples that are known in this branch of painting'. If one considers Cotes's carefully worded opinion of himself, from both an historical and an aesthetic point of view, it is difficult to find fault with it. His influence as a pastellist was not international, as in the case of Rosalba, La Tour, and Liotard. Nevertheless, he exerted a considerable force within Britain. In fact, he raised

British pastels to the most prestigious level they had ever attained, and, in doing so, paved the way for his pupil, John Russell, and for Daniel Gardiner, even though their pastels rarely equalled his own. He often surpassed Rosalba, Mengs, and Perroneau, and frequently came up to the level of La Tour and Liotard. In the light of history, therefore, it cannot be 'deemed to much presumption' on Cotes's part that he accurately assessed his standing as a major eighteenth-century pastellist.

We have no idea what he thought he had achieved as an oil painter. No statement of his survives on the subject, but perhaps that in itself is significant. As an oil painter, he was a minor master. During his lifetime he enjoyed a moderate degree of fame and was able to earn a comfortable living, although he contributed little to the development of oil portraiture in Britain except as a popularizer of Ramsay's and Reynolds's ideas. His innovations in oils were mainly confined to a personal struggle to preserve his own sensibility and the rudiments of his conservative style in an age that was often hostile to both. The results he achieved in this struggle were not significant enough to deeply influence oil painters who came after him. Walpole was right: 'Cotes succeeded much better in crayons than in oils' (Appendix III, 1767).

He and Ramsay had enough in common so that his adjustment to the types of pictures Ramsay was painting was not problematic, and generally proved quite successful. Cotes and Reynolds, on the other hand, were not at all alike. When Cotes came too close to the precedents Reynolds had established, his paintings, though attractive, looked decidedly second-rate, but when he took only a few superficial characteristics from Reynolds's portraits and went on to assert his own temperament and taste in a forceful manner, his work in oils was of much higher quality. This did, in fact, happen frequently, especially in the final phase of his career; therefore, among his oil portraits one finds many exceedingly fine pictures. These oils and his pastels make up an extensive body of work which richly deserves recognition.

NOTES

1. Carl Winter, 'Francis Cotes, R.A.', 2 Parts, *The Connoisseur*, Vol. 88, no. 361, Sept. 1931, pp. 170–177, and Vol. 88, no. 362, Oct. 1931, pp. 244–252.
2. *St. Mary-le-Strand Parish Register*, in MS., now kept at the Westminster Public Library, London, May 29, 1726. Cotes's birth date and baptism date, May 20, 1726, and May 29, 1726, respectively, are recorded in the register.
3. John Nichols, *The History and Antiquities of the County of Leicester*, Vol. IV, Part I, London, John Nichols and Son, 1807, p. 35. Hereafter, Vol. IV, Part I is understood whenever this work is cited. Cotes's family tree, which appears on p. 35, is reproduced in Appendix I.
4. *The Case of Robert Cotes, Esq., Mayor, and John Staunton, Esq., Recorder of Gallway. On Behalf of Themselves, and the Majority of the Corporation of Gallway. In Answer to a Petition Preferr'd To the Honourable House of Commons By Thomas Simcocks and Edward Barrett, Aldermen*, Dublin, 1717, pp. 1–22. The original pamphlet is kept at the British Museum. It gives a full account of Robert Cotes's conduct as Mayor and of the political difficulties he encountered.
5. Anon., 'Samuel Cotes, Esq.', *The Gentleman's Magazine*, March, 1814, p. 276. The author said of Robert Cotes that after his Irish trial, he 'came to London to lay his case before the Queen (Anne) in Council, in which appeal his conduct was honourably borne out'.
6. Nichols, p. 35, cf. Appendix I.
7. *Ibid.*
8. *St. Mary-le-Strand Parish Register*, May 29, 1726.
9. Nichols, p. 35, cf. Appendix I.
10. *Ibid.*
11. Edward Edwards, *Anecdotes of Painters*, London, Leigh and Sotheby, W. J. and J. Richardson, R. Faulder, T. Payne and J. White, 1808, p. 34.
12. *The London Advertiser*, Monday, April 6, 1752, front page. His residence is given as Cork Street. From this address he sold prints after his own pastel portraits.
13. Edwards, p. 34.
14. Anon., 'Samuel Cotes, Esq.,' *The Gentleman's Magazine*, March, 1814, p. 403. The career of Robert Cotes, the father of Samuel and Francis, is referred to as that of 'Medicine'.
15. Edwards, p. 34.
16. John Russell, *Elements of Painting with Crayons*, London, J. Wilkie and J. Walter, 1772, pp. ii, 35–45.
17. Horace Walpole, *Anecdotes of Painting in England*, edited by the Rev. James Dallaway, Vol. IV, London, John Major and Robert Jennings, 1828, p. 111. This edition is used throughout the text. Walpole speaks of Cotes as a 'scholar of Knapton'; he does not give the date of Cotes's entry into Knapton's studio. The actual date remains a matter of conjecture. Cotes probably entered the studio when he was fourteen or fifteen, the usual age at which apprentices were bound to their masters.
18. *Ibid.*
19. William T. Whitley, *Artists and Their Friends in England*, Vol. I, London, The Medici Society, 1928, p. 137.
20. Oliver Millar, *The Tudor, Stuart and Early Georgian Pictures in the Collection of Her Majesty The Queen*, Vol. I, London, Phaidon Press, 1963, no. 573.
21. Walpole, *Anecdotes*, Vol. IV, p. 110, note 2. Dallaway mentions that Knapton's essay appeared in the *Philosophical Transcactions*, 1740, no. 468.
22. Mark Girouard, 'Coffee at Slaughter's—English Art and the Rococo, Part I', *Country Life*, Vol. 139, no. 3593, Jan. 13, 1966, pp. 58–61; 'Hogarth and His Friends—English Art and the Rococo, Part II', Vol. 139, no. 3595, Jan. 27, 1966, pp. 188–190; 'The Two Worlds of St. Martin's Lane—English Art and the Rococo, Part III', Vol. 139, no. 3596, Feb. 3, 1966, pp. 224–255. Girouard fully discusses the English artists who were involved with the rococo aesthetic.
23. George Vertue, *Notebooks, The Walpole Society*, Vol. XXII, Oxford, The University Press, 1934, Vol. III of the Notebooks for 1741, II. 109, 110. Vertue remarks on the popularity of crayon painting in England.
24. P. J. Mariette, *Abécédario de P. J. Mariette*, edited by P. De Chennevières and A. De Montaiglon, Vol. 6, Paris, J. B. Dumoulin, 1854–1856, p. 69. Mariette recalls that Maurice-Quentin de la Tour advertised himself as a pastellist who could execute portraits quickly so as not to fatigue the sitters. The rapidity with which an artist could finish a pastel portrait was a decided advantage.
25. Michael Levey, *Painting in XVIII Century Venice*, London, Phaidon Press, 1959, p. 144. Levey says that Rosalba's 'postbag' revealed that she was 'besieged by potential patrons in England.' Her name was so familiar that it was even anglicized to 'Roselby'. The English constantly demanded portraits from her until she became blind c. 1746.
26. Strawberry Hill Sale Catalogue, George Robbins, Strawberry Hill, May 9, 1842, lot 1; May 18, 1842, lots 1, 2, 73, 73*, 86. These lots were pastel portraits by Rosalba from the collection of Horace Walpole and his family at Strawberry Hill.
27. Walpole, *Anecdotes*, Vol. IV, p. 177.
28. Levey, p. 141, fig. 66, p. 142; Michael Levey, *The Later Italian Pictures in the Collection of Her Majesty The Queen*, London, Phaidon Press, 1964, No. 446, Plate 212.
29. Russell, *Elements of Painting with Crayons*, pp. ii, 35–45.
30. *Ibid.*, p. ii.
31. *Ibid.*, p. 19.
32. *Ibid.*, pp. 19–20.
33. *Ibid.*, p. 27.
34. Anon., 'Samuel Cotes, Esq.', *The Gentleman's Magazine*, March, 1814, p. 276.
35. Russell, *Elements of Painting with Crayons*, p. ii.
36. Walpole, *Anecdotes*, Vol. IV, p. 111.
37. Russell, *Elements of Painting with Crayons*, p. 20.
38. Girouard, 'The Two Worlds of St. Martin's Lane', p. 224.
39. Russell, *Elements of Painting with Crayons*, p. 27.
40. George Anne Bellamy, *An Apology for the Life of George Anne Bellamy, Late of Covent-Garden Theatre*, Vol. I, London, J. Bell, 1786, pp. 196–202.
41. W. S. Lewis, Warren Hunting Smith, and George L. Lam (editors), *Horace Walpole's Correspondence*, Vol. 20, New Haven, Yale University Press, 1960, p. 260.
42. *Ibid.*, Vol. 22, p. 311.
43. Walpole, *Anecdotes*, Vol. IV, p. 177.
44. Allan Ramsay, *Dialogue on Taste*, London, 1762 edition, p. 20.

45. Arno Schönberger and Halldor Soehner, *The Rococo Age*, London, McGraw-Hill, 1960, pp. 78–80, a discussion of the theme of the triumph of love in rococo art.
46. Joseph Farington, *The Farington Diary*, edited by James Greig, Vol. 5, London, Hutchinson and Co., 1925, p. 37.
47. Edwards, p. 54.
48. *Ibid.*
49. *The Gazeteer and London Daily Advertiser*, February 14, 1771, p. 3. An advertisement in this newspaper described Cotes's lease.
50. Humphrey Ward and W. Roberts, *Romney*, London, Thomas Agnew and Sons, 1904, p. 43.
51. Edwards, p. 51.
52. *Ibid.*
53. Walpole, *Anecdotes*, Vol. IV, p. 111.
54. Edward Johnson, 'Cotes at Nottingham', *The Burlington Magazine*, No. 826, Vol. CXIV, Jan. 1972, p. 52.
55. *The Oxford English Dictionary*, Vol. XI, Oxford, The Clarendon Press, 1933, p. 357.
56. E. K. Waterhouse, *Reynolds*, London, Kegan Paul, Trench, Trubner and Co., 1941, pp. 13, 14.
57. Cf. catalogue entry 208, where the bill to the Duke of Portland is reproduced in full.
58. *The Public Advertiser*, May 2, 1764, front page.
59. Waterhouse, *Reynolds*, p. 9.
60. Frederick Cummings and Allen Staley, *Romantic Art in Britain, Paintings and Drawings 1760–1860* (exhibition catalogue), Philadelphia, Philadelphia Museum of Art, 1968, pp. 39, 40, no. 6. Cummings fully explains the symbolism in Reynolds's portrait of Lady Sarah Bunbury.
61. *Ibid.*, p. 40.
62. Waterhouse, *Reynolds*, p. 16.
63. Anon., 'Pictures from Yorkshire Houses', *The Connoisseur*, Vol. 142, no. 571, Aug. 1958, p. 26. Professor E. K. Waterhouse believes that the portrait (no. 250) was connected with the private theatricals put on at the house of Lady Stanhope's brother, Sir Francis Blake Delaval.
64. Hester W. Chapman, *Caroline Matilda, Queen of Denmark, 1751–75*, London, Jonathan Cape, 1971, pp. 177–209.
65. Horace Walpole, *Journal of Visits to Country Seats, The Walpole Society*, Vol. XVI, Oxford, The University Press, 1928, p. 79.
66. *A Copy of the Royal Charter and Statutes of the Society of Artists of Great Britain*, London, By Order of the Society, 1769, pp. 5–6, 9–10.
67. Hester Lynch Thrale, *Thraliana, The Diary of Hester Lynch Thrale* (*Later Mrs. Piozzi*), edited by Katherine C. Balderston, Vol. I, Oxford, Clarendon Press, 1951, p. 268.
68. Whitley, Vol. I, p. 219.
69. Edwards, p. 54.
70. *Ibid.*
71. Russell, *Diary*, Vol. I, p. 51.
72. *Ibid.*, p. 62.
73. *Ibid.*, p. 85.
74. Anon., *The Conduct of the Royal Academicians*, London, 1771; also cf. Whitley, p. 223.
75. *The London Chronicle*, May 5–7, 1767, p. 440.
76. Edwards, p. 40.
77. Russell, *Diary*, Vol. III, p. 81.
78. James Northcote, R.A., *The Life of Sir Joshua Reynolds*, Vol. I, London, Henry Colburn, 1819, p. 165.
79. *Royal Academy of Arts, General Assembly Minute Books*, Vol. I, in MS., 1768–1796, now kept at the Royal Academy of Arts, London, minutes for Dec. 14, 1768 and Jan. 2, 1769.
80. Russell, *Diary*, Vol. IV, p. 28.
81. *Ibid.*
82. *Ibid.*, Vol. IV, pp. 40, 41.
83. *The Gazetteer and New Daily Advertiser*, Wednesday, July 25, 1770, p. 2.
84. John Thomas Smith, *Nollekens and His Times*, London, Richard Bentley and Son, 1895, p. 82. The letter from Mary Moser to Henry Fuseli is reproduced here.
85. Katherine Ada Esdaille, *The Life and Works of Louis François Roubiliac*, Oxford, Oxford University Press, 1928, pp. 88, 89.

CATALOGUE

ABBREVIATIONS

b. born.

BPP. Spielman, M. H. *British Portrait Painting to the Opening of the Nineteenth Century*. Vol. I. London: The Berlin Photographic Co., 1910.

CAN. Johnson, Edward Mead. 'Cotes at Nottingham,' *The Burlington Magazine*. Vol. CXIV. No. 826. Jan. 1972, pp. 51–52.

cat. catalogue.

CC18. Cunnington, C. Willet and Cunnington, Phillis. *Handbook of English Costume in the Eighteenth Century*. London: Faber and Faber, 1957.

CS. Smith, John Challoner. *British Mezzotinto Portraits*. 5 vols. and a portfolio of plates. London: Henry Sotheran and Co., 1878–1883.

CWO. Winter, Carl. 'Francis Cotes, R.A.' Part II, *The Connoisseur*. Vol. 88. No. 362. Oct. 1931, pp. 244–252.

CWS. Winter, Carl. 'Francis Cotes, R.A.' Part I, *The Connoisseur*. Vol. 88. No. 361. Sept. 1931, pp. 170–177.

d. died.

EG. Gosse, Edmond. *British Portrait Painters and Engravers of the Eighteenth Century, Kneller to Reynolds*. London: Goupil and Co., 1906.

F.L. Full-length.

GP. Goulding, Richard W. *Catalogue of the Pictures Belonging to His Grace The Duke of Portland, K.G., at Welbeck Abbey, 17 Hill Street, London, and Langwell House*. Cambridge: The University Press, 1936.

H.L. Half-length.

H.S. Head and shoulders. In this catalogue the term head and shoulders includes the long bust length.

illus. illustrated.

LB. Binyon, Laurence. *Catalogue of Drawings by British Artists and Artists of Foreign Origins Working in Great Britain, Preserved in the Department of Prints and Drawings in the British Museum*. London: The British Museum, 1898.

n.d. no date.

NTH. St. John Gore, Robert. 'Pictures in National Trust Houses,' *The Burlington Magazine*. Vol. CXI. No. 793. Apr. 1969, pp. 237–262.

O'D. O'Donoghue, Freeman, and Hake, Sir Henry M. *Catalogue of Engraved British Portraits . . . in the British Museum*. 6 vols. London: The British Museum, 1908–1925.

OML. Millar, Oliver. *The Later Georgian Pictures in the Collection of Her Majesty The Queen*. 2 vols. London: Phaidon Press, 1969.

PFC. Heil, Walter. 'Portraits by Francis Cotes,' *Art in America*. Vol. XX. No. I. Dec. 1931, pp. 2–12.

PIB. Waterhouse, Ellis K. *Painting in Britain, 1530–1790*. London and Baltimore: Penguin Books, pp. 153, 182.

PN. Duleep Singh, Prince Frederick. *Portraits in Norfolk Houses*. 2 vols. Norwich: Jarrold and Sons, 1928.

PS. Farrer, Rev. Edmund. *Portraits in Suffolk Houses (East)*. 5 vols. in MS., deposited at the Ipswich Public Library, n.d.

PSW. Farrer, Rev. Edmund. *Portraits in Suffolk Houses (West)*. London: Bernard Quaritch, 1908.

PW. Steegman, John. *A Survey of Portraits in Welsh Houses*. 2 vols. Cardiff: National Museum of Wales, Vol. I, 1957; Vol. II, 1962.

RSC. Keyes, Homer Eaton. 'The Rising Star of Francis Cotes,' *Antiques*. Vol. 19. Mar. 1931, pp. 217–220.

RTG. Russell, Constance Lady. *Three Generations of Fascinating Women*. London: Longmans, Green, and Co., 1904.

T.Q.L. Three-quarter length.

WA. Walpole, Horace (Earl of Orford). *Anecdotes of Painting*. Edited by the Rev. James Dallaway. Vol. IV. London: John Major and Robert Jennings, 1828.

WW. Whitley, William T. *Artists and their Friends in England*. Vol. I. London: The Medici Society, 1928.

Other Terms

Left and right. These refer to the viewer's left and right, unless otherwise stated.

A plain background. A background without any design or figure.

The Arrangement of the Catalogue

The Catalogue is arranged chronologically and alphabetically. Signed and dated works precede those that are not signed and dated. Pastels precede oils. If a portrait has been engraved, only the principal eighteenth-century engravings are mentioned.

1747: Portraits in pastel, signed and dated, nos. 1, 2.

1. **A Gentleman** (fig. 4). Leicestershire Museums and Art Galleries, Belgrave House, Leicester. Pastel on paper, 23½ × 17 in. Signed and dated at the lower left: FCotes pinx^t / 1747. F and C in monogram. Condition: Excellent.
H.S., to the left, wearing a blue coat with a gold design of a stag's head and a blue hat; a plain background. The costume is probably that of a Master of Staghounds.

PROVENANCE: J. H. Fitzhenry, Esq., U.K., 1911; Mrs. Mary Mitchison, London; Lady Strathcarron Sale (on behalf of Mary Mitchison), Christie's, Feb. 25, 1938 (lot 121), bought by the present owner.

EXHIBITIONS: 'Expositions des Pastellistes Anglais du XVIIIe Siècle', Galeries Brunner, Paris, Apr. 8 – Je. 15, 1911, no. 72 (lent by J. H. Fitzhenry, Esq.). The portrait was incorrectly attributed to George Knapton, Cotes's teacher; it was entitled 'Officer of the Marine' because the stag's head design on the sitter's frock coat was thought to be a naval insignia. No such naval insignia was in use when the portrait was done.
'Introducing Francis Cotes, R.A.', Nottingham University Art Gallery, Nov. 5–27, 1971, no. 2 (lent by the present owner); illus. in cat., Pl. III.

REFERENCES: Anon., The Leicester Museum Quarterly, no. 57, Jul., 1938, p. 4; no. 58, Oct., 1938, p. 2, cover (illus.); *CAN.*, p. 52; *CC18.*, p. 84, Pl. 21; J. R. K. Duff, 'The Place of Pastel Paintings', *The Art Journal*, Annual Vol., Nov. 1911, p. 397 (illus.); *PIB.*, pp. 153, 182.

2. **Catherine Wilson** (fig. 5). Capt. John Litchfield, R.N., U.K. Pastel on paper, 23 × 17 in. Signed and dated at the middle right: FCotes pinx^t / 1747. F and C in monogram. Condition: Good, slight damage in spots.
Catherine Wilson, c. 1718–1780, the daughter of Robert Wilson of Park Prospect, St. James's, London; c. 1758 she married William Speer, Esq., of Kent.
H.S., to the left, wearing a pink dress; a plain background.

PROVENANCE: By family descent from the sitter to the present owner.

1748: Portraits in pastel, signed and dated, nos. 3–5.

3. **A Lady.** Present whereabouts unknown. Pastel on paper, 23½ × 17½ in. Signed and dated at the middle left: FCotes pinx^t / 1748. F and C in monogram. Condition: Unknown.
H.S., head slightly to the left, shoulders to the right, wearing a white dress; a plain background.

PROVENANCE: Arthur Cane, Esq., London; Arthur Cane Sale, Christie's, Nov. 20, 1936 (lot 10), bought by Collings.

4. **Lady Ilchester.** Lady Teresa Agnew, Melbury House, Dorchester, Dorset. Pastel on paper, 23 × 17 in. Signed and dated at the right, opposite the sitter's shoulder: FCotes px^t / 1748. F and C in monogram. Condition: Good, minor damage in spots.
Lady Ilchester, later 1st Countess of Ilchester, 1722/23–1792; she was born Elizabeth Strangeways-Horner; in 1735 she married Stephen Fox-Strangeways, who was elevated to the peerage in 1741 and became 1st Earl of Ilchester in 1756.
H.S., to the left, wearing a pink dress; a plain background.
Pendant to no. 6.

PROVENANCE: By family descent from the sitter to the present owner.

EXHIBITIONS: 'Introducing Francis Cotes, R.A.', Nottingham University Art Gallery, Nov. 5–27, 1971, no. 4 (lent by the owner).

5. **Matthew Hale,** also called Matthew Hall. Present whereabouts unknown. Pastel on paper, 23 × 17½ in. Signed and dated at the lower right: FCotes px^t / 1748. F and C in monogram. Condition: Unknown.
The sitter is probably Matthew Hale of Bristol Bank, d. 1764.
H.S., to the right, wearing an olive coat; a plain background.
Pendant to no. 7.

PROVENANCE: Anon. Sale, Christie's, Jul. 4, 1919 (lot 37); this lot included the portrait of Mrs. Hale (no. 7); both pictures were bought by P. and D. Colnaghi and Co., London. M. Knoedler and Co., London, 1919–1924. Knoedler sold both pictures back to Colnaghi in 1924. A. S. Drey Sale, Graupe, Berlin, Je. 17–18, 1936 (lot 10), buyer unknown. In the Drey Sale catalogue and in *Art in America* the pictures were said to have been signed and dated 1749. In the 1919 sale at Christie's there had been some confusion over the date (reported as either 1748 or 1749) because at that time the last digit was not legible. There is another slight discrepancy between the 1919 catalogue and the later references. In the 1919 catalogue the sitters were referred to as 'Mr. and Mrs. Matthew Hale', whereas in *Art in America* and in the Drey Sale catalogue they were called 'Mr. and Mrs. Matthew Hall'. Nothing more is known about their identity.

REFERENCES: *PFC.*, p. 4.

c. 1748: A portrait in pastel apparently neither signed nor dated, no. 6.

6. **Stephen Fox-Strangeways, Lord Ilchester and Stavordale.** Lady Teresa Agnew, Melbury House, Dorchester, Dorset. Pastel on paper, 23 × 17 in. Neither signed nor dated as far as one can see; a signature and date may be hidden in the background, which has darkened. Condition: Good, minor damage in spots.
Lord Ilchester, later 1st Earl of Ilchester, 1704–1776, cf. no. 4.
H.S., to the right, wearing a brown jacket; a plain background.
Pendant to no. 4.

DATE: The style of the portrait, stiff and precise, is typical of Cotes's earliest pastels. The closest parallels are no. 1, signed and dated 1747, and no. 4, signed and dated 1748. The type of wig the sitter wears was popular in the 1740's. A date of c. 1748 is suggested.

PROVENANCE: By family descent from the sitter to the present owner.

EXHIBITIONS: 'Introducing Francis Cotes, R.A.', Nottingham University Art Gallery, Nov. 5–27, 1971, no. 3 (lent by the owner).

REFERENCES: *CAN.*, p. 52.

1748–1750: See Supplement no. 1.

1749: A portrait in pastel, signed and dated, no. 7.

7. **Mrs. Matthew Hale,** also called Mrs. Matthew Hall. Present whereabouts unknown. Pastel on paper, 23 × 17½ in. Signed and dated at the lower left: FCotes px[t] / 1749. F and C in monogram. Condition: Unknown.
The sitter is probably Mary, daughter of John Harding, and wife of Matthew Hale of Bristol Bank.
H.S., to the left, wearing a yellow dress; a plain background.
Pendant to no. 5.

PROVENANCE: cf. no. 5.

REFERENCES: *PFC.*, p. 2.

1750: Portraits in pastel, signed and dated, nos. 8–10.

8. **A Gentleman.** The Victoria and Albert Museum, London. Pastel on paper, 24 × 17⅝ in. Signed and dated at the lower right: FCotes px[t] / 1750. F and C in monogram. Condition: Excellent.
H.S., to the right, wearing a brown coat; a plain background.

PROVENANCE: Claude D. Rotch, Esq., U.K.; Mr. Rotch bequeathed the portrait to the Victoria and Albert Museum in 1962.

EXHIBITIONS: The portrait has been publicly exhibited at the Victoria and Albert Museum.

9. **Elizabeth Ryves.** Present whereabouts unknown, possibly in the collection of Mr. Eric Benjamin, New York. Pastel on paper, 24 × 17¾ in. Inscribed at the upper left: Miss Elizabeth Ryves. Signed and dated at the upper left: FCotes px 1750. F and C in monogram. Condition: Unknown.
Elizabeth Ryves, of Ranston, Blandford, Dorset; b. 1726, the daughter of Sir Anthony Abdy, 3rd Bt; in 1749 she married Thomas Ryves (no. 10).
H.S., to the left, wearing a pink dress with a blue and gold scarf; a plain background.
Pendant to no. 10. No. 44 is a later portrait of the same sitter. For other family portraits, cf. Appendix V, nos. 52, 53, 55.

PROVENANCE: Mr. Jules Porges, Paris; Mr. Emile Gross; Mr. Xavier Haas, Paris; and Sig. Salvator; The Salvator Sale, Anderson Galleries, New York, Jan. 20–21, 1927 (lot 53), illus.; Mr. Francis Kelly, New York; Mr. Eric Benjamin, New York (1943).

10. **Thomas Ryves.** Present whereabouts unknown. Pastel on paper, 23 × 17 in. Inscribed at the top left: Tho. Ryves Esq. A'tat: 29. 1750. Signed and dated at the lower right: FCotes px[t] 1750. F and C in monogram. Condition: Unknown.
Thomas Ryves, of Ranston, Blandford, Dorset; in 1749 he married Elizabeth, daughter of Sir Anthony Abdy, 3rd Bt. His dates are unknown.
H.S., to the right, wearing a Van Dyck costume composed of a yellow coat and a red cloak; a plain background.
Pendant to no. 9.

PROVENANCE: Colonel R. Malthus, U.K.; Colonel Malthus Sale, Christie's, Dec. 16, 1938 (lot 16), bought by Moore.

EXHIBITIONS: 'Expositions des Pastellistes Anglais du XVIIIe Siècle', Galeries Brunner, Paris, Apr. 8 – Je. 15, 1911, no. 18 (loaned by Colonel R. Malthus).

1750: A lost portrait, known only through an eighteenth-century engraving, no. 11.

11. **Dr. Charles Chauncy (or Chauncey), M.D.** Present whereabouts unknown. Probably pastel on paper, as Cotes is not known to have done oil portraits at this date; measurements unknown. Signed and dated 1750. Condition: Unknown.
Engraved by Caroline Watson and inscribed: Francis Cotes pinx[t] 1750 Caroline Watson sculp[t] Engraver to Her Majesty / Charles Chauncy / M.D. F.R.S. / Obiit 25 Dec 1777 / Aetatis 68.
Charles Chauncy, 1706–1777.
H.S., to the left, wearing a jacket, holding a large book under his right arm; a plain background.

REFERENCES: *O'D.*, Vol. I, p. 420, no. 1.
For Cotes's other portraits of medical doctors, cf. nos. 77, 81, and 139. For Samuel Richardson's correspondence with and about the sitter, cf. Supplement no. 1.

175(?): A portrait in pastel, signed and dated, no. 12.

12. **The Hon. Bridget Gunning.** Edward Croft-Murray, Esq., Richmond, Surrey. Pastel on paper, 23 × 17 in. Signed and dated at the middle left, opposite the sitter's right shoulder: FCotes px[t] / 175(?). F and C in monogram. The last digit of the date, said to be 8, is indecipherable. Condition: Surface worn away in spots.
The Hon. Bridget Gunning, 1711–1767; she was the daughter of Theobald Bourke, 6th Viscount Bourke of Mayo; in 1731 she married John Gunning of Castlecoote, County Roscommon; her children were Maria, Elizabeth, Catherine, and John.
H.L., seated, head to the front, shoulders to the left, wearing a blue dress with touches of green; a plain background.

PROVENANCE: By family descent from the sitter to her daughter, Elizabeth, Duchess of Argyll, then by descent to John Campbell, 9th Duke of Argyll; Roseneath Castle Sale, Dowell's, Edinburgh, Oct. 7–11, 1940 (lot 1313), bought by Appleby Brothers, London; purchased by the present owner in 1941.

EXHIBITIONS: 'Introducing Francis Cotes, R.A.', Nottingham University Art Gallery, Nov. 5–27, 1971, no. 10 (lent by the present owner).
Cotes did pastel portraits of Bridget's husband (no. 17), of her three daughters (nos. 15, 16, 19, 31, 33, Supplement no. 7), and of her son (no. 18). Nos. 15, 16, 17, 18, and 19 are signed and dated 1751, and nos. 31 and 33 were done around 1751. Supplement no. 7 is signed and dated 1758. The portrait of Bridget Gunning belongs to this group of family pictures.

1751: Portraits in pastel, signed and dated, nos. 16–30 [see also Supplement no. 2].

13. **A Boy.** Present whereabouts unknown. Pastel on paper, 23 × 17 in. Signed and dated at the lower right, opposite the sitter's left shoulder: FCotes px[t] / 1751. F and C in monogram. Condition: Unknown.
H.S., to the right, wearing a Van Dyck jacket and a cloak; a plain background.

PROVENANCE: P. M. Turner, London (formerly).

14. **Thomas Cooke.** Present whereabouts unknown. Pastel on paper, 23 × 17½ in. Signed and dated at the lower left: FCotes px[t] / 1751. F and C in monogram. Condition: Unknown.
Thomas Cooke, son of Thomas Cooke of Painstown, County Carlow, and Helen, daughter of Nicholas Purcell, brother of Anne, wife of the 4th Viscount Kenmare.
H.S., to the right, wearing a jacket; a plain background.

PROVENANCE: By family descent from the sitter to Elizabeth, Countess of Kenmare; Elizabeth, Countess of Kenmare Sale, Sotheby's, London, Jul. 11, 1945 (lot 62), bought by Cullen.

15. **Catherine Gunning.** Present whereabouts unknown. Pastel on paper, approximately 25½ × 17½ in. Originally signed and dated 1751.
Engraved in mezzotint by Richard Houston and published in 1755, with the following inscription composed by the sitter's two sisters:

> This youngest Grace, so like her Sisters' Frame!
> Her kindred Features tell from whence she came:
> Tis needless once to mention Gunning's name.
> Duchess of Hamilton and Countess of Coventry

There is a second mezzotint by C. Spooner.
Catherine Gunning, 1735–1773, the youngest daughter of John and Bridget Gunning; in 1769 she married Robert Travis (or Travers).
H.S., head slightly to the right, shoulders to the left, wearing a low-cut dress with a scarf; a landscape background.

PROVENANCE: By family descent from the sitter to Constance, Lady Russell (1905). When Lady Russell published the portrait in 1905, she said: 'The writer has a beautiful pastelle of Kitty Gunning, painted and signed by Cotes in 1751, which was engraved by Houston.' Her portrait was illustrated in *Three Generations of Fascinating Women.* It appears to be exactly like Agnew's portrait of Catherine Gunning (Supplement no. 7), which came from the Russell collection; however, Agnew's pastel is signed and dated 1758, not 1751. Two possibilities should be considered: either the date on Agnew's pastel was originally 1751 and was subsequently changed to 1758, or Cotes simply did two versions of the same picture, one in 1751 and another in 1758. At the present time, one cannot determine which alternative is correct. Since Cotes is known to have frequently made two versions of a pastel portrait, it has been thought prudent to catalogue the pictures separately.

REFERENCES: Ruth M. Bleackley, 'The Beautiful Misses Gunning', Part I, *The Connoisseur*, Vol. 12, no. 47, Jul. 1905, p. 161. *CS.*, Vol. II, p. 664, no. 55; Vol. III, p. 1341, no. 21; *O'D.*, Vol. IV, p. 302, no. 1; *RTG.*, pp. 135, 139.

16. **Elizabeth Gunning.** National Portrait Gallery, London. Pastel on paper, 23½ × 16¼ in. Signed and dated at the lower right: FCotes px[t] / 1751. F and C in monogram. Condition: Good.
Engraved in mezzotint by James McArdell in 1752, after the sitter had become the Duchess of Hamilton and Brandon. Also engraved by Richard Houston.
Elizabeth Gunning, later Duchess of Hamilton and Brandon, Duchess of Argyll, and Baroness Hamilton of Hambledon, 1733–1790, the second daughter of John and Bridget Gunning.
H.S., head slightly to the left, shoulders to the right, wearing a pink, gold, and blue dress; a plain background.

PROVENANCE: By family descent from the sitter to Marjorie, Lady Russell, Little Struan, Pangbourne, Berkshire; Anon. Sale (Property of a Lady), Christie's, Je. 6, 1972 (lot 104), bought by Leggatt Brothers for the National Portrait Gallery.

EXHIBITIONS: 'A Century of British Art, 1737–1837', The Grosvenor Gallery, London, Summer, 1889, no. 230 (lent by Sir George Russell).
'Exhibition of British Art, c. 1000–1869', R.A., London, 1934, no. 808 (lent by Arthur Russell).

REFERENCES: *CS.*, Vol. II, p. 871, no. 97; Vol. II, p. 667, no. 59; *The London Advertiser*, Apr. 6, 1752, front page (engraving advertised by Cotes and McArdell).

There is a copy in oils of no. 16 in the collection of the Duke of Argyll, Inveraray Castle, Argyllshire.

17. **John Gunning.** Present whereabouts unknown. Pastel on paper, 23 × 17 in. Signed and dated at the lower right: FCotes px[t] / 1751. F and C in monogram. Condition: Good.
John Gunning, of Castlecoote, Co. Roscommon, the father of Maria, Elizabeth, Catherine, and John Gunning, Jr.
H.S., to the right, wearing a double-breasted jacket with blue lapels; a plain background.

PROVENANCE: By family descent from the sitter to Marjorie, Lady Russell, Little Struan, Pangbourne, Berkshire; Anon. Sale (Property of a Lady), Christie's, Je. 6, 1972 (lot 106), bought by Collin.

REFERENCES: *RTG.*, pp. 99–102; illus. opposite p. 99.

18. **John Gunning, Jr.** Present whereabouts unknown. Pastel on paper, 23 × 17 in. Originally signed and dated at the lower left: FCotes px[t] / 1751. F and C in monogram. At some time after 1905 the date was changed to 1744. Condition: Good (1972).
John Gunning, Jr., 1742–1797, later Major General Gunning; he was the youngest child of John and Bridget Gunning and the brother of Maria, Elizabeth, and Catherine Gunning.

PROVENANCE: By family descent from the sitter to Marjorie, Lady Russell, Little Struan, Pangbourne, Berkshire; Anon Sale (Property of a Lady), Christie's, Je. 6, 1972 (lot 105), said to be dated 1744. The sitter appears to be about nine years old. In 1744 he was only two; consequently, that date should be treated as spurious. When Constance, Lady Russell, published the portrait in 1905, she noted that it was 'done in 1751'.

REFERENCES: *RTG.*, pp. 135–136 (illus. opposite), p. 140 (footnote 2).

19. **Maria Gunning** (fig. 6). The Duke of Argyll, Inveraray Castle, Inveraray, Argyllshire. Pastel on paper, 23½ × 17½. Signed and dated at the lower left: FCotes px[t]: / 1751. F and C in monogram. Condition: Excellent.
Engraved in mezzotint by Richard Houston and by James McArdell.
Maria Gunning, later Countess of Coventry, 1732–1760, the eldest daughter of John and Bridget Gunning.
H.S., to the left, wearing a pink and white dress and a cloak; a plain background.

PROVENANCE: By family descent from the sitter to the present owner.

EXHIBITIONS: 'Introducing Francis Cotes, R.A.', Nottingham University Art Gallery, Nov. 5–27, 1971, no. 5 (lent by the owner); illus. in cat. (Pl. XVIII). The portrait is on exhibit at Inveraray Castle, which is open to the public at certain times of the year.

REFERENCES: Ruth M. Bleackley, 'The Beautiful Misses Gunning', Part II, *The Connoisseur*, Vol. 12, no. 48, Aug. 1905, p. 232; *EG.*, Pl. 27. *The London Advertiser*, Apr. 6, 1752, front page; *O'D.*, Vol. I, p. 503, no. 2.

There are two copies in oils of no. 19, one at Inveraray Castle, the other at the National Gallery of Ireland (Appendix VI, no. 9).

20. **Sir Charles Kent.** Captain Sir Anthony Thorold, Bt., R.N., Syston Old Hall, Grantham, Lincolnshire. Pastel on paper, 23½ × 17½ in. Signed and dated at the lower left: FCotes px[t] / 1751. F and C in monogram. Condition: Right eye of figure painted over; surface damage in spots.
Sir Charles Kent; dates unknown.
H.S., to the left, wearing a Van Dyck costume composed of a blue jacket and a cloak; a plain background.

PROVENANCE: In the Thorold collection since the early 1900's.

21. **A Lady.** Present whereabouts unknown. Pastel on paper 23 × 17 in. Signed and dated at the middle left: FCotes px[t] / 1751. F and C in monogram. Condition: Unknown.
H.S., head tilted slightly to the left, shoulders to the right, wearing a dress with a lace tippet and a lace ruff; a plain background.
Pendant to Supplement no. 2.

PROVENANCE: Jules Féral, Paris (1936).

22. **A Lady** (fig. 37). Henry E. Huntington Library and Art Gallery, San Marino, California. Pastel on paper, 23 × 17½ in. Signed and dated at the lower right: FCotes px[t]: / 1751. F and C in monogram. Condition: Excellent.
H.S., to the right, wearing a brown dress and a rose and blue cloak; a plain background.

PROVENANCE: Anon. Sale, Christie's, Feb. 7, 1903 (lot 105), bought by C. J. Wertheimer, Esq., London; M. Knoedler and Co., London, purchased the picture from Mr. Wertheimer in 1908, and sold it in 1911 to Mr. Henry E. Huntington.

EXHIBITIONS: 'Cent Pastels', Galerie George Petit, Paris, May–Je. 1908, no. 9, incorrectly identified as Lady Frances Bridges (lent by Charles Wertheimer).
The picture is on permanent exhibition at the Henry E. Huntington Library and Art Gallery.

REFERENCES: C. H. Collins Baker, *Catalogue of British Paintings in the Henry E. Huntington Library and Art Gallery*, San Marino, California, Published by the Library, 1936, p. 36, Pl. III; *CWS.*, p. 176, fig. no. IV; R. A. Riches, 'Sir William Chambers and Francis Cotes', *The Connoisseur*, Vol. 94, Sept. 1934, pp. 142–145.

The Huntington Lady is not Lady Frances Bridges. Cotes's portrait of Lady Frances (no. 254) makes this quite evident, nor is R. A. Riches's theory that she is Mrs. E. Morton Pleydell convincing. He illustrates a portrait of Mrs. Pleydell along with that of the Huntington Lady, and, clearly, the features of the two sitters are very different.

23. **A Lady.** Present whereabouts unknown. Pastel on paper, 23½ × 17 in. Signed and dated at the middle left: FCotes px[t] / 1751. F and C in monogram. Condition: Unknown.
H.S., head to the front, shoulders to the left, wearing a blue dress with a brown scarf; a plain background.

PROVENANCE: Anon. Sale, Christie's, Feb. 1, 1924 (lot 67), signature and date not noted, bought by Grenfell.

24. **William Northey.** Present whereabouts unknown. Pastel on paper, 23 × 17½ in. Signed and dated at the lower right: FCotes px[t] / 1751. F and C in monogram. Condition: Unknown.
William Northey, of Compton Bassett and Ivy House, Wiltshire, d. 1770.
H.S., to the right, wearing a grey coat; a plain background.

PROVENANCE: The Lord Boston, Hedsor, Buckinghamshire; The Lord Boston Sale, Christie's, Mar. 6, 1942 (lot 46), bought by Cooling. No record of the present owner has been discovered at the Cooling Galleries, London.

25. **The Rev. Baptist Proby.** Major Sir Richard Proby, Bt., Elton Hall, Peterborough, Northamptonshire. Pastel on paper, 23½ × 17½ in. Signed and dated on the lower right: FCotes px[t] / 1751. F and C in monogram. Condition: Good.
The Rev. Baptist Proby, 1726–1807, son of John Proby of Elton, Huntingdonshire, and brother of John, Thomas, and Caroline Proby.
H.S., to the right, wearing a black gown; a plain background.

PROVENANCE: By family descent from the sitter to the present owner.

REFERENCES: Tancred Borenius and J. V. Hodgson, *A Catalogue of the Pictures at Elton Hall in Huntingdonshire in the Possession of Colonel Douglas James Proby*, London, The Medici Society, 1924, no. 77.

26. **Sir John Proby.** Major Sir Richard Proby, Bt., Elton Hall, Peterborough, Northamptonshire. Pastel on paper, 23½ × 17½ in. Signed and dated at the lower right: FCotes px[t] / 1751. F and C in monogram. Condition: Good, some minor damage in spots.
Sir John Proby, 1720–1772, brother of Baptist, Caroline, and Thomas Proby, was created 1st Baron Carysfort in 1752, and became one of the Lords of the Admiralty. He may have introduced Cotes to his naval colleagues. Cotes was to develop a clientele of naval officers in the 1760's, culminating with three famous sitters, Admiral Keppel (no. 168), Admiral Hawke, later 1st Baron Hawke (nos. 238 and 239), and Captain John Jervis, later Admiral Jervis and 1st Earl of St. Vincent (no. 281).
H.S., to the right, wearing a blue jacket; a plain background.

PROVENANCE: By family descent from the sitter to the present owner.

REFERENCES: Tancred Borenius and J. V. Hodgson, *A Catalogue of the Pictures at Elton Hall in Huntingdonshire in the Possession of Colonel Douglas James Proby*, London, The Medici Society, 1924, no. 75.

27. **A Lady of the Proby Family.** Major Sir Richard Proby, Bt., Elton Hall, Peterborough, Northamptonshire. Pastel on paper, 23½ × 17½ in. Signed and dated at the lower left: FCotes px / 1751. F and C in monogram. Condition: Good, minor damage in spots.
The sitter, possibly Caroline Proby, b. 1723, the daughter of John Proby of Elton, Huntingdonshire, and the sister of Baptist, John, and Thomas Proby.
H.S., to the left, wearing a yellow and black dress; a plain background.

PROVENANCE: By family descent from the sitter to the present owner.

REFERENCES: Tancred Borenius and J. V. Hodgson, *A Catalogue of the Pictures at Elton Hall in Huntingdonshire in the Possession of Colonel Douglas James Proby*, London, The Medici Society, 1924, no. 78 (identified as Caroline Proby).
No. 28 is almost identical to this portrait.

28. **A Lady of the Proby Family.** The University of Michigan Museum of Art, Ann Arbor, Michigan. Pastel on paper, 23½ × 17½ in. Signed and dated at the lower left: FCotes px[t] / 1751. F and C in monogram. Condition: Excellent.
The sitter is possibly Caroline Proby, b. 1723; cf. no. 27 for her genealogy.
Cf. no. 27; the pose of the sitter and the design of the costume are repeated in this portrait; a plain background.

PROVENANCE: The University of Michigan acquired the picture in 1965.

REFERENCES: Anon., 'Accessions of American and Canadian Museums', *The Art Quarterly*, Vol. 28, no. 3, 1965, pp. 212, 217 (illus.), incorrectly identified as Elizabeth, Lady Carysfort, daughter of the Viscount Allen.
No. 28 is almost exactly like no. 27.

29. **Major Thomas Proby.** Major Sir Richard Proby, Bt., Elton Hall, Peterborough, Northamptonshire. Pastel on paper, 23½ × 17½ in. Signed and dated at the lower left: FCotes px / 1751 F and C in monogram. Condition: Good, slight smearing in spots.
Major Thomas Proby, 1723–1756, the brother of Baptist, John, and Caroline Proby.
H.S., to the left, wearing a red military jacket; a plain background.

PROVENANCE: By family descent from the sitter to the present owner.

REFERENCES: Tancred Borenius and J. V. Hodgson, *A Catalogue of the Pictures at Elton Hall in Huntingdonshire in the Possession of Colonel Douglas James Proby*, London, The Medici Society, 1924, no. 76.

30. **Anne Wordsworth.** Present whereabouts unknown. Pastel on paper, 23 × 17 in. Signed and dated at the lower right: FCotes px[t] / 1751. F and C in monogram. Condition: Unknown.
Anne Wordsworth, wife of J. Wordsworth of Wadworth, Yorkshire; dates unknown.
H.S., to the right, wearing a popular type of Van Dyck costume composed of a black dress with a lace collar; a plain background.

PROVENANCE: Anon. Sale, Christie's, May 13, 1948 (lot 93), bought by Frost and Reed, London.

REFERENCES: J. L. Nevinson, 'Van Dyke Dress', *The Connoisseur*, Vol. 157, no. 633, Nov. 1964, pp. 166–171; Stella Mary Pearce. 'The Study of Costume in Painting', *Studies in Conservation*, Vol. 4, Nov. 1959, pp. 134–137; John Steegman, 'A Drapery Painter of the Eighteenth Century', *The Connoisseur*, Vol. 97, no. 418, Je. 1936, pp. 309–315.
The particular type of Van Dyck costume Anne Wordsworth was painted in was especially popular in British portraits between 1730 and 1760. The original model for the costume was supplied by Rubens's full-length portrait of his second wife, Hélène Fourment, which came into the collection of Sir Robert Walpole and was erroneously catalogued by Horace Walpole as a Van Dyck. When the collection was sold, the portrait went to Russia and eventually to the Hermitage. The Hermitage sold it to the Calouste Gulbenkian Foundation in Lisbon, where it is today.

c. 1751: A lost portrait known only through an engraving, no. 31.

31. **Elizabeth Gunning.** Present whereabouts unknown. The medium is almost certainly pastel on paper because Cotes did not work in oils in 1751. Measurements unknown. Possibly signed and dated. Condition: Unknown.
Engraved in mezzotint by Richard Houston and inscribed with the sitter's name at the time of publication, Elizabeth, Duchess of Hamilton and Brandon. She became the Duchess of Hamilton and Brandon in 1752.
For the sitter's genealogy, cf. no. 16.
H.L., head slightly to the left, shoulders to the right, wearing a dress trimmed with fur on the sleeves and a cloak; a plain background.

DATE: The style of this portrait, seen by means of Houston's engraving, corresponds exactly to that of the other Gunning portraits of 1751, and, as in the case of nos. 16 and 19, it was probably engraved after the sitter had married and acquired a title.

PROVENANCE: Unknown.

REFERENCES: Ruth M. Bleackley, 'The Beautiful Misses Gunning', Part I, *The Connoisseur*, Vol. 12, no. 47, July 1905, p. 162 (engraving illustrated). Bleackley thought that Houston's engraving was after a portrait by Gavin Hamilton. The style of the original picture, as far as one can judge from an engraving, is not at all typical of Hamilton, but strongly suggests the hand of Cotes; consequently, Challoner Smith and O'Donaghue, cf. below, catalogued the engraving as after Cotes. This seems the more logical opinion, especially in view of Cotes's other portraits of the Gunnings. *CS.*, Vol. II, p. 667, no. 59; *O'D.*, Vol. I, p. 69, no. I.

c. 1751 – c. 1754: Portraits in pastel, nos. 32–34 [see also Supplement no. 3].

32. **Richard Acland.** The National Trust, Stourhead House, Stourton, Wiltshire. Pastel on paper, in an oval, 22½ × 18 in. Neither signed nor dated. Condition: Excellent.
Richard Acland (dates unknown), the son of Richard Acland (brother of Sir Hugh Acland, 6th Bt.). Frances Ann Acland, second wife of Sir Richard Hoare, 1st Bt., was the sitter's sister.
H.S., to the left, wearing a blue jacket; a plain background.

DATE: Male portraits of this quality and with the fashionably small head type occur in Cotes's work from about 1751 to about 1754. Some notable examples are no. 24, signed and dated 1751; no. 39, signed and dated 1752; and no. 48, signed and dated 1754. The portrait of Richard Acland definitely fits into this group.

PROVENANCE: The portrait was in the Hoare family until 1946, when Sir Henry Hoare, 6th Bt., presented Stourhead to the National Trust.

EXHIBITIONS: The picture is on exhibit at Stourhead House.

REFERENCES: *NTH.*, p. 254.

At Stourhead there are also pastel portraits by Cotes of Richard Acland's sister, no. 204, of his brother-in-law, no. 76, and of his brother-in-law's first wife, no. 72.

33. **Catherine Gunning.** National Gallery of Scotland, Edinburgh. Pastel on paper, 23 × 17 in. Neither signed nor dated. Condition: Excellent.
For genealogy cf. no. 15.
H.S., to the right, wearing a Van Dyck costume composed of a dress with slashed sleeves and a lace collar; a plain background.

DATE: This portrait of Catherine Gunning shows a rather rough technique in combination with the young artist's newly found sense for the suppleness of the female figure. These are exactly the qualities that characterize his signed and dated pastels of the Gunning sisters, nos. 15, 16, and 19, all done in 1751. After 1754 Cotes developed a smoother style; therefore, this portrait belongs in the period from about 1751 to about 1754.

PROVENANCE: Miss A. C. Watson, Edinburgh; Miss Watson bequeathed the portrait to the National Gallery of Scotland in 1967.

34. **Captain Nugent.** Present whereabouts unknown. Pastel on paper, 23 × 17 in. It is not known whether the portrait is signed and dated. Condition: Unknown.
Captain Nugent, dates unknown.
H.S., to the left, wearing a Van Dyck costume composed of a jacket with slashed sleeves; a plain background.

DATE: The quality of work and the style of this portrait indicate that it was done in the early 1750's. The wooden appearance of the figure, the angular drapery, the hard outlines, and the pattern of sharp highlights are characteristic of the artist's work from this period. Close parallels are offered by no. 13, signed and dated 1751, and no. 35, signed and dated 1752. A date of c. 1751 – c. 1754 is suggested.

PROVENANCE: Unknown.

1752: Portraits in pastel, signed and dated, nos. 35–42.

35. **The Hon. George Keppel.** Private collection, U.K. Pastel on paper 23½ × 17½ in. Signed and dated at the lower left: FCotes px[t] / 1752. F and C in monogram. Condition: Excellent.
The Hon. George Keppel, later 3rd Earl of Albemarle, 1724–1772.
H.S., to the left, wearing a Van Dyck costume composed of a black doublet and a red cloak; a plain background.

PROVENANCE: By family descent from the sitter to the present owner.

REFERENCES: *PN.*, Vol. II, p. 152, no. 28. Duleep Singh gives the measurements as 35½ × 20½ in.; this may include the frame. He also notes an inscription: 'George, 3rd Earl of Albemarle aet 22'. In 1752 George Keppel was 28, not 22. The inscription does not appear on the front of the picture; it may have been on the back.

36. **A Lady.** Jeremy, Ltd., London. Pastel on paper, 23 × 17 in. Signed and dated at the lower left: FCotes px[t] / 1752. F and C in monogram. Condition: Excellent.
The sitter is possibly Henrietta Freston; dates unknown.
H.S., to the left, wearing a pink dress with a blue and gold scarf; a plain background.

PROVENANCE: Anon. Sale, Christie's, Jul. 25, 1919 (lot 47); Arthur Ackerman and Son, New York; the present owner.

REFERENCES: *The Connoisseur*, Vol. LIV, no. 216, Aug., 1919, p. 205 (illus.).

37. **A Lady.** Major C. Fellowes, Shotesham Park, Norwich, Norfolk. Pastel on paper, 23 × 18 in. Signed and dated at the middle left: FCotes px[t]: 1752. F and C in monogram. Condition: Excellent.
H.S., to the right, wearing a white dress with a blue and gold scarf; a plain background.

PROVENANCE: The portrait has been in the Fellowes collection at Shotesham since the early 1900's.

REFERENCES: *PN.*, Vol. II, p. 297, no. 38. Duleep Singh published the signature and date as: F Cotes ft 1752; this is incorrect.

38. **A Lady.** Present whereabouts unknown. Pastel on paper, 23 × 17 in. Signed and dated at the lower left: FCotes px[t]: / 1752. F and C in monogram. Condition: Unknown.
H.S., to the left, wearing a dress with a stomacher of crisscrossed ribbons; a plain background.

PROVENANCE: Maresco Pearce, London (formerly).

39. **Sir John Ripton** (fig. 8). Mr. and Mrs. Rockwell Gardiner, Stamford, Connecticut. Pastel on paper, 23 × 17 in. Signed and dated at the lower left: FCotes px[t] / 1752. F and C in monogram. Condition: Excellent.

Sir John Ripton, dates unknown.
H.S., to the left, wearing a grey jacket; a plain background.

PROVENANCE: The Lady Benthall, Lindridge, Bishopsteignton, Teignmouth, Devon; The Lady Benthall Sale, Sotheby's, Jul. 18, 1962 (lot 72), bought by Holcroft; Pawsey and Paine, London; an anonymous dealer, New York, who sold the picture to the present owners.
In the Benthall sale a companion portrait of 'Lady Ripton', neither signed nor dated, was lot 71. There is no further record of the portrait, and no judgement is made about its authenticity.

40. **Jane Robinson.** The Victoria and Albert Museum, London. Pastel on paper, 24 × 18 in. Signed and dated at the lower right: FCotes px[t] / 1752. F and C in monogram. Condition: Excellent.
Jane Robinson, born Jane Greenland, was the wife of Morris Robinson, who died in 1777.
H.S., to the right, wearing a blue dress and a pink cloak; a plain background.

PROVENANCE: Anon. Sale, Christie's, Je. 25, 1904 (lot 27), bought by Helft; Anon. Sale, Christie's, Mar. 14, 1952 (lot 47), bought by the present owner.

EXHIBITIONS: 'European Masters of the Eighteenth Century', R.A., London, Winter Exhibition, 1954–55, no. 375 (lent by the Victoria and Albert Museum).

41. **Elizabeth Webber.** Present whereabouts unknown. Pastel on paper, 23½ × 17¾ in. Signed and dated: FCotes px[t] 1752. F and C in monogram. Condition: Unknown.
Elizabeth Webber, later Lady Teynham, 1727–1793, the second wife of Henry Roper, 11th Baron Teynham of Lynsted Park, Kent.
H.S., head slightly to the left, shoulders to the right, wearing a dress with a stomacher of crisscrossed ribbons; a plain background.

PROVENANCE: By family descent from the sitter to Mrs. Roper-Lumley-Holland of Lynsted Park, Kent. The picture has not been located among the descendants of Mrs. Roper-Lumley-Holland and is believed to have been sold privately in America.

EXHIBITIONS: 'Old Masters from Houses in Kent', Tower House, Canterbury, Je. 11 – Jul. 9, 1937, no. 81 (lent by Mrs. Roper-Lumley-Holland).

42. **Charlotte Tulliedeph** (fig. 7). Sir David Ogilvy, Bt., Winton House, Pencaitland, East Lothian. Pastel on paper, 23½ × 17½ in. Signed and dated at the lower right: FCotes px[t]: / 1752. F and C in monogram. Condition: Excellent.
Charlotte Tulliedeph, b. 1737, the daughter of Walter Tulliedeph of Baldovan and Balgay, and his wife, Mary Burroughs; in 1754 the sitter married Sir John Ogilvy, 5th Bt.
H.S., to the right, wearing a pink dress and a blue shawl; a plain background.

PROVENANCE: By family descent from the sitter to the present owner.

EXHIBITIONS: 'The British Association Exhibition', Dundee, 1867, no. 168c (lent from the Ogilvy collection).
'Introducing Francis Cotes, R.A.', Nottingham University Art Gallery, Nov. 5–27, 1971, no. 8 (lent by the owner).

REFERENCES: *CAN.*, pp. 50 (fig. 43), 51.

1753: Portraits in pastel, signed and dated, nos. 43–46.

43. **Lady Fitzgerald.** Present whereabouts unknown. Pastel on paper, 23½ × 17½ in. Signed and dated at the lower left: FCotes px[t]: / 1753. F and C in monogram. Condition: Unknown.
Lady Fitzgerald, possibly Anne Fitzmaurice, daughter of the 2nd Earl of Kerry, who married Maurice Fitzgerald, Knight of Kerry, in 1764.
H.L., seated, to the left, wearing a blue dress and a lace cap; a plain background.

PROVENANCE: Anon. Sale (Property of a Lady), Sotheby's, Dec. 10, 1930 (lot 100), bought by Hutton.

44. **Elizabeth Ryves.** Present whereabouts unknown. Pastel on paper, 23 × 17 in. Inscribed at the top left: Eliz: Wife of Tho. Ryves Esq. Aetat: 27. 1753. Signed and dated at the lower left: FCotes px[t]: / 1753. F and C in monogram. Condition: Unknown.
Elizabeth Ryves, b. 1726, the daughter of Sir Anthony Abdy, 3rd Bt.; in 1749 she married Thomas Ryves of Ranston, Blandford, Dorset.
H.S., to the left, wearing a grey and gold dress and holding her pearl necklace; a plain background.

PROVENANCE: Colonel R. Malthus, U.K.; Colonel R. Malthus Sale, Christie's, Dec. 16, 1938 (lot 17), bought by Fletcher.

EXHIBITIONS: 'Expositions des Pastellistes Anglais du XVIIIe Siècle', Galeries Brunner, Paris, Apr. 8 – Je. 15, 1911, no. 19 (lent by Colonel R. Malthus).
For the other Ryves portraits, cf. nos. 9 and 10.

45. **A Gentleman.** Ralph Edwards, Esq., London. Pastel on paper, 23 × 17¼ in. Signed and dated at the lower right: FCotes px[t] / 1753. F and C in monogram. Condition: The contours of the figure have been blurred in spots.
A gentleman, possibly a member of the Vallaston family of Castel, Mereilly-sur-Seine.
H.S., to the right, wearing a brown jacket; a plain background.
Pendant to no. 46.

PROVENANCE: M. Jacques Seligman, Paris; M. Knoedler and Co., London (1917); Anon. Sale, Christie's, Jul. 11, 1930 (lot 83), bought by the King Galleries, London; The Squires Gallery, London (1932); the present owner.

EXHIBITIONS: 'Introducing Francis Cotes, R.A.', Nottingham University Art Gallery, Nov. 5–27, 1971, no. 6 (lent by the owner).

46. **A Lady** (fig. 13). Ralph Edwards, Esq., London. Pastel on paper, 23 × 17¼ in. Signed and dated at the middle left: FCotes px[t]: / 1753. F and C in monogram. Condition: Good, minor surface damage in spots.
A lady, possibly a member of the Vallaston family of Castel, Mereilly-sur-Seine.
H.S., head slightly to the left, shoulders to the right, wearing a yellow dress and a mauve scarf; a plain background.
Pendant to no. 45.

PROVENANCE: M. Jacques Seligman, Paris; M. Knoedler and Co., London (1917); Anon. Sale, Christie's, Jul. 11, 1930 (lot 83), bought by the King Galleries, London; The Squires Gallery, London (1932); the present owner.

EXHIBITIONS: 'Introducing Francis Cotes, R.A.', Nottingham University Art Gallery, Nov. 5–27, 1971, no. 7 (lent by the owner).

1753: A portrait in oils, signed and dated, no. 47.

47. **A Lady** (fig. 12). The Croome Estate Trustees, U.K. Oil on canvas, $24\frac{1}{4} \times 18\frac{1}{2}$ in. Signed and dated: FCotes px[t] / 1753. F and C in monogram. Condition: Good, minor damage in the background. H.S., head slightly to the left, shoulders to the right, wearing a gold dress and a gold scarf; a plain background.

PROVENANCE: By family descent from the sitter to the present estate trust.

EXHIBITIONS: 'An Exhibition of Treasures from Midland Homes', Birmingham Museum and Art Gallery, Birmingham, Nov. 2 – Dec. 2, 1938, no. 96 (lent by the Earl of Coventry). Here the sitter is identified as Barbara, Countess of Coventry, but this identification is no longer accepted by the present owner. If one compares the portrait with Cotes's pastel of Barbara, Countess of Coventry (no. 207) it becomes evident that the two sitters are not the same person.

This portrait is Cotes's earliest known oil painting.

1754: A portrait in pastel, signed and dated, no. 48 [see also Supplement no. 4].

48. **Midshipman George Cherry, R.N.** Private Collection, County Durham, England. Pastel on paper, 24×18 in. Signed and dated at the lower left: FCotes px[t]: / 1754. F and C in monogram. Condition: Excellent.
George Cherry, 1731–1815, later Judge Advocate General of Gibraltar and officer in charge of victualling the Royal Navy.
H.S., to the left, wearing the blue uniform of an ensign of the Fleet; a plain background.

PROVENANCE: By family descent from the sitter to the present owner.

1754: A portrait in pastel, dated, no. 49.

49. **John Gulston.** Private Collection, U.K. Pastel on brown paper, $17 \times 14\frac{1}{2}$ in. Inscribed at the lower left: Gulston delin / 1754. Condition: Excellent.
John Gulston, 1750–1764, the son of Joseph Gulston of Ealing Grove.
H.S., to the left, wearing a maroon and white costume; a plain background.

PROVENANCE: By family descent from the sitter to the present owner.
This sketch is a preliminary study of the head and shoulders of John Gulston, made in preparation for the pastel portrait of John and his brother, Joseph, which Cotes did in 1755 (no. 52).

c. 1754 – c. 1762: A lost portrait, known only through an engraving, no. 50.

50. **Miss Smith.** Present whereabouts unknown. Medium and measurements unknown. Possibly signed and dated. Condition: Unknown.
Engraved in mezzotint in the latter half of the eighteenth century by C. Spooner and inscribed: Cotes pinx[t] C. Spooner fecit. Miss Smith.
No further information is available on the sitter.
H.S., to the left, in an oval, wearing a low-necked dress and a cloak, holding the cloak with her right hand; a plain background.

DATE: The style of the portrait, as seen by means of the engraving, and the sitter's hair style would place the portrait in the period c. 1754 – c. 1762.

PROVENANCE: Unknown.

REFERENCES: *O'D.*, Vol. I, p. 136, no. 1.

1755: Portraits in pastel, signed and dated, nos. 51–57.

51. **Elizabeth Chaplin.** Sir Westrow Hulse, Bt., Breamore House, Breamore, Hampshire. Pastel on paper, approximately $23\frac{1}{2} \times 17\frac{1}{2}$ in. Signed and dated at the lower left: FCotes px[t] / 1755. F and C in monogram. Condition: Excellent.
Elizabeth Chaplin, b. 1730, the daughter of Robert Thoroton of Screveton Hall, Lincolnshire; in 1755 she married Charles Chaplin of Tathwell, Lincolnshire. See also nos. 60 and 62.
H.S., to the left, wearing a pink and blue dress; a plain background.

PROVENANCE: By family descent from the sitter to the present owner.

EXHIBITIONS: The picture is on exhibit at Breamore House, which is open to the public at certain times of the year.

52. **Joseph Gulston and John Gulston** (fig. 24). Private Collection, U.K. Pastel on paper, $27 \times 33\frac{1}{2}$ in. Signed and dated at the bottom left: FCotes px[t] 1755. F and C in monogram. Condition: Excellent.
Engraved in mezzotint by Valentine Green and published in 1771.
Joseph and John Gulston, 1745–1786 and 1750–1764, the children of Joseph Gulston of Ealing Grove.
H.L. figures; Joseph faces to the right, John to the left; both in Van Dyck costumes, Joseph in brown with a blue cloak, John in white; Joseph holds his cloak, John a straw basket filled with flowers; a landscape background.

PROVENANCE: By family descent from the sitters to the present owner.

EXHIBITIONS: The portrait is exhibited at the National Museum of Wales, Cardiff, on loan from the present owner.
It was probably exhibited with the Society of Artists in 1761, no. 19, described in the catalogue as a pastel portrait of 'Two children'. (cf. Appendix III.) No. 52 is the only known pastel portrait by Cotes of two children.

REFERENCES: *CS.*, Vol. II, p. 559, no. 59; *O'D.*, Vol. II, p. 400, no. 1; *PW.*, Vol. II, p. 53, no. 35.

This is Cotes's earliest known double portrait. For the preparatory drawing of John Gulston's head, cf. no. 49.

53. **Mary Anne Gulston.** Private Collection, U.K. Pastel on paper, $27 \times 33\frac{1}{2}$ in. Signed and dated at the middle left: FCotes px[t] / 1755. F and C in monogram. Condition: Excellent.
Mary Anne Gulston, d. 1798, the daughter of Thomas Gulston of Ealing Grove; she married Charles Colmore.
H.S., head to the left, shoulders to the right, wearing a black dress; a plain background.

PROVENANCE: By family descent from the sitter to the present owner.

EXHIBITIONS: The portrait is exhibited at the National Museum of Wales, on loan from the present owner.

REFERENCES: *PW.*, Vol. II, p. 53, no. 36.
No. 151 is a later portrait in oils of the sitter; no. 157 is of her husband.

54. **Mericas Gulston.** Private Collection, U.K. Pastel on paper, 23½ × 17½ in. Signed and dated at the middle right: FCotes px[t] / 1755. F and C in monogram. Condition: Good, but some damage to the surface; the object in the sitter's right hand can no longer be distinguished.
Mericas Gulston, 1715–1799, born Da Silva, wife of Joseph Gulston of Ealing Grove, the father of Joseph and John Gulston (no. 52).
H.L., seated to the right, wearing a pink cloak and a lace cap, and holding an object in her right hand; a plain background.

PROVENANCE: By family descent from the sitter to the present owner.

EXHIBITIONS: The portrait is exhibited at the National Museum of Wales, Cardiff, on loan from the present owner.

REFERENCES: *PW.*, Vol. II, p. 52, no. 34.

55. **Mrs. Howe.** Present whereabouts unknown. Pastel on paper, 24 × 17½ in. Signed and dated at the lower left: FCotes px[t] / 1755. F and C in monogram. Condition: Unknown.
Mrs. Howe, later Mrs. Barnard, dates unknown.
H.S., to the left, wearing a blue and white dress; a plain background.

PROVENANCE: Anon. Sale, Christie's, Feb. 23, 1923 (lot 10).

56. **Elizabeth Hulse** (fig. 14). Ralph B. Verney, Esq., Claydon House, Bletchley, Buckinghamshire. Pastel on paper 23½ × 17½ in. Signed and dated at the lower left: FCotes px[t] / 1755. F and C in monogram. Condition: Excellent.
Elizabeth Hulse, 1732–1807, daughter of Sir Edward Hulse, 1st Bt.; in 1757 she married John Calvert of Oldbury Hall, Hertfordshire.
H.L., seated, to the left, wearing a grey dress, a black lace shawl, and a blue and white hat; a plain background.

PROVENANCE: By family descent from the sitter to the present owner.
For another portrait of the sitter see no. 67.

57. **Lady Mary Radcliffe.** Cleveland Museum of Art, Cleveland, Ohio. Pastel on vellum, 23⅞ × 18 in. Signed and dated at the lower left: FCotes px[t] / 1755. F and C in monogram. Condition: Excellent.
Lady Mary Radcliffe, dates unknown, married Francis Eyre; she was possibly a member of the family of Sir Everard Radcliffe of Rudding Park, Harrogate, Yorkshire, whose ancestors were related to the Eyres.
H.S., to the left, wearing a fancy dress costume composed of a low-necked dress and a blue mantle with gold flowers on the sleeves; a plain background.

PROVENANCE: Colonel H. H. Mulliner, Clifton Court, Rugby, Warwickshire; Colonel H. H. Mulliner Sale, Christie's, Jul. 18, 1924 (lot 2), bought by P. and D. Colnaghi, London; W. M. Mensing Sale, Mensing and Sons, Amsterdam, Apr. 27, 1937 (lot 148), illus.; bought by A. Seligman and Rey, Paris, for E. B. Greene, U.S.A.; Mr. Greene gave the picture to the Cleveland Museum in 1946.

REFERENCES: *PFC.*, p. 5.

1755: A lost portrait, known only through an engraving, no. 58.

58. **Elizabeth Sandby.** Present whereabouts unknown. Medium and measurements unknown. Possibly signed and dated. Condition: Unknown.
Engraved in mezzotint by James McArdell and published in 1756 with the following inscription: F Cotes Pinx[t] 1755.
Elizabeth Sandby, 1733–1782, born Elizabeth Venables; in 1753 she married, as his second wife, Thomas Sandby, the brother of Paul Sandby.
T.Q.L., seated, to the right, wearing a dress with crisscrossed ribbons, and holding the thread from a ball of yarn resting in her lap; a plain background.

PROVENANCE: Unknown.

REFERENCES: *O'D.*, Vol. IV, p. 20, no. 1; William Sandby, *Thomas and Paul Sandby, Royal Academicians*, London, Seeley and Company, 1892, p. 176 (illus. opposite), p. 196.

c. 1755: A portrait in pastel, signed, no. 59.

59. **The Countess of Fauconberg.** V. M. G. Wombwell, Newburgh Priory, Coxwold, Yorkshire. Pastel on paper, 25 × 19 in. Signed at the middle right: FCotes. F and C in monogram. A more complete inscription may have existed at one time. Condition: Deterioration of the surface in spots.
The Countess of Fauconberg, daughter of John Beltham; in 1726 she married Thomas Bellasis, 1st Earl of Fauconberg.
H.L., seated, to the right, wearing a pink cloak, a dress with a high lace collar, and a lace cap; a plain background.

DATE: The closest parallel is no. 54, signed and dated 1755; the style and quality of the portrait of the Countess of Fauconberg place it in about the same year.

PROVENANCE: By family descent from the sitter to the present owner.

c. 1755: Portraits in pastel, neither signed nor dated, nos. 60, 61.

60. **Mary Gould.** Sir Westrow Hulse, Bt., Breamore House, Breamore, Hampshire. Pastel on paper, approximately 23½ × 19½ in. Neither signed nor dated. Condition: Good.
Mary Gould, b. 1725, the daughter of Robert Thoroton of Screveton Hall, Lincolnshire; in 1745 she married Edward Gould of Much Hadham, Hertfordshire. For portraits of her sister Elizabeth see nos. 51 and 62.
H.S., to the right, wearing a white dress and a blue cloak; a plain background.

DATE: The portrait is similar in quality to Cotes's work of c. 1755; the closest parallel to no. 60 is no. 51, the portrait of the sitter's sister, signed and dated 1755.

PROVENANCE: By family descent from the sitter to the present owner.

EXHIBITIONS: The portrait is on exhibit at Breamore House, which is open to the public at certain times of the year.

61. **Lady Elizabeth Keppel.** Present whereabouts unknown. Pastel on paper, 25½ × 20½ in. Neither signed nor dated. Condition: Unknown.

Lady Elizabeth Keppel, d. 1768; in 1764 she married Francis Russell, Marquess of Tavistock.
H.L., seated, to the left, wearing a blue dress, her right hand raised to her face; a plain background.

DATE: Seated figures, like the one in this picture, were first painted by Cotes c. 1755, and the sitter's hair style is also of this period.

PROVENANCE: Unknown.

No. 171 is of the sitter's husband.
For Reynolds's portrait of the sitter of 1761–62, cf. fig. 34.

c. 1755 – c. 1764: Portraits in pastel, neither signed nor dated, nos. 62–64.

62. **Elizabeth Chaplin.** The Sutton Estates, London. Pastel on paper, 24 × 18 in. Neither signed nor dated. Condition: Excellent.
Elizabeth Chaplin, b. 1730, daughter of Robert Thoroton of Screveton Hall, Lincolnshire; in 1755 she married Charles Chaplin of Tathwell, Lincolnshire. See also nos. 51 and 60.
H.S., head to the left, shoulders to the right, wearing a blue dress and a grey cloak; a plain background.

DATE: The closest parallel to this portrait is no. 66, signed and dated 1756. The sitter's hair style was worn from about 1755–1764; therefore, a date of c. 1755 – c. 1764 is suggested.

PROVENANCE: By family descent from the sitter to the Sutton Estates.

This picture is exactly like no. 63 except for differences in the colours of the costume.

63. **Elizabeth Chaplin.** Group Captain H. L. Hamner, Westhorpe Hall, Southwell, Nottinghamshire. Pastel on paper, 24 × 18 in. Neither signed nor dated. Condition: Good.
For genealogy, cf. no. 62.
H.S., head to the left, shoulders to the right, wearing a grey dress and a pink cloak; a plain background.

DATE: Cf. no. 62, which is exactly like no. 63, except for differences in the colours of the costume.

PROVENANCE: By family descent from the sitter to the present owner.

64. **A Lady.** The Victoria and Albert Museum, London. Pastel on paper, 23¾ × 18 in. Neither signed nor dated. Condition: Good.
H.S., to the right, wearing a blue dress, a blue and white cloak, and a white hat; a plain background.

DATE: Pastel portraits of this high quality and naturalness did not begin to occur in Cotes's work before c. 1755. The way the hair is combed back close to the head and tucked under a white mob hat would have been unusual by 1764, when hair styles had become much fuller and higher. A date of c. 1755 – c. 1764 is suggested.

PROVENANCE: Claude D. Rotch, Esq., U.K.; Mr. Rotch gave the portrait to the Victoria and Albert Museum in 1962.

EXHIBITIONS: 'Old Master Drawings', P. and D. Colnaghi, London, 1952, no. 70.

c. 1755 – c. 1765: A wash drawing, inscribed, no. 65.

65. **A Lady** (fig. 107). The Victoria and Albert Museum, London. Pencil and wash with slight watercolour on paper, 10⅜ × 6⅞ in. Inscribed in pencil at the lower left: Mr. F. Cotes. On the back of the sheet at the lower left are the initials of Benjamin West: BW. Condition: Good, minor damage in spots.
A lady, possibly Sarah Cotes, the artist's wife. Her genealogy is unknown. She married Cotes in 1765 and is mentioned in his will as sole executrix and chief beneficiary.
F.L., seated, head to the left, shoulders to the right, wearing a dress, shawl, and cap, and holding a closed fan; a plain background.

DATE: The sitter's hair style was worn from c. 1755 – c. 1764. She was married to Cotes in 1765. A date of c. 1755 – c. 1765 is suggested.

PROVENANCE: Benjamin West, Esq., London; The Rev. Alexander Dyce, London; The South Kensington Museum (now the Victoria and Albert Museum) acquired the drawing in 1869.

EXHIBITIONS: 'Introducing Francis Cotes, R.A.', Nottingham University Art Gallery, Nov. 5–27, 1971, no. 40 (lent by the Victoria and Albert Museum).

REFERENCES: Anon., *The Dyce Collection, A Catalogue of Paintings, Miniatures, Drawings, Engravings, Rings, and Miscellaneous Objects Bequeathed by the Reverend Alexander Dyce*, South Kensington Museum, London, Her Majesty's Stationery Office, 1874, p. 93, no. 627; Anon., *Portrait Drawings at the Victoria and Albert Museum*, London, Her Majesty's Stationery Office, 1948, fig. 15, n.d.; *CWO.*, p. 247.

For other portraits by Cotes considered to be of his wife, cf. nos. 296 (fig. 109) and 297 (fig. 108).

1756: Portraits in pastel, signed and dated, nos. 66–70.

66. **The Hon. Elizabeth Gregory.** Sir Andrew Forbes-Leith, Bt., Fyvie Castle, Aberdeenshire. Pastel on paper, 24 × 19 in. Signed and dated at the lower left: FCotes px[t] / 1756. F and C in monogram. Condition: Excellent.
The Hon. Elizabeth Gregory, d. 1761, the daughter of William, 14th Baron Forbes; in 1752 she married Dr. John Gregory.
H.S., to the left, wearing a brown and blue dress; a plain background.

PROVENANCE: By family descent from the sitter to the present owner.
Cotes's portrait of the sitter's husband, Dr. John Gregory, is no. 139.

67. **Elizabeth Hulse.** Sir Westrow Hulse, Bt., Breamore House, Breamore, Hampshire. Pastel on paper, approximately 23½ × 17½ in. Signed and dated at the top right: Cotes px / 1756. Condition: Excellent.
Elizabeth Hulse, 1732–1807, the daughter of Sir Edward Hulse, 1st Bt.; in 1757 she married John Calvert of Oldbury Hall, Hertfordshire.
H.L., seated, to the right, wearing a brown dress and a headscarf, and resting her head on her left hand; a plain background.

PROVENANCE: By family descent from the sitter to the present owner.

EXHIBITIONS: This portrait is on exhibit at Breamore House, which is open to the public at certain times of the year.

68. **James Rivington.** The New York Historical Society, New York. Pastel on paper, 25 × 20 in. Signed and dated at the lower right: FCotes px[t] / 1756. F and C in monogram. Condition: Excellent.

James Rivington, c. 1724–1802, bookseller and printer in London and New York, publisher of *Rivington's New York Review*, *The Gazette*, and *The Royal Gazette*.
H.S., to the right; a plain background.

PROVENANCE: Mrs. Augustus Van Horne Ellis, New York; Mrs. Ellis gave the picture to the New York Historical Society in 1940.

EXHIBITIONS: The portrait is on exhibit at the New York Historical Society.

REFERENCES: Anon., *The New York Historical Society Quarterly Bulletin*, Vol. XXIV, no. 3, Jul. 1940, cover (illus.); *Catalogue of the New York Historical Society*, New York, The New York Historical Society, p. 254, no. 623.

69. **Lady Anne Somerset and Lady Louisa Greville.** The Duke of Beaufort, Badminton House, Badminton, Gloucestershire. Pastel on paper, 26¾ × 23½ in. Signed and dated at the top left: FCotes px[t] / 1756. Condition: Good, slight damage in spots.
Lady Anne Somerset, later Countess of Northampton, was the daughter of Charles Noel Somerset, 4th Duke of Beaufort. Lady Louisa Greville, later Countess of Warwick, was the daughter of Francis Greville, 1st Earl Brooke.
Both figures H.L., seated; Lady Anne, wearing a dress with full sleeves and a stomacher of ribbons, faces to the left; Lady Louisa, wearing a dress with a striped scarf over the shoulder, faces to the right. Lady Anne holds her embroidery on her lap; she is copying a painting on an easel in front of her. The background is plain.

PROVENANCE: By family descent from the sitter to the present owner.

70. **Lady Anne Hope-Vere.** The Lord Barnard, Raby Castle, Staindrop, Darlington, Co. Durham. Pastel on paper, 23 × 17½ in. Signed and dated at the lower right: FCotes px[t] / 1756. F and C in monogram. Condition: Surface damage in several spots.
Lady Anne Hope-Vere, daughter of Henry Vane, 3rd Baron Barnard and 1st Earl of Darlington; the sitter married first Charles Hope-Vere, brother of the 2nd Earl of Hopetoun, and secondly Brigadier General Charles George Monson.
H.S., to the right, wearing a white dress with a blue and white striped scarf; a plain background.

PROVENANCE: By family descent from the sitter to the present owner.

EXHIBITIONS: The portrait is on exhibit at Raby Castle, which is open to the public at certain times of the year.

1756: A landscape watercolour, signed and dated, no. 71.

71. **A View of Purley Hall in Berkshire** (fig. 25). Victoria and Albert Museum, London. Watercolour on paper, 14½ × 21⅛ in. Signed and dated in pencil at the bottom right: FCotes delt / 1756. F and C in monogram. Condition: Good, slight foxing in spots.
In the foreground are figures and trees; to the right are two children and a dog, to the left is another dog, three ladies (one of which is seated), and a gentleman. The gentleman points to Purley Hall in the distance. The house is in the middle ground. In front of it is a lawn with vases and statues commissioned by the owner, Francis Hawes, Esq., in 1720, from Andries Carpentière (167?–1737). Behind the house the landscape fades into the distance. The dominant colours throughout are soft, pale greys, greens, and browns.

PROVENANCE: Walker's Galleries, London; the Victoria and Albert Museum purchased the drawing from Walker's Galleries in 1932.

EXHIBITIONS: 'Introducing Francis Cotes, R.A.', Nottingham University Art Gallery, Nov. 5–27, 1971, no. 42 (lent by the Victoria and Albert Museum); illus. in the cat. (Pl. XVI).

REFERENCES: Rupert Gunnis, *Dictionary of British Sculptors, 1600–1851*, London, The Abbey Library, 1969, p. 83; *The Victoria and Albert Museum Annual Review*, 1932, Pl. 16; *Walker's Monthly*, no. 60, Dec. 1932, p. 3 (illus.).
This picture and no. 80 are the only known signed and dated drawings by Cotes, and they are the only works in which he used 'delt' (drew) after his signature. Both are watercolours.

c. 1756–1759: A portrait in pastel, neither signed nor dated, no. 72.

72. **Lady Hoare.** National Trust, Stourhead House, Stourton, Wiltshire. Pastel on paper, 29½ × 25½ in. Neither signed nor dated.
Lady Hoare, 1737–1759, Anne, daughter of Henry Hoare of Stourhead, Wiltshire; in 1756 she married her cousin, Sir Richard Hoare, of Barn Elms, Wiltshire.
H.L., seated to the left, wearing a white and blue dress and playing a guitar; a plain background.
Pendant to no. 76.

DATE: The companion picture, no. 76, is signed and dated 1757. Cotes did similar pastels between 1755 and 1760. A date of c. 1756 – c. 1759, the year of the sitter's death, is suggested.

PROVENANCE: By family descent from the sitter to Sir Henry Hoare, 6th Bt., who in 1946 gave Stourhead House to the National Trust.

EXHIBITIONS: The portrait is on exhibit at Stourhead House, which is open to the public at certain times of the year.

REFERENCES: Sir Richard Colt Hoare, *A List of the Contents of Stourhead*, c. 1818, no. 43; *NTH.*, p. 254.

A copy in oils by Samuel Woodforde is also at Stourhead House.

c. 1756 – c. 1763: A lost portrait, known only through an engraving, no. 73.

73. **Thomas Pownall.** Present whereabouts unknown. Medium and measurements unknown. Possibly signed and dated. Condition: Unknown. Engraved in mezzotint by L. Earlom and published in 1777 with the following inscription: Cotes pinxit Earlom fecit / Thomas Pownall, Esq., Member of Parliament / Late Governor-Captain General and Commander in Chief and Vice Admiral / of His Majesty's provinces Massachusetts Bay and South Carolina and Lieu.[t] Governor of New Jersey.
Thomas Pownall, c. 1720–1805. He was in America between 1753 and 1761, when he held various positions in the colonies which are listed on Earlom's engraving after the portrait.
H.L., seated, to the left, probably in an oval, wearing a jacket with deep cuffs and long button holes; a plain background.

DATE: Long button holes in the jacket were popular c. 1756. Deep cuffs were worn until c. 1763. A date of c. 1756 – c. 1763 is suggested. Pownall returned to England from America in 1761. If the portrait was done before 1761, Cotes probably would have studied the likeness from a miniature sent back to England or supplied by a relative at home.

PROVENANCE: According to the records of the Massachusetts Historical Society, the provenance is as follows: The Pownall family; the Earl of Orford, Norfolk; Harold Noat, Esq., Manchester (1929); present whereabouts unknown.

REFERENCES: *CC18.*, pp. 57 (fig. f), 93, 184, 244 (fig. b); *CS.*, p. 255, no. 33. The National Maritime Museum, Greenwich, has Earlom's engraving.

Copies in oils after the Earlom engraving are at the Massachusetts Historical Society; the State House, Augusta, Maine; and in the collection of the Rev. C. C. Beaty-Pownall, Bedfordshire.

1757: Portraits in pastel, signed and dated, nos. 74–79 [see also Supplement nos. 5, 6].

74. **The Hon. Anne Burges.** Present whereabouts unknown. Pastel on paper, 23½ × 17½ in. Signed and dated at the middle left: FCotes px[t] / 1757. F and C in monogram. Condition: Unknown.
The Hon. Anne Burges, born Anne Wichenover, daughter of the 13th Lord Somerville; she married George Burges, Esq.
H.S., head to the front, shoulders to the left, wearing a white dress with a blue bow; a plain background.

PROVENANCE: Sir Charles Lamb, U.K.; Anon. Sale, Christie's, Mar. 11, 1960 (lot 16).

75. **Robert Cotes** (fig. 17). Royal Academy of Arts, London. Pastel on paper, 23½ × 17½ in. Signed and dated at the middle right: FCotes px[t] / 1757. F and C in monogram. Condition: Good.
Robert Cotes, d. 1774, the son of William Cotes of Co. Roscommon, and the father of Francis Cotes, cf. Appendix I.
H.S., to the right, wearing a grey dressing gown, a red jacket, and a black night hat; a plain background.

PROVENANCE: By family descent from the sitter to his son, Samuel Cotes, who presented the picture to the Royal Academy in 1817.

EXHIBITIONS: 'Exhibition of British Art c. 1000–1860', R.A., London, 1934, no. 785 (lent by the Royal Academy).
'Introducing Francis Cotes, R.A.', Nottingham University Art Gallery, Nov. 5–27, 1971, no. 9 (lent by the Royal Academy); illus. in cat. (Pl. IV).

REFERENCES: Francis Cotes, R.A. (untitled), notes on crayon painting, *The European Magazine*, Feb. 1797, pp. 84–85, cf. Appendix IV; *CWS.*, p. 173 (fig. no. II), p. 176; John Nichols, *The History and Antiquities of the County of Leicester*, Vol. IV, Part I, London, John Nichols and Son, 1807, p. 35, cf. Appendix I; William Sandby, *The History of the Royal Academy*, Vol. II, London, Longman, Green, Longman, Roberts, and Green, 1862, p. 409; W. T. Whitley, *Artists and their Friends in England*, Vol. I, London, The Medici Society, 1928, p. 268.

76. **Sir Richard Hoare** (fig. 21). National Trust, Stourhead House, Stourton, Wiltshire. Pastel on paper, 29½ × 25½ in. Signed and dated at the bottom left: FCotes px[t] / 1757. F and C in monogram. Condition: Excellent.
Sir Richard Hoare, 1734/35–1787; he first married his cousin, Anne Hoare, daughter of Henry Hoare of Stourhead; she died in 1759; in 1761 he married Frances Ann Acland, daughter of Richard Acland, Sr.; the sitter was created a baronet in 1786.
H.L., to the right, wearing a tan and blue coat, and holding a quill pen and a sheet of paper in his right hand; he rests his left hand on his hip. In the background there is a window and a wall covered with a red and brown patterned material.
Pendant to no. 72.

PROVENANCE: By family descent from the sitter to Sir Henry Hoare, 6th Bt., who gave Stourhead House to the National Trust in 1946.

EXHIBITIONS: The portrait is on exhibit at Stourhead House, which is open to the public at certain times of the year.

REFERENCES: Sir Richard Colt Hoare, *A List of the Contents of Stourhead*, c. 1818, no. 42; *NTH.*, p. 254.

A copy in oils by Samuel Woodforde is also at Stourhead House.

77. **Sir Edward Hulse, 1st Bt.** (fig. 18). Sir Westrow Hulse, Bt., Breamore House, Breamore, Hampshire. Pastel on paper, 25 × 20 in. Signed and dated at the middle left: FCotes px[t] / 1757. F and C in monogram.
Engraved in mezzotint by James Watson in the latter half of the eighteenth century.
Sir Edward Hulse, 1682–1759, Physician-in-Ordinary to Queen Anne, George I, and George II.
H.S., seated, to the right, wearing a brown jacket; a plain background.

PROVENANCE: By family descent from the sitter to the present owner.

EXHIBITIONS: Society of Artists, 1760, no. 12 (cf. Appendix III). 'British Portraits', R.A., London, Winter, 1956–57, no. 647 (lent by Sir Westrow Hulse, Bt.).
The portrait is on exhibit at Breamore House, which is open to the public at certain times of the year.

REFERENCES: *O'D.*, Vol. II, p. 583, no. 1; Arthur Oswald, 'Breamore House—Hampshire', Part II, *Country Life*, Vol. CXXI, no. 3153, Je. 20, 1957, p. 1271 (fig. 10).

There is a copy in oils at Breamore House.

78. **Mrs. George Pitt.** Present whereabouts unknown. Pastel on paper, 25 × 20 in. Signed and dated at the middle right: FCotes px[t] / 1757. F and C in monogram. Condition: Unknown.
Mrs. George Pitt, b. Penelope Atkins, daughter of Sir Henry Atkins; in 1745–1746 she married George Pitt, who was created Lord Rivers in 1776.
H.S., to the right, wearing a blue dress and a white scarf and resting her head on her left hand; a plain background.

PROVENANCE: Anon. Sale, Christie's, Jul. 25, 1919 (lot 60), bought by Tooth; Mrs. Maud Melville, Crawley Manor, Crawley, Bedfordshire; Anon. Sale, Christie's, Dec. 16, 1949 (lot 8), bought by Edwards.

79. **Francis Vernon.** Frick Collection, New York. Pastel on paper, 24 × 17⅞ in. Signed and dated at the bottom right: FCotes px[t] / 1757. F and C in monogram. Condition: Excellent.
Francis Vernon, 1752–1760, son of Francis Vernon of Orwell Park, Suffolk, who in 1762 became the 1st Earl of Shipbrooke.
H.L., to the left, in a painted oval, wearing a blue jacket and a rose cloak; a plain background.

PROVENANCE: Charles Edmund Dashwood, Esq., Wherstead Park, Ipswich, Suffolk; Charles Edmund Dashwood Sale, Christie's, Je. 26, 1914 (lot 90), bought by Thomas Agnew and Son, London; M. Knoedler and Co., London; Knoedler's sold the picture in 1915 to Mr. Henry Clay Frick, New York.

REFERENCES: Anon., *The Frick Collection, An Illustrated Catalogue*, Vol. I, New York, The Frick Collection, 1968, pp. 40, 41 (illus.); *PS.*, Vol. III, p. 179, no. 53.

This picture is not on exhibition to the public. It is in the part of the museum reserved for the staff.

1757: A portrait in India ink and wash, signed and dated, no. 80.

80. **Dr. John Hill.** British Museum, London. India ink and wash on paper, 8½ × 7½ in. Signed at the lower right: F Cotes ad ... / delt 17. ... Condition: The paper has been cut away on the right, and part of the original inscription has been destroyed; it read: F Cotes ad vivum / delt 1757.
Engraved in mezzotint by Richard Houston with the inscription: Dr. John Hill. F. Cotes ad vivum delt 1757. R. Houston fecit.
Dr. John Hill, c. 1716–1775, an apothecary and botanist, Superintendent of the Gardens at Kew; in 1774 he received the Order of Vasa from the King of Sweden, and was known afterwards as Sir John Hill.
H.S., to the right, in an oval, wearing a grey jacket; a plain background.

PROVENANCE: Dr. John Percy, U.K.; Dr. John Percy Sale, Sotheby's, May 12, 1890 (lot 264), bought by the British Museum.

REFERENCES: Laurence Binyon, *Catalogue of Drawings by British Artists in the British Museum*, London, The British Museum, 1898, p. 258, no. 1; *CS.*, Vol. II, p. 668, no. 64; *O'D.*, Vol. II, p. 527, no. 1.

For a discussion of Cotes's use of 'delt' cf. no. 71, and for his portrait of another famous botanist, Sir Joseph Banks, cf. no. 129.

c. 1757: A portrait in pastel, no. 81.

81. **Dr. William Bromfield, M.D.** Royal Academy of Arts, London. Pastel on paper, 24¼ × 21¼ in. Neither signed nor dated. Condition: Good.
Dr. William Bromfield, M.D., 1712–1792, Surgeon to Queen Charlotte.
H.S., to the right, wearing a red jacket; a plain background.

DATE: The face is exceptionally realistic. Realism in Cotes's pastel portraits of male sitters occurred mainly c. 1757; cf. nos. 75, 77, 80, and 86. The closest parallel is no. 77, the portrait of Dr. Bromfield's colleague, Sir Edward Hulse, signed and dated 1757.

PROVENANCE: Sir J. Wright, U.K. This owner gave the portrait to the Royal Academy in 1796.

REFERENCES: *CWS.*, pp. 174, 176 (fig. no. III); William Sandby, *The History of the Royal Academy*, Vol. II, London, Longman, Green, Longman, Roberts and Green, 1892, p. 409; Sandby incorrectly identified the sitter as Surgeon Bloomfield.

c. 1757–1762: A portrait in pastel, neither signed nor dated, no. 82.

82. **Louis François Roubiliac.** David Drey, Esq., London. Pastel on paper, 24½ × 21½ in. Neither signed nor dated. Condition: Good.
Louis François Roubiliac, the sculptor, 1705–1762.
H.S., head to the right, shoulders to the left, wearing a green dressing gown and a green night hat, resting his arms on the marble bust of a woman, and holding a pair of calipers in his right hand; a plain background.

DATE: The realistic representation of the face would place the portrait c. 1757; cf. no. 81. The sitter died in 1762. A date of c. 1757 – 1762 is suggested.

PROVENANCE: By family descent from the sitter to his daughter, Mrs. Roger Thomas. In 1870 the picture was owned by the sitter's great-great grandson, who permitted it to be published in *The Art Journal*. Anon. sale, Christie's, Mar. 20, 1953 (lot 53), sold as by Maurice-Quentin de la Tour; the present owner.

REFERENCES: Anon., untitled review, *The Art Journal*, Jul. 1870, p. 259; Katherine Ada Esdaile, *The Life and Work of Louis François Roubiliac*, Oxford, Oxford University Press, 1928, pp. 85, 189–190, 198.
Mrs. Esdaile dated the portrait 1752; but Cotes was not doing work of this nature or quality in 1752.
Mrs. Esdaile points out that the sculptured head bears some similarity to the head of Britannia from Roubiliac's monument to Admiral Sir Peter Warren in Westminster Abbey (Esdaile, Pl. XXII). Elizabeth Crosby, who married Roubiliac in 1752, shortly before he completed the Warren monument in the early part of 1753, is said to have posed for the Britannia. The sculptured head in Cotes's portrait, therefore, may represent Roubiliac's wife.
Other important pictures of Roubiliac which also show him *en negligé* are Andrea Soldi's portrait of the sculptor modelling the bust of David Garrick, signed and dated 1758, now at the Garrick Club in London, and Andries Carpentière's portrait of Roubiliac modelling a statuette of Shakespeare, signed and dated 1761, now in the National Portrait Gallery, London. Mrs. Esdaile illustrates both of these (Plates XLIIa and XLVa). Cotes's picture is in the same mood and yet significantly different in the pose and the style. At one time it was attributed to Hogarth, but it bears no resemblance to Hogarth's work; the style is characteristic of Cotes c. 1757.

1758: Portraits in pastel: signed and dated, nos. 83–86 [see also Supplement no. 7].

83. **A Lady.** Present whereabouts unknown. Pastel on paper, 23¼ × 17¾ in. Signed and dated 1758. Condition: Unknown.
H.S., to the left, a plain background.
No. 84 is the pendant to this portrait.

PROVENANCE: The Earl of Sandwich; The Earl of Sandwich Sale, Christie's, Mar. 4, 1927 (lot 1), bought by Clements; The Viscount Hinchingbrooke; The Viscount Hinchingbrooke Sale, Sotheby's, Dec. 4, 1957 (lot 168), bought by Twining.

84. **A Lady.** Present whereabouts unknown. Pastel on paper, 23¼ × 17¼ in. Signed and dated 1758. Condition: Unknown.
H.S., to the left, wearing a white and blue dress and a shawl; a plain background.
No. 83 is the pendant to this portrait.

PROVENANCE: The Viscount Hinchingbrooke; The Viscount Hinchingbrooke Sale, Sotheby's, Dec. 4, 1957 (lot 168).

85. **Margaret Payler.** Private Collection, Kent. Pastel on paper, 24 × 18 in. Signed and dated at the middle right: FCotes . . . / 1758. F and C in monogram. Condition: Good.
Margaret Payler, 1744–1780. In 1769 the sitter married the Rev. Patrick Taylor of Bifrons, Patrixbourne, Kent.
H.S., to the right, wearing a white dress; a plain background.

PROVENANCE: By family descent from the sitter to the present owner.

REFERENCES: Sir Herbert Taylor, *The Taylor Papers*, London, Longmans, Green and Co., 1913, pp. 2, 3, illus. opposite p. 4.

86. **Taylor White** (Pl. I). Thomas Coram Foundation for Children (the Foundling Hospital), London. Pastel on paper, approximately 30 × 25 in. Signed and dated at the lower left: FCotes px[t] / 1758. F and C in monogram. Condition: Excellent.
Taylor White, 1701–1772, Barrister-at-Law, Judge of Chester, Recorder of Stamford, and Treasurer of the Foundling Hospital (1745–1771).
H.L., seated at a desk covered with blue felt on which there is an ink stand, facing to the left, wearing a red jacket, and holding a quill pen and a piece of paper; a plain background.

PROVENANCE: Humphrey Cotes, Esq., London. In 1759 Humphrey Cotes presented the picture to the Foundling Hospital.

EXHIBITIONS: 'Introducing Francis Cotes, R.A.', Nottingham University Art Gallery, Nov. 5–27, 1971, no. 11 (lent by the Thomas Coram Foundation). The portrait is on exhibition at the Thomas Coram Foundation, which is open to the public on certain days of the month.

REFERENCES: *CAN.*, pp. 50 (fig. 44), 51; General Court Minutes of the Foundling Hospital, in MS., Feb. 21, 1759. *The Foundling Hospital Catalogue of Pictures, Relics, and Works of Art*, London, The Foundling Hospital, 1946, p. 3, no. 33.

1758: A portrait in oils, signed and dated, no. 87.

87. **The Rev. William Romaine.** National Portrait Gallery, London. Oil on canvas, 49 × 39 in. Signed and dated at the bottom left: FCotes px[t] / 1758. F and C in monogram. Condition: Somewhat darkened and discoloured.
Engraved in mezzotint by Richard Houston in the latter half of the eighteenth century and inscribed: Painted from the life by F Cotes 1758. R. Houston sculp. The Rev. Mr. William Romaine, A.M.
The Rev. William Romaine, 1714–1795, a leader of the evangelical movement within the Church of England and a famous preacher.
T.Q.L., seated at a desk, on which there is a book and a piece of paper, facing to the left, wearing black clerical robes; his right hand slightly raised; a column and the wall of an interior in the background.

PROVENANCE: The portrait remained in the Romaine family until it was purchased by the National Portrait Gallery in 1924.

EXHIBITIONS: 'National Portraits Commencing with the Fortieth Year of the Reign of George The Third and ending with the Year 1868', South Kensington Museum, Apr. 13, 1868, no. 889 (lent by W. G. Romaine, Esq.).
'Introducing Francis Cotes, R.A.', Nottingham University Art Gallery, Nov. 5–27, 1971, no. 12 (lent by the National Portrait Gallery); illus. in cat. (Pl. V).

REFERENCES: Anon., *The National Portrait Gallery, 1856–1947*, London, National Portrait Gallery, 1949, no. 2036; *CS.*, Vol. II, p. 685, no. 105; *CWO.*, pp. 246, 252 (fig. no. III).

c. 1758 – c. 1762: Portraits in oils, neither signed nor dated, nos. 88–90.

88. **A Gentleman.** The Viscount Allendale, Bywell Hall, Stocksfield-on-Tyne, Northumberland. Oil on canvas, approximately 30 × 25 in. Neither signed nor dated. Condition: Good, paint has run in spots.
H.S., to the left in a painted oval, wearing a red jacket; a plain background.

DATE: Between c. 1758 and c. 1762 Cotes was beginning to develop his own personal way of painting in oils. As one might expect, he was strongly influenced by his experience as a pastellist. The dry, smooth painting and fine lines of his oil portraits from this period often vividly recall his work in pastels. This particular portrait is a case in point; therefore, a date of c. 1758 – c. 1762 is suggested.

PROVENANCE: It is not known when the picture came into the Allendale Collection.

89. **Captain Edward Knowles, R.N.** Present whereabouts unknown. Oil on canvas, 50 × 40 in. Neither signed nor dated. Condition: Unknown.
Captain Edward Knowles, 1742–1762, the son of Admiral Sir Charles Knowles, Bt.
T.Q.L., to the left, wearing a blue naval uniform and a three-cornered hat, standing on the deck of a ship and pointing to a battle between two other ships, which is going on in the background.

DATE: The picture is in the style Cotes used between c. 1758 and c. 1762; cf. no. 88.

PROVENANCE: Spink and Son, London (1931); Spencer Bickerton, New York (1932); M. Harris and Sons, London; Mr. W. G. Loewe, New York; Anon. Sale (W. G. Loewe), Parke-Bernet, New York, Apr. 26–28, 1956 (lot 320), illus., bought by P. Bader. At this sale the sitter was incorrectly identified as Captain Charles Knowles.

EXHIBITIONS: International Art Galleries, London, Jan. 1931, no. 146.

REFERENCES: *Art News*, Vol. 29, no. 19, Feb. 7, 1931, p. 19.

90. **Sir Robert Pigot.** Sir Robert Pigot, Bt., Yarlington Lodge, Wincanton, Somerset. Oil on canvas, 56 × 46 in. Neither signed nor dated. Condition: Excellent.
Sir Robert Pigot, 1720–1796. After the Battle of Bunker Hill in 1775, Sir Robert Pigot was made a colonel in the 38th Regiment of Foot Guards; subsequently, he became a Lieutenant General.
T.Q.L., to the left, wearing a red army officer's uniform, holding a three-cornered hat in his right hand, leaning his left arm on a mound of earth, pointing to a fort in the background.

DATE: The picture is in the style Cotes used between c. 1758 and c. 1762; cf. no. 88.

PROVENANCE: By family descent from the sitter to the present owner.

1759: Portraits in pastel, signed and dated, nos. 91–94.

91. **Thomas Cripps.** The Earl Kitchener of Khartoum and of Broome, London. Pastel on paper, approximately 25 × 17 in. Signed and dated at the lower right: FCotes px[t] / 1759. F and C in monogram. Condition: Good, slight damage in spots.
Thomas Cripps, 1738–1794; in 1759 the sitter married Catherine Buck, daughter of William Buck of Carneby, Yorkshire.
H.S., to the right, wearing a blue coat; a plain background.
Pendant to no. 92.

PROVENANCE: By family descent from the sitter to the present owner.

REFERENCES: F. H. Cripps-Day, 'Cripps and Kitchener', *The Connoisseur*, Vol. 90, no. 372, Aug. 1932, pp. 76 (illus.), 77–81, 95.

92. **Catherine Cripps.** The Earl Kitchener of Khartoum and of Broome, London. Pastel on paper, approximately 25 × 17 in. Signed and dated at the lower left: FCotes px[t] / 1759. F and C in monogram. Condition: Excellent.
Catherine Cripps, d. 1853, the daughter of William Buck of Carneby, Yorkshire; in 1759 the sitter married Thomas Cripps.
H.S. to the left, wearing a brown brocade dress and a blue cloak; a plain background.
Pendant to no. 91.

PROVENANCE: By family descent from the sitter to the present owner.

REFERENCES: F. H. Cripps-Day, 'Cripps and Kitchener', *The Connoisseur*, Vol. 90, no. 372, Aug. 1932, pp. 76–81, 95 (illus.).

93. **A Lady,** probably of the Hulse family. Sir Westrow Hulse, Bt., Breamore House, Breamore, Hampshire. Pastel on paper, approximately 23½ × 17½ in. Signed and dated at the lower left: FCotes px[t] / 1759. F and C in monogram. Condition: Excellent.
H.S., to the left, wearing a blue dress and shawl; a plain background.

PROVENANCE: By family descent from the sitter to the present owner.

EXHIBITIONS: The portrait is on exhibit at Breamore House, which is open to the public at certain times of the year.

It has been thought that the sitter might be Mary Blackbourne, born in 1713, the daughter of Abraham Blackbourne and the wife of Captain Charles Newton. This theory must be discounted because Mary Blackbourne would have been forty-six years old in 1759, and the sitter in Cotes's picture appears to be much younger. A painting by J. Whood of Mary Blackbourne does exist in the collection of Myles Thoroton Hildyard of Flintham Hall, Newark, Nottinghamshire, in which she looks quite different from the sitter in the portrait by Cotes.

94. **A Lady.** Present whereabouts unknown. Pastel on paper, 24 × 18 in. Signed and dated at the middle left: FCotes px[t] / 1759. F and C in monogram. Condition: Unknown.
H.S., to the right, wearing a white dress; a plain background.

PROVENANCE: The Countess de la Béraudière, Paris; The Countess de la Béraudière Sale, American Art Association—Anderson Galleries, New York, Dec. 11–13, 1930 (lot 292), bought by J. J. Bodell.

EXHIBITIONS: 'Expositions des Pastellistes Anglais du XVIIIe Siècle', Galeries Brunner, Paris, Apr. 8 – Je. 15, 1911, no. 15 (lent by the Countess de la Béraudière.

REFERENCES: *RSC.*, p. 220 (fig. 4); R. R. M. Sée, *English Pastels, 1750–1830*, London, G. Bell and Sons, 1911, p. 71.

1759: A portrait in oils, not signed but dated by an inscription, no. 95.

95. **Paul Sandby** (Frontispiece). Tate Gallery, London. Oil on canvas, 49½ × 39½ in. Neither signed nor dated. Inscribed on the back: Paul Sandby, aged 34. Condition: Good.
Engraved in mezzotint by Edward Fisher and published in 1763 with the following inscription: Fras. Cotes pinxit. E. Fisher fecit. Paulus Sandby. Ruralium Prospectuum Pictor.
Paul Sandby, the painter, 1725–1809; in 1768 he became a founding member of the Royal Academy.
T.Q.L., seated, to the right, wearing a brown coat, sketching by an open window; a landscape in the right background.
Possibly pendant to no. 96.

DATE: According to the inscription on the back of the canvas the painting was done when Sandby was 34; this would have been in 1759. The style of the picture is typical of Cotes's work in the late 1750's.

PROVENANCE: By family descent from the sitter to W. A. Sandby, Esq., London. Mr. Sandby bequeathed the picture to the National Gallery in 1904. It was transferred to the Tate Gallery in 1919.

EXHIBITIONS: Society of Artists, 1761, no. 21 (cf. Appendix III). In the catalogue the portrait was described as a half length; in fact, it is closer to a three-quarter length.
'Introducing Francis Cotes, R.A.', Nottingham University Art Gallery, Nov. 5–27, 1971, no. 13 (lent by the present owner); illus. in the cat. (Pl. x).
The picture is on exhibit at the Tate Gallery.

REFERENCES: Anon., *National Gallery Catalogue*, London, Printed for the Trustees, 1912, pp. 177–178; Mary Chamot, *The Tate Gallery*, British School, London, Printed for the Trustees, 1953, p. 50, no. 1943; *CWO.*, p. 246; *PFC.*, pp. 5, 10 (fig. 2); William Sandby, *Thomas and Paul Sandby*, London, Seeley and Co., 1890, p. 192; Fisher's engraving is illustrated opposite p. 1.

1759: A portrait in oils, apparently neither signed nor dated, no. 96.

96. **Anne Sandby as 'Emma the Nut-Brown Maid'** (from Matthew Prior's poem *Henry and Emma*). Present whereabouts unknown. Oil on canvas, measurements unknown. Apparently neither signed nor dated. Condition: Unknown.
Engraved in mezzotint by Edward Fisher (fig. 23) and published in 1763 with the following inscription: 'Fras. Cotes pinxit. E. Fisher Fisher fecit. The Nut brown Maid.' Four lines from Matthew Prior's poem *Henry and Emma* were also included:

> As potent Nature shed her kindly Showr's,
> And decked the various Mead with opening Flow'rs,
> Upon this Tree the Nymph's obliging Care,
> Had left a fragrant Wreath of Henry's Hair.
>
> Prior

Anne Sandby, 1736–1797, born Anne Stogden; she married Paul Sandby, the painter.

T.Q.L., to the left, wearing a dress with a bow on her left sleeve and a cloak over her right shoulder and placing on the branch of a tree a wreath of Henry's hair entwined with flowers; a landscape background.

DATE: This portrait was exhibited in 1760; it was possibly the pendant to no. 95, which was done in 1759; therefore, a date of 1759 is suggested. The details of the costume agree with this dating.

PROVENANCE: Unknown.

EXHIBITIONS: Society of Artists, 1760, no. 13, cf. Appendix III. Mrs. Sandby is not named in the catalogue. The exhibited portrait is merely described as: 'Half length in Oil of a Young Lady in the Character of Emma, or the Nut-brown Maid.' The portrait of Mrs. Sandy (no. 96) was Cotes's only picture of this nature which could have been exhibited in 1760. In the catalogue it was described as a half-length, but judging from Fisher's engraving, it was between a half-length and a three-quarter length, being closer to the latter measurement.

REFERENCES: *CS.*, Vol. II, p. 505, no. 54; *CWO.*, p. 249; *O'D.*, Vol. IV, p. 20, no. 1; William Sandby, *The History of the Royal Academy*, Vol. I, London, Longman, Green, Longman, Roberts, and Green, 1867, p. 96; William Sandby, *Thomas and Paul Sandby*, London, Seeley and Co., 1892, p. 192; an engraving by McArdell after the portrait is illustrated opposite p. 186.

1760: A portrait in oils, signed and dated, no. 97.

97. **Sir Edward Hulse, 2nd Bt.** Sir Westrow Hulse, Bt., Breamore House, Breamore, Hampshire. Oil on canvas, approximately 30 × 25 in. Signed and dated at the lower left: FCotes px[t] / 1760. F and C in monogram. Condition: On the figure's jacket the paint has run in spots.
Sir Edward Hulse, 2nd Bt., 1715–1800, High Sheriff of Hampshire (1765–66).
H.S., to the left, wearing a plum-coloured jacket; a plain background.

PROVENANCE: By family descent from the sitter to the present owner.

EXHIBITIONS: 'Introducing Francis Cotes, R.A.', Nottingham University Art Gallery, Nov. 5–27, 1971, no. 14 (lent by the present owner)
The portrait is on exhibit at Breamore House, which is open to the public at certain times of the year.

REFERENCES: Arthur Oswald, 'Breamore House—Hampshire', Part III, *Country Life*, Vol. CXXI, no. 3154, Je. 27, 1957, p. 1320.

1760 – c. 1765: A portrait in pastel, signed and dated, no. 98.

98. **The Countess of Kildare.** The Earl of Roden, Bryansford, County Down, Northern Ireland. Pastel on paper, 24 × 18½ in. Signed and dated: FCotes px 176(?). The last digit of the date cannot be deciphered. It is possibly '5'. Condition: Good, surface damage in spots.
The Countess of Kildare, b. Lady Emilia Mary Lennox in 1731; in 1747 she married James, Marquess of Kildare, who was created 1st Duke of Leinster in 1766.
H.S., head to the left, shoulders to the right, wearing a dress with a dark shawl over her shoulders and a small lace cap; a plain background.

DATE: The picture is dated 176(?). The sitter's hair style was fashionable until c. 1765; therefore, a date of 1760 – c. 1765 is suggested.

PROVENANCE: By family descent from the sitter to the present owner.

EXHIBITIONS: 'Pictures from Ulster Houses', Belfast Museum and Art Gallery, Belfast, May 10 – Jul. 15, 1961, no. 172 (lent by the Earl of Roden).

1761: Portraits in oils, signed and dated, nos. 99–102.

99. **Frances Burdett as 'Emma''** (from Matthew Prior's poem *Henry and Emma*). Present whereabouts unknown. Oil on canvas, 51 × 40½ in. Signed and dated at the lower left: FCotes px[t] / 1761. F and C in monogram. Condition: Unknown.
Frances Burdett, daughter of Sir Robert Burdett, 4th Bt.
T.Q.L., to the left, wearing a grey dress with a green cloak. The portrait is almost identical to Fisher's engraving of Cotes's picture of Anne Sandby (no. 96).

PROVENANCE: Mr. Alfred H. Mulliken, Chicago and New Canaan, Conn.; Alfred H. Mulliken Sale, American Art Association—Anderson Galleries, New York, Jan. 5–7, 1933 (lot 14), bought in by the Ehrich Galleries, New York, on behalf of Mr. Mulliken; Alfred H. Mulliken Sale, American Art Association—Anderson Galleries, New York, April 12–13, 1935 (lot 134), bought by E. B. Harper. In the sale catalogues the sitter's last name is spelled 'Burdette'; it should be 'Burdett'. Either a copy or a damaged version of this picture appeared in the following sale: Anon. Sale (Connecticut Private Collector), Parke-Bernet, New York, Nov. 3, 1954, lot 42 (illus.). The heavy trunk of a tree in the left foreground, which was present when the picture was sold in the 1930's, was missing in 1954.

100. **David Gavin.** Armorer, Countess of Breadalbane, Invereil, Dirleton, East Lothian. Oil on panel, 30 × 24½ in. Signed and dated at the lower right: FCotes px / 1761. F and C in monogram. Condition: The paint has run in several places.
David Gavin of Langton House, Berwickshire; he first married Christina Maria Hirsce, who died in 1767, and then Lady Elizabeth Maitland, daughter of the 7th Earl of Lauderdale.
H.L., head to the front, shoulders to the left, wearing a blue jacket, and resting his left arm on the back of a chair; a plain background.

PROVENANCE: By family descent from the sitter to the present owner.

101. **Richard Hulse.** Sir Westrow Hulse, Breamore House, Breamore, Hampshire. Oil on canvas, approximately 30 × 25 in. Signed and dated at the middle right: FCotes px[t]. / 1761. F and C in monogram. Condition: Good.
Richard Hulse, 1727/28–1805, of Blackheath and Baldwins, Kent; in 1768 he was High Sheriff of Kent, and later he became Deputy Governor of the Hudson Bay Company.

H.L., seated, to the left, wearing a blue coat; a plain background.

PROVENANCE: By family descent from the sitter to the present owner.

REFERENCES: Arthur Oswald, 'Breamore House—Hampshire', Part III, *Country Life*, Vol. CXXI, no. 3154, Je. 27, 1957, p. 1321.

102. **Colonel Kinnear.** The Earl of Bradford, Weston Park, Shifnal, Shropshire. Oil on canvas, 29½ × 24½ in. Signed and dated at the lower left: FCotes pxt / 1761. F and C in monogram. Condition: Good.
Col. Kinnear of the 50th Regiment of Foot Guards.
H.S., to the left, wearing a blue jacket; a plain background.

PROVENANCE: The picture has been at Weston Park for many years; when it was acquired is not known.

1762: Portraits in oils, signed and dated, nos. 103–108 [see also Supplement nos. 10, 11].

103. **Elizabeth Adams** (fig. 28). The Earl Cawdor, Golden Grove House, Broad Oak, Carmarthenshire. Oil on canvas, 50 × 40 in. Signed and dated at the middle right: FCotes pxt / 1762. F and C in monogram. Condition: Good.
Elizabeth Adams, d. 1816, the daughter of John Campbell; she married Major Joseph Adams of Holyland, Pembrokeshire.
T.Q.L., head to the right, shoulders slightly to the left. The sitter is wearing a yellow wrapping gown, a striped sash, and a blue cloak. Her hair is arranged in the 1762–1770 manner and trimmed with pearls. She holds a rose in her left hand. There is a landscape background with a garden urn.

PROVENANCE: By family descent from the sitter to the present owner.

REFERENCES: *PW.*, Vol. II, p. 201, no. 11.

104. **Pryse Campbell.** The Earl Cawdor, Golden Grove House, Broad Oak, Carmarthenshire. Oil on canvas, 50 × 40 in. Signed and dated at the middle right: FCotes pxt / 1762. F and C in monogram. Condition: Good.
Pryse Campbell of Cawdor, Nairn and Stackpole Court, Carmarthenshire, the brother of Elizabeth Adams (no. 103).
T.Q.L., head to the right, shoulders to the left, wearing a tartan jacket, kilt, and cloak, and resting his right hand on the hilt of his broad sword; a landscape background.

PROVENANCE: By family descent from the sitter to the present owner.

REFERENCES: *PW.*, Vol. II, p. 201, no. 7. The date is incorrectly given as 1763.

105. **Sarah Campbell.** The Earl Cawdor, Golden Grove House, Broad Oak, Carmarthenshire. Oil on canvas, 50 × 40 in. Signed and dated at the bottom left: FCotes pxt 1762. F and C in monogram. Condition: Good.
Sarah Campbell, d. 1767; she was born Sarah Bacon, the daughter of Sir Edmund Bacon, Bt.; in 1752 she married Pryse Campbell of Cawdor and Stackpole.
T.Q.L., seated, to the right, wearing a white dress and a blue cloak, holding a wreath of flowers in her right hand, and resting her right arm on a stone parapet; a landscape background.

PROVENANCE: By family descent from the sitter to the present owner.

EXHIBITION: 'Cent Portraits de Femmes des Écoles Anglaise et Française', Galerie Georges Petit, Paris, 1910, no. 2 (lent by the Earl Cawdor);
'Introducing Francis Cotes, R.A.', Nottingham University Art Gallery, Nov. 5–27, 1971, no. 21 (lent by the owner); illus. in cat. Pl. VI).

REFERENCES: *CAN.*, p. 52; *PW.*, Vol. II, p. 201, no. 8. The date is incorrectly given as 1763.

106. **John Campbell Hooke.** The Earl Cawdor, Golden Grove House, Broad Oak, Carmarthenshire. Oil on canvas, 50 × 40 in. Signed and dated at the bottom left: FCotes pxt 1762. F and C in monogram. Condition: Good.
John Campbell-Hooke, born Hooke (the name Campbell assumed later) of Bangeston and Co. Pembroke, Lyon King of Arms from 1754, married Eustacia, daughter of Francis Basset.
T.Q.L., to the left, wearing a jacket and the cloak and insignia of the Lord Lyon of Scotland, resting his right arm on a pedestal, and holding a wooden cane in his right hand; a column and an arch in the background.

PROVENANCE: By family descent from the sitter to the present owner.

107. **Captain Timothy Edwards, R.N.** Major R. Harden, Nanhoran, Pwllheli, Caernarvonshire. Oil on canvas, 50 × 40 in. Signed and dated at the bottom right: FCotes pxt / 1762. F and C in monogram. Condition: Unknown.
Captain Timothy Edwards of Nanhoran, 1731–1780.
T.Q.L., to the left, wearing a blue naval officer's jacket, and a blue, three-cornered hat, and holding a drawn sword in his right hand; a longboat filled with men in the middleground and a ship in the background.

PROVENANCE: By family descent from the sitter to Mrs. Alan Gough (1957); the present owner.

EXHIBITIONS: 'Pictures from Welsh Private Collections', National Museum of Wales, Cardiff, and Glynn Vivian Gallery, Swansea, 1951, no. 14 (lent by Mrs. Alan Gough).

REFERENCES: David Piper, 'Pictures from Welsh Private Collections', *The Burlington Magazine*, Vol. 93, Nov. 1951, p. 355; *PW.*, Vol. I, p. 55, no. 13.
For a portrait of Richard Edwards of Nanhoran, a member of the sitter's family, cf. Appendix V, no. 17.

108. **Lady Fortescue.** Present whereabouts unknown. Oil on canvas, 50 × 40 in. Signed and dated 1762. Condition: Unknown.
Lady Fortescue, 1730–1812, born Anne Campbell; in 1752 she married Matthew Fortescue, 2nd Baron Fortescue.
T.Q.L., to the left, wearing a dress and cloak edged with ermine, and holding a coronet in her right hand; a church interior in the background. Probably the portrait commemorates the sitters' presence at the Coronation of George III in 1760.
Pendant to no. 124. For another portrait by Cotes of the same sitter, cf. no. 113.

PROVENANCE: By family descent from the sitter to the Earl Cawdor; The Viscount Emlyn Sale, Sotheby's, Jul. 12, 1967 (lot 91), bought by Liddell; Anon. Sale, Sotheby's, Jul. 19, 1972 (lot 48).

EXHIBITIONS: 'Cent Portraits de Femmes des Écoles Anglaise et Française', Galerie Georges Petit, Paris, 1910, no. 1 (lent by the Earl Cawdor).

REFERENCES: *PW.*, Vol. II, p. 201, no. 12.

c. 1762: Portraits in oils, neither signed nor dated, nos. 109 and 110.

109. **Henry Paulet, 6th Duke of Bolton** (fig. 30). The Metropolitan Museum of Art, New York. Oil on canvas, 50 × 40 in

Neither signed nor dated. Inscribed on the back: Henry 6th and last Duke of Bolton / Grandfather of Viscountess Templetown. Condition: Good, but the varnish is somewhat discoloured.
Henry Paulet, 6th Duke of Bolton, 1719–94.
T.Q.L., to the right, wearing a blue naval officer's jacket, resting his left hand on an anchor and holding a three-cornered hat in his right hand; to the left in the background is a mound of earth and rock, and to the right a coastline.

DATE: The style of the portrait places it at c. 1762. Its closest parallels are nos. 104 and 107. Cotes may have taken the composition from Reynolds's portrait of George Brydges, Lord Rodney (1761), at Petworth. Reynolds's portrait was engraved by James Watson and the engraving was exhibited at the Society of Artists in 1762. Cotes, who showed works in the same exhibition, would have known of the engraving.

PROVENANCE: By family descent from the sitter to the 3rd Viscount Templetown, Castle Upton, Co. Antrim, Ireland; Arthur Sanderson, Esq., Edinburgh; M. Knoedler and Co., London; Scott and Fowles, New York; Mr. Jacob Ruppert, New York (1912); Mr. Ruppert bequeathed the painting to the Metropolitan Museum of Art in 1939.

EXHIBITIONS: The portrait has been shown at the Metropolitan Museum of Art.

REFERENCES: *The Metropolitan Museum of Art Bulletin*, Vol. 34, no. 7, Jul. 1939, p. 168.

110. **Captain Robert Boyle Nicholas, R.N.** National Trust, Montacute House, Montacute, Somerset. Oil on canvas, 49½ × 40 in. Neither signed nor dated. Condition: Good.
The label on the frame reads: 1744 Captain Robert Boyle Nicholas, R.N. 1780 / Post Captain in H.M.S. 'Thunderer' / 1726 Francis Cotes R.A. 1770 / Seascape with his yacht 'Nepaul' by D. Serres R.A.
Capt. Robert Boyle Nicholas, 1744–1780.
T.Q.L., to the right, wearing a scarlet coat, leaning against a stone parapet to his left, holding a wooden walking stick in his right hand and a black hat in his left hand; a seascape background with his yacht, 'Nepaul'.

DATE: The style of the picture places it c. 1762; it is similar to no. 109.

PROVENANCE: By family descent to the Marquis del Moral; Leggatt Brothers, London; Sir Malcolm Stewart, U.K.; Sir Malcolm Stewart bequeathed the picture to the National Trust at Montacute in 1960.

REFERENCES: *CWO.*, pp. 250 (fig. no. v), 251; *NTH.*, p. 248.

Dominic Serres, the marine painter, 1722–1793, arrived in England c. 1758. Along with Cotes he became a founding member of the Royal Academy. It is interesting to note that among Cotes's posessions sold after his death was 'A sea piece by Seres' (cf. Appendix II, p. 12, lot 38).

1762–1763: Portraits in oils, neither signed nor dated, nos. 111 and 112.

111. **Colonel Robert Dalrymple-Horne-Elphinstone.** The Earl of Glasgow, Kelburn, Fairlie, Ayrshire. Oil on canvas, 30 × 25 in. Neither signed nor dated. Condition: Unknown.
Col. Robert Dalrymple-Horne-Elphinstone, 1718–1794, son of Hew Dalrymple, Lord Drummore; in 1770 he became Major General of the 53rd Regiment of Foot Guards.
H.S., head to the left, shoulders to the right, wearing a colonel's uniform of the 120th Regiment of Foot Guards; a plain background. Pendant to no. 112.

DATE: The sitter was made a colonel in the 120th Regiment of Foot Guards in 1762; the regiment was disbanded in 1763. The style of the picture would place it in the period of 1762–1763.

PROVENANCE: The Elphinstone family; N. Forbes Robertson, Esq., London; N. Forbes Robertson Sale, Christie's, May 19, 1911 (lot 102), bought by Arthur Tooth, London; the present owner.

EXHIBITIONS: 'National Portraits Commencing with the Fortieth Year of the Reign of George The Third and Ending with the Year 1867', South Kensington Museum, London, Apr. 13, 1868, no. 781 (lent by Sir James Dalrymple-Horne-Elphinstone, Bt.).

REFERENCES: P. W. Reynolds, *Military Costume of the 18th and 19th Centuries*, in MS. at the Victoria and Albert Museum Library, London, n.d., Vol. III, p. 285.

112. **Mary Dalrymple-Horne-Elphinstone.** The Earl of Glasgow, Kelburn, Fairlie, Ayrshire. Oil on canvas, 30 × 25 in. Neither signed nor dated. Condition: Unknown.
Mary Dalrymple-Horne-Elphinstone, d. 1776, born Mary Elphinstone; in 1753 she married Colonel Robert Dalrymple of Horne, who assumed the name of Dalrymple-Horne-Elphinstone.
H.S., to the right, wearing a yellow dress; a plain background. Pendant to no. 111.

DATE: The style of the picture is similar to that of its companion portrait, no. 111.

PROVENANCE: The Elphinstone family; N. Forbes Robertson, Esq., London; N. Forbes Robertson Sale, Christie's, May 19, 1911 (lot 101), bought by Boyle; the present owner.

EXHIBITIONS: 'National Portraits Commencing with the Fortieth Year of the Reign of George The Third and Ending with the Year 1867', South Kensington Museum, London, Apr. 13, 1868, no. 782 (lent by Sir James Dalrymple-Horne-Elphinstone, Bt.).

c. 1762–1763: Portraits in oils, neither signed nor dated, nos. 113 and 114.

113. **Lady Fortescue** (fig. 33). Lady Margaret Fortescue, Castle Hill, Barnstaple, Devonshire. Oil on canvas, 49 × 39 in. Neither signed nor dated. Condition: Excellent.
Engraved in mezzotint by James Watson in the latter half of the eighteenth century with the following inscription: F Cotes pinx^{t} James Watson Sculp^{t} / The Right Honble Lady Fortescue.
Lady Fortescue, 1730–1812, born Anne Campbell; in 1752 she married Matthew Fortescue, 2nd Baron Fortescue.
T.Q.L., seated head to the right, shoulders to the left, wearing a blue dress, a striped sash, and a brown mantle, leaning her left arm on a bank of earth; a landscape background.

DATE: The portrait is similar to the Campbell portraits of 1762 and 1763; cf. nos. 103–106, 123, and 124.

PROVENANCE: The portrait was purchased by the Earl Fortescue c. 1920 and passed by family descent to the present owner.

REFERENCES: *O'D.*, Vol. II, p. 238.

For Cotes's other portrait of Lady Fortescue, cf. no. 108.

114. **Colonel Campbell Dalrymple.** The Earl of Stair, Lochinch Castle, Stranaer, Wigtownshire. Oil on canvas, 30 × 25 in. Neither signed nor dated. Condition: Excellent.
Col. Campbell Dalrymple, 1725–1767, son of Hew Dalrymple, Lord Drummore.
H.L., to the left, wearing a scarlet jacket; a plain background.

DATE: The portrait is similar to the pictures of Colonel and Mrs. Dalrymple-Horne-Elphinstone of 1762–1763, nos. 111 and 112, and of the same quality as the Campbell portraits of 1762 and 1763, nos. 103–106, 123 and 124.

PROVENANCE: The portrait was purchased in 1903 by the family of the present owner.

c. 1762–1770: Portraits in oils, neither signed nor dated, nos. 115 and 116.

115. **Francis Vernon, Baron Orwell of Newry.** Present whereabouts unknown. Oil on canvas, 49½ × 39½ in. Neither signed nor dated. Condition: Unknown.
Lord Orwell, c. 1715–1783; in 1747/48 he married Alice Ibbetson, daughter of Samuel Ibbetson of Denton, Yorkshire; in 1762 he was created Baron Orwell of Newry; in 1776 he became Viscount Orwell, and in 1777, Earl of Shipbrooke.
T.Q.L., to the left, wearing a brown jacket, a scarlet cloak trimmed with ermine, and a sword at his left side, and resting his left hand on his hip; an architectural background consisting of a column with red drapery and a balcony.
Pendant to no. 116.

DATE: The style and quality of the picture are in keeping with Cotes's work between c. 1762 and his death in 1770. The sitter is wearing the robes of a peer, to which he was not entitled until 1762.

PROVENANCE: Charles Edmund Dashwood, Esq., Wherstead Park, Ipswich Suffolk; Charles Edmund Dashwood Sale, Christie's, Je. 26, 1914 (lot 96), bought in by Lacey on behalf of Mr. Dashwood; Charles Edmund Dashwood Sale, Sotheby's, Dec. 11, 1929 (lot 60), illus., bought by Warwick.

REFERENCES: *PS.*, Vol. III, p. 177, no. 49.

116. **Lady Orwell.** Present whereabouts unknown. Oil on canvas, 49½ × 39 in. Neither signed nor dated. Condition: Unknown.
Lady Orwell, 1730–1808, born Alice Ibbetson, daughter of Samuel Ibbetson of Denton, Yorkshire; in 1747/48 she married Francis Vernon, who was created Baron Orwell of Newry in 1762, Viscount Orwell in 1776, and Earl of Shipbrooke in 1777.
T.Q.L., seated, to the right, wearing a white and gold wrapping gown, a blue sash, and a blue cloak edged with ermine; a rose bush and an expanse of sky in the background.
Pendant to no. 115.

DATE: The portrait could have been done at any time between c. 1762 and 1770. It is the companion picture to no. 115, which is also of c. 1762–1770.

PROVENANCE: Charles Edmund Dashwood, Esq., Wherstead Park, Ipswich, Suffolk; Charles Edmund Dashwood Sale, Christie's, Je. 26, 1914 (lot 95), bought by Gooden and Fox, London; The Marquess Curzon, Kedleston, Derbyshire; The Marquess Curzon Sale, Christie's, Dec. 22, 1927 (lot 87), illus., bought by Benjamin De Casseres, London; Mr. W. G. Loew, New York; The Palatial Mansion Sale (W. G. Loew), Parke-Bernet, Apr. 26–28, 1956 (lot 317), illus., bought by P. Bader.

REFERENCES: *CWO.*, p. 250; *PS.*, Vol. III, p. 173, no. 41.

1763: Portraits in pastel, signed and dated, nos. 117–121.

117. **Cornelia Chambers.** Victoria and Albert Museum, London. Pastel on paper, 21⅞ × 17⅞ in. Signed and dated at the middle left: FCotes px[t] / 1763. F and C in monogram. Condition: Good, minor surface damage in several spots.
Cornelia Chambers, 1753–1795, the daughter of Sir William Chambers; in 1775 she married John Millbanke.
H.S., to the right, in an oval. The sitter is wearing a pink dress with lace at the bodice and on the sleeves. Her hair is arranged in the 1755–1764 manner and trimmed with flowers and a ribbon. The background is plain.

PROVENANCE: By family descent from the sitter to Miss E. F. E. Pebardy. Miss Pebardy gave the picture to the National Portrait Gallery, London. It has since been transferred to the Victoria and Albert Museum.

EXHIBITIONS: The picture is on exhibit at Osterley Park, Osterley, Middlesex.

REFERENCES: John Harris, *Sir William Chambers, Knight of the Polar Star*, London, A. Zwemmer, 1970, pp. 6, 14.

118. **Elizabeth Chudleigh.** Present whereabouts unknown. Pastel on paper, 23 × 17 in. Signed and dated at the middle right: FCotes px[t] / 1763. F and C in monogram. Condition: Unknown.
Elizabeth Chudleigh, 1720–1788; in 1744 she married Captain Hervey, later Earl of Bristol, but was immediately separated from him; in 1769 she married the Duke of Kingston.
H.S., slightly to the right, wearing a blue dress; a plain background.

PROVENANCE: In 1868 the picture was in the collection of Clifford Chaplin, Esq., U.K.

EXHIBITIONS: 'National Portraits Commencing with the Reign of George The Third and Ending with the Year 1867', South Kensington Museum, London, Apr. 13, 1868, no. 791 (lent by Clifford Chaplin).
Fig. 32 is of Reynolds's portrait of the sitter's first husband.

119. **A Lady** (fig. 38). The Henry E. Hungtington Library and Art Gallery, San Marino, California. Pastel on paper, 23½ × 17½ in. Signed and dated at the middle right: FCotes px[t]/1763. F and C in monogram. Condition: Excellent.
A lady, possibly of the Marquess of Normanby's family.
H.S., to the right, wearing a white dress, rose cloak, and a tiara, her right hand raised to her breast; a plain background.

PROVENANCE: The Rev. Canon the Marquess of Normanby, Mulgrave Castle, Whitby, Yorkshire; The Rev. Canon the Marquess of Normanby Sale, Christie's, May 8, 1897 (lot 91), bought by Charles Wertheimer, Esq., London. M. Knoedler and Co., London, purchased the picture from the Wertheimer estate in 1908, and sold it to Mr. Henry E. Huntington in 1911.

EXHIBITIONS: 'Cent Pastels', Galerie Georges Petit, Paris, May–Je. 1908, no. 11 (lent by Charles Wertheimer).
The portrait is on exhibit at the Henry E. Huntington Library and Art Gallery.

REFERENCES: C. H. Collins Baker, *Catalogue of British Paintings in the Henry E. Huntington Library and Art Gallery*, San Marino, California. Published by the Library, 1936, p. 37, Pl. III.

120. **William O'Brien** (fig. 44). Lady Teresa Agnew, Melbury House, Dorchester, Dorset. Pastel on paper, 25½ × 21½ in. Signed and dated at the lower right: FCotes px[t] / 1763. F and C in monogram. Condition: Good, but somewhat smeared in spots.
Engraved by James Watson and published in the latter half of the eighteenth century.
William O'Brien, the actor, d. 1815; in 1764 he married Lady Susan Fox-Strangeways.
H.S., to the right, in an oval, wearing a red coat, his arms folded across his chest; a plain background.
Pendant to no. 128.

PROVENANCE: By family descent from the sitter to the present owner.

EXHIBITIONS: Society of Artists, 1763, no. 26. Walpole thought that this was 'the best picture in the exhibition', (cf. Appendix III). 'Introducing Francis Cotes, R.A.', Nottingham University Art Gallery, Nov. 5–27, 1971; no. 17 (lent by the present owner); illus. in cat. (Pl. VIII).

REFERENCES: The Countess of Ilchester and Lord Stavordale (ed.), *The Life and Letters of Lady Sarah Lennox, 1745–1826*, Vol. I, London, John Murray, 1901, p. 148; Watson's engraving is reproduced opposite p. 148; William Sandby, *The History of the Royal Academy*, Vol. I, London, Longman, Green, Longman, Roberts, and Green, 1862, p. 96; *O'D.*, Vol. II, p. 364; *WA.*, Vol. IV, p. iii; *WW.*, pp. 181–182.

121. **Martha Seymer.** Present whereabouts unknown. Pastel on paper, 23½ × 17½ in. Signed and dated at the lower right: FCotes px[t] / 1763. F and C in monogram. Condition: Unknown.
Martha Seymer, wife of Francis Steward, dates unknown.
H.S., to the right, wearing a white dress and a white and gold cloak; a plain background.

PROVENANCE: Anon. Sale, Christie's, Jul. 4, 1930 (lot 146), bought by Popoff; Van Gelder Sale, Moos, Geneva, Oct. 7, 1933 (lot 94).

1763: Portraits in oils, signed and dated, nos. 122–126.

122. **Richard Beaumont.** Present whereabouts unknown. Oil on canvas, 30 × 24½ in. Signed and dated at the lower right: FCotes px[t] 1763. F and C in monogram. Inscribed with the name of the sitter at the lower left. Condition: Unknown.
Richard Beaumont, d. 1764.
H.S., to the left, in a painted oval, wearing a blue jacket; a plain background.

PROVENANCE: P. and D. Colnaghi, London (1926); M. Knoedler and Co., London; Private Collection, New York; Anon. Sale, Parke-Bernet, New York, Mar. 12, 1969 (lot 91), bought by Rambert.

EXHIBITIONS: Kansas City Art Institute, Oct. 5–27, 1930, no. 21. California Palace of the Legion of Honor, Je. – Jul. 1933, no. 7 (lent by M. Knoedler and Co.).

123. **Lieutenant-Colonel Alexander Campbell** (fig. 31). The Earl Cawdor, Golden Grove House, Broad Oak, Carmarthenshire. Oil on canvas, 50 × 40 in. Signed and dated at the bottom right: FCotes px[t] / 1763. F and C in monogram. Condition: Excellent.
Lieutenant-Colonel Alexander Campbell, 1737–1785, the third son of John Campbell of Cawdor and Stackpole.
T.Q.L., to the left, wearing the scarlet uniform of the 1st Regiment of Foot Guards and a black, three cornered hat, holding a pike across his chest; in the background beside an estuary, a steepled church, and hills.

PROVENANCE: By family descent from the sitter to the present owner.

EXHIBITIONS: 'Introducing Francis Cotes, R.A.', Nottingham University Art Gallery, Nov. 5–27, 1971, no. 19 (lent by the present owner); illus. in cat. (Pl. VII).

REFERENCES: *PW.*, Vol. II, p. 201, no. 10.

124. **Matthew Fortescue, 2nd Baron Fortescue.** The Earl Cawdor, Golden Grove House, Broad Oak, Carmarthenshire. Oil on canvas, 50 × 40 in. Signed and dated at the bottom right: FCotes px[t] / 1763. F and C in monogram. Condition: Unknown.
Lord Fortescue, 1719–1785; in 1752 he married Anne Campbell.
T.Q.L., to the right, wearing a gold jacket, a scarlet cloak edged with ermine, a sword at his left side, leaning his left arm against the base of a column and holding a coronet in his left hand; a plain wall of an interior in the background. The picture probably commemorates the presence of the sitter at the coronation of George III.
Pendant to no. 108.

PROVENANCE: By family descent from the sitter to the present owner.

EXHIBITIONS: 'Introducing Francis Cotes, R.A.', Nottingham University Art Gallery, Nov. 5–27, 1971, no. 20 (lent by the present owner).

REFERENCES: *PW.*, Vol. II, p. 202, no. 13.

125. **Sir Hector Monro.** Mr. Philip Rieff, Philadelphia. Oil on canvas, 37½ × 25½ in. Signed and dated at the lower right: FCotes px[t] / 1763. F and C in monogram. Condition: Good.
Sir Hector Monro, dates unknown.
H.L., to the left, wearing a scarlet coat with a green collar, his arms folded across his chest, holding a glove in his right hand which rests on the top of a cane; a plain background.
Pendant to no. 126.

PROVENANCE: Lionel Clark, Esq., London; Lionel Clark Sale, Sotheby's, Jul. 24, 1929 (lot 48), bought by Asscher; Mr. Leo M. Flesh, Piqua, Ohio; Leo M. Flesh Sale, Christie's, Nov. 17, 1967 (lot 94), bought by Leyland; Anon. Sale, Sotheby's, Mar. 12, 1969 (lot 134); the present owner.

126. **Lady Monro.** Present whereabouts unknown. Oil on canvas, 36 × 28 in. Signed and dated at the middle right: FCotes px[t] / 1763. F and C in monogram. Condition: Unknown.
Lady Monro, dates unknown, wife of Sir Hector Monro.
H.L., to the right, wearing a blue dress and a lace shawl; a plain background.
Pendant to no. 125.

PROVENANCE: Lionel Clark, Esq., London; Lionel Clark Sale, Sotheby's, Jul. 24, 1929 (lot 48), bought by Asscher; Arthur Edwin Bye, Philadelphia; Mr. George Horace Lorimer, Philadelphia; Mr. George Burford Lorimer, Philadelphia; George Burford Lorimer Sale, Parke-Bernet, New York, Apr. 1, 1944 (lot 757), illus., bought by Julius Weitzner.

Exhibited in 1763: A lost portrait, no. 127.

127. **The Countess of Macclesfield.** Present whereabouts unknown. Oil on canvas, measurements unknown. Possibly signed and dated. Condition: Unknown.
The sitter is probably Mary Heathcote, who married Thomas, 3rd Earl of Macclesfield, in 1749 and died in 1812.
F.L., wearing her peeress's robes; a view of Westminster Abbey in the background. The portrait was probably intended to commemorate the sitter's presence at the coronation of George III in 1760.

PROVENANCE: Unknown.

EXHIBITIONS: Society of Artists, 1763, no. 23. Walpole writes: 'very good. Countess of Macclesfield, with a view of Westminster Abbey'. (cf. Appendix III.)

1763–1764: A portrait in pastel, neither signed nor dated, no. 128.

128. **Lady Susan Fox-Strangeways** (fig. 42). Lady Teresa Agnew, Melbury House, Dorchester, Dorset. Pastel on paper, $25\frac{1}{2} \times 21\frac{1}{2}$ in. Neither signed nor dated. Condition: Good.
Engraved in mezzotint by James Watson and published in 1772.
Lady Susan Fox-Strangeways, 1744–1827, the daughter of Stephen Fox-Strangeways, 1st Earl of Ilchester; in 1764 she married William O'Brien, the actor.
H.L., to the left, wearing a blue and pink dress with a black lace shawl, resting both arms in front of her on a stone wall partially covered by drapery; her right hand is raised to her cheek; a plain background.
Pendant to no. 120.

DATE: The companion picture of the sitter's husband, no. 120, is signed and dated 1763. The commission to paint the crayon portrait of Lady Susan may have been given to Cotes at approximately the same date; however, he took a long time to actually finish the portrait. A year later Lady Sarah Bunbury, writing to Lady Susan, informed her that 'that devil Mr. Coates has not finished your picture yet'. A date of 1763–1764 is suggested.

PROVENANCE: By family descent from the sitter to the present owner.

EXHIBITIONS: 'Introducing Francis Cotes, R.A.', Nottingham University Art Gallery, Nov. 5–27, 1971, no. 18 (lent by the present owner); illus. in cat. (Pl. IX).

REFERENCES: The Countess of Ilchester and Lord Stavordale (ed.), *The Life and Letters of Lady Sarah Lennox, 1745–1826*, Vol. I, London, John Murray, 1901, p. 144; Watson's engraving is illustrated between pp. 144 and 145; *O'D.*, Vol. II, p. 364; *WW.*, pp. 181–182.

c. 1763: Portraits in oils, neither signed nor dated, nos. 129–131.

129. **Sir Joseph Banks.** D. W. Hughes, Esq., London. Oil on canvas, $36 \times 27\frac{1}{2}$ in. Neither signed nor dated. Condition: Good.
Sir Joseph Banks, 1743–1820, the famous botanist and traveller.
H.L., to the right, wearing a buff coat with a green collar, and resting one hand on his hip, the other on a pedestal; a garden with a pavilion by a lake beyond.

PROVENANCE: Anon. Sale, Christie's, Je. 3, 1932 (lot 56), bought by Freeman. Guinevere, Countess of Midleton, Hersey. Countess of Midleton Sale, Christie's, Nov. 21, 1975 (lot 91), bought by the present owner.
For Cotes's portrait of another botanist, Dr. John Hill, cf. no. 80.

130. **Thomas Estcourt.** Present whereabouts unknown. Oil on canvas, $28\frac{1}{2} \times 23\frac{1}{2}$ in. Neither signed nor dated. Condition: Unknown.
Thomas Estcourt, dates unknown.
H.S., to the right, wearing a green coat, and holding a hat under his left arm and a gold-tipped cane in his left hand; a plain background.

DATE: The style of the picture would place it c. 1763. Its closest parallel is no. 125.

PROVENANCE: By family descent from the sitter to Captain T. E. Souteron-Estcourt, Tetbury, Gloucestershire; Captain T. E. Souteron-Estcourt Sale, Christie's, Dec. 9, 1927 (lot 87), sold as 'Portrait of a Gentleman', bought by DeCasseres; John Levy Galleries, New York; Chester H. Johnson Galleries Chicago; Chester H. Johnson Galleries Sale, American Art Association—Anderson Galleries, Nov. 14, 1934 (lot 74); Mrs. M. E. Martineau, Princeton, New Jersey; Anon. Sale, Sotheby's, May 2, 1962 (lot 151), bought by the Leger Galleries, London.

131. **Thomas Twisleton, 13th Baron Saye and Sele.** Present whereabouts unknown. Oil on canvas, $29\frac{1}{2} \times 24\frac{1}{2}$ in. Neither signed nor dated. Inscribed at the top left: Lord Saye and Sele. Condition: Unknown.
The sitter joined the 32nd Brigade of Foot Guards in 1754 and later became an officer. Eventually he was promoted to the rank of colonel in the 9th Regiment of Foot Guards, and finally to that of Major-General.
H.S., to the left, wearing the uniform of an officer in the 32nd Brigade of Foot Guards, a scarlet and blue coat trimmed in gold; he holds a hat under his left arm; the background is plain except for the sitter's name, inscribed in the upper left-hand corner.

DATE: The style of the picture places it c. 1763.

PROVENANCE: By family descent from the sitter to the Lords Saye and Sele; Lord Saye and Sele Sale, Christie's, Je. 23, 1933 (lot 42), illus., bought by Asscher; B. L. Bisgood, Esq., U.K. (1934).

EXHIBITIONS: The Scots Guards Loan Exhibition, Edinburgh, 1934, lent by B. L. Bisgood, Esq.

REFERENCES: William Gladstone Menzies, 'Art in the Salerooms', *Apollo*, Vol. 18, no. 103, Jul. 1933, pp. 59–66; P. W. Reynolds, *Military Costume of the 18th and 19th Centuries*, in MS. at the Victoria and Albert Museum, not dated, Vol. III, p. 38 (illus.).

c. 1763–1765: Portraits in oils, neither signed nor dated, nos. 132 and 133.

132. **Elizabeth Booth.** Present whereabouts unknown. Oil on canvas, 30×25 in. Neither signed nor dated. Condition: Unknown.
Elizabeth Booth, 1744–1765, the daughter of Nathaniel Booth, 4th Baron Delamere, and his wife, Margaret Jones, daughter of Richard Jones of Ramsbury Manor, Wiltshire.
H.S., to the right, in a painted oval, wearing a white dress; a plain background.

DATE: The paint is laid on in a rather rough manner. The sharp edges of the drapery and the highlights are emphasized. The closest parallels are no. 112, 1762–1763, and no. 150, signed and dated 1764. The sitter died in 1765. A date of c. 1763–1765 is suggested.

PROVENANCE: Anon. Sale, Christie's, Dec. 19, 1913 (lot 110), bought by Agnew, London; W. Lockett Agnew Sale, Christie's, Je. 15, 1923, lot 6; Leggatt Brothers, London; Arthur Ackermann and Son, London; The Leger Galleries, London (1932).

For another portrait by Cotes of the same sitter, cf. no. 133.

133. **Elizabeth Booth.** Private Collection, U.K. Oil on canvas, 49½ × 39½ in. Neither signed nor dated. Condition: Excellent.
For genealogy, cf. no. 132.

T.Q.L., to the right, wearing the same costume as in no. 132, but in this picture the dress is pink instead of white. She rests her left arm on a pedestal covered by red drapery. The background consists of a column, a stone wall, and a patch of sky.

DATE: c. 1763–1765. Cf. no. 132.

PROVENANCE: By family descent to Sir Francis Burdett, Bt., Ramsbury Manor, Wiltshire; Sir Francis Burdett Sale, Sotheby's, Dec. 2, 1953 (lot 53), sold as 'after Cotes', bought by Leggatt Brothers, London, who sold the picture to the present owner.

REFERENCES: Anon. 'Works of Art Now on the Market', *The Connoisseur*, Vol. 135, no. 534, Feb. 1955, p. 50, fig. 2.

c. 1763 – c. 1766: Portraits in oils, neither signed nor dated, nos. 134 and 135.

134. **Elizabeth Knight.** Private Collection, U.K. Oil on canvas, 29½ × 24 in. Neither signed nor dated. Condition: Excellent.
Elizabeth Knight, 1737–1809, one of the three daughters of Thomas Knight of Chawton House, Alton, Hampshire.
H.L., to the left, in a painted oval, wearing the same dress as that of Elizabeth Booth in no. 133, but the bows on the dress are green instead of blue, and a lace tippet has been added; a plain background.

DATE: The style is typical of much of Cotes's work in the mid-1760's. The closest parallels are no. 132, dated c. 1763–1765, and the two portraits of the sitter's sisters, nos. 198 and 199, signed and dated 1766. A date, therefore, of c. 1763 – c. 1766 is suggested.

PROVENANCE: By family descent from the sitter to Edward Knight, Esq., Chawton House, Alton, Hampshire; Edward Knight Sale, Sotheby's, Jul. 17, 1935 (lot 146), bought by Vicars Brothers, London; Anon. Sale, Christie's, Je. 18, 1937 (lot 128), incorrectly identified as Anne Knight, bought by Varle; Vicars Brothers, London (1948); purchased from Vicars Brothers by the present owner.

135. **A Lady.** Present whereabout unknown. Oil on canvas, 30 × 25 in. Neither signed nor dated. Condition: Unknown.
H.L., head to the left, shoulders to the right, in a painted oval, wearing a light-coloured dress with embroidered flower sprigs, a dark sash, and a cloak; a plain background.

DATE: The style and the costume are similar to nos. 132 and 134; therefore, a date of c. 1763 – c. 1766 is suggested.

PROVENANCE: A. J. Sulley, Esq., London (formerly).

1764: Portraits in pastel, signed and dated, nos. 136–143.

136. **Selina Chambers** (Pl. II). The Victoria and Albert Museum, London. Pastel on paper, 21⅞ × 18⅛ in. Signed and dated at the middle right: FCotes px[t] / 1764. F and C in monogram. Condition: Excellent.
Selina Chambers, b. 1754/55, the daughter of Sir William Chambers; in 1788 she married William Innes.
H.L., to the left, in an oval, wearing a blue, green, and white dress, holding a doll in her arms; a plain background.

PROVENANCE: By family descent from the sitter to Miss E. F. E. Pebardy, U.K. Miss Pebardy gave the picture to the National Portrait Gallery, London. It has since been transferred to the Victoria and Albert Museum, London.

EXHIBITIONS: The picture is on exhibit at Osterley Park, Osterley, Middlesex, a National Trust house administered by the Victoria and Albert Museum.

REFERENCES: John Harris, *Sir William Chambers, Knight of the Polar Star*, London, A. Zwemmer, 1970, pp. 6, 15.

137. **William Chambers** (fig. 46). Scottish National Portrait Gallery, Edinburgh. Pastel on paper, 23½ × 17½ in. Signed and dated at the middle right: FCotes px[t] / 1764. F and C in monogram. Condition: Good.
Engraved in mezzotint by Richard Houston and published in 1771.
William Chambers, 1726–1796, the architect, subsequently Sir William Chambers, R.A., Knight of the Polar Star.
H.S., to the right, wearing a claret-coloured dressing gown with blue lapels; a plain background.

PROVENANCE: General Sir Redvers Buller, U.K.; Leggatt Brothers, London; Leggatt Brothers sold the picture to the present owner in 1904.

EXHIBITIONS: The portrait is on exhibit at the Scottish National Portrait Gallery.

REFERENCES: Anon., *Scottish National Portrait Gallery* (Catalogue), Edinburgh, By Order of the Trustees, 1951, p. 31, no. 629; *BPP.*, p. 75; *O'D.*, Vol. I, p. 377, no. 1; R. A. Riches, 'Sir William Chambers and Francis Cotes', *The Connoisseur*, Vol. 94, no. 397, Sept. 1934, pp. 143–145.

For versions of this portrait which are not by Cotes, cf. Appendix VI, nos. 5, 6, 33.
Mr. Riches claimed the oil portrait at Somerset House (Appendix VI, no. 6) was the original of Houston's engraving, In fact, the engraving corresponds only to the signed and dated Scottish pastel. In the Scottish pastel and the engraving Chambers's face is fatter in the cheeks, and his mouth is smaller with bigger lips and deeper dimples than in the other versions. The other versions, which were probably done at Chambers's instigation, are definitely copies of the original portrait by Cotes.

138. **The Countess Fitzwilliam.** The Earl of Bessborough, Stansted Park, Rowlands Castle, Hampshire. Pastel on paper, 25 × 20 in. Signed and dated at the lower right: FCotes px[t] / 1764. F and C in monogram. Condition: Good.
The Countess Fitzwilliam, d. 1822, born Lady Charlotte Ponsonby, daughter of the 2nd Earl of Bessborough.
H.S., seated, to the right, wearing a blue dress; a plain background.

PROVENANCE: By family descent from the sitter to the present owner.

139. **Dr. John Gregory, M.D.** (fig. 45). Sir Andrew Forbes-Leith, Bt., Fyvie Castle, Aberdeenshire. Pastel on paper, 24½ × 18½ in. Signed and dated at the lower right: FCotes px[t] / 1764. F and C in monogram. Condition: Excellent.
Engraved in the stipple manner by J. Bengo and published in 1788.
Dr. John Gregory, 1724–1773; in 1752 he married Elizabeth Forbes, daughter of William, 14th Baron Forbes (see no. 66).
H.S., to the right, wearing a plum dressing gown with blue lapels; a plain background.

PROVENANCE: By family descent from the sitter to the present owner.

REFERENCES: *O'D.*, Vol. II, p. 381, no. 3.

The costume and pose of the sitter are quite similar to no. 137. For an oil portrait by Cotes, said to be of John Gregory, cf. Appendix V, no. 24.
For Cotes's other portraits of medical doctors, cf. no. 11.

140. **Lieutenant-General William Keppel.** Private Collection, U.K. Pastel on paper, 23¾ × 17¼ in. Signed and dated at the lower right: FCotes px / 1764. F and C in monogram. Condition: Excellent.
Lieut.-General William Keppel, 1727–1782.
H.S., to the right, wearing a scarlet army uniform with a silver gorget; a plain background.

PROVENANCE: By family descent from the sitter to the present owner.

EXHIBITIONS: Society of Artists, 1764, no. 21. Walpole writes: 'good, General Keppel.' (cf. Appendix III.)

REFERENCES: *PN.*, Vol. II, p. 158, no. 49.

141. **Frances Lascelles.** The Earl of Harewood, Harewood House, Leeds, Yorkshire. Pastel on paper, 23½ × 17¼ in. Signed and dated 1764. Condition: Good.
Engraved in mezzotint by James Watson in the latter half of the eighteenth century.
Frances Lascelles, 1762–1817, daughter of Edward Lascelles, 1st Earl of Harewood; she married John Douglas, son of James Douglas, 16th Earl of Morton.
T.Q.L., to the right, wearing a dress with buttons down the front, a sash, and a lace-trimmed cap, and holding a scarf around the neck of a greyhound, which rests its paws on her skirt; a plain background.

PROVENANCE: By family descent from the sitter to the present owner.

EXHIBITIONS: Society of Artists, 1765, no. 20. A child playing with a greyhound. Walpole writes: 'very pretty' (cf. Appendix III). The only known picture by Cotes of this description which could have been exhibited in 1765 was the portrait of Frances Lascelles.

REFERENCES: *O'D.*, Vol. II, p. 78, no. 1; Tancred Borenius, *Catalogue . . . Harewood House*, 1936, no. 238.

Another portrait of the sitter by Cotes was in the sale of the artist's personal effects in 1771; cf. Appendix II, Lot 23 on p. 11: Two ditto (heads in crayon), the Queen of Denmark and Miss Lassels.

142. **Rebecca Tucker.** Mrs. Douglas H. Gordon, Baltimore, Maryland. Pastel on paper, 23¼ × 17¼ in. Signed and dated at the lower left: FCotes px[t] / 1764. F and C in monogram. Condition: Excellent.
Rebecca Tucker, daughter of Richard Tucker and wife of Gabriel Steward of the East India Company.
H.S., head to the left, shoulders to the right, wearing a blue dress almost identical to the one Cotes used for the portrait of the Countess Fitzwilliam, no. 138; a plain background.

PROVENANCE: Anon. Sale, Christie's, Jul. 4, 1930 (lot 147), bought by Popoff; F. R. Meatyard, Esq., London; the present owner.

143. **Maria, Dowager Countess of Waldegrave** (fig. 41). Private Collection, U.K. Pastel on paper, 25¼ × 20½ in. Signed and dated at the lower left: FCotes px[t] / 1764. F and C in monogram. Condition: Some darkening and surface damage.
Maria, Dowager Countess of Waldegrave, 1736–1807, the natural daughter of Sir Edward Walpole and Dorothy Clements; in 1759 she married James, 2nd Earl of Waldegrave (fig. 61), who died in 1762; in 1766 she married William Henry, Duke of Gloucester (no. 273, fig. 110).
H.S., to the right, wearing a pink dress with a black lace shawl, and touching her pearl necklace with her right hand; a plain background.

PROVENANCE: By family descent from the sitter to the present owner.

REFERENCES: *PN.*, Vol. II, p. 159, no. 53.

1764: Portraits in oils, signed and dated, nos. 144–152.

144. **Lady Alston** (fig. 40). Present whereabouts unknown. Oil on canvas, 34 × 38½ in. Signed and dated 1764. Condition: Unknown.
Lady Alston, born Margaret Lee; she married Sir Thomas Alston, Bt., of Odell Castle, Bedfordshire.
T.Q.L., seated, to the left, wearing a yellow wrapping gown, a blue and gold sash, and a blue cloak, touching her pearl necklace with her left hand, resting her left arm on a stone parapet covered by drapery, and extending her right hand; a landscape background.

PROVENANCE: Anon. Sale, Christie's, Jul. 14, 1911 (lot 54), bought by Howard; M. Knoedler and Co., London; Scott and Fowles, New York; Charles F. Fowles Estate Sale, Parke-Bernet, New York, Jan. 17, 1922 (lot 17), illus., bought by Duveen Brothers, New York; Anon. Sale, Sotheby's, Nov. 17, 1971 (lot 87), bought by Douglas.

145. **A Boy of the Barwell Family** (fig. 50). Mrs. Jackson Martindell, U.S.A. Oil on canvas, 35 × 27 in. Signed and dated at the middle left: FCotes px[t] / 1764. F and C in monogram. Condition: Unknown.
The boy in this picture and the boy in no. 146 may have been related to Richard Barwell (1741–1804), an Anglo-Indian, who made a fortune in India and retired in England. He was married in 1776 and was painted by Reynolds with his son in 1780/81.
H.L., to the left, wearing a blue naval officer's coat and a sword at his left side, resting his right arm on a table and holding in his right hand a map of the city and harbour of Havana; a plain background. Pendant to no. 146.

PROVENANCE: Samuel Hood Cowper-Coles, Esq., Pennyorth, Crickhowell, Brecknockshire; Samuel Hood Cowper-Coles Sale, Christie's, Je. 7, 1912 (lot 124), bought by A. Wertheimer, Esq., London; M. Knoedler and Co., London; the present owner.

146. **A Boy of the Barwell Family** (fig. 48). Mrs. J. B. Campbell, New York. Oil on canvas, 35 × 27 in. Signed and dated at the lower right: FCotes px[t] / 1764. F and C in monogram. Condition: Unknown.
H.L., to the right, wearing a crimson coat, resting both arms on a brass instrument to the right, possibly an azimuth, and holding an open book in his left hand; the book contains columns of numbers and what appear to be mathematical calculations; a background of sky and foliage.
Pendant to no. 145.

PROVENANCE: Samuel Hood Cowper-Coles, Esq., Pennyorth, Crickhowell, Brecknockshire; Samuel Hood Cowper-Coles Sale, Christie's, Je. 7, 1912 (lot 125), bought by A. Wertheimer, Esq., London; M. Knoedler and Co., London; the present owner.

REFERENCES: Anon. 'Collectors' Questions', *Country Life*, Vol. 135, no. 3498, Mar. 19, 1964, pp. 98–99.

147. **Francis Burdett** (fig. 54). The Ferens Art Gallery, Hull, Yorkshire. Oil on canvas, 49½ × 39¼ in. Signed and dated at the middle left on a tree trunk in the background: FCotes px[t] 1764. F and C in monogram. Condition: Excellent.
Francis Burdett, 1743–1794, son of Sir Robert Burdett, 4th Bt.; the sitter married Mary Eleanor Jones, daughter of William Jones of Ramsbury Manor, Ramsbury, Wiltshire.
T.Q.L., to the right, wearing a buff-coloured coat, and holding a walking stick and a black three-cornered hat; a landscape background.

PROVENANCE: By family descent from the sitter to Sir Francis Burdett, 7th Bt., Ramsbury Manor, Ramsbury, Wiltshire; Sir Francis Burdett Sale, Sotheby's, Dec. 2, 1953 (lot 43), illus., bought by the Leger Galleries, London; the present owner.

EXHIBITIONS: The picture is on exhibit at the Ferens Art Gallery, Hull.

REFERENCES: *CAN.*, p. 52; *The Connoisseur*, Vol. 133, no. 537, Apr. 1954, p. 181 (illus.).

For an almost identical portrait cf. no. 156.

148. **Francis Burdett.** K. R. Thomson, Esq., London. Oil on canvas, 29½ × 24½ in. Signed and dated at the lower left: FCotes px[t] / 1764. F and C in monogram. Condition: Excellent.
For the sitter's genealogy, cf. no. 147.
H.S., to the right, wearing a grey coat, and resting his right hand in the front of his coat; a background of sky and foliage.

PROVENANCE: By family descent from the sitter to Sir Francis Burdett, 7th Bt., Ramsbury Manor, Ramsbury, Wiltshire; Sir Francis Burdett Sale, Sotheby's, Dec. 2, 1953 (lot 46), bought by the Leger Galleries, London, from whom the picture was purchased by the present owner in 1954.

For an almost identical portrait, cf. no. 149.

149. **Francis Burdett.** Present whereabouts unknown. Oil on canvas, 29½ × 24½ in. Signed and dated: FCotes px[t] / 1764. F and C in monogram. Condition: badly crackled paint (1953).
For the sitter's genealogy, cf. no. 147.
The picture is exactly like no. 148, except that the sitter wears a blue coat.

PROVENANCE: By family descent from the sitter to Sir Francis Burdett, 7th Bt., Ramsbury Manor, Ramsbury, Wiltshire; Sir Francis Burdett Sale, Sotheby's, Dec. 2, 1953 (lot 47), bought by T. Turner.

150. **Eleanor Burdett.** Private Collection, England. Oil on canvas 29½ × 24½ in. Signed and dated at the middle left: FCotes px[t] / 1764. F and C in monogram. Condition: Unknown.
Eleanor Burdett, d. 1783, daughter of William Jones of Ramsbury Manor, Ramsbury, Wiltshire, and wife of Francis Burdett.
H.S., to the right, wearing a white dress and a maroon mantle; a plain background except for a curtain at the right.

PROVENANCE: By family descent from the sitter to Sir Francis Burdett, 7th Bt., Ramsbury Manor, Ramsbury, Wiltshire; Sir Francis Burdett Sale, Sotheby's, Dec. 2, 1953 (lot 48), bought by Leggatt Brothers, London, from whom the picture was purchased by the present owner.

151. **Mary Anne Colmore.** Leger Galleries, London. Oil on canvas, 48 × 39 in. Signed and dated at the lower right: FCotes px[t] / 1764. F and C in monogram. Inscribed at the bottom right: Mary, wife of Charles Colmore, Esq., and Dau. of To. Gulston, Esq. ob. 1798. Condition: Excellent.
Mary Anne Colmore, d. 1798; she was born Mary Anne Gulston, the daughter of Thomas Gulston of Ealing Grove, Carmarthenshire; she married Charles Colmore.
T.Q.L., to the right, wearing a green dress and a pink mantle, and resting her right hand on the back of a chair; the background consists of an open doorway to the left and a wall covered in a patterned material.

PROVENANCE: Brigadier A. F. L. Clive, U.K.; Brigadier A. F. L. Clive Sale, Christie's, Apr. 2, 1965 (lot 38), bought by the Leger Galleries, London.

REFERENCES: Adrian Bury, 'In the Galleries', *The Connoisseur*, Vol 164, Mar. 1967, p. 176.

For Cotes's other portrait of the sitter cf. no. 53; for the portrait of her husband cf. no. 157.

152. **The Hon. Booth Grey.** Dr. and Mrs. Edgar M. Bick, U.S.A. Oil on canvas, 29½ × 24 in. Signed and dated at the lower right on the painted oval: FCotes px[t] 1764. F and C in monogram. Condition: Excellent.
The Hon. Booth Grey, 1740–1802, son of the 4th Earl of Stamford.
H.S., to the left, in a painted oval, wearing a scarlet coat, and resting his right hand in the front of his jacket; a plain background.

PROVENANCE: By family descent from the sitter to Sir John Foley Grey, Bt., Enville Hall, Enville, Staffordshire; Sir John Foley Grey Sale, Christie's, Je. 15, 1928 (lot 9), illus., bought by Arthur Ackermann and Son, London, and transferred to their branch in New York. It hung in the apartment of the president of the New York office until recently, when it was sold to the present owners.

REFERENCES: *CWO.*, pp. 249, 251 (fig. no. VI); *RSC.*, p. 217 (fig. 2).

Cotes's portrait of the sitter's brother is no. 181.

1764, or possibly earlier: A lost portrait, known only through an engraving, no. 153.

153. **William Campbell Skinner.** Present whereabouts unknown. Medium and measurements unknown. Possibly signed and dated.

Condition: Unknown.
Engraved in mezzotint before 1770 by James Watson (fig. 47) and inscribed: F. Cotes pinx^{t} / Jas. Watson fecit / William Campbell Skinner, Aetat 5.
Watson exhibited the engraving at the Society of Artists in 1764, no. 207. This was the first instance in which an engraving after one of Cotes's portraits was publicly shown.
William Campbell Skinner, son of General William Skinner.
H.S., head to the left, shoulders to the right, in an oval, wearing a jacket, a waistcoat, and an open-necked shirt edged with lace; a background of sky and foliage.

DATE: It was Watson's custom to exhibit engravings after recent portraits by British artists; consequently, one would assume that the portrait by Cotes was done in 1764 or slightly earlier.

PROVENANCE: Possibly as follows: Humphrey Roberts, Esq., London; Humphrey Roberts Sale, Christie's, May 21–23, 1908 (lot 195), sold as by Gainsborough, bought by Thomas Agnew and Sons, London, who considered the portrait to be by Cotes. It is not known to whom Agnew's sold the picture, nor whether it was the original from which Watson's engraving was made. In the Roberts sale catalogue, it was said to be oil on canvas, but neither a signature nor a date was mentioned.

REFERENCES: *O'D.*, Vol. IV, p. 155, nos. 1–3.

c. 1764: A portrait in pastel, signed and dated, but with the last two digits illegible, no. 154.

154. **A Lady.** V. M. G. Wombwell, Newburgh Priory, Coxwold, Yorkshire. Pastel on paper, 24 × 18 in. Signed and dated at the middle left: FCotes px^{t} / 17– –. F and C in monogram. Condition: Surface damage in several places.
H.S., head to the front, shoulders slightly to the right, wearing a white and pink dress; a plain background.

DATE: The hair style suggests a date of c. 1764. A close parallel is offered by no. 155, also from c. 1764.

PROVENANCE: It is not known when the picture came to the Newburgh Priory.

c. 1764: A portrait in pastel, neither signed nor dated, no. 155.

155. **Laura (Louisa) Keppel** (fig. 43). Private Collection, U.K. Pastel on paper, 23 × 17 in. Neither signed nor dated. Condition: Good.
Laura Keppel, the natural daughter of Sir Edward Walpole; in 1758 she married the Rev. Frederick Keppel.
H.S., head to the left, shoulders to the right, wearing a green dress and a cream and white lace mantle; a plain background.

DATE: The hair style suggests a date of c. 1764. The closest parallels are nos. 143 and 142.

PROVENANCE: By family descent from the sitter to the present owner.

No. 169 is of the sitter's husband.

c. 1764: Portraits in oils, neither signed nor dated, nos. 156–160.

156. **Francis Burdett.** Hammerson Group of Companies, London. Oil on canvas, 49½ × 39½ in. Neither signed nor dated. Condition: Excellent.
For the sitter's genealogy, cf. no. 147.
T.Q.L., to the right. The portrait is exactly like no. 147, except for the colours of the costume. In this picture the coat is green.

DATE: The close relationship between this portrait and no. 147, signed and dated 1764, suggests that the two pictures were painted at approximately the same time.

PROVENANCE: By family descent from the sitter to Sir Francis Burdett, 7th Bt., Ramsbury, Manor Ramsbury, Wiltshire; Sir Francis Burdett Sale, Sotheby's, Dec. 2, 1953 (lot 44), bought by Frank Partridge, London; Mrs. Margaret Louise Van Alen Bruguiere, Wakehurst, Newport, Rhode Island; Margaret Louise Van Alen Bruguiere Sale, Christie's, Nov. 28, 1969 (lot 187); the present owner.

EXHIBITIONS: 'Introducing Francis Cotes, R.A.', Nottingham University Art Gallery, Nov. 5–27, 1971, no. 22 (lent by the present owner), incorrectly said to have been signed and dated 1764.

REFERENCES: *CAN.*, p. 52.

157. **Charles Colmore** (fig. 56). Present whereabouts unknown. Oil on canvas, 49 × 39 in. Neither signed nor dated. Condition: Unknown.
Charles Colmore, husband of Mary Anne Colmore, born Gulston, cf. no. 151.
T.Q.L., to the right, wearing a brown coat, holding a three-cornered hat in his right hand and a walking stick in his left; a landscape background.

DATE: The closest parallels to this picture are the three-quarter length portraits of Francis Burdett, no. 147, signed and dated 1764, and no. 156, c. 1764. The portrait by Cotes of the sitter's wife, no. 151, is also signed and dated 1764.

PROVENANCE: The Marquess of Hertford, Ragley Hall, Alcester, Warwickshire; The Marquess of Hertford Sale, Christie's, Jul. 1, 1921 (lot 132), bought by Jones.

EXHIBITIONS: In the sale catalogue mentioned above the picture is said to have been exhibited at the 'Worcester Exhibition of 1882'.

158. **Admiral Thomas Craven.** Present whereabouts unknown. Oil on canvas, 30 × 25½ in. Neither signed nor dated. Condition: Excellent.
Admiral Thomas Craven, son of William, 2nd Baron Craven, M.P. for Berkshire 1766–72, d. 1772.
H.S., to the right, in a painted oval, wearing a blue and white naval uniform and holding a hat under his left arm; a background of sky.

DATE: The closest parallels to this picture are the two small portraits of Francis Burdett, nos. 148 and 149, both signed and dated 1764.

PROVENANCE: By family descent from the sitter to Collier Thornhill, Esq., Kingston Lisle, Berkshire. The picture was in the Thornhill collection in the 19th century; it descended to Eleana Thornhill, who married J. A. Fane of Wormsley in 1860. Anon. Sale, Sotheby's, Mar. 12, 1969 (lot 135), bought by the Leger Galleries London; The Baroncino de Piro d'Amico Inquanez, Valetta, Malta; Anon. Sale, Christie's, Mar. 17, 1972 (lot 43), bought by Woodhouse.

EXHIBITIONS: The Leger Galleries, London, Oct. 1 – Nov. 1, 1969, no. 4 (lent by the gallery).

159. **William Jones** (fig. 55). Aitken Collection, U.S.A. Oil on canvas, 50 × 40 in. Neither signed nor dated. Condition: Excellent.
William Jones, d. 1766, of Ramsbury Manor, Ramsbury, Wiltshire; he was the father of Mary Eleanor Jones (no. 150), who married Francis Burdett.
T.Q.L., head to the left, shoulders to the right, wearing a red coat, and holding a wooden walking stick in his right hand and a black hat in his left; a landscape background.

DATE: The picture is similar to portraits of Francis Burdett, no. 147, signed and dated 1764, and no. 156, c. 1764. A date of c. 1764 is therefore suggested.

PROVENANCE: By family descent from the sitter to Sir Francis Burdett, 7th Bt., Ramsbury Manor, Ramsbury, Wiltshire; Sir Francis Burdett Sale, Sotheby's, Dec. 2, 1953 (lot 45), sold as Francis Burdett, bought by Frank Partridge, London; Mrs. Margaret Louise Van Alen Bruguiere, Wakehurst, Newport, Rhode Island; Margaret Louise Van Alen Bruguiere Sale, Christie's, Nov. 28, 1969 (lot 188), incorrectly identified as Francis Burdett; the Leger Galleries, London; the present owner.

EXHIBITIONS: 'An Exhibition of English Paintings, 1750–1900', The Leger Galleries, London, Oct. 7–31, 1970, no. 4 (lent by the gallery).
It is interesting to note the considerable increase in Cotes's prices which has taken place in recent years. In the Sotheby's sale of 1953, this portrait fetched 480 pounds; in the Christie's sale of 1969, it made 7,500 guineas.

160. **Henrietta Molesworth.** National Trust, Springhill, County Derry, Northern Ireland. Oil on canvas, 35¼ × 28¼ in. Neither signed nor dated. Condition: Good.
Henrietta Molesworth, 1745–1812, daughter of the 3rd Viscount Molesworth; in 1774 she married John Staples of Lissan, County Tyrone.
H.L., seated, to the right, wearing a crimson dress and a white lace mantle, and resting her right arm on a polished wooden table, which reflects the ruffles of her right sleeve; a plain background.

DATE: The style of the picture is typical of Cotes's work of c. 1764.

PROVENANCE: By family descent from the sitter to her daughter, Charlotte Melosina, who in 1819 married William Lenox Conyingham of Springhill. The picture has remained at Springhill.

EXHIBITIONS: Possibly shown with the Society of Artists in 1764, no. 22, described in the exhibition catalogue as 'A lady in oil, kit cat'. Walpole added: 'Leaning on a table, which reflects her ruffles,' (cf. Appendix III). A kitcat was 36 × 28 in. Also cf. Supplement, no. 23.
'Pictures in Ulster Houses', Belfast Museum and Art Gallery, Belfast, May 10 – Jul. 15, 1961, no. 65, illus. in the cat (Pl. VI).

1764–1767: Portraits in oils, neither signed nor dated, nos. 161–164.

161. **A Gentleman.** The Leger Galleries, London. Oil on canvas, 30 × 25 in. Neither signed nor dated. Condition: Excellent.
H.L., to the right, wearing a red jacket and black academic robes with a white collar; a plain background.
Pendant to no. 163.

DATE: The closest parallels to this portrait, nos. 148, 149, and 152, are all signed and dated 1764. After 1767 Cotes's small oils are more refined; therefore, a date of 1764–1767 is suggested.

PROVENANCE: Unknown.

EXHIBITIONS: 'Introducing Francis Cotes, R.A.', Nottingham University Art Gallery, Nov. 5–27, 1971, no. 23 (lent by the Leger Galleries).

162. **Anne Harrison.** Colonial Williamsburg, Williamsburg, Virginia. Oil on canvas, 30¼ × 23⅞ in. Neither signed nor dated. Condition: Excellent.
Anne Harrison, d. 1767, born Anne Randolf, the first wife of Benjamin Harrison of Brandon, in Virginia.
H.L., head to the left, shoulders to the right, in a painted oval, wearing a white dress, a pink sash, and a blue cloak; a plain background.

DATE: The closest parallels to the portrait are no. 150, signed and dated 1764, and no. 198, signed and dated 1766. Small portraits of this type, boldly, but somewhat crudely painted, occur in Cotes's work between 1764 and 1767. A date of 1764–1767 is, therefore, suggested.

PROVENANCE: Unknown.

EXHIBITIONS: The portrait is on exhibit at Williamsburg.

163. **A Lady.** Forty Hall Museum and Art Gallery, Forty Hill, Enfield, Middlesex. Oil on canvas, 30 × 25 in. Neither signed nor dated. Condition: Excellent.
H.L., slightly to the right, wearing a wrapping gown, a sash, and a cloak; a plain background.

DATE: The portrait is quite similar to no. 162 and was painted in the same period. The companion picture, no. 161, is also of 1764–1767.

PROVENANCE: Unknown.

EXHIBITIONS: 'The Gracious Age', The Leger Galleries, London, Mar. 1967. The portrait is on exhibit at Forty Hall.

REFERENCES: Benedict Nicolson, 'Current and Forthcoming Exhibitions', *The Burlington Magazine*, Vol. CIX, no. 768, Mar. 1967, pp. 176 (fig. 98), 180.

164. **Captain Collingwood Roddam.** Private Collection, Canada. Oil on canvas, 29½ × 24½ in. Neither signed nor dated. Condition: Unknown.
Capt. Collingwood Roddam, b. between 1731 and 1734, d. 1806, the fourth son of Edward Roddam of Hebburn and Roddam.
H.L., to the right, wearing the uniform of a captain in the East India Company, a scarlet jacket with blue lapels, and resting his left hand in the front of his jacket; a background of sky and foliage.

DATE: The closest parallels are nos. 148 and 149, both signed and dated 1764. The quality of the portrait suggests that it was painted at some time between 1764 and 1767.

PROVENANCE: The Lord Roddam, U.K.; Sir Herbert Hadfield, Bt., U.K., Ehrich Galleries, New York (Mar. 1931); Anon. Sale, American Art Association—Anderson Galleries, Mar. 15 – Apr. 4, 1931 (lot 39); The Cooling Galleries, London (May 1941); the present owner.

REFERENCES: *Art News*, Vol. 99, Mar. 28, 1931, cover (illus.); H. Granville Fell, 'Some Topics of Moment', *The Connoisseur*,

Vol. 107, May, 1941, p. 219, cover (illus.); *PFC.*, p. 6; *RSC.*, p. 217, fig. 1.

1764–1768: A portrait in oils, neither signed nor dated, no. 165.

165. **Lady Campbell.** Present whereabouts unknown. Oil on canvas, 36 × 28 in. Neither signed nor dated. Condition: Unknown. Genealogy unknown.
T.Q.L., seated, to the right, wearing a wrapping gown and a sash, resting her left arm on the back of her chair: her left hand is raised to her cheek; a plain background, except for a piece of drapery across the top.

DATE: The closest parallels to the portrait are nos. 263 and 264, both signed and dated 1768. The bold, slightly crude brushwork occurs sporadically between 1764 and 1768. A date of 1764–1768 is, therefore, suggested.

PROVENANCE: Arthur Tooth and Sons, London (1915).

1764–1770: Portraits in oils, neither signed nor dated, nos. 166 and 167.

166. **Arthur Maister.** University Galleries, University of Southern California, Los Angeles. Oil on canvas, 29 × 24¼ in. Neither signed nor dated. Condition: Excellent.
Arthur Maister, 1738–1791, son of Henry Maister, Sheriff and M.P. for Hull; in 1772 he married Esther Thompson, the natural daughter of John Rickaby of Bridlington Quay, Yorkshire.
H.L., to the right, wearing a jacket and waistcoat beneath a heavy, fur-lined, scarlet cloak; a bare wall in the background.

DATE: The boldness with which the picture was painted could have occurred as early as 1764. It recalls the Burdett portraits of that year, nos. 147–150; however, the paint is laid on with a confidence and finesse that one finds in Cotes's late portraits. A date of 1764–1770 is suggested.

PROVENANCE: By family descent from the sitter to Mrs. Hugh Dryden Corbet, Sundorne Castle, Shrewsbury, Shropshire; Hugh Dryden Corbet Sale, Sotheby's, May 21, 1935 (lot 151), illus., bought by Ellis and Smith, London; The Newhouse Galleries, New York; Mrs. Elizabeth Holmes Fisher, California. Mrs. Fisher gave the portrait to the University of Southern California in 1940.

EXHIBITIONS: The picture is on exhibit at the University Galleries, University of Southern California.

REFERENCES: Maister Family Papers, in the possession of Colonel R. A. Alec-Smith, Winestead, Hull; the sitter's costume is described as 'the garb of a Russian merchant'; Colonel R. A. Alec-Smith, 'The Maisters of Hull', *Country Life*, Vol. CVII, no. 2765, Jan. 13, 1950, p. 95 (illus.); T. Tindall Wildridge, *Old and New Hull*, Hull, M. C. Peck and Son, 1884, pp. 121–124; a drawing after Cotes's portrait is illustrated opposite p. 121 as Pl. XLVII.

In the Hugh Dryden Corbet Sale Catalogue it was stated that Arthur Maister was the Lord Mayor of Hull, and that Cotes painted him in his robes of office. In fact, Maister never held the post of Lord Mayor. The mayors of Hull date from 1330, but the city did not have a Lord Mayor until 1914. The unusual cloak Arthur Maister wears is not associated with mayoral attire; it is merely a heavy garment which he wore for warmth in the cold climate of St. Petersburg, where he lived for some years, looking after his family's business interests.
For a portrait of the sitter's wife, cf. Appendix V, no. 25.

167. **A Boy.** A. W. Moss, Esq., Tocknells Court, Painswick, Gloucestershire. Oil on canvas, 30 × 25 in. Neither signed nor dated. Condition: Excellent.
H.L., to the left, wearing a green coat with a red collar, and leaning both arms on a stone parapet; a black, three-cornered hat in front of his hands; a background of sky and foliage.

DATE: The closest parallels to this portrait are nos. 145 and 146, both signed and dated 1764; and no. 195, signed and dated 1766; however, since the style of the portrait could have occurred at any time between 1764 and 1770, and since up until Cotes's death child portraiture remained one of his specialties, a rather broad dating of 1764–1770 is suggested.

PROVENANCE: Eggan and Co., Farnham, Surrey; Thomas Agnew and Sons, London; the present owner.

EXHIBITIONS: 'Realism and Romance in English Painting', Thomas Agnew and Sons, London, Nov. 14 – Dec. 10, 1966, no. 27 (lent by the gallery).
'Introducing Francis Cotes, R.A.', Nottingham University Art Gallery, Nov. 5–27, 1971, no. 23 (lent by the present owner); illus. in the cat. (Pl. XIII).

1765: Portraits in pastel, signed and dated, nos. 168–171.

168. **Admiral Augustus Keppel** (fig. 57). Private Collection, U.K. Pastel on paper, 22¾ × 19¾ in. Signed and dated at the lower left: FCotes pinx[t] 1765. F and C in monogram. Condition: Excellent.
Admiral Augustus Keppel, later Viscount Keppel, 1725–1782.
H.S., head to the right, shoulders to the left, in an oval, wearing a blue, white, and gold admiral's uniform; a plain background.

PROVENANCE: By family descent from the sitter to the present owner.

EXHIBITIONS: Society of Artists, 1765, no. 21, cf. Appendix III.

REFERENCES: *PN.*, Vol. II, p. 150, no. 21.

169. **The Right Rev. Frederick Keppel, Bishop of Exeter and Dean of Windsor.** Private Collection, U.K. Pastel on paper, 23¾ × 19¾ in. Signed and dated at the lower right: FCotes px[t] / 1765. F and C in monogram. Condition: Excellent.
Frederick Keppel, 1728–1777; in 1758 he married Laura (Louisa) Walpole, the natural daughter of Sir Edward Walpole.
H.S., to the right, in an oval, wearing a white alb, a black stole, and a clerical collar; a plain background.

PROVENANCE: By family descent from the sitter to the present owner.

REFERENCES: *PN.*, Vol. II, p. 152, no. 26.

No. 155 is of the sitter's wife.

170. **Mary Provis.** The Lord Ducie, Tortworth House, Tortworth, Gloucestershire. Pastel on paper, 26 × 22 in. Signed and dated at the middle right: FCotes px[t] / 1765. F and C in monogram. Condition: Surface damage in spots.
Mary Provis, 1755–1789, the daughter of T. Provis of Shepton Mallet, Somerset; in 1774 she married Francis Reynolds, 3rd Baron Ducie, as his first wife.
H.S., to the left, in an oval, wearing a pink, white, and grey dress

and a mantle, resting her right arm on a table; her right hand is raised to her face; a plain background.

PROVENANCE: By family descent from the sitter to the present owner.

For Cotes's portrait of Lord Ducie's second wife, cf. nos. 190 and 201.

171. **Francis Russell, Marquess of Tavistock.** Private Collection, U.K. Pastel on paper, 23½ × 17½ in. Signed and dated at the lower left: FCotes px[t] / 1765. F and C in monogram. Condition: Good.
Francis Russell, Marquess of Tavistock, 1739–1767; in 1764 he married Lady Elizabeth Keppel.
H.S., to the right, wearing a scarlet coat; a plain background.

PROVENANCE: By family descent from the sitter to the present owner.

REFERENCES: *PN.*, Vol. II, p. 161, no. 58.

No. 61 is of the sitter's wife.

1765: Portraits in oils, signed and dated, nos. 172–175.

172. **The Hon. Mrs. Campbell.** Present whereabouts unknown. Oil on canvas, 50 × 40 in. Signed and dated 1765. Condition: Unknown.
The Hon. Mrs. Campbell, wife of John Campbell of Congerston, Pembrokeshire, dates unknown
T.Q.L., head to the front, shoulders slightly to the right, wearing a purple wrapping gown and a blue sash, resting her left arm on a pedestal surmounted by a garden urn; with her left hand she holds a straw basket filled with flowers; her right hand touches her sash; a background of sky and foliage.

PROVENANCE: Elizabeth, Countess of Kenmare, U.K.; Elizabeth, Countess of Kenmare Sale, Sotheby's, Jul. 11, 1945 (lot 59).

173. **James Duff, 2nd Earl of Fife** (fig. 60). North Carolina Museum of Art, Raleigh, North Carolina. Oil on canvas, 93½ × 56½ in. Signed and dated at the lower left: FCotes px[t] / 1765. F and C in monogram. Condition: Some of the original paint has faded or been replaced.
James Duff, 2nd Earl of Fife, 1729.
F.L., to the right, wearing a gold jacket, a red cloak trimmed with ermine, a sword at his left side, resting his right hand on his hip and his left hand on a table; an architectural background consisting of a column covered with red drapery and a wall.

PROVENANCE: By family descent to the Earls of Fife; the Princess Royal Sale, Christie's, Jul. 18, 1924 (lot 97), bought by Gooden and Fox, London; The Viscount Leverhulme, U.K.; The Viscount Leverhulme Sale, Anderson Galleries, New York, Feb. 17–19, 1926 (lot 43b), bought by the Vose Galleries, Boston, from where it was purchased by Edward I. Farmer, New York; Edward I. Farmer, Inc. Sale, Parke-Bernet, New York, Apr. 16–19, 1947 (lot 897); the present owner.

EXHIBITIONS: Society of Artists, 1765, no. 17, cf. Appendix III. The picture is on exhibit at the North Carolina Museum of Art.

REFERENCES: W. R. Valentiner, *Catalogue of Paintings, North Carolina Museum of Art*, Raleigh, By Order of the Trustees, 1956, p. 16.

174. **A Gentleman** (formerly called John Simpson of Esslington). Tate Gallery, London. Oil on canvas, 35½ × 27¼ in. Signed and dated: FCotes px[t] 1765. F and C in monogram. Condition: Serious damage and discolouration; a pentimento in the hat.
H.L., to the right, wearing a claret-coloured coat, resting both hands on a wooden walking stick and holding a black, three-cornered hat; a background of sky.

PROVENANCE: Sir George Lindsay Holford, Westonbirt House, Westonbirt, Gloucestershire; Sir George Lindsay Holford Sale, Christie's, May 17–18, 1928 (lot 99), bought by the National Gallery, London, and transferred to the Tate Gallery in 1949.

EXHIBITIONS: 'Meisterwerke Englischer Malerei aus drei Jahrhunderten', Secession, Vienna, Sept. 8 – Nov. 13, 1927, no. 5 (lent by Sir George Holford).
'Introducing Francis Cotes, R.A.', Nottingham University Art Gallery, Nov. 5–27, 1971, no. 27, lent by the Tate.

REFERENCES: Mary Chamot, *The Tate Gallery, British School*, London, Printed for the Trustees, 1953, p. 50, no. 1943; *CWO.*, p. 249; Martin Davies, *British School*, National Gallery Catalogue, London, 1946, pp. 40–41; C. Reginald Grundy, *English Art in the Eighteenth Century*, London, The Studio Ltd., 1928, Pl. XXII; Franz Ottman, 'Meisterwerke Englischer Malerei aus drei Jahrhunderten', *Belvedere*, Vol. 11, no. 60, pp. 165–167; *PFC.*, pp. 5–6, 8 (fig. 3).

When the portrait was in the Holford collection there was a tradition that the sitter was John Simpson of Esslington. This identification has never been substantiated.
A copy of the portrait was in the collection of the late Lady Hamilton, Paisley Cottage, Selsea, Chichester, Sussex. It was sold at Sotheby's on Jan. 30, 1963, lot 96, as by J. Reynolds, and was bought by the Sabin Galleries, London; it is now in a private American collection. At the Sotheby's sale the sitter was identified as Mr. Fox, the husband of Miss Hamilton of Chilston Park, Kent.

175. **Richard Glover.** The Earl of Verulam, Gorhambury House, St. Albans, Hertfordshire. Oil on canvas, 31 × 26 in. Signed and dated at the lower left: FCotes px[t] / 1765. F and C in monogram. Condition: Good.
Richard Glover, of Redbourne Mills, Hertfordshire, the brother of the first wife of the Hon. George Grimston (1714–1782).
H.S., head to the right, shoulders to the left, wearing a Van Dyck costume composed of a jacket with slashed sleeves, an open-neck shirt and a cloak; he holds the cloak with his right hand; a plain background.

PROVENANCE: By family descent from the sitter to the present owner.

EXHIBITIONS: 'British Portraits', R.A., London, Winter Exhibition, 1956–57, no. 217 (lent by the present owner).
The portrait is on exhibit at Gorhambury, which is open to the public at certain times of the year.

REFERENCES Anon., *Gorhambury* (a guide with an inventory of pictures), privately printed, 1938, p. 14.

1765: A portrait in oils, not signed, but dated by an inscription, no. 176.

176. **Lady Cunliffe** (fig. 76). Walker Art Gallery, Liverpool. Oil on canvas, 49½ × 40 in. Neither signed nor dated. Inscribed at the top right: Mary wife of / Sir Rob.[t] Cunliffe Bar.[t] 1765. Condition: Excellent.

Lady Cunliffe, 1723–1791, born Mary Wright; in 1752 she married Sir Robert Cunliffe, who succeeded his brother as second baronet in 1767.
T.Q.L., seated, to the left, wearing a pink and grey gown, resting her head on her right hand and her right arm on a stone parapet; a background of sky and trees.

PROVENANCE: By family descent from the sitter to Sir Foster Cunliffe, Bt., Acton Hall, Wrexham, Denbighshire; Sir Foster Cunliffe Sale, Sotheby's, Feb. 1, 1950 (lot 109), bought by Thomas Agnew and Sons, London; The Walker Art Gallery (1950).

EXHIBITIONS: 'Selected Acquisitions of the Walker Art Gallery, Liverpool, 1945–1955', Thomas Agnew and Sons, London, 1955, no. 26. The portrait is on exhibit at the Walker Art Gallery.

For Cotes's portrait of the sitter's niece, cf. no. 196; for the portrait of her husband, cf. no. 258.

1765: A lost portrait, known only through an engraving, no. 177.

177. **Samuel Foote.** Present whereabouts unknown. Medium and measurements unknown. Possibly signed and dated. Condition: Unknown.
Engraved in mezzotint by R. Brookshaw and published in Paris in 1773 with the following inscription: F. Cotes Pinx[t] Londini 1765. R. Brookshaw fecit Paris 1773.
Samuel Foote, 1720–1777, the actor.
H.S., to the right, in an oval, wearing a frock coat; a plain background.

PROVENANCE: Unknown.

REFERENCES: *CS.*, p. 101, no. 10; *O'D.*, Vol. II, p. 231, no. 5.

For the pastel drawing of the head of Samuel Foote, once attributed to Cotes, cf. Appendix VI, no. 13.

1765, or possibly earlier: A lost portrait, no. 178.

178. **Mr. Milner or Mr. Mills.** Present whereabouts unknown. Oil on canvas, measurements unknown. Possibly signed and dated. Condition: Unknown.
Both names have been given to the sitter, his dates are unknown.

PROVENANCE: Unknown.

EXHIBITIONS: Society of Artists, 1765, no. 18, cf. Appendix III. Different copies of Walpole's catalogues give different identifications of the sitter; the copy cited by Gatty has 'Mr. Milner, an old gentleman'; the copy cited by Graves has 'Mr. Mills, Engineer to New River Company'.

c. 1765: Portraits in oils, neither signed nor dated, nos. 179–184.

179. **Mary Coleby as 'Emma, The Nut-Brown Maid'** (from Matthew Prior's poem *Henry and Emma*). Cheltenham Art Gallery and Museum, Cheltenham, Gloucestershire. Oil on canvas, 108 × 72 in. Neither signed nor dated. Condition: Excellent.
Mary Coleby, 1745–1774, the daughter of Captain Charles Coleby, Commissioner of Gibraltar; she married John Lewis of Harpton Court, Radnorshire.
F.L., to the left, wearing a cream wrapping gown with a blue sash; with her right hand she places on the branch of a tree a wreath of Henry's hair intertwined with flowers, and holds her skirt with her left hand; a landscape background with a building in the distance.

DATE: The portrait was possibly exhibited at the Society of Artists in 1765. The costume and style would agree with this date.

PROVENANCE: By family descent from the sitter to Guy Whinyates, Esq., Buckfast, Devonshire. Mr. Whinyates gave the portrait to the Cheltenham Art Gallery in 1956.

EXHIBITIONS: The picture may have been exhibited with the Society of Artists, 1765, no. 16, cf. Appendix III. The catalogue description could refer to no. 179 or no. 183.
'The Whinyates Collection', Cheltenham Art Gallery and Museum, Jan. 25 – Feb. 8, 1969, unnumbered entry (lent by the Gallery).

For Cotes's other portraits in which the *Henry and Emma* theme is used cf. nos. 96, 99 and 183.
For other portraits of Mary Coleby cf. Appendix V no. 20, and Appendix VI, nos. 7, 8.

180. **Dr. Connell** (fig. 66). Private Collection, U.K. Oil on canvas, 50 × 40 in. Neither signed nor dated. Condition: Excellent.
Dr. Connell, the husband of Lady Phillipa Hamilton, dates unknown.
T.Q.L., to the left, wearing a blue coat, holding a three-cornered hat, resting his right hand on a walking stick, and leaning against the trunk of a tree to the right; a landscape background.

DATE: The portrait is very similar to certain works by Cotes from the mid-1760's: no. 147, signed and dated 1764, and nos. 156, 157, and 159, all c. 1764. In addition, it is important to note that in the mid-1760's it became fashionable for fairly young men like Dr. Connell to dispense with wigs (cf. *CC18*, p. 241). Cotes's portraits from the middle of the decade clearly illustrate this trend, cf. nos. 137, 139, 152, all signed and dated 1764, and nos. 181 and 182, from c. 1765. The portrait of Dr. Connell was done at approximately the same date.

PROVENANCE: The Leger Galleries, London; the present owner.

181. **George, Lord Grey de Groby.** Present whereabouts unknown. Oil on canvas, 35½ × 27½ in. Neither signed nor dated. Condition: Unknown.
Lord Grey, 1737–1819; in 1763 he married Lady Henrietta Cavendish Bentinck, daughter of William, 2nd Duke of Portland. In 1768 he succeeded as 5th Earl of Stamford; in 1796 he was created Baron Delamere and 7th Earl of Warrington.
T.Q.L., seated, to the left, wearing a claret-coloured coat and a black academic gown, holding an open book, which rests on the arm of his chair; a plain background.

DATE: The style of the picture as well as the noticeable absence of a wig suggest a date of c. 1765; also cf. No. 180. From the fact that the sitter is wearing an academic gown one might suppose that the portrait was done while he was at university; he attended Queen's College, Cambridge, between 1755 and 1758. The style, however, is far bolder than Cotes was accustomed to in the 1750's; it is, in fact, typical of his work in the mid-1760's.

PROVENANCE: By family descent from the sitter to Sir John Foley Grey, Bt., Enville Hall, Enville, Staffordshire; Sir John Foley Grey Sale, Christie's, Je. 15, 1928 (lot 10), bought by P. and D. Colnaghi, London; M. Knoedler and Company, London (1928); P. and D. Colnaghi, London (1937); Anon. Sale, Sotheby's, Nov. 22, 1961 (lot 98), bought by the Leger Galleries, London.

Various copies exist; one is at Queen's College, Cambridge (incorrectly identified as of J. L. Hubbertsy, Esq.); another was sold at Sotheby's (Anon. Sale, May 23, 1962, lot 105); a third was in the collection of Sylvia Levey, Fairlawn House, Teston, Maidstone, Kent (incorrectly identified as the Earl of Westmorland); cf. *Country Life*, Vol. CXI, no. 2872, Feb. 1, 1952, p. 285, illus.
For the portrait of Lord Grey's brother, cf. no. 152, and for other family portraits, cf. nos. 211 and 212.

182. **An Army Officer.** Present whereabouts unknown. Oil on canvas, 30 × 25 in. Neither signed nor dated. Condition: Unknown.
H.S., to the left, wearing a scarlet army uniform with gold gorget, and holding a hat under his left arm; a landscape background.

DATE: The closest parallels are nos. 148 and 149, both signed and dated 1764. The absence of a wig also indicates that the picture was probably done in the mid-1760's; cf. no. 180.

PROVENANCE: Mr. Alfred H. Mulliken, Chicago and New Canaan, Conn.; Alfred H. Mulliken Sale, American Art Association—Anderson Galleries, New York, Jan. 5, 1933 (lot 26), illus., bought by Averell House.

REFERENCES: *Antiques*, Vol. 23, no. 1, Jan. 1933, p. 25 (illus.).

183. **Anne Sandby as 'Emma, The Nut-Brown Maid'** (from *Henry and Emma*, the poem by Matthew Prior), fig. 82. Mrs. M. Smiley, Scotland. Oil on canvas, 48 × 38 in. Neither signed nor dated. Condition: Paint badly crackled (1959).
Anne Sandby, 1736–1797, born Anne Stogden; she married Paul Sandby, the painter.
F.L., to the left. The costume, hair style, and pose of the sitter and the background are the same as in no. 179.

DATE: The picture was possibly exhibited at the Society of Artists in 1765. The costume and style would agree with this date.

PROVENANCE: Francis Cotes Sale, Langford and Son, London, Feb. 23, 1771, p. 12, lot 30, 'A small whole length of Emma', cf. Appendix II. The only portrait in Cotes's oeuvre which is known to fit this description is no. 183. The buyer at the Cotes sale may have been the artist's friend, Paul Sandby, R.A. In the nineteenth century the portrait was in the possession of Paul Sandby's descendant, William Sandby, Esq. Hubert Peake, Esq., U.K.; Hubert Peake Sale, Christie's, Mar. 24, 1959 (lot 5), bought by Betts for Gooden and Fox, London; the present owner.

EXHIBITIONS: The picture may have been exhibited with the Society of Artists, 1765, no. 16, cf. Appendix III. The catalogue description could refer to no. 179 or no. 183.

REFERENCES: William Sandby, *Thomas and Paul Sandby*, London, Seeley and Co., 1890, p. 192.

For Cotes's use of the *Henry and Emma* theme in other portraits, cf. nos. 96, 99, and 179.

184. **Mary Anne Yates.** Garrick Club, London. Oil on canvas, 49¼ × 39½ in. Neither signed nor dated. Condition: Good, some crackling of the paint.
Mary Ann Yates, c. 1728–1787, the actress, born Mary Ann Graham, the second wife of Richard Yates, the actor.
T.Q.L., to the left, wearing a yellow dress, a blue sash, and a brown mantle, resting her right arm on a stone parapet, and holding a book, possibly the script of a play, in her right hand; the background consists of a wall with sky and trees beyond.

DATE: The closest parallel to this picture is no. 172, signed and dated 1765. A date, therefore, of c. 1765 is suggested.

PROVENANCE: The history of the picture before it was acquired by the Garrick Club and the date of acquisition are unknown. It does appear in the Club's 1936 catalogue.

REFERENCES: Anon., *A Catalogue of the Pictures in the Garrick Club*, London, Published by the Club, 1936, pp. 7–8, no. 21, p. 265; *BPP.*, p. 73, Pl. 53.

c. 1765–1770: Portraits in oils, neither signed nor dated, nos. 185–187.

185. **Henry Cope.** Alexander Collection, Aubrey House, London. Oil on canvas, 30 × 24 in. Neither signed nor dated. Condition: Excellent.
Henry Cope of Bramshill, Hampshire; he was known as 'the Green Man', because in his old age he would parade about at Brighton dressed entirely in green.
H.L., to the right, wearing a green coat and holding a ring in his right hand; a bare wall in the background.

DATE: The ring may indicate that the portrait commemorates the marriage of the sitter; unfortunately, the date of his marriage is not known. His hair is dressed high off the forehead in the manner that was popular in the late 1760's. The picture is very carefully and smoothly painted. It has the refinement of Cotes's small portraits done between 1765 and 1770. A date of c. 1765–1770 is, therefore, suggested.

PROVENANCE: Doyne C. Bell, Esq., London (1876); W. C. Alexander, Esq., London; the present collection.

EXHIBITIONS: 'Exhibition of Works by Old Masters and Deceased Masters of the British School', R.A., London, Winter Exhibition, 1876, no. 5 (lent by Doyne C. Bell, Esq.).
'Spring Exhibition, 1906, Illustrating Georgian England', Whitechapel Art Gallery, London, 1906, no. 69, upper gallery (lent by W. C. Alexander, Esq.).

REFERENCES: Joan Penelope Cope, *Bramshill, the Memoirs of Joan Penelope Cope*, Bungay, Richard Clay and Co., 1938, pp. 14–16; *The Globe*, Oct. 8, 1806.

186. **Frances Davis.** Present whereabouts unknown. Oil on canvas, 29 × 24½ in. Neither signed nor dated. Condition: Unknown.
Frances Davis, daughter of the Rev. John Davis, vicar of West Farleigh and Rector of Mereworth, dates unknown.

H.L., seated, head to the front, shoulders to the left, wearing a pink dress, leaning on the arm of her chair, and resting her head on her right hand; a plain background.

DATE: The closest parallel to this portrait is no. 176, dated 1765. Pictures of this high quality, boldly painted, yet intimate, occur in Cotes's oeuvre between 1765 and 1770. A date of c.1765–1770 is, therefore, suggested.

PROVENANCE: Anon. Sale, Christie's, May 14, 1920 (lot 62), bought by Thomas Agnew and Sons, London; John Levey Galleries, New York; M. Knoedler and Co., London. The portrait was purchased from Knoedler's in 1933 by Mr. R. B. Mellon, Pittsburgh. Mrs. Sarah Mellon Scaife, Pittsburgh; Sarah Mellon Scaife Sale, Sotheby's, Jul. 13, 1966 (lot 159), illus., bought by Maggs.

EXHIBITIONS: Kansas City Art Institute, Oct. 5–27, 1930, no. 22.

187. **Mary Watson.** Present whereabouts unknown. Oil on canvas, 35 × 27 in. Neither signed nor dated. Condition: Unknown.
Mary Watson, 1734–1795; she married John Parker.
T.Q.L., to the front, wearing a simple, low-necked dress and a cloak, resting her arms on a balustrade in front of her; a background of sky.

DATE: The combination of intimacy and elegance in this portrait is typical of Cotes's work from 1765 to 1770.

PROVENANCE: By family descent from the sitter to Major Parker Leighton, Sweeney Hall, Oswestry, Shropshire. The contents of Sweeney Hall were sold in 1969.

EXHIBITIONS: Shrewsbury Art Gallery, 1951, no. 1 (lent by Major Parker Leighton).

1766: Portraits in pastel, signed and dated, nos. 188–191.

188. **Princess Caroline Matilda** (fig. 99). S. K. H. der Prinz von Hannover, Herzog zu Braunschweig und Lüneburg; the picture is on loan to the Bomann-Museum, Celle, Lower Saxony. Pastel on paper, 24 × 19½ in. Signed and dated at the middle right: FCotes px[t] / 1766. F and C in monogram. Condition: Excellent.
Engraved in mezzotint by James Watson and Richard Brookshaw in the latter half of the eighteenth century.
Princess Caroline Matilda, 1751–1775, the youngest daughter of Frederick, Prince of Wales; in 1766 she married Christian VII, King of Denmark. This portrait and no. 189 were probably painted before her departure for Denmark in October of 1766.
H.S., head to the left, shoulders to the front, wearing a dress with pearls and a cloak of silk and ermine; a plain background.

PROVENANCE: By family descent from the sitter to the present owner. The portrait was recorded as being in the Bedchamber in George III's inventory of Buckingham House of c. 1790–1795. Afterwards it was not mentioned in the royal documents. Evidently, in the late 18th or early 19th century the portrait was transferred to Hanover; cf. References, *OML*.

EXHIBITIONS: 'The Brunswick Art Treasures', Victoria and Albert Museum, London, Aug. 1952 (lent by the present owner).
'Die Königin Caroline Mathilde und ihr Kreis', Schloss Celle, Celle, Apr. 10 – Je. 30, 1960, no. 76 (lent by the present owner).

REFERENCES: Hester W. Chapman, *Caroline Matilda, Queen of Denmark*, London, Jonathan Cape, 1971, frontispiece; *CS.*, Vol. I, p. 100, no. 4; *O'D.*, Vol. I, p. 349, nos. 1 and ff; Oliver Millar, 'The Brunswick Art Treasures at the Victoria and Albert Museum: the Pictures', *The Burlington Magazine*, Vol. 94, no. 594, Sept. 1952, pp. 267–268; *OML.*, Vol. I, pp. xx and xxi, cf. fig. 1; p. 21, no. 720.

This pastel portrait was probably used by Cotes as a preparatory study for the head of Queen Caroline in no. 220.

189. **Princess Caroline Matilda.** Nationalhistoriske Museum, Frederiksborg, Denmark. Pastel on paper, 24 × 17 in. Signed and dated at the middle right: FCotes px[t] 176(?). The last digit has been read variously: it is generally interpreted as '6'. F and C in monogram. Condition: Excellent.
For the sitter see under no. 188.
The portrait is like no. 188, but there are more black-tipped ermine tails on the cloak, and the folds in the left sleeve are more complex.

PROVENANCE: Possibly from the collection of the artist. At the Francis Cotes Sale, Langford and Son, London, Feb. 23, 1771 (lot 23), p. 11, the catalogue reads: 'Two ditto (heads in crayon), the Queen of Denmark and Miss Lassels.' Cf. Appendix II. Possibly in the collection of Alfred Morrison, Esq., in 1894; cf. Exhibitions. In 1920 the museum acquired the portrait from England through a Danish dealer.

EXHIBITIONS: The picture was possibly in the following exhibition: 'Fair Women', The Grafton Galleries, London, Summer 1894, no. 210, 'Caroline Matilda, Queen of Denmark' (lent by Alfred Morrison, Esq.).
The picture is on exhibit at the Nationalhistoriske Museum.

REFERENCES: O. Andrup, *Det Nationalhistoriske Museum pi Frederiksborg. Et. udvalg af Museets Erhvervelser, 1913–1925*, Frederiksborg, 1925, p. 101; O. Andrup, *Katalog over de udstillerde Portraetter og Genstande paa Frederiksborg*, Frederiksborg, 1943, p. 253; *OML.*, Vol. I, p. 22, under no. 720.

190. **Sarah Child** (fig. 78). The Earl of Jersey, Radier Manor, Longueville, Jersey. Pastel on paper, 38 × 28 in. Signed and dated at the lower right: FCotes px[t] / 1766. F and C in monogram. Condition: Excellent.
Sarah Child, d. 1793, born Jodrell; she first married Robert Child of Osterley Park, and later (1791) Francis Reynolds, 3rd Baron Ducie.
H.L., to the left, in an oval, wearing a green wrapping gown with a blue sash, and resting her head on her right hand; immediately behind the sitter to the right is a stone pedestal surmounted by what is probably a garden urn; a background of sky and trees.

PROVENANCE: By family descent from the sitter to the present owner.

EXHIBITIONS: Society of Artists, 1766, no. 29, cf. Appendix III.

REFERENCES: Francis Cotes, notes on crayon painting, *The European Magazine*, Feb. 1797, pp. 84–85, cf. Appendix IV; William Sandby, *The History of the Royal Academy*, London, Longman, Green, Longman, Roberts and Green, 1862, p. 96; WA., Vol. IV, p. 111.

191. **A Gentleman.** Private Collection, Nottingham. Pastel on paper, 23½ × 17½ in. Signed and dated at the lower left: FCotes px[t] / 1766. F and C in monogram. Condition: Good.
H.S., to the left, wearing a brown jacket; a plain background.

PROVENANCE: Anon. Sale, Bonham's, London, Feb. 13, 1969 (lot 238), bought by Arthur Grogan, Esq.; Abbot and Holder, London, from whom the present owner purchased the picture in 1970.

EXHIBITIONS: 'Introducing Francis Cotes, R.A.', Nottingham University Art Gallery, Nov. 5–27, 1971, no. 26 (lent by the present owner).

1766: Portraits in oils, signed and dated, nos. 192–199.

192. **Elizabeth Diana Bosville.** The Viscount Allendale, Bywell Hall, Stocksfield-on-Tyne, Northumberland. Oil on canvas, 50 × 40 in. Signed and dated at the lower left: FCotes px[t] 1766. F and C in monogram. Condition: Excellent.
Elizabeth Diana Bosville, c. 1748–1789, the daughter of Godfrey

Bosville of Gunthwaite, Yorkshire; in 1768 she married Sir Alexander Macdonald.
T.Q.L., to the left, wearing a simple, low-necked dress with a sash; to the left is a garden seat and a tree with a flowering vine; she picks a flower from the vine; a background of sky and foliage.

PROVENANCE: By family descent from the sitter to the present owner.

EXHIBITIONS: 'The Yorkshire Loan Exhibition of Pictures', Judges' Lodging, York, Jul. 24 – Aug. 8, 1934, no. 11 (lent by the Viscount Allendale).
The picture was exhibited at Temple Newsam, Leeds in 1947 (lent by The Viscount Allendale).
'Mr. Boswell', National Portrait Gallery, London, 1967, no. 29 (lent by the present owner). The portrait was incorrectly dated 1767. The signature and date appear at the lower left, in the background, on the tree trunk, above the arm of the garden chair. The date is 1766.

A small copy in oils is in a private collection in Washington, D.C.

193. **John Hobart, 2nd Earl of Buckinghamshire** (fig. 58). The Marquess of Lothian, Melbourne Hall, Derby. Oil on canvas, 30 × 25 in. Signed and dated at the lower right: FCotes px[t] / 1766. F and C in monogram. Condition: Excellent.
John Hobart, 2nd Earl of Buckinghamshire, 1723–1793.
H.S., head to the left, shoulders to the right, wearing a red jacket and a black waistcoat; a plain background.

PROVENANCE: By family descent from the sitter to the present owner.

EXHIBITIONS: 'Bicentenary Exhibition 1768–1968', R.A., London, Winter, 1968/69, no. 32 (lent by the present owner).

REFERENCES: *Inventory of Pictures at Newbattle Abbey and Crailing House*, 1883, no. 243.

A copy was formerly in the collection of the Earl of Mount Edgcumbe, Cornwall, and is believed to have been destroyed by fire in 1941.

194. **Elizabeth Burdett.** H. J. Hyams, Esq., Ramsbury Manor, Ramsbury, Wiltshire. Oil on canvas, 29½ × 24½ in. Signed and dated at the lower right on the painted oval: FCotes px[t] 1766. F and C in monogram. Condition: Unknown.
Elizabeth Burdett, daughter of Sir Robert Burdett, 4th Bt.; she married Francis Munday, Esq.
H.S., to the front in a painted oval, wearing a pink and white dress and a black mantle; a plain background.

PROVENANCE: By family descent from the sitter to Sir Francis Burdett, 7th Bt., Ramsbury Manor, Ramsbury, Wiltshire; Sir Francis Burdett Sale, Sotheby's, Dec. 2, 1953 (lot 51), bought by the Earl of Wilton, who also purchased Ramsbury Manor, to which the portrait was returned. The Manor and the portrait then passed by successive sales to the Lord Rootes and the present owner.

195. **Charles Collyer** (fig. 70). Mr. and Mrs. Paul Mellon Collection, U.S.A. Oil on canvas, 35¾ × 27¾ in. Signed and dated at the lower left: FCotes px[t] 1766. F and C in monogram. Condition: Excellent.
Charles Collyer, 1755–1830, the second son of Daniel Collyer of Wroxham Hall, Norfolk; he married Sarah, eldest daughter of Sir Jacob Astley, Bt.; in 1798 he became Rector of Gunthorpe.
H.L., head to the right, shoulders to the left, wearing a white, open-neck shirt, a green waistcoat, and green breeches, holding a cricket bat in his right hand and a black hat in his left hand; a background of sky and trees.

PROVENANCE: By family descent from the sitter to Brigadier General J. J. Collyer, who sold the picture in 1930 to Thomas Agnew and Sons, London. It was purchased from Agnew's in 1931 by Mr. Langdon K. Thorne, U.S.A. M. Knoedler and Co., London; Thomas Agnew and Sons, London, from whom it was purchased in 1966 by the present owners.

REFERENCES: *PFC.*, p. 6; *PN.*, Vol. I, p. 202, no. 10.

For Cotes's portrait of the sitter's brother, cf. no. 202.

196. **Mary Cunliffe.** The Dowager Viscountess Galway, Serlby Hall, Bawtry, Doncaster, Yorkshire. Oil on canvas, approximately 30 × 25 in. Signed and dated at the lower right: FCotes px[t] / 1766. F and C in monogram. Condition: Excellent.
Engraved in mezzotint by James Watson in the latter half of the eighteenth century with the inscription: F. Cotes pinx.[t] Watson fecit. / Miss Cunliffe.
Mary Cunliffe, d. 1804, the daughter of Sir Ellis Cunliffe, Bt.; she married Sir Drummond Smith, Bt., of Tring Park, Tring, Hertfordshire. In the portrait she appears to be between five and ten years old.
T.Q.L., head to the front, shoulders to the left, wearing a cream dress with a pink sash and a lace cap, holding her skirt with her right hand and resting her left hand on the neck of a greyhound; a landscape background.

PROVENANCE: By family descent from the sitter to the present owner.

EXHIBITIONS: In the past, the portrait has been on exhibit at Serlby Hall when the house was open to the public.

REFERENCES: *O'D.*, Vol. IV, p. 128, no. 1.

A similar composition was used in Cotes's portrait of Frances Lascelles, no. 141. For the portraits of the sitter's aunt and uncle, cf. nos. 176 and 258.

197. **The Countess of Donegall.** National Gallery of Ireland, Dublin. Oil on canvas, 93 × 58 in. Signed and dated at the lower left: FCotes px[t] 1766. F and C in monogram. Condition: Excellent.
The Countess of Donegall, 1738–1780, born Lady Anne Douglas Hamilton; in 1761 she married, as his first wife, Arthur Chichester, Earl and later 1st Marquess of Donegall.
F.L., head to the front, shoulders slightly to the left, wearing a white wrapping gown and a red cloak, holding her cloak with her left hand resting her right arm on the base of a column; an architectural background with sky and foliage.

PROVENANCE: The Duke of Somerset, U.K.; The Duke of Somerset Sale, Christie's, Je. 28, 1890 (lot 26), illus., sold as by Reynolds, bought by Doyle for the National Gallery of Ireland.

EXHIBITIONS: The portrait is on exhibit at the National Gallery of Ireland.

REFERENCES: Anon., *Concise Catalogue of the Oil Paintings, National Gallery of Ireland*, Dublin, The Stationery Office, 1963, p. 23, no. 373; Ellen Duncan, 'The Irish National Portrait Collection', *The Burlington Magazine*, Vol. 12, Oct. 1907, pp. 14–15.

For another portrait of the sitter, cf. no. 203, and for the portrait of Lord Donegall's second wife, cf. no. 249.

198. **Anne Knight.** Present whereabouts unknown. Oil on canvas, 30×25 in. Signed and dated 1766. FCotes px[t] / 1766. F and C in monogram. Condition: Unknown.
Anne Knight, 1733–1773, daughter of Thomas Knight, Esq.
H.S., to the right, in a painted oval, wearing a blue dress; a plain background.

PROVENANCE: By family descent from the sitter to Edward Knight, Esq., Chawton House, Alton, Hampshire; Edward Knight Sale, Sotheby's, Jul. 17, 1935 (lot 144), bought by Vicars Brothers, London; Anon. Sale, Christie's, Je. 18, 1937 (lot 127), incorrectly identified as Elizabeth Knight, bought by Greene.

For Cotes's portraits of the sitter's sisters, cf. nos. 134 and 199.

199. **Jane Knight.** Present whereabouts unknown. Oil on canvas, 29½×24½ in. Signed and dated 1766. Condition: Unknown.
Jane Knight, 1730–1793, daughter of Thomas Knight, Esq.
H.S., head to the left, shoulders to the right, in a painted oval, wearing a brocade dress and a blue cloak; a plain background.

PROVENANCE: Edward Knight, Esq., Chawton House, Alton, Hampshire; Edward Knight Sale, Sotheby's, Jul. 17, 1935 (lot 145), bought by F. Howard; Leggatt Brothers, London (1936); Anon. Sale, Sotheby's, May 30, 1951 (lot 115); Anon. Sale, Sotheby's, Je. 15, 1960 (lot 174).

1766: A portrait in oils, neither signed nor dated, no. 200.

200. **Colonel William Phillips.** Present whereabouts unknown. Oil on canvas, 50×40 in. Neither signed nor dated. Condition: Unknown.
Engraved in mezzotint by Valentine Green and published in 1785 with the inscription: 'Painted by F. Cotes, R.A. Engraved by V. Green, Mezzotinto Engraver to his Majesty and to the Elector Palatine. Major General Phillips. To the Officers of the Royal Regiment of Artillery.' Beneath Phillips's hand is a letter addressed to 'An Col Phillips Commandant de l'Artillerie Britt Almayne' and signed 'Granby and Ferdinand Duc d Br. & L.'.
Col. William Phillips, 1731–1781. He saw service in Germany, Canada, and America, and is chiefly remembered for conducting the retreat from Saratoga in 1777. At some time after this portrait was painted he was made a Major General.
T.Q.L., head to the right, shoulders to the left, wearing a blue and red uniform, holding two letters on a table beneath his right hand; the writing on one of these is cited above; a background of brown drapery and sky.

DATE: The picture was exhibited in 1766; its bold style is typical of Cotes's work at that time. The brush work is very close to what one finds in portraits like nos. 192–199, signed and dated 1766.

PROVENANCE: Anon. Sale, Christie's, Dec. 7, 1928 (lot 55), bought by Glen; Lord Gerald Wellesley, U.K.; Ehrich Galleries, New York (1931); Anon. Sale, Christie's, Jul. 2, 1937 (lot 80), bought by Mayes; Anon. Sale, Robinson and Fisher, London, Jan. 20, 1938 (lot 152).

EXHIBITIONS: Society of Artists, 1766, no. 26, cf. Appendix III. In the exhibition catalogue the portrait is described as a half length; it is closer to a three-quarter length.

REFERENCES: *CS.*, Vol. II, p. 578, no. 103; *PFC.*, p. 5.

c. 1766: Portraits in oils, neither signed nor dated, nos. 201 and 202.

201. **Sarah Child.** The Hon. Mrs. James Innes, Larkenshaw, Chobham, Surrey. Oil on canvas, approximately 38×28 in. Neither signed nor dated. Condition: Excellent.
For the sitter, cf. no. 190.
H.L., to the right. The portrait is like no. 190, except for the medium and the fact that the sitter faces in the opposite direction. It is not a copy, but a version in oils of the composition Cotes previously developed in pastels in no. 190.

DATE: The style is typical of Cotes's oil portraits of 1766, and the composition is very close to that of no. 190, signed and dated 1766.

PROVENANCE: By family descent from the sitter to the present owner.

202. **Daniel Collyer.** Present whereabouts unknown. Oil on canvas, approximately 35×27 in. Apparently neither signed nor dated. Condition: Unknown.
Daniel Collyer, 1752–1819, eldest son of Daniel Collyer of Wroxham Hall, Norfolk; in 1774 he married Catherine Bedingford, and in 1776 he became Rector of Wroxham.
T.Q.L., head to the front, shoulders slightly to the left, wearing a Van Dyck costume, a grey jacket and a gold cloak, resting his left arm on a pedestal surmounted by a broken column; a background of sky.

DATE: The closest parallel to this picture is the companion portrait of the sitter's brother, no. 195, signed and dated 1766. A date, therefore, of c. 1766 is suggested.

PROVENANCE: By family descent from the sitter to General J. J. Collyer, who sold the picture in 1930 to Thomas Agnew and Sons, London. It was purchased from Agnew's in 1931 by Mr. Langdon K. Thorne, U.S.A.

REFERENCES: *PFC.*, pp. 6, 8 (fig. 4); *PN.*, Vol. I, p. 202, no. 12.

c. 1766: A portrait in oils by Cotes, neither signed nor dated, with the head repainted between c. 1778 and 1780, no. 203.

203. **The Countess of Donegall.** The Lord Templemore, Dunbrody Park, Arthurstown, Co. Wexford, Ireland. Oil on canvas, 93×58 in. Neither signed nor dated. Condition: Good, but the head repainted.
The Countess of Donegall, see no. 197.

DATE: c. 1766, with the head probably repainted by Gainsborough c. 1778–1780. With the exception of the head, the picture is a repetition by Cotes of no. 197, signed and dated 1766. The head is obviously at variance with the rest of the picture. The hair style is of a later period (late 1770's – early 1780's), and Lady Donegall's face has aged considerably. Evidently, in this second version of Cotes's portrait of her she had her head repainted by another artist. For the part of the picture that still reveals Cotes's hand a date of c. 1766 is suggested. Lady Donegall died in 1780. She probably had the head repainted c. 1778–80. The style is that of Gainsborough.

PROVENANCE: By family descent from the sitter to the present owner.

c. 1766–1770: A portrait in pastels, neither signed nor dated, no. 204.

204. **Lady Hoare** (fig. 80). National Trust, Stourhead House, Stourton, Wiltshire. Pastel on paper, 29½ × 25½ in. Neither signed nor dated. Condition: Excellent.
Lady Hoare, d. 1800, born Frances Ann Acland; in 1761 she married, as his second wife, Sir Richard Hoare.
H.L., seated, to the front, shoulders to the right, wearing a blue and white dress and a white scarf, holding thread in her left hand, a spinning wheel in front of her; a background with red drapery.

DATE: Carefully balanced forms in tightly-knit compositions such as this appear in Cotes's pastels after c. 1766. Especially noteworthy in this respect is no. 190, signed and dated 1766, no. 205, signed and dated 1767, and no. 206 of 1767. A date of c. 1766–70 is suggested.

PROVENANCE: By family descent from the sitter to Sir Henry Hoare, 6th Bt., who gave Stourhead House to the National Trust in 1946.

EXHIBITIONS: The portrait is on exhibit at Stourhead House, which is open to the public at certain times of the year.

REFERENCES: *NTH.*, p. 254.

1767: A portrait in pastel, signed and dated, no. 205.

205. **Queen Charlotte with Charlotte, Princess Royal** (fig. 103). H.M. The Queen, Buckingham Palace. Pastel on paper, 35⅞ × 33¼ in. Signed and dated at the middle right: FCotes px[t] / 1767. F and C in monogram. Condition: Surface damage in several spots.
Queen Charlotte, 1744–1818, born Charlotte Sophia of Mecklenburg-Strelitz; in 1761 she married George III.
Princess Charlotte, 1766–1828, Princess Charlotte Augusta Matilda, the 4th child of George III and Queen Charlotte; in 1797 she married Prince Frederick William of Würtemberg.
T.Q.L., to the right, in an oval, wearing a low-necked dress with trim and a cloak edged with fur, holding the sleeping Princess in her lap, her right hand raised, as if to silence the onlooker; drapery and a column in the background.

PROVENANCE: By family descent from the sitters to H.M. The Queen. For the inventories and other documents in which the picture was recorded at Buckingham House, Windsor Castle, and Buckingham Palace, cf. References, *OML.*

EXHIBITIONS: Society of Artists, 1767, no. 32, cf. Appendix III.

REFERENCES: Anon., *The Conduct of the Royal Academicians*, London, The Incorporated Society of Artists of Great Britain, 1770; Francis Cotes, notes on crayon painting, *The European Magazine*, Feb. 1797, pp. 84–85, cf. Appendix IV. Cotes may be referring to either no. 205 or no. 206; *CWO.*, p. 249; *OML.*, Vol. I, p. 22, no. 717; Horace Walpole, 'Journal of Visits to Country Seats', *The Walpole Society*, Vol. XVI, Oxford, The University Press, 1928, p. 79; Rev. John Wool (ed.), *Biographical Memoirs of the Late Rev[d] Joseph Warton, D.D.*, London, T. Cadell and W. Davies, 1806, p. 317, Letter LXIX, James Harris to Dr. Warton, May 8, 1767. Harris notes that in the Society of Artists exhibition of 1767 'a portrait of the Queen and her daughter by Coates, is universally admired . . .'; *WW.*, p. 222.

This portrait and no. 206 are quite similar, as discussed on p. 37 above.

1767: A portrait in pastel, apparently neither signed nor dated, no. 206.

206. **Queen Charlotte with Charlotte, Princess Royal** (fig. 104). The Duke of Northumberland, Syon House, Brentford, Middlesex. Pastel on paper, 37½ × 31½ in. Apparently neither signed nor dated. Condition: Excellent, but background somewhat darkened.
For the sitters, cf. no. 205.
The composition is the same as in no. 205, with one exception: the stripes around Queen Charlotte's right sleeve are much thinner in the Syon House version. It is also interesting to note that the dress the Queen wears in the Syon House version is repeated exactly in no. 215. This leads one to suspect that the Syon House pastel was used as a preparatory study for no. 215.

DATE: The portrait was probably in the possession of the Duchess of Northumberland in 1767 (cf. Provenance). Considering its close similarity to no. 205, a date of 1767 is suggested.

PROVENANCE: Queen Charlotte; the Duchess of Northumberland. Walpole noted in his Society of Artists Catalogue of 1767 that the Queen had given the portrait to the Duchess of Northumberland. By family descent to the present owner.

EXHIBITIONS: 'The Second Special Exhibition of National Portraits Commencing with the Reign of William and Mary and Ending with the Year 1800,' South Kensington Museum, May 1, 1867, no. 459 (lent by the Duke of Northumberland).

REFERENCES: Charles Henry Collins Baker, 'Portraits at Syon House', *The Connoisseur*, Vol. 55, Sept. 1919, pp. 7, 8, 13 (illus.); *BPP.*, p. 75; Francis Cotes, notes on crayon painting by the artist, *The European Magazine*, Feb. 1797, pp. 84–85, cf. Appendix IV. Cotes may be referring to either no. 205 or no. 206; *CWO.*, p. 249; *OML.*, Vol. I, p. 22, under no. 717; *WA.*, Vol. IV, p. 11; Horace Walpole, 'Journal of Visits to Country Seats', *The Walpole Society*, Vol. XVI, Oxford, The University Press, 1928, p. 79.

1767: Portraits in pastel, signed and dated, nos. 207–212.

207. **The Countess of Coventry.** Present whereabouts unknown. Pastel on paper, 30 × 23½ in. Signed and dated at the middle left: FCotes px[t] / 1767. F and C in monogram. Condition: Unknown.
The Countess of Coventry, born the Hon. Barbara St. John Bletsoe; in 1764 she married, as his second wife, the 6th Earl of Coventry.
H.L., head to the left, shoulders slightly to the right, wearing a white dress and a pink cloak, holding a dove; a background of sky and trees.

PROVENANCE: By family descent from the sitter to the Hon. John Coventry, Burgate Manor, Fordingbridge, Wiltshire; John Coventry Sale, Sotheby's, May 15, 1929 (lot 80), illus., bought by West; Private Collection, England (1931).

REFERENCES: *PFC.*, p. 6.

For Cotes's portrait of the 6th Earl of Coventry's first wife, Maria Gunning, cf. no. 19.

208. **William Cavendish, 5th Duke of Devonshire.** Present whereabouts unknown. Pastel on paper, 25½ × 19¼ in. Signed and dated: FCotes px[t] 1767. F and C in monogram. Condition: Unknown.
The 5th Duke of Devonshire, 1748–1811.
H.S., to the left, wearing a brown coat; a plain background.

PROVENANCE: By family descent from the sitter to the Duke of Portland. Welbeck Abbey, Welbeck, Nottinghamshire (1936). At the present time the picture has not been located in the Portland collection.

REFERENCES: *GP.*, p. 140, no. 356. The special importance of Goulding's catalogue is that it contains Cotes's only bill known to have survived. This is reproduced here:

> My Lord, Pursuant to Orders have sent your Grace's and the Dutchess's Pictures, with the Duke of Devonshire's, which I hope will give satisfaction; annexed is the Account, and am with the greatest Deference, my Lord, Your Grace's Most obedient humble servant,
>
> Fra^s^ Cotes
>
> Cavendish Square
> May 7, 1768

His Grace the Duke of Portland			
Dr to Fras Cotes			
Your Grace's own Picture in Crayons	26	5	0
The Dutchess of Portland's Do	26	5	0
The Duke of Devonshire's Do	26	5	0
Three Italian burr'd Frames at 3 Guineas each	9	9	0
Three Plate Glasses at 1 5 0	3	15	0
	£91	19	0
May 4, 1767			
Rece^d^ in part for the Dutchess's P.	13	2	6
Rece^d^ Do for the Duke of Devonshire's	13	2	6
Rece^d^ Do for your Grace's	13	2	6
	£39	7	6
Remains due	£52	11	6

For the portraits of the Duke and Duchess of Portland, cf. nos. 211 and 212. The Duchess of Portland, born Lady Dorothy Cavendish, was the 5th Duke of Devonshire's sister.

209. **Elizabetha Gulston.** Private Collection, U.K. Pastel on paper, 23½ × 17½ in. Signed and dated at the lower left: FCotes px^t^ / 1767. F and C in monogram. Condition: Good, some surface damage.
Elizabetha Gulston, 1749–1780, the daughter of Sir Thomas Stepney, Bt.; in 1767 she married Joseph Gulston. (no. 52).
H.S., to the front, wearing a white dress; a plain background.

PROVENANCE: By family descent from the sitter to the present owner.

EXHIBITIONS: The portrait is exhibited at the National Museum of Wales, Cardiff, on loan from the present owner.

REFERENCES: *PW.*, Vol. I, p. 53, no. 7.

No. 52 is an earlier portrait of the sitter's husband.

210. **A Lady.** The Lord Petre, Ingatestone Hall, Essex. Pastel on paper, 23¼ × 17¼ in. Signed and dated at the middle left: FCotes px^t^ / 1767. F and C in monogram. Condition: Unknown.
H.L., wearing a white dress and a blue cloak; a plain background.

PROVENANCE: It is not known when the picture came into the Petre collection.

211. **William Henry Cavendish Bentinck, 3rd Duke of Portland.** Present whereabouts unknown. Pastel on paper, 24¾ × 19½ in. Signed and dated: FCotes px^t^ 1767. F and C in monogram. Condition: Unknown.
The 3rd Duke of Portland, 1738–1809; in 1766 he married Lady Dorothy Cavendish, daughter of the 4th Duke of Devonshire.
H.S., to the left, wearing a crimson velvet coat; a plain background.

PROVENANCE: By family descent from the sitter to the Duke of Portland, Welbeck Abbey, Welbeck, Nottinghamshire (1936). At the present time the picture has not been located in the Portland collection.

REFERENCES: *GP.*, p. 140, no. 357.

For Cotes's bill to the Duke of Portland, cf. no. 208.

212. **The Duchess of Portland.** Present whereabouts unknown. Pastel on paper, 25¾ × 19½ in. Signed and dated: FCotes px^t^ 1767. F and C in monogram. Condition: Unknown.
The Duchess of Portland, born Lady Dorothy Cavendish, daughter of the 4th Duke of Devonshire; in 1766 she married the 3rd Duke of Portland.
H.S., to the right, wearing a black dress; a plain background.

PROVENANCE: By family descent from the sitter to the Duke of Portland, Welbeck Abbey, Welbeck, Nottinghamshire (1936). At the present time the portrait has not been located in the Portland collection.

REFERENCES: *GP.*, p. 140, no. 355.
For Cotes's bill, cf. no. 208.

1767: Portraits in oils, signed and dated, nos. 213–222.

213. **Elizabeth Burdett.** Hammerson Group of Companies, London. Oil on canvas, 50 × 40 in. Signed and dated at the middle left: FCotes px^t^ 1767. F and C in monogram. Condition: Excellent.
Elizabeth Burdett, daughter of Sir Robert Burdett, 4th Bt.; she married Francis Munday, Esq.
T.Q.L., to the left, wearing a green dress, resting her right arm on a pedestal surmounted by a garden urn, and holding a hat in her right hand; a background of sky and trees.

PROVENANCE: By family descent from the sitter to Sir Francis Burdett, 7th Bt., Ramsbury Manor, Ramsbury, Wiltshire; Sir Francis Burdett Sale, Sotheby's, Dec. 2, 1953 (lot 50), illus., bought by Frank Partridge, London; Mrs. Margaret Van Alen Bruguiere, Wakehurst, Newport, Rhode Island; Margaret Louise Van Alen Bruguiere Sale, Christie's, Nov. 27, 1969 (lot 186), incorrectly identified as Elizabeth Sedley, Sir Robert Burdett's first wife, who died in 1747.

EXHIBITIONS: 'Introducing Francis Cotes, R.A.', Nottingham University Art Gallery, Nov. 5–27, 1971, no. 30 (lent by the present owner).
As an indication of the increasing value of works by Francis Cotes, it is interesting to note that in 1953 this portrait brought £450, and in 1969 it was sold for 3000 guineas.

214. **Sir Robert Burdett, 4th Bt.** (fig. 62). G. F. Pinney, Esq., England. Oil on canvas, 49½ × 39½ in. Signed and dated at the lower right: FCotes px^t^ / 1767. F and C in monogram. Condition: Excellent.
Sir Robert Burdett, 4th Bt., 1716–1797.
T.Q.L., to the right, wearing a red jacket with a sword at his left side, resting his right hand on a table, and holding a black hat

under his left arm; a plain background except for a green curtain to the left.

PROVENANCE: By family descent from the sitter to Sir Francis Burdett, 7th Bt., Ramsbury Manor, Ramsbury, Wiltshire; Sir Francis Burdett Sale, Sotheby's, Dec. 2, 1953 (lot 41), bought by Leggatt Brothers, London; Gooden and Fox, London; the present owner.

REFERENCES: C. H. Collins Baker, *British Painting*, London, The Medici Society, Pl. 61 (top), incorrectly identified as Sir Francis Burdett.

215. **Queen Charlotte with Charlotte, Princess Royal** (fig. 105). H.M. The Queen, Windsor Castle. Oil on canvas, 94 × 58¼ in. Signed and dated: FCotes px[t] 1767. F and C in monogram. Condition: Excellent. In the 19th century it was reduced to a half-length by folding the canvas under the stretcher. In 1901 it was restretched to its original size.
Engraved by W. Wynne Ryland and published in 1770.
For the sitters cf. no. 205.
F.L., seated, to the right. The sitters are wearing the same dresses as in no. 206, and their poses are the same as in nos. 205 and 206, but extended to full-length. On the floor is a patterned carpet; in the background a crown resting on a table, drapery, and a column.

PROVENANCE: By family descent from the sitters to H.M. The Queen. For the inventories and other documents in which the picture was recorded at Buckingham House, Carlton House, and Windsor Castle, cf. References, *OML*; in 1816 and 1819 the picture was incorrectly attributed to Allan Ramsay, and the child was erroneously identified as the Prince of Wales; this mistaken identification of the child was repeated in H. Adlard's engraving of the portrait published in 1830.

REFERENCES: *CWO*., p. 249; Edward Edwards, *Anecdotes of Painters*, London, Leigh and Sotheby, W. J. and J. Richardson, R. Faulder, T. Payne, and J. White, 1808, p. 34; *O'D*., Vol. I, p. 409, nos. 1–7; *OML*., Vol. I, p. 22, no. 718; Vol. II, Pl. 15; William Sandby, *The History of the Royal Academy*, Vol. I, London, Longman, Green, Longman, Roberts, and Green, 1862, p. 96; Society of Artists Catalogue, 1767, no. 32, with a note by Horace Walpole, cf. Appendix III; *WA*., Vol. IV, p. 111.

This picture is an enlargement of the basic composition in nos. 205 and 206, one or both of which may have been used as preparatory studies.

216. **Thomas and Isabel Crathorne** (figs. 89, 90, and 91). Henry E. Huntington Library and Art Gallery, San Marino, California. Oil on canvas, 52½ × 59½ in. Signed and dated at the lower left on the end of a rolled-up sheet of paper lying on a chair: FCotes px[t]. F and C in monogram. Formerly the signature and the date were: FCotes px[t] / 1767. Condition: Excellent, but date removed.
Thomas Crathorne of Crathorne and Ness Hall, Yorkshire, died in 1764; therefore, the portrait of him is posthumous. He was survived by his wife Isabel, daughter of Sir John Swinburne, 3rd Bt., and great-grand aunt of the poet Algernon Swinburne.
T.Q.L. Thomas Crathorne: standing, head to the right, shoulders to the front, wearing a white Van Dyck costume with a pink cloak, leaning on the back of a yellow brocade chair, on which there is a book, a folder containing sheets of paper, and a piece of paper rolled up and tied with a ribbon. Isabel Crathorne: seated, head to the front, shoulders to the left, wearing a blue wrapping gown with a lace collar and cuffs, and a pink sash; her lace collar and cuffs are touches of 17th century fashion which correspond to her husband's Van Dyck costume; she holds a drawing pen in her right hand and rests her left hand on an open book, which is on a table; in the book there is a drawing of Cupid; a bare wall and a curtain in the background.

DATE: After the Sotheby sale in March of 1964, the date of '1767', which had been inscribed directly below the signature, was removed. When the portrait arrived at the Huntington Gallery, no date appeared on the canvas. In retrospect, the removal of the date does not seem justified. The noticeable exploitation of highlights is a characteristic of Cotes's work which appears sporadically in his oil paintings between c. 1764 and 1770. It reaches its peak c. 1766/67 in portraits like that of the Countess of Donegall (no. 197) and that of the Crathornes. In addition, it is interesting to note that double portraits in oils by Cotes are exclusively associated with the latter half of the 1760's. Besides the pictures of the Crathornes, some other known examples of such double portraits are nos. 284 and 287, both signed and dated 1769, and no. 250 of c. 1767–70. Considering the Crathornes' picture, therefore, both from the viewpoint of style and composition, a date in the late 1760's is definitely suggested. The date of 1767 is what one would expect; it need not be rejected because the portrait of Thomas Crathorne would then be posthumous. Cotes could have copied his features from a miniature or from another portrait in the possession of the family. The date of '1767' which was accepted as genuine in publications appearing in 1929, 1934, and 1964, should continue to be regarded as valid.

PROVENANCE: Purchased in 1928 by Sir Gomer Berry, Bt., Chandos House, London; by family descent from Sir Gomer Berry to the 2nd Viscount Kemsley; Anon. Sale, Sotheby's, Mar. 18, 1964 (lot 85), bought by Thomas Agnew and Sons, London, for the Henry E. Huntington Library and Art Gallery.

EXHIBITIONS: 'Daily Telegraph Exhibition', London, 1928, no. x8.
'Exhibition of British Art c. 1000–1860', R.A. London, 1934, no. 267 (lent by Sir Gomer Berry, Bt.).
The picture is on exhibit at the Henry E. Huntington Library and Art Gallery.

REFERENCES: Anon., 'Accessions of American and Canadian Museums', *The Art Quarterly*, Vol. 27, no. 4, 1964, p. 492; Hugh Aveling, O.S.B., *Northern Catholics, the Catholic Recusants of the North Riding of Yorkshire, 1558–1790*, London, Geoffrey Chapman, 1966, illus. between pp. 224 and 225. Below the illustration the death date of Thomas Crathorne is given as 1764. Aveling is the chief authority on the Crathorne family. In this book he traces its history from 1568 to the late eighteenth century; Ruth Davidson 'In the Museums', *Antiques*, Vol. 87, no. 4, Apr. 1965, p. 468 (illus.); Frank Rutter, 'Sir Gomer Berry's Paintings at Chandos House', *The Connoisseur*, Vol. LXXXIII, no. 333, May, 1929, p. 277 (illus.); Frank Rutter, 'Fame Returns to Francis Cotes', *The Antique Collector*, Vol. VI, no. 2, Jul. 18, 1931, pp. 170, 171 (illus.).

217. **Lady Dering.** Carnegie Institute, Pittsburgh. Oil on canvas, 53½ × 40¼ in. Signed and dated at the lower left: FCotes px[t] 1767. F and C in monogram. Inscribed at the top right: Deborah Winchester, Lady Dering. Condition: Excellent.
Lady Dering, c. 1745–1818, the daughter of John Winchester,

M.D., of Nethersole House, Barham Downs, Kent; in 1765 she married Sir Edward Dering, 6th Bt.
T.Q.L., to the right, wearing a wrapping gown and a mantle, leaning her right arm on a balustrade; a background of trees and sky.

PROVENANCE: By family descent from the sitter to Sir Henry Dering, 10th Bt., Surrenden Park, Kent; M. Knoedler and Co., London, purchased the picture from the Dering collection in 1919, and sold it in the same year to the John Levy Galleries, New York; Mrs. J. Willis Dalzell of Pittsburgh purchased the picture from the John Levy Galleries in 1921; in 1929 she gave it to the Carnegie Institute.

EXHIBITIONS: 'Permanent Collection of Paintings', Carnegie Institute, Pittsburgh, Feb. 1945, no. 72.

REFERENCES: W. Roberts, *Deborah, Lady Dering by Francis Cotes, R.A.*, London, The Chiswick Press, 1920, pp. 1–8.

218. **Catherine Eld.** Birmingham Museum and Art Gallery, Birmingham. Oil on canvas, 94 × 57 in. Signed and dated at the left on a well: FCotes px[t] 1767. F and C in monogram. Condition: Good, but with varnish somewhat discoloured.
Catherine Eld, daughter of John Eld of Seighford Hall, Staffordshire.
F.L., to the right, wearing a white dress and a blue cloak, resting her right hand on a gold pitcher, which is on the rim of a well; a landscape background.

PROVENANCE: By family descent from the sitter to Major R. C. Eld, Seighford Hall, Staffordshire; Major R. C. Eld Sale, Christie's, Mar. 11, 1959 (lot 109), illus., bought in; Major R. C. Eld Sale, Christie's, Mar. 24, 1961 (lot 78), bought in; The Birmingham Museum and Art Gallery purchased the picture in 1961 after the sale.

EXHIBITIONS: 'British Painting and Watercolours', Municipal Museum, Lyon, 1966, no. 26 (lent by the Birmingham Museum and Art Gallery).

219. **The Duchess of Hamilton as Venus, Queen of Beauty** (fig. 83). The Duke of Argyll, Inveraray Castle, Inveraray, Argyllshire. Oil on canvas, 96 × 57 in. Signed and dated at the lower left on the base of a pedestal: FCotes px[t] 1767. F and C in monogram. Condition: Excellent.
The Duchess of Hamilton, 1733–1790, born Elizabeth Gunning, cf. no. 16. After her marriage to the Duke of Hamilton, which lasted from 1753 until his death in 1758, she married, in 1759, Col. John Campbell, who soon succeeded as Marquess of Lorne, and in 1770, became Duke of Argyll.
F.L., to the right, wearing a green wrapping gown and a pink cloak, leaning against a pedestal surmounted by a garden urn; to the right is a sunflower that turns to her instead of the sun, an allusion to her unsurpassed radiance as the Queen of Beauty; a landscape background.

PROVENANCE: By family descent from the sitter to the present owner.

EXHIBITIONS: Society of Artists, 1767, no. 35, cf. Appendix III. 'Introducing Francis Cotes, R.A.', Nottingham University Art Gallery, Nov. 5–27, 1971, no. 29 (lent by the owner).

REFERENCES: Anon., *The Conduct of the Royal Academicians*, London, Incorporated Society of Artists of Great Britain, 1770; *CWO.*, p. 249; *PIB.*, p. 183; *RTG.*, p. 133; Ellis Kirkham Waterhouse, *Three Decades of British Art, 1740–1770*, Jayne Lectures for 1964, Philadelphia, American Philosophical Society, 1965, p. 69; *WW.*, Vol. I, p. 222.

For a similar portrait of the sitter cf. Appendix V, no. 28.

220. **Princess Louisa and Queen Caroline Matilda** (fig. 102). H.M. The Queen, Buckingham Palace. Oil on canvas, 104⅝ × 73½ in. Signed and dated: FCotes px[t] 1767. F and C in monogram. Condition: Excellent.
Louisa Ann, 1749–1768, daughter of Frederick, Prince of Wales. Caroline Matilda, cf. no. 188. By the time this portrait was painted Princess Caroline had become Queen of Denmark.
F.L. Princess Louisa: seated in front of a music stand, head to the front, shoulders to the left, wearing a blue dress; with her right hand she points to a line of music in an open book on her lap, and with her left she holds a guitern or English guitar. Queen Caroline: standing, to the left, wearing a white and pink dress, resting her right hand on the back of Princess Louisa's chair, her fingers gently touching Louisa's shoulder; in her left hand she holds rolled-up sheets of music; her eyes are fixed upon a score on the music stand; an organ, a column, and drapery in the background.

PROVENANCE: By family descent from the sitters to H.M. The Queen. For the inventories and other documents in which the picture was recorded at various royal residences, cf. References, *OML*; note that Horace Walpole may have seen this picture at Melcomb House and incorrectly attributed it to Angelica Kauffman, and that it was listed at Carlton House in 1816 as by Allan Ramsay.

EXHIBITIONS: 'Exhibition of Works by the Old Masters and by Deceased Masters of the British School', R.A., London, Winter Exhibition, 1881, no. 142 (lent by Queen Victoria).
'Exhibition of the King's Pictures', R.A., London, 1946–1947, no. 109 (lent by King George VI).

REFERENCES: *CWO.*, p. 249; *OML.*, Vol. I, p. 22, no. 720; Vol. II, Pl. 14.

In this picture the head of Queen Caroline is almost exactly as in the pastel of 1766, no. 188. The head and costume of Princess Louisa are as they appear in no. 227, a small, half-length oil portrait. The motif of two ladies before a music stand, one with a guitar, is also present in no. 225, a pen and wash drawing. Nos. 188, 227, and 225 were probably used as preparatory studies for no. 220.

221. **Richard Milles.** Present whereabouts unknown. Oil on canvas, 30 × 24 in. Signed and dated: FCotes px[t] 1767. F and C in monogram. Condition: Unknown.
Richard Milles, 1730–1820, son of Christopher Milles and Mary, daughter of Richard Warner of Elmham Hall, Norfolk.
H.L., seated, to the right, wearing a brown coat and holding a gold-tipped cane and a black hat under his right arm; a plain background.

PROVENANCE: By family descent from the sitter to the Earl Sondes, Elmham Hall, Norfolk (1927); Earl Sondes Sale, Christie's, Mar. 17, 1972 (lot 8), bought by Reichmeyd, identified as of 'a Gentleman'.

REFERENCES: *PN.*, Vol. I, p. 143, no. 2.

222. **Lady Wolseley.** Sir Charles Wolseley, Bt., Wolseley, Staffordshire. Oil on canvas, 50 × 40 in. Signed and dated at the lower right: FCotes R.A. px[t] / 1767. F and C in monogram. The

Royal Academy was not founded until December of 1768; presumably Cotes painted the picture in 1767, but signed it after the foundation of the Academy. Condition: Excellent.

Lady Wolseley, born Charlotte Barbara Chambers, the only child of Zachary Chambers of Wimbledon; in 1765 she married Sir William Wolseley, 6th Bt.
T.Q.L., to the left, wearing a blue-grey wrapping gown, resting her left hand on an urn and her right hand on her hip; part of a wall, trees, and sky in the background.

PROVENANCE: By family descent from the sitter to the present owner.

EXHIBITIONS: 'Commemorative Exhibition of the Art Treasures of the Midlands', City of Birmingham Museum and Art Gallery, 1934, no. 448 (lent by Sir Edric Wolseley, Bt.).
'Introducing Francis Cotes, R.A.', Nottingham University Art Gallery, Nov. 5–27, 1971, no. 31 (lent by the present owner); illus. in cat. (Pl. XIV).

Exhibited in 1767: A lost portrait in pastel, no. 223.

223. **George Knapton.** Present whereabouts unknown. Pastel on paper, measurements unknown. Possibly signed and dated. Condition: Unknown.

PROVENANCE: Unknown.

EXHIBITIONS: Society of Artists, 1767, no. 33, cf. Appendix III.

REFERENCES: Francis Cotes, notes on crayon painting, *The European Magazine*, Feb. 1797, pp. 84, 85, cf. Appendix IV.

c. 1767: Drawings, pen and wash, neither signed nor dated, nos. 224 and 225.

224. **Queen Charlotte with Charlotte, Princess Royal, and the Duchess of Ancaster.** British Museum, London. Pen and wash, tinted with watercolour, on paper, $9\frac{1}{2} \times 6\frac{5}{8}$ in. Neither signed nor dated. Condition: Good, slight fading of the colours.
For Queen Charlotte and Charlotte, Princess Royal, cf. no. 205.

Mary, Duchess of Ancaster, born Mary Panton, d. 1793.
F.L. The poses of Queen Charlotte and the Princess Royal are exactly as in nos. 205, 206, and 215. The Queen is wearing a white dress with yellow stripes. The design of her skirt is slightly different than in no. 215. Princess Charlotte is dressed, as in other portraits, in a white dress with a blue sash and a white bonnet with a blue bow. The Duchess of Ancaster stands on the Queen's right. She wears a blue dress, rests her left hand on the back of the Queen's chair, and looks down at the baby. In the background the drapery comes directly behind the heads of the Queen and the Duchess of Ancaster. This arrangement of the drapery is similar to that in nos. 205 and 206. To the right in the background is the crown on a table, as in no. 215.

DATE: The similarity between this drawing and no. 215 suggests a date of c. 1767. Whether or not it was used as a preparatory drawing for no. 215 is impossible to determine at present.

PROVENANCE: Edward Cheney, Esq., U.K Edward Cheney Sale, place unknown, May 9, 1885 (lot 298), bought by the British Museum.

REFERENCES: *CC18.*, p. 275, fig. 98; *CWO.*, p. 249; Randal Davies, *English Society of the Eighteenth Century in Contemporary Art*, London, 1907, frontispiece; *EG.*, Pl. 22; *LB.*, pp. 257–258, no. 3; *OML.*, Vol. I, p. 22, under 718.

225. **Two Ladies at Music** (fig. 101). Henry E. Huntington Library and Art Gallery, San Marino, California. Pen and wash on paper, $9\frac{1}{4} \times 7\frac{1}{2}$ in. Neither signed nor dated. Inscribed on the mount at the back: Francis Cotes. Condition: Excellent.
F.L., one figure standing, the other sitting; their heads to the left, their shoulders to the right. Both sitters have dresses and hair styles similar to those of Princess Louisa and Queen Caroline in no. 220. As in no. 220 there is a music stand to the left. The overall composition, however, is somewhat different. In the drawing the standing figure, who holds a sheet of music in one hand, is nearest to the stand, while the seated figure, who sings and plays the guitar, is farther away. The drawing is probably a preparatory study for no. 220.

DATE: The similarity between the drawing and no. 220 suggests a date of c. 1767.

PROVENANCE: Ingram Collection, U.K.; P. and D. Colnaghi, London; Henry E. Huntington Library and Art Gallery.

c. 1767: Portraits in oils, neither signed nor dated, nos. 226 and 227.

226. **Elizabeth Burdett.** R. F. Popham, Esq., England. Oil on canvas, $29 \times 24\frac{1}{2}$ in. Neither signed nor dated. Condition: Excellent.
Elizabeth Burdett, daughter of Sir Robert Burdett, 4th Bt.; she married Francis Munday, Esq.
H.L., a plain background.

DATE: The head in this portrait is very similar to that in the signed and dated picture of Elizabeth Burdett, no. 213 (1767). A date of c. 1767 is therefore suggested.

PROVENANCE: By family descent from the sitter to Sir Francis Burdett, 7th Bt., Ramsbury Manor, Ramsbury, Wiltshire; Sir Francis Burdett Sale, Sotheby's, Dec. 2, 1953 (lot 52), bought by Sabin; Leggatt Brothers, London; Gooden and Fox, London; the present owner.

227. **Princess Louisa Ann** (fig. 100). H.M. Queen Elizabeth The Queen Mother, Clarence House, London. Oil on canvas, $28\frac{1}{2} \times 24$ in. Neither signed nor dated. Condition: Excellent.
Princess Louisa Ann, 1749–1768, daughter of Frederick, Prince of Wales.
H.L., seated, head slightly to the right, shoulders to the left, wearing the same dress and hair style as in no. 220, holding a fan in her right hand and a glove in her left hand; the background is plain, except for a curtain to the left.

DATE: The close similarity between this portrait and the figure of Princess Louisa in no. 220, signed and dated 1767, suggests a date of c. 1767.

PROVENANCE: Anon. Sale, Christie's, Nov. 10, 1950 (lot 117), bought by Marsh; H.M. Queen Elizabeth The Queen Mother.

EXHIBITIONS: 'Introducing Francis Cotes, R.A.', Nottingham University Art Gallery, Nov. 5–27, 1971, no. 32 (lent by H.M. Queen Elizabeth The Queen Mother); illus. in cat. (Pl. XII).

This portrait was probably used as a preparatory study for the figure of Princess Louisa in no. 220. There are compositional differences, however, which should be noted: in no. 227, the Princess holds a glove and a fan, whereas in no. 220 she points to a line of music and holds a guitar.

1767/68: A portrait in oils, neither signed nor dated, no. 228.

228. **Agneta Yorke** (fig. 85). Private Collection, U.K. Oil on canvas, 50 × 40 in. Neither signed nor dated. Condition: Excellent. Engraved in mezzotint by Valentine Green and published in 1768. Agneta Yorke, d. 1820, the daughter of Henry Johnson of Great Berkhamstead, Hertfordshire; in 1762 she married, as his second wife, the Hon. Charles Yorke, son of the 1st Earl of Hardwicke.
T.Q.L., head to the left, shoulders to the right, wearing a red and blue wrapping gown, resting her left hand on the top of an urn and her right hand on her hip; in the background an oval mirror, a column, and green drapery.

DATE: The pose of the sitter and the style of the painting is very similar to no. 222, signed and dated 1767. The engraving was published at approximately the same time, 1768. A date, therefore, of 1767/68 is suggested.

PROVENANCE: By family descent from the sitter to the present owner's wife.

REFERENCES: *CS.*, Vol. II, p. 595, no. 143; *O'D.*, Vol. IV, p. 563, no. 1.

A copy in oils of the head of Agneta Yorke, made after this portrait, has had the following provenance: Anon. Sale, Christie's, May 20, 1927 (lot 75), bought by the Raeburn Gallery; The Ehrich Galleries New York; The Ehrich Galleries Sale, American Art Association-Anderson Galleries, New York, Nov. 29, 1931 (lot 13), bought by R. C. Vose of the Vose Gallery, Boston; Anon. Sale, American Art Association-Anderson Galleries, Dec. 14, 1933 (lot 50); The Ehrich Galleries, New York; The Ehrich Galleries Sale, American Art Association-Anderson Galleries, New York, Apr. 18, 1934 (lot 100).

c. 1767–1770: Drawings, pen and wash, neither signed nor dated, nos. 229 and 230.

229. **A Lady with a Greyhound.** Present whereabouts unknown. Pen and wash, tinted with watercolour, on paper, 12⅛ × 8 in. Neither signed nor dated. Inscribed on the back with Cotes's monogram: FC. Condition: Unknown.
F.L., to the left, wearing a dress with bows at the bodice and a flounce at each sleeve, holding her skirt with her left hand and extending her right hand towards her greyhound, who looks up at her; a landscape background with a garden urn on a pedestal to the right.

DATE: Drawings of female figures such as this one, full-length, in grand compositions, occur in Cotes's work c. 1767, cf. nos. 224 and 225. The hair style of this sitter also indicates a date in the later 1760's; therefore a date of c. 1767–1770 is suggested.

PROVENANCE: Herbert Horne, Esq., U.K.; Edward Marsh, Esq., purchased the drawing from Herbert Horne in 1904, and was still in possession of it in 1934.

EXHIBITIONS: 'Exhibition of the Herbert Horne Collection of Drawing', Burlington Fine Arts Club, London, 1916, no. 51 (lent by Edward Marsh, Esq.).
'Exhibition of British Art c. 1000–1860', R.A., London, 1934, no. 1110 (lent by Edward Marsh, Esq.).

230. **Three Children with a Dog.** British Museum, London. Pen and wash, tinted with watercolour, on paper, 7¾ × 6 in. Neither signed nor dated. Inscribed at the lower right with Cotes's monogram composed of F and C, and at the lower left with 'T Th', probably the initials of Thomas Thane, Esq., a 19th-century collector of English portraits and drawings. Condition: Good, slight fading of the colours.
Three full-length figures: a girl to the left (head to the left, shoulders to the right, wearing a low-necked dress with a sash, and holding a flower in her right hand); a girl in the centre (head to the left, shoulders to the front, seated on a balustrade in front of a garden urn, wearing a dress with a sash and a broad-brimmed hat with a feather); and a boy to the right (head to the front, shoulders to the left, wearing a suit with a waistcoat, holding a dog by a lead, and pointing to the two girls). In the background a balustrade, a garden urn, and a landscape. The figures are done in a predominantly grey wash.

DATE: The only known full-length views of children in Cotes's work occur in the late 1760's: no. 255, signed and dated 1768, and no. 270, c. 1768–1770. The style of the drawing corresponds to that in no. 229, c. 1767–1770. A date of c. 1767–1770 is therefore suggested.

PROVENANCE: Probably from the collection of Thomas Thane, Esq., London (1782–1846), who initialled his drawings in a similar manner. Thomas Thane's extensive collection was sold at Sotheby's in 1846 in three sales: April 2–3, May 25–30, and Je. 16–20. This drawing was not mentioned specifically, but it may have been included in lot 320 on May 26, under the heading 'Miscellaneous Drawings'. The British Museum purchased the drawing at a sale on March 5, 1847, lot 5. Further information on the sale has not come to light.

REFERENCES: *LB.*, p. 257, no. 1; Frits Lugt, *Les Marques de Collections de Dessins et d'Estampes*, Amsterdam, Vereenigde Drukkerijen, 1921, pp. 450–451, 459.

c. 1767–1770: Portraits in oils, neither signed nor dated, nos. 231–250.

231. **Anne Blackwell.** Present whereabouts unknown. Oil on canvas, 50 × 40 in. Neither signed nor dated. Condition: Unknown. Anne Blackwell, d. 1827, born Anne Dutton; in 1760 she married Samuel Blackwell of Ampney Park, Gloucestershire.
T.Q.L., seated, to the left, wearing a wrapping gown, leaning her right arm on a stone parapet, and resting her head on her right hand; a background of trees and sky.

DATE: The head in profile to the left and resting on the hand is a pose Cotes used in no. 190, signed and dated 1766, and in no. 254, signed and dated 1768. The quality of the painting and the structure of the background are similar in no. 259, signed and dated 1768. The sitter's hair is dressed rather high, a fashion popular in the late 1760's. A date of c. 1767–1770 is suggested.

PROVENANCE: By family descent from the sitter to E. J. Blackwell, Esq., Ampney Park, Gloucestershire; Lord Tweedmouth Sale, Je. 3, 1905 (lot 44), incorrectly attributed to Reynolds, bought by Colnaghi; P. and D. Colnaghi, London; Mr. Nathaniel Thayer, U.S.A.; Nathanial Thayer Sale, American Art Association-Anderson Galleries, New York, Apr. 25, 1935 (lot 68), bought by W. W. Seaman.

232. **Harriet Brocas.** Tate Gallery, London. Oil on canvas, 29¼ × 24½ in. Neither signed nor dated. Condition: Good, some discolouration.
The lady is apparently a member of the Brocas family; the name 'Harriet Brocas' is a traditional identification that has yet to be substantiated.
H.L., to the left, in a painted oval, wearing a white wrapping gown and a blue-grey mantle; a plain background.

DATE: This portrait is very similar to Cotes's picture of the Duchess of Beaufort, no. 295, signed and dated 1770. The hair style could be as early as c. 1767; therefore, a date of c. 1767–1770 is suggested.

PROVENANCE: The portrait remained in the Brocas family until 1887; Brocas Sale, Jul. 29, 1887 (lot 162), bought by Thomas Agnew and Sons, London, who sold the picture in 1888 to George Holt, Esq., U.K. George Holt presented it to the National Gallery, London, 1889; it has since been transferred to the Tate Gallery.

EXHIBITIONS: 'A Century of British Art from 1737 to 1837', Grosvenor Gallery, London, Summer, 1889, no. 78 (lent by George Holt, Esq.).

REFERENCES: *BPP.*, Vol. I, p. 74, Pl. 54; *CWO.*, p. 250; Martin Davies, *British School*, National Gallery Catalogue, London, Printed for the Trustees, 1946, p. 40, no. 1281. The date of the Brocas sale is given incorrectly; *EG.*, Pl. 16.

233. **Lady Broughton** (fig. 79). National Trust, Attingham Park, Atcham, Shropshire. Oil on canvas, 39 × 31¾ in. Neither signed nor dated. Condition: Excellent.
Engraved in mezzotint by J. Finlayson and published in 1772.
Lady Broughton, d. 1785, born Maria Wicker; she married the Rev. Sir Thomas Broughton, Bt. This identification is given by Finlayson in his mezzotint of 1772. In recent years the sitter has been referred to as Susanna Maria Hill, wife of Sir Brian Broughton-Delves, Bt. (1740–1766).
T.Q.L., seated to the left, in an oval, wearing a wrapping gown, a sash, and a turban, leaning her right arm on a stone parapet and resting her head on her right hand; a background of sky and trees.

DATE: The pose of the sitter, the hair style, and the mode of painting suggest a date of c. 1767–1770; cf. no. 231.

PROVENANCE: Teresa, Lady Berwick, Attingham Park; it is not known when the portrait came into the Berwick collection; National Trust.

REFERENCES: *NTH.*, p. 240, under 'Attingham Park—Pictures not on View', identified as Susanna Hill; *O'D.*, Vol. I, p. 254, no. 1.

234. **Anne Cust.** Leger Galleries, London. Oil on canvas, 50 × 40 in. Neither signed nor dated. Condition: Excellent.
Anne Cust, daughter of Sir John Cust, 3rd Bt.; in 1777 she married Jacob Reynardson of Holywell Hall, Stamford, Lincolnshire.
T.Q.L., head to the front, shoulders to the left, wearing a pink wrapping gown, holding her skirt with her left hand, and resting her right arm on the base of a stone pedestal surmounted by a garden urn; a background of sky and trees.

DATE: The sitter's hair is arranged in the style of the late 1760's. Her pose is also found in nos. 241 and 247, both of c. 1767–1770. A date of c. 1767–1770 is therefore suggested.

PROVENANCE: By family descent from the sitter to Mrs. Mountjoy Fane, The Old Rectory, Careby, Lincolnshire; Mrs. Alexander Laughlin, Sewickley, Pennsylvania; Leggatt Brothers, London (1961); M. Knoedler and Co., London; Leger Galleries, London.

EXHIBITIONS: 'Allan Ramsay, His Masters and Rivals', National Gallery of Scotland, Edinburgh, Aug.–Sept. 1963 (no. 91).
For the portrait of the sitter's sister, cf. no. 235.

235. **Elizabeth Cust.** Philip Yorke, Esq., Erddig, Wrexham, Denbighshire. Oil on canvas, 50 × 40 in. Neither signed nor dated. Condition: Excellent.
Elizabeth Cust, 1749/50–1779, daughter of Sir John Cust, 3rd Bt.; in 1770 she married Philip Yorke of Erddig.
T.Q.L., head to the left, shoulders to the right, posing as a shepherdess, wearing a pink dress with a white apron, holding a shepherd's crook in her right hand, and resting her left hand on her hip; a landscape background.

DATE: The hair is arranged in the style of the late 1760's. The quality of the picture is similar to that of no. 234, Cotes's portrait of the sitter's sister, c. 1767–1770. The same date is suggested here.

PROVENANCE: By family descent from the sitter to the present owner.

REFERENCES: Albinia Lucy Cust, *The Chronicles of Erddig on the Wyke*, London, John Lane, 1914, p. 205; *PW.*, Vol. I, p. 95, no. 11. A small copy, 11½ × 9¾ in., attributed to Gainsborough, appeared in the Anon. Sale, Sotheby's, Mar. 2, 1966 (lot 171), bought by Klein.

236. **Mary Fletcher.** Private Collection, U.K. Oil on canvas, 49 × 38½ in. Neither signed nor dated. Condition: At some point between the 1936 sale and the acquisition of the painting by the present owner the garden urn was changed into a garden vase with a plant. The original urn has been restored, and the picture is now in good condition.
The identification was made by the present owner. T.Q.L., head to the left, shoulders to the right, wearing a pink and white wrapping gown and sash, resting her left hand on a garden urn, and holding a bracelet with an inset portrait miniature of a lady in her right.

DATE: The formality of the composition indicates a date of c. 1767–1770.

PROVENANCE: C. H. T. Hawkins, Esq., U.K.; C. H. T. Hawkins Sale, Oct. 30, 1936 (lot 48), bought by Ellis and Smith, London, who sold the picture to the present owner, after June of 1939.

EXHIBITIONS: 'In the Days of Queen Charlotte', The Luton Public Museum, May 11 – Je. 11, 1939, no. 7, identified as 'Portrait of a Lady' (lent by Ellis and Smith, London).
'Works of Art from Midland Houses', City of Birmingham Museum and Art Gallery, Jul. 18 – Sept. 6, 1953, no. 6, identified as 'Portrait of a Lady' (lent by the present owner).

237. (Erratum). **Lady Gage.** The Viscount Gage, Firle Place, Lewes, Sussex. Oil on canvas, 82 × 57 in. Neither signed nor dated. Condition: Excellent. Formerly thought to be by Cotes, now attributed to Benjamin West.

238. **Admiral Sir Edward Hawke.** The Earl of Rosse, Womersley Park, Doncaster, Yorkshire. Oil on canvas, 50 × 40 in. Neither signed nor dated. Condition; Good.
Engraved by J. Hall and published in 1793. Hall's line engraving is not after no. 239, the well-known portrait of Hawke at Greenwich. A comparison between the Hall engraving and nos. 238 and 239 leaves no doubt that no. 238 was the portrait Hall saw.

Admiral Sir Edward Hawke, 1705–81; from 1766–71 he was First Lord of the Admiralty, and in 1776 he was created Baron Hawke of Towton.

T.Q.L., head to the left, shoulders to the right, wearing a blue, white, and gold naval uniform, holding a hat in his left hand and resting his right hand on a sword; the background consists of a mound of earth and rock, and a seascape with ships in the distance.

DATE: The cuffs on the uniform appear to be of the fairly narrow variety that came into use on flag officer's jackets after 1767. The closest parallel to this portrait among Cotes's signed and dated works is also from the late 1760's and also of a great naval officer, Captain John Jervis, later Admiral and Earl of St. Vincent, no. 281 (1769). For Hawke's portrait a date of c. 1767–1770 is suggested.

PROVENANCE: By family descent from the sitter to the present owner.

EXHIBITIONS: 'The British Empire Exhibition', Palace of Arts, Wembley, 1924, no. N13 (lent by the Earl of Rosse).

REFERENCES: *O'D.*, Vol. VI, p. 209, no. 1 and ff. O'Donoghue identified the Greenwich portrait, no. 239, as the original from which Hall's engraving was made. This is unlikely.

239. **Admiral Sir Edward Hawke** (fig. 67). National Maritime Museum, Greenwich. Oil on canvas, 50 × 40 in. Neither signed nor dated. Condition: Good. In the 19th century the portrait was extended so that more of the legs was showing. In 1937 it was restored to its original proportions.

For biographical dates, cf. no. 238.

The pose, the costume, and the background are as in no. 238. The face, however, is not as elongated.

DATE: The quality of the painting is not as distinguished as in no. 238. Both pictures come from the same period, c. 1767–1770.

PROVENANCE: By family descent from the sitter to Lord Hawke, who gave the portrait to the National Maritime Museum in 1825.

EXHIBITIONS: 'Portraits of Yorkshire Worthies', Leeds, 1868, no. 3160 (lent by the National Maritime Museum).

The picture is on exhibit at the National Maritime Museum.

REFERENCES: Anon., *Concise Catalogue of Paintings, National Maritime Museum*, London, Her Majesty's Stationery Office, 1958, no. 10; *The Connoisseur*, Vol. LVI, Jan. 1920, p. 55 (illus.). The illustration shows the portrait extended beyond its proper proportions; *CWO.*, p. 250; *The Illustrated London News*, Apr. 17, 1937, p. 657 (illus., top right). This illustration shows the painting shortly after it was restored to its original size; *O'D.*, Vol. IV, p. 209, no. 1 and ff., cf. no. 238.

240. **A Lady.** Biggs of Maidenhead, Maidenhead, Berkshire. Oil on canvas, 15½ × 13 in. Neither signed nor dated. Condition: Restored, but the paint is still badly crackled in spots.

T.Q.L., seated, to the left, wearing a pink and white wrapping gown and a blue sash, sitting on a stone wall, leaning her left arm on a stone parapet, and resting her head in her left hand; a background of sky and trees.

DATE: The pose recalls that of Anne Blackwell, no. 231, c. 1767–1770, and the hair style is of the same period; consequently, a date of c. 1767–1770 is suggested.

PROVENANCE: Unknown.

EXHIBITIONS: Antiques Fair, Grosvenor House, London, Je. 1969 exhibited by Biggs of Maidenhead.

241. **Lady Elizabeth Lee.** Mrs. Eugenio Annovazzi, Rome. Oil on canvas, 49½ × 39½ in. Neither signed nor dated. Condition: Unknown.

Lady Elizabeth Lee, daughter of the 1st Earl of Harcourt; in 1763 she married Sir William Lee, 4th Bt.

T.Q.L., head to the front, shoulders to the left, wearing a blue wrapping gown and a brown sash, holding her skirt with her left hand and a flower with her right hand; her right arm rests on a stone pedestal surmounted by a garden urn; a background of sky and trees.

DATE: In style and composition this portrait is quite similar to no. 234, c. 1767–1770. The sitter's hair style indicates a corresponding date.

PROVENANCE: Colonel H. H. Mulliner, U.K.; Colonel H. H. Mulliner Sale, Christie's, Jul. 18, 1924 (lot 10), bought by P. and D. Colnaghi, London; The Viscount Rothermere, London; Anon. Sale, Christie's, Nov. 19, 1965 (lot 156), sold as by Reynolds, bought by the Leger Galleries, London; the present owner.

242. **Lady Leicester.** Lieutenant Colonel J. L. B. Leicester-Warren, Tabley House, Knutsford, Cheshire. Oil on canvas, 94½ × 59 in. Neither signed nor dated. Condition: Excellent.

Lady Leicester, Catherine, daughter of Sir William Fleming of Rydal; in 1755 she married Sir Peter Leicester, Bt.

F.L., seated, head to the left, shoulders to the right, wearing a long-sleeved satin dress with a sash, a satin cloak, and a scarf around her head, resting her left arm on a table, holding her sash in her left hand and an open book in her right hand; the background consists of a curtain and a wall with a landscape painting in a round frame.

DATE: Highly formal, full-length portraits of ladies occur in Cotes's work after 1766. This picture with its very carefully balanced forms around the sitter recalls the painting of Queen Charlotte and the Princess Royal, no. 215 (1767). The contrast of the rounded form of a frame with the other shapes in the composition also appears in no. 228 (1767/68). The sitter's hair style indicates the late 1760's. A date of c. 1767–1770 is therefore suggested.

PROVENANCE: By family descent from the sitter to the present owner.

EXHIBITIONS: 'Works of Art from Private Collections', City of Manchester Art Gallery, Sept. 21 – Oct. 30, 1960, no. 111 (lent by the present owner).

243. **Mrs. Macrae.** Present whereabouts unknown. Oil on canvas, 48 × 39½ in. Neither signed nor dated. Condition: Unknown.

Mrs. Macrae, born Roche; no other biographical data are available.

T.Q.L., to the right, wearing a white wrapping gown and a blue sash, supporting her left arm on a pedestal surmounted by a garden urn, and resting her head on her left hand; a background of sky and trees.

DATE: For similar portraits cf. no. 217, signed and dated 1767, and no. 254, signed and dated 1768. This kind of portrait, of a meditative lady leaning on a pedestal in a woodland scene, often occurs in Cotes's work between c. 1767 and 1770.

PROVENANCE: Anon. Sale, Christie's, Jul. 8, 1910 (lot 122), bought by A. Wertheimer, Esq., London; Mr. William H. Sage, U.S.A.; William H. Sage Sale, American Art Association-Anderson Galleries, New York, Nov. 15, 1935 (lot 34), illus., bought by Emil Schwartzhaupt.

244. **A Lady, possibly of the Milles Family.** Present whereabouts unknown. Oil on canvas, 50 × 40 in. Neither signed nor dated. Condition: Unknown.
The sitter has been identified as Mary Milles (1765–1818), wife of Lewis Watson, 2nd Baron Sondes. Since she appears to be about twenty years old in the portrait, this identification is impossible; Mary Milles was only five years old when Cotes died in 1770.
T.Q.L., to the left, wearing a white wrapping gown and a blue and gold sash and holding flowers in her left hand, which she rests on a fountain sculptured in the form of a dolphin; a landscape background.

DATE: From the late 1800's until the 1920's the portrait was attributed to Reynolds, and even appears in the catalogue of Reynolds's work by Graves and Cronin (1901). In more recent times it has been given to Cotes. The style and quality of the painting strongly indicate Cotes's hand. One recalls portraits by Cotes, such as that of Lady Dering, no. 217, signed and dated 1767, and that of Mary Fletcher, no. 236, c. 1767–1770, in which the sitter is posed in a similar attitude and painted in a like manner. A date of c. 1767–1770 is suggested.

PROVENANCE: The Earl Sondes, Elmham Hall, Norfolk; The Earl Sondes Sale, Christie's, May 9, 1896 (lot 126), illus., sold as by Reynolds, bought in; Anon. Sale, Christie's, May 8, 1897 (lot 40), as by Reynolds, bought in; Anon. Sale, Christie's, Je. 3, 1905 (lot 84), as by Reynolds, bought by P. and D. Colnaghi, London; L. H. McCormick, Esq., London; L. H. McCormick Sale, Christie's, Dec. 1, 1922 (lot 17), illus., bought by Lady Bullough; by family descent to Hermione, Countess of Durham, U.K.; Countess of Durham Sale, Christie's, Nov. 21, 1975 (lot 77).

EXHIBITIONS: 'The British Empire Exhibition', Palace of Arts, Wembley, 1924, no. v. 29 (lent by Lady Bullough).

REFERENCES: Algernon Graves and William Vine Cronin, *A History of the Works of Sir Joshua Reynolds, P.R.A.*, Vol. II, London, 1901, p. 647, catalogued as by Reynolds.

245. **Richard Myddelton** (fig. 63). Lieutenant-Colonel Ririd Myddelton, Chirk Castle, Chirk, Denbighshire. Oil on canvas, 50 × 40 in. Neither signed nor dated. Condition: Excellent.
Richard Myddelton of Chirk Castle, 1725–1795, son of John Myddelton.
T.Q.L., to the front, wearing a red jacket and holding a black hat under his left arm, which he rests on the back of a green chair; his left hand is open, in a gesture that one might make in conversation; a green curtain in the background.
Pendant to no. 246.

DATE: The casual elegance of the pose, and the care and precision with which the picture is painted, are characteristic of Cotes's best male portraits from c. 1767–1770; e.g. no. 279 (1769).

PROVENANCE: By family descent from the sitter to the present owner.

EXHIBITIONS: 'Introducing Francis Cotes, R.A.', Nottingham University Art Gallery, Nov. 5–27, 1971, no. 33 (lent by the present owner); illus. in cat. (frontispiece).

REFERENCES: *CAN.*, pp. 50 (fig. 45), 51; *PW.*, Vol. I, p. 86, no. 26 and Pl. 15c.

246. **Elizabeth Myddelton.** Lieutenant-Colonel Ririd Myddelton, Chirk Castle, Chirk, Denbighshire. Oil on canvas, 50 × 40 in. Neither signed nor dated. Condition: Excellent.
Elizabeth Myddelton, daughter of Sir John Rushout, 4th Bt., and wife of Richard Myddelton of Chirk Castle; cf. no. 245.
T.Q.L., to the left, wearing a blue wrapping gown and a blue cloak, resting her left arm on a pedestal, near the base of a column, and holding a pink turban in her left hand; a background of sky and trees.

DATE: The pose of the sitter and the quality of the painting recall similar pictures by Cotes; e.g. no. 217, signed and dated 1767, and nos. 236 and 244, both from c. 1767–1770. A date of c. 1767–1770 is therefore suggested.

PROVENANCE: By family descent from the sitter to the present owner.

EXHIBITIONS: 'Introducing Francis Cotes, R.A.', Nottingham University Art Gallery, Nov. 5–27, 1971, no. 34 (lent by the present owner).

REFERENCES: *PW.*, Vol. I, p. 86, no. 27.

A half-length copy in oils was sold anonymously at Christie's, Nov. 18, 1966 (lot 98). The sitter was incorrectly identified as 'Lady Lascelles'.

247. **Anne Sawbridge.** Present whereabouts unknown. Oil on canvas, 50 × 40 in. Neither signed nor dated. Condition: Unknown.
Anne Sawbridge, d. 1805, the daughter of Sir William Stephenson; in 1766 she married, as his second wife, John Sawbridge of Olantigh, Kent, who became Lord Mayor of London in 1775.
T.Q.L., to the front, wearing a white wrapping gown with a blue and gold sash, resting her left arm on a stone pedestal surmounted by a garden urn, and holding her skirt with her right hand; a background of sky and trees.

DATE: The portrait is very similar to nos. 234 and 241, both from c. 1767–1770. The same date is suggested here.

PROVENANCE: A. Hirsch, Esq., England; Thomas Agnew and Sons, London, purchased the picture in 1900, and in the same year sold it to M. Eugene Fischhof, Paris; Mr. P. A. B. Widener, Philadelphia; P. A. B. Widener Sale, Philadelphia, Je. 20–24, 1944 (lot 426), bought by Freeman and Co., Philadelphia.

For Cotes's other portrait of Mrs. Sawbridge, cf. no. 301.

248. **Miss Somerville (Summerville).** California Palace of the Legion of Honor, San Francisco, California. Oil on canvas, 30¼ × 25¼ in. Neither signed nor dated. Condition: Some damage to the paint due possibly to overcleaning.
The identification of the sitter, with either spelling, is traditional; nothing is known of its nature or source.
H.L., to the left, wearing a blue wrapping gown and a white cloak; a plain background.

DATE: The style of the portrait is similar to that of other small half-length oil paintings Cotes did between c. 1766 and 1770; cf. nos. 232 and 249, both c. 1767–1770, and no. 295, signed and dated 1770. A date of c. 1767–1770 is therefore suggested.

PROVENANCE: W. Lockett Agnew, Esq., London (c. 1898–1918); purchased from Mrs. W. Lockett Agnew in 1918 by M. Knoedler and Co., London; purchased from Knoedler's in 1919 by Scott and Fowles, New York; Scott and Fowles Sale, American Art Association-Anderson Galleries, New York, Nov. 19, 1926 (lot 68), illus., identified as Miss Summerville, bought by Lewis and Simmons, U.S.A.; Dr. D. Vandergrift, Chicago; John Levy Galleries, New York; purchased from the Levy Galleries by

Mr. H. K. S. Williams, U.S.A. for the Mildred Anna Williams Collection. In 1943 the picture became part of the Williams Collection at the California Palace of the Legion of Honor.

EXHIBITIONS: 'A Loan Exhibition of Portraits', City of Birmingham Museum and Art Gallery, 1903, no. 42, illus. (lent by W. Lockett Agnew), identified as 'Miss Somerville'.

249. **Charlotte Spencer.** The Lord Templemore, Dunbrody Park, Arthurstown, Co. Wexford, Ireland. Oil on canvas, 29½ × 24 in. Neither signed nor dated. Condition: Excellent.
Charlotte Spencer, d. 1789, the daughter of Conway Spencer of Tremary; in 1788 she married as his second wife Arthur Chichester, Earl and later 1st Marquess of Donegall.
H.L., head to the right, shoulders to the front, wearing a dress with lace ruffles at the sleeves and an ermine cloak; a bare wall in the background.

DATE: Like no. 248, this portrait is illustrative of the type of small half-length oil paintings Cotes did between c. 1767 and 1770; in quality and style it is particularly close to no. 295, signed and dated 1770. A date of c. 1767–1770 is therefore suggested.

PROVENANCE: By family descent from the sitter to the present owner.

250. **Lady Stanhope and Lady Effingham as Diana and Her Companion** (fig. 86). The Earl of Mexborough, Methley Park, Leeds, Yorkshire. The portrait has been on loan to Temple Newsam House, Leeds, since 1957. Oil on canvas, 94½ × 60 in. Neither signed nor dated. Inscribed with the sitters' names, on the ground at the feet of each figure:

THE HON[able] LADY STANHOPE
KATH[n] COUNT[s] OF EFFINGHAM.

Condition: The figures are well-preserved but the background is somewhat marred by creases in the canvas, which appear to have resulted from a stretching, in which a wide border along the edges of the portrait was folded behind a frame. The present frame, a highly elaborate and fascinating creation in itself, is a version of the one made about 1762 for Reynolds's portrait of Lord and Lady Pollington. Exactly when Cotes's portrait was put into this particular frame is not known.
Lady Stanhope, born Anne Hussey Delaval (d. 1812), was the third wife of Sir William Stanhope.
The Countess of Effingham, born Catherine Proctor, 1746–1791, married Thomas, 3rd Earl of Effingham, in 1765.
F.L. Lady Stanhope, as Diana the huntress, head to the right, shoulders to the left, wearing a pink and yellow wrapping gown with a sash; in her right hand she holds a spear, and with her left hand she points to a stag in the background. Lady Effingham is facing to the left, wearing a blue wrapping gown with a white and gold sash; at Diana's command she unleashes a hound, which is about to give chase to the stag in the distance; in the middle ground is a mound of earth and rock; in the background a landscape with the stag.

DATE: Grand, full-length portraits of women occur in Cotes's work between 1766 and 1770. His first signed and dated double portrait in oils, no. 216, was done in 1767. The style and quality of this picture recalls no. 219, signed and dated 1767. A date of c. 1767–1770 is therefore suggested.

PROVENANCE: By family descent from Lady Stanhope to her sister, Lady Mexborough, and thence to the present owner.

EXHIBITIONS: The picture has been on exhibit at Temple Newsam House, Leeds, since 1957.

REFERENCES: Anon., 'Pictures from Yorkshire Houses', *The Connoisseur*, Vol. 142, no. 571, Aug. 1958, p. 26 (illus., top left). Under the illustration is a note on Professor E. K. Waterhouse's interpretation of the meaning of the picture; cf. below; Anon., 'A Portrait by Francis Cotes', *Leeds Art Calendar*, Vol. 12, no. 39, Spring, 1958, pp. 25, 26 (Pl. 14), 27 (Pl. 15); Anon., 'The Prince's Room at Temple Newsam', *Leeds Art Calendar*, Vol. 12, no. 38, Winter, 1957, pp. 23–25; E. K. Waterhouse, *Three Decades of British Art, 1740–1770*, Jayne Lectures for 1964, Philadelphia, American Philosophical Society, 1965, p. 69 and fig. 17.
Lady Stanhope had separated from her husband in 1763. It is thought that she went to live with her sister Lady Mexborough. In Prof. Waterhouse's opinion, this portrait is probably related to the private theatricals staged by Lady Stanhope's and Lady Mexborough's brother, Sir Francis Blake Delaval.
For other portraits by Cotes with literary or allegorical themes, cf. nos. 96, 99, 179, 183, and 219.

c. 1767–1770: Lost portraits, known only through engravings, nos. 251 and 252.

251. **Lady Catherine Beauclerk.** Present whereabouts unknown. Medium and measurements unknown. Possibly signed and dated. Condition: Unknown.
Engraved by Francesco Bartolozzi and published in 1778 with the following inscription: F Cotes pinxit. F. Bartolozzi delin[t] et sculpsit. / The Right Honorable Lady Catherine Beauclerk.
Lady Catherine Beauclerk, d. 1789, born Lady Catherine Ponsonby, daughter of the 2nd Earl of Bessborough; in 1763 she married Aubrey Beauclerk, who succeeded in 1787 as Duke of St. Albans.
H.L., head to the right, shoulders to the left, in an oval, wearing a wrapping gown, a sash, and a cloak edged with fur; a plain background.

DATE: The sitter's hair style has the egg-like shape that was popular in the late 1760's. The original portrait was of the same type as that of Mrs. Brocas, no. 232, c. 1767–1770. A date of c. 1767–1770 is suggested.

PROVENANCE: Unknown.

REFERENCES: A. de Vesme and A. Calabi, *Francesco Bartolozzi, Catalogue des Estampes*, Milan, Guido Modiano, 1928, p. 270, no. 1041.

252. **Admiral Sir Edward Hawke.** Present whereabouts unknown. Medium and measurements unknown. Possibly signed and dated. Condition: Unknown.
Engraved by Francesco Bartolozzi and published in 1796 with the following inscription: Painted by Coates Engraved by F. Bartolozzi / Lord Hawke / From a Painting by Coates the Property / of William Locker Esq. / Lieut Gov[r] of Greenwich Hospital.
Cf. nos. 238 and 239.
H.S., head to the left, shoulders to the front, wearing the same costume as in nos. 238 and 239.

DATE: The similarity between this picture and nos. 238 and 239 suggests a date of c. 1767–1770.

PROVENANCE: William Locker, Esq., Greenwich Hospital (1796).

REFERENCES: A. de Vesme and A. Calabi, *Francesco Bartolozzi, Catalogue des Estampes*, Milan, Guido Modiano, 1928, p. 231, no. 835; *O'D.*, Vol. VI, p. 209, no. 3. O'Donoghue assumed that the source of Bartolozzi's engraving was the same as Hall's. This is false. Hall engraved no. 238, Bartolozzi, no. 252.

1768: Portraits in oils, signed and dated, nos. 253–264.

253. **Lady Boynton.** Dr. and Mrs. Henry Clay Frick, Alpine, New Jersey. Oil on canvas, 94½ × 58 in. Signed and dated at the lower left: FCotes px[t] 1768. F and C in monogram. Condition: Excellent.
Engraved in mezzotint by James Watson and published in 1770.
Lady Boynton, d. 1815, born Mary Heblethwayte; in 1768 she married, as his second wife, Sir Griffith Boynton, 6th Bt., of Barmston, Yorkshire. After his death in 1778, she married John Parkhurst of Catesby Abbey, Yorkshire.
F.L., head to the front, shoulders to the left, wearing a rose, brown, and gold dress, holding her skirt with her left hand and a bouquet of flowers in her right hand; her right arm rests on a stone pedestal; a background of sky and trees.
Pendant to no. 279.

PROVENANCE: By family descent from the sitter to Capt. T. L. Wickham Boynton, Burton Agnes Hall, Driffield, Yorkshire; E. Trevelyan Turner, Esq., U.K.; Thomas Agnew and Sons, London, purchased the portrait from Mr. Turner in 1911, and in the same year sold it to M. Knoedler and Co., London. It was purchased from Knoedler's in New York in 1915 by Mr. Henry Clay Frick, Eagle Rock, Pride's Crossing, Massachusetts; Miss Helen Clay Frick, Pride's Crossing; the present owners received the portrait from Miss Frick in 1959.

EXHIBITIONS: 'Exhibitions of English Masters', M. Knoedler and Co., London, 1911, no. 12 (lent by the gallery).
'The Inaugural Exhibition', The Minneapolis Institute of Arts, 1915, no. 72 (lent by M. Knoedler and Co., New York).

REFERENCES: *CWO.*, p. 250; *O'D.*, Vol. I, p. 227; *EG.*, Pl. 15.

254. **Lady Bridges.** The Lord Fitzwalter, Goodnestone Park, Canterbury, Kent. Oil on canvas, 50 × 40 in. Signed and dated at the lower left: FCotes R.A. px[t] 1768. F and C in monogram. Condition: Unknown.
Engraved in mezzotint by James Watson and published in 1769.
Lady Bridges, 1746–1825, born Frances Fowler, the daughter of Edmund Fowler of Graces, Essex; in 1765 she married Sir Brook Bridges, 3rd Bt.
T.Q.L., to the left, wearing a pink wrapping gown and a green cloak, leaning her right arm on a sculptured stone pedestal and resting her head on her right hand; with her left hand she holds her skirt; a background of sky and trees.

PROVENANCE: By family descent from the sitter to the present owner.

EXHIBITIONS: 'The Second Special Exhibition of National Portraits Commencing with the Reign of William and Mary and Ending with the Year MDCCC', London, The South Kensington Museum, May 1, 1867, no. 777 (lent by Sir Brook Bridges).
'An Exhibition of Old Masters from Houses in Kent', Tower House, Canterbury, Je. 11 – Jul. 8, 1937, no. 46 (lent by Mrs. George Plumptre).

REFERENCES: *BPP.*, p. 74; *O'D.*, Vol. I, p. 238, no. 1.

255. **Lewis Cage** (fig. 72). Private Collection, U.K. Oil on canvas, 66½ × 43½ in. Inscribed, signed and dated at the lower left on the cricket bat: Lewis Cage Aet: 15 / FCotes R.A. px[t] 1768. F and C in monogram. Condition: Excellent.
Engraved in mezzotint by L. Busière.
Lewis Cage of Milgate Park, Maidstone, Kent, b. 1753.
F.L., head to the right, shoulders slightly to the left, wearing an unbuttoned green waistcoat, a white shirt open at the neck, and green breeches that have come unbuttoned at his left knee. He stands in a pose which Van Dyck was fond of using. His left foot is forward, and his left hand rests on his hip. In his right hand he holds a cricket bat. In the background is a ball, a wicket made of twigs, and a landscape.

PROVENANCE: By family descent from the sitter to Lord Brocket, Brocket Hall, Welwyn, Hertfordshire; Lord Brocket Sale, Sotheby's, Jul. 16, 1952 (lot 20), bought in through Delafont; the present owner.

EXHIBITIONS: Probably exhibited at the R.A., 1769, no. 23, cf. Appendix III for the original entry and for Walpole's remark: 'Very pretty.' Northcote also refers to 'a boy playing at cricket by Mr. Cotes' as being exhibited at the Royal Academy in 1769. Judging from the catalogue descriptions of the exhibited paintings, the portrait would have had to be no. 23.
'Exhibition of British Art, c. 1000–1860', R.A., London, 1934, no. 368 (lent by Lord Brocket).
'British Painting in the 18th Century', Arts Council Exhibition, Montreal Museum of Fine Art, Montreal, 1957; National Gallery, Ottawa, 1957–58; Art Gallery of Toronto, 1958; Museum of Fine Arts, Toledo, 1958, no. 5 (lent by Lord Brocket).

REFERENCES: James Northcote, R.A., *The Life of Sir Joshua Reynolds*, Vol. I, London, Henry Colburn, 1819, p. 184.

There is a copy at Lords Cricket Grounds, London. Another copy is in the collection of Sir Oliver Crosthwaite-Eyre, Warrens, Lyndhurst, Hampshire. This picture was scheduled to be sold at Christie's in 1973 (Anon. Sale, Je. 22, 1973, lot 72) but was withdrawn when it was seen to be a copy.

256. **Mrs. William Colquhoun** (fig. 84). Present whereabouts unknown. Oil on canvas, 93 × 56½ in. Inscribed, signed and dated at the right on a pedestal: Mrs. Colquhoun, mother of Mrs. Edward Coke / Francis Cotes R.A. px[t] / 1768. F and C in monogram. Condition: Unknown.
Mrs. William Colquhoun, the wife of William Colquhoun of Wrotham, Norfolk.
F.L., head to the left, shoulders to the front, wearing a lilac wrapping gown, a green sash, and a green cloak, leaning her left arm on a stone pedestal surmounted by a garden urn, and resting her head on her left hand; with her right hand she holds her skirt; a background of sky and trees.

PROVENANCE: By family descent from the sitter to the Hon. Edward Keppel Coke, Longford Hall, Longford, Derbyshire; Hon. Edward Keppel Coke Sale, Christie's, Apr. 27, 1917 (lot 129), bought by A. Wertheimer, Esq., London; M. Knoedler and Co., New York (1924).

EXHIBITIONS: 'Exhibition of English Eighteenth-Century Portraits', Rhode Island School of Design, Providence, Nov. 12–30, 1932, no. 7 (lent by M. Knoedler and Co., New York).

REFERENCES: *CWO.*, p. 250.

257. **William Craven, 6th Baron Craven** (Pl. IV). Worcester Art Museum, Worcester, Massachusetts. Oil on canvas, 49½ × 39¾ in. Signed and dated at the lower left on a piece of wood nailed to a tree: FCotes px^{t} 1768. F and C in monogram. Condition: Excellent.
Lord Craven, 1738–1791; in 1767 he married Elizabeth, daughter of Augustus, 4th Earl of Berkeley.
T.Q.L., seated, to the right, wearing a green coat, holding a hunting whip under his left arm, a black hat in his left hand, and a scarf in his right hand; a landscape background.

PROVENANCE: Mrs. Arabella Laura Prichard of Athgaine, The Parade, Budleigh Salterton, Devon; Arabella Laura Prichard Sale, Christie's, May 9, 1958 (lot 33), incorrectly identified as Lord Charles Craven, bought by Mr. H. Sperling of F. Kleinberger and Co., New York, on behalf of Mr. and Mrs. Chester D. Heywood of Worcester, Massachusetts, who gave the portrait to the museum in 1962.

EXHIBITIONS: 'Seventy-five Masterworks', Portland Art Museum, Portland, Oregon, Dec. 12 – Jan. 21, 1968 (lent by the Worcester Art Museum).

REFERENCES: Anon., 'La Chronique des Arts', *Supplément à la Gazette des Beaux-Arts*, no. 1129, Feb. 1963, p. 67; Anon. *Worcester Art Museum Annual Report*, Worcester, 1963, pp. ix, xiii; Ruth Davidson, 'In the Museum', *Antiques*, Vol. 83, no. 4, Apr. 1963, p. 464 (illus.); Daniel Catton Rich, 'A Splendid Portrait by Francis Cotes', *Worcester Art Museum News Bulletin and Calendar*, Vol. XXVIII, no. 1, Oct. 1962, pp. 1, 2.

258. **Sir Robert Cunliffe, 2nd Bt.** Walker Art Gallery, Liverpool. Oil on canvas, 50¼ × 40 in. Signed and dated: FCotes px^{t} / 1768. F and C in monogram. Condition: Restored, after being badly damaged by fire in 1953.
Sir Robert Cunliffe, 2nd Bt., 1719–1778; in 1752 he married Mary, daughter of Ichabod Wright of Nottingham, cf. no. 176; he succeeded as 2nd baronet in 1767.
T.Q.L., to the right, wearing a plum-coloured jacket and a sword at his left side, resting his left hand on a wooden walking stick, and holding a hat in his right hand; a background of sky and trees.

PROVENANCE: By family descent from the sitter to Sir Foster Cunliffe, Bt., Acton Hall, near Wrexham, Denbighshire; Sir Foster Cunliffe Sale, Sotheby's, Feb. 1, 1950 (lot 108), bought by Thomas Agnew and Sons, London; Mr. Cunliffe Fraser, U.K.; Walker Art Gallery (1953).

EXHIBITIONS: 'Selected Acquisitions of the Walker Art Gallery, Liverpool, 1945–1955', Thomas Agnew and Sons, London, 1955, no. 26 (lent by the Walker Art Gallery).

259. **A Lady** (fig. 77). National Gallery, London; a life interest being reserved for a private collector. Oil on canvas, 50 × 40 in. Signed and dated at the middle right on the trunk of a tree: FCotes R.A. px^{t} / 1768. F and C in monogram. Condition: Good.
The sitter was traditionally believed to be Kitty Fisher. In 1953 Professor Waterhouse pointed out that Kitty Fisher died in 1767, and did not resemble this sitter (cf. below, Waterhouse). The old identification should definitely be discarded. Since the picture originally came from the collection of the Earl of Hardwicke, one suspects that the sitter was a member of the Yorke family (Yorke being the family name of the Earls of Hardwicke). In this connection, it is interesting to note that Cotes painted Agneta Yorke in 1767/68, no. 228. She was the second wife of the Hon. Charles Yorke, second son of the 1st Earl of Hardwicke.
T.Q.L., seated, to the left, wearing a pink and white dress; a background of sky and trees.

PROVENANCE: The Earl of Hardwicke; The Earl of Hardwicke Sale, Christie's, Je. 30, 1883 (lot 52), bought by Murray; Charles Butler, Esq., U.K., who exhibited the picture in 1889 and 1891; James Orrock, Esq., who exhibited the picture in 1904; James Orrock Sale, Christie's, Je. 4, 1904 (lot 75), illus., bought by Thomas Agnew and Sons, London; Sir Edward Stern, London, who bequeathed the portrait to the National Gallery, London, in 1933, reserving a life interest for a private collector.

EXHIBITIONS: 'Exhibition of Works by the Old Masters and by Deceased Masters of the British School', R.A., London, Winter, 1889, no. 146 (lent by Charles Butler, Esq.).
'Exhibition of the Royal House of Guelph', The New Gallery, London, 1891, no. 236 (lent by Charles Butler, Esq.).
'Pictures, Decorative Furniture, and Other Works of Art', The Burlington Fine Arts Club, London, 1904, no. 24 (lent by Sir Edward Stern).

REFERENCES: Tancred Borenius, *La Peinture Anglaise au XVIIIme Siècle*, Paris, Hyperion, 1938, Pl. 44; H. Isherwood Kay, 'The Stern Bequest to the National Gallery', *The Connoisseur*, Vol. 92, no. 386, Oct. 1933, pp. 271–274; Martin Davies, *British School*, National Gallery Catalogues, London, 1946, p. 41, no. 4689; *PFC.*, pp. 6, 10 (fig. 6); *PIB.*, p. 183, and Pl. 162B.

260. **A Lady.** Private Collection, England. Oil on canvas, 35 × 25 in. Signed and dated at the lower left: FCotes px^{t} / 1768. F and C in monogram. Condition: Excellent.
H.L., seated, to the left, wearing a dress with bows at the sleeves, a shawl over her shoulders, and a lace bonnet; a plain background.

PROVENANCE: P. and D. Colnaghi, London; Gooden and Fox, London. The present owner purchased the painting from Gooden and Fox in 1967.

261. **Charles Howard, 10th Duke of Norfolk.** Simon Birch, Esq., Brantham Glebe, Manningtree, Essex. Oil on canvas, 49 × 39 in. Signed and dated at the middle right on a column base: FCotes px^{t} 1768. F and C in monogram. Condition: Good.
The 10th Duke of Norfolk, 1720–1786.
A certain amount of difficulty has arisen concerning the identity of the sitter. At the Norfolk Sale he was merely called a 'Gentleman'. In a private collection in Washington, D.C., where there is a copy of the portrait, the sitter was called Alderman Boydell, even though he looked nothing like Boydell. Opie's picture of Charles Howard, 10th Duke of Norfolk, published by Lady Victoria Manners in 1926, is very clearly of the same person who sat to Cotes for this portrait.

T.Q.L., seated, head to the left, shoulders to the right, wearing a maroon jacket, resting his left arm on some papers that lie on a desk; also on the desk are a silver ink stand and two books, one marked 'Shakespeare', the other, 'Milton'; in his right hand he holds a quill pen; the background is plain except for a column on the right.

PROVENANCE: By family descent from the sitter to the Duke of Norfolk (1938); the Duke of Norfolk Sale, Christie's, Feb. 11, 1938 (lot 76) sold as 'Portrait of a Gentleman', bought by the father of the present owner.

REFERENCES: Lady Victoria Manners, 'The Later Historical Portraits in the Collection of the Duke of Norfolk, E.M., at Arundel Castle', *The Connoisseur*, Je. 1926, Vol. LXXV, no. 298, p. 79, Pl. III (John Opie's portrait of the 10th Duke of Norfolk).

262. **Margaret Rogers.** Present whereabouts unknown. Oil on canvas, 50 × 40 in. Signed and dated at the middle left on a tree: FCotes px[t] 1768. F and C in monogram. Condition: Unknown. The portrait is illustrated in the Arthur Tooth and Sons sale catalogue of 1925. At the Witt and Frick Libraries there are also photographs of the portrait which were taken when it was in the Meinhard collection. By comparing the catalogue illustration with the library photographs, one can see that the head was repainted at some point after the Tooth sale and before the Meinhard photographs were taken. In the Tooth illustration the face is quite plump and relatively plain; in the later photographs it has been transformed into that of a much younger and more attractive woman. Margaret Rogers, c. 1727–1786, daughter of Jonathan Tyers, founder of Vauxhall Gardens; she married George Rogers of Southampton.

PROVENANCE: Lieutenant-Colonel C. P. Boyd Hamilton, Brandon House, Brandon, Essex; C. P. Boyd-Hamilton Sale, Brandon House, Sept. 5, 1919 (lot 612), illus., bought by Arthur Tooth and Sons, London; Arthur Tooth and Sons Sale, American Art Association, New York, Feb. 19, 1925 (lot 74), illus.; Leggatt Brothers, London; Mr. William Johns Ralston, New York; William Johns Ralston Sale, American Art Association, New York, March 12, 1926 (lot 81), bought by Mrs. Morton H. Meinhard, New York; Mrs. Meinhard still owned the picture in 1949, but its present whereabouts are unknown.

263. **Benjamin Vaughan.** Museum of Fine Arts, Boston. Oil on canvas, 50 × 40 in. Signed and dated at the middle left: FCotes px[t] 1768. F and C in monogram. Condition: Good.
Benjamin Vaughan, 1713–86, born in Ballyhoe, Co. Tipperary; in 1736 he married Hannah Halfhide (cf. no. 264). The sitter was a scrivener in London. He is buried at Great Parndon, Essex.
T.Q.L., head to the right, shoulders to the left, wearing a brown jacket, on his lap he holds a large book marked 'Ledger'; the top part of the book rests against a desk, which has an inkstand on it; red drapery in the background.
Pendant to no. 264.

PROVENANCE: The Vaughan family of Great Parndon, Essex; the portrait was purchased between 1900 and 1905 by an American relative, Mr. Benjamin Vaughan, Cambridge, Massachusetts; thence by family descent to Mr. Samuel Vaughan and Mrs. Mary Vaughan Marvin, who gave the picture to the Museum of Fine Arts in 1948.

EXHIBITIONS: 'British Painting in the Eighteenth Century', Arts Council Exhibition, Montreal Museum of Fine Arts, 1957; National Gallery, Ottawa, 1957–58; Art Gallery of Toronto, 1958; Museum of Fine Arts, Toledo, 1958; no. 4 (lent by the Museum of Fine Arts, Boston).

264. **Hannah Vaughan.** Museum of Fine Arts, Boston. Oil on canvas, 50 × 40 in. Signed and dated at the lower left: FCotes px[t] 1768. F and C in monogram. Condition: Good.
Hannah Vaughan, d. 1787, born Hannah Halfhide, the wife of Benjamin Vaughan (no. 263).
T.Q.L., seated, to the left, wearing a mauve dress, a green cloak and a lace bonnet; green drapery in the background.
Pendant to no. 263.

PROVENANCE: As in no. 263.

Exhibited in 1768: A portrait in pastels, no. 265.

265. **Polly Jones.** Present whereabouts unknown. Pastel on paper, measurements unknown. Possibly signed and dated. Condition: Unknown.
Miss Kennedy, alias Polly Jones, the famous courtesan.

PROVENANCE: Francis Cotes Sale, Langford and Son, London, Feb. 23, 1771, p. 12, lot 25, 'One ditto (head in crayons) of Miss Jones, fram'd and glaz'd.' Cf. Appendix II.

EXHIBITIONS: Society of Artists, 1768, no. 32, 'A lady's head in crayons'. Walpole added, 'Polly Jones,' Cf. Appendix III.

REFERENCES: Francis Cotes, notes on crayon painting, *The European Magazine*, Feb. 1797, p. 84, cf. Appendix IV; *WA.*, p. 111.

For a portrait of Polly Jones incorrectly attributed to Cotes, cf. Appendix VI, no. 43.

c. 1768–1770: Portraits in oils, neither signed nor dated, nos. 266–270.

266. **An Artist.** Mr. and Mrs. Paul Mellon Collection, U.S.A. Oil on canvas, 44¼ × 34⅝ in. Neither signed nor dated. Condition: Excellent.
Traditionally, this picture has been known as a self-portrait by Francis Cotes. The only reliable portrait of Cotes which has come to light is D. P. Pariset's engraving of 1768 (Pl. III). Clearly, the sitter in the Mellon picture does not resemble Francis Cotes.
T.Q.L., seated, to the left, wearing a green coat; with his left hand he supports a portfolio of drawings, which rests on his right leg; on the back of the portfolio is a sheet of paper, on which he is sketching a landscape with a large tree in the foreground; the sketching pen is in his left hand; a landscape background.

DATE: The portrait is from Cotes's latest period. Two close parallels are offered from among the artist's signed and dated works: the portrait of Lord Craven at Worcester, no. 257 (1768), and the portrait of Sir William Jones, Bt., no. 282 (1769). A date of c. 1768–1770 is suggested.

PROVENANCE: Anon. Sale, Christie's, Mar. 13, 1905 (lot 24), as a self-portrait by Francis Cotes, bought by Turner; Anon. Sale, Sotheby's, Jul. 7, 1964 (lot 83), illus., as a self-portrait by Francis Cotes, bought by P. and D. Colnaghi, London; the present owner.

REFERENCES: *The Burlington Magazine*, Vol. 107, no. 747, Je. 1965, p. xiii (illus.).

For another so-called self-portrait, falsely attributed to Cotes, cf. Appendix VI, no. 62.

267. **A Baby as Cupid.** H.M. The Queen, Windsor Castle. Oil on canvas, 50¼ × 40⅜ in. Neither signed nor dated. Condition: Good.
A baby, probably Prince Edward, later Duke of Kent, 1767–1820, son of George III and Queen Charlotte, and father of Queen

Victoria. This tentative identification was suggested in 1969 by Oliver Millar, cf. References, *OML.*

F.L., seated, to the left. The baby is nude and has the wings of Cupid. He sits on a rock, which is covered by drapery. In his right hand he holds a festoon of flowers. His right foot rests on a straw basket that he has toppled over, allowing the flowers inside to spill out. Beneath the basket is his quiver of arrows. There is a landscape background.

DATE: The style is indicative of Cotes's work in the late 1760's. The baby appears to be about a year old. If he is Prince Edward, born in 1767, Cotes would have painted him between c. 1768 and 1770.

PROVENANCE: Probably by family descent to H.M. The Queen. For the inventories and other documents in which the portrait is recorded in the royal collection, cf. References, *OML.* It is especially interesting to note that the portrait was probably listed in 1872 in the collection of Queen Victoria at Frogmore House as a painting by Copley. The attribution to Copley was rightly discarded in 1969 by Oliver Millar.

REFERENCES: *OML.*, Vol. I, p. 23, no. 721; Vol. II, Pl. 35.

For a lost portrait by Cotes of Prince Edward, cf. Supplement, no. 16.

268. **Sir James Langham, 7th Bt.** Private Collection. Oil on canvas, 49½ × 39½ in. Neither signed nor dated. Condition: Excellent.
Sir James Langham, 7th Bt., 1736–1795.
T.Q.L., to the left, wearing an army officer's uniform, resting his right arm on a stone wall, and holding a three-cornered hat in his right hand; his left hand is in his left pocket; a background of sky and trees.

DATE: This portrait has a refinement and clarity which one finds in Cotes's paintings from c. 1768 to 1770. Among his signed and dated pictures, the portrait of Lord Craven, no. 257 (1768), best illustrates these qualities. A date of c. 1768–1770 is suggested.

PROVENANCE: Unknown.

269. **An Officer.** Christ Church, Oxford. Oil on canvas, 30 × 25 in. Neither signed nor dated. Condition: Excellent.
H.S., to the right, wearing an army officer's uniform; a plain background.

DATE: In style and quality the portrait recalls no. 294, signed and dated 1770. It is from Cotes's latest period. A date of c. 1768–1770 is suggested.

PROVENANCE: The Earl of Rosslyn, U.K.; Leggatt Brothers, London; in 1955 the portrait was purchased by Sir Richard Nosworthy, U.K.; Nosworthy Bequest to Christ Church (1966).

EXHIBITIONS: 'Old Masters and Scottish National Portraits', Edinburgh 1883, no. 137, without the name of the artist or the sitter.

REFERENCES: J. Byam Shaw, *Paintings by Old Masters at Christ Church, Oxford*, London, Phaidon Press, 1967, p. 133, no. 265.

270. **Master Smith** (fig. 75). The Lord Burton's Trustees, U.K. Oil on canvas, 67½ × 44 in. Neither signed nor dated. Condition: Excellent.
The identification is traditional; its nature and source are unknown.
F.L., to the left, wearing an open jacket and waistcoat and a white shirt open at the neck, holding a kite in his right hand; a landscape background.

DATE: This picture is quite similar to Cotes's earliest known full-length portrait of a child, that of Lewis Cage, no. 255, signed and dated 1768. A date of c. 1768–1770 is suggested.

PROVENANCE: It is not known exactly when the picture came into the Burton collection, but it was there as early as 1894.

EXHIBITIONS: 'Exhibition of Works by the Old Masters and by Deceased Masters of the British School', R.A., London, Winter, 1894, no. 38 (lent by Lord Burton of Rangemore and Burton-on-Trent).

Possibly 1768: A lost portrait, known only through an engraving, no. 271.

271. **The Right Rev. Charles Lyttleton, Bishop of Carlisle and President of the Society of Antiquaries.** Present whereabouts unknown. Medium and measurements unknown. Possibly signed and dated. Condition: Unknown.
Engraved in mezzotint by James Watson and published in 1770 with the inscription: F. Cotes pinx[t] J. Watson fecit. / Reverendus Admodum Carolus Lyttleton / Nuper Episcopus Carlislensis et Societatis Antiquariorum Praefes / Honoris et Gratitudinis Ergo / Voluit Soc. Art. Lond. 1770.
Charles Lyttleton, 1714–68.
T.Q.L., seated, head to the right, shoulders to the left, wearing a white alb and a stole; on his lap he holds an open book; a column and drapery in the background.

DATE: The original portrait was similar to nos. 261 and 263, both signed and dated 1768. Possibly it was done shortly before the sitter's death in 1768.

PROVENANCE: Unknown.

REFERENCES: *O'D.*, Vol. III, p. 113, no. 1.

1769: Portraits in pastel, signed and dated, nos. 272 and 273.

272. **Prince Ernst of Mecklenburg-Strelitz.** S. K. H. der Prinz von Hannover, Herzog zu Braunschweig und Lüneburg; the picture is on loan to the Bomann-Museum, Celle, Lower Saxony. Pastel on paper, 18¾ × 24½ in. Signed and dated at the middle right: FCotes R.A. / px[t] 1769. F and C in monogram. Condition: Excellent.
Prince Ernst, 1742–1814.
H.S., head to the left, shoulders to the right, wearing a jacket with insignia and a waistcoat with a ribbon across the chest; a plain background.

PROVENANCE: By family descent from the sitter to the present owner. The portrait was recorded in the Bedchamber in George III's inventory of Buckingham House, c. 1790–1795. It is not mentioned in later royal documents. Evidently, in the late 18th or early 19th century it was transferred to Hanover.

EXHIBITIONS: 'The Brunswick Art Treasures', The Victoria and Albert Museum, London, Aug. 1952 (lent by the present owner). 'Die Königin Caroline Mathilde und ihr Kreis', Bomann-Museum, Celle, Apr. 10 – Je. 30, 1960, no. 216 (lent by the present owner).

REFERENCES: Hester W. Chapman, *Caroline Matilda, Queen of Denmark*, London, Jonathan Cape, 1971, pp. 171, 180; Oliver Millar, 'The Brunswick Art Treasures at the Victoria and Alber

Museum: the Pictures', *The Burlington Magazine*, Vol. 94, no. 594, Sept. 1952, p. 266 (fig. 24, incorrectly identified as Christian VII of Denmark), p. 268; *OML.*, Vol. I, between pp. xx and xxi, fig. II, correctly identified as Prince Ernst of Mecklenburg-Strelitz, p. 21.

273. **Prince William Henry, Duke of Gloucester** (fig. 110). H.M. The Queen, Windsor Castle. Pastel on paper, 24 × 18 in. Signed and dated at the middle right: FCotes px[t] / 1769. F and C in monogram. Condition: Excellent.
The Duke of Gloucester, 1743–1805, son of Frederick, Prince of Wales; in 1766 he married Maria, Countess Dowager of Waldegrave (no. 143).
H.S., head to the left, shoulders to the front, wearing the scarlet and gold uniform of a colonel of the First Regiment of Foot Guards and the ribbon and star of the Garter; a plain background.

PROVENANCE: John Ambler, Esq., Thorpe Underwood Hall, Ouseburn, Yorkshire; John Ambler Sale, Christie's, May 4, 1933 (lot 101), bought by Lister for the royal collection.

EXHIBITIONS: Royal Academy, 1769, no. 27; Walpole remarked in his catalogue, 'Exceedingly like'; cf. Appendix III.
'Exhibition of the King's Pictures, R.A.', London, 1946–47, no. 78 (lent by King George VI).

REFERENCES: Oliver Millar, 'The Brunswick Art Treasures at the Victoria and Albert Museum: the Pictures', *The Burlington Magazine*, Vol. 94, no. 594, Sept. 1952, p. 268; *OML.*, Vol. I, p. 22, no. 719; Vol. II, Pl. 13.

1769: Portraits in oils, signed and dated, nos. 274–289 [see also Supplement nos. 17–19].

274. **Samuel Allpress.** Quentin Crewe, Esq., Netherset Hey, Madeley, Crewe, Cheshire. Oil on canvas, 36 × 28 in. Signed and dated at the left: FCotes R.A. / px[t] 1769. F and C in monogram. Condition: The background has been damaged somewhat, and the contours of the figure have lost their original sharpness.
Samuel Allpress was of the family of the Marquess of Crewe, but his precise genealogy is unknown.
H.L., to the right, wearing a green coat, holding a hat under his left arm, and resting his hand on a cane; a background of sky and foliage.
Pendant to no. 275.

PROVENANCE: By family descent from the sitter to the present owner.

EXHIBITIONS: 'An Exhibition of Treasures from Midland Homes', City of Birmingham Museum and Art Gallery, Nov. 2 – Dec. 2, 1938, no. 136 (lent by the Marquess of Crewe).
'Introducing Francis Cotes, R.A.', Nottingham University Art Gallery, Nov. 5–27, 1971, no. 35 (lent by the present owner).

275. **Mrs. Samuel Allpress.** Quentin Crewe, Esq., Netherset Hey, Madeley, Crewe, Cheshire. Oil on canvas, 36 × 28 in. Signed and dated at the lower left: FCotes R.A. / px[t] 1769. F and C in monogram. Condition: The paint has discoloured with age. The hair has been repainted in the style of the late 1770's and early 1780's.
For her husband, cf. no. 274.
H.L., seated, to the left, wearing a pink dress, resting both arms on a polished wooden table, which reflects her ruffles; a plain background.
Pendant to no. 274.

PROVENANCE: By family descent from the sitter to the present owner.

EXHIBITIONS: 'An Exhibition of Treasures from Midland Homes', City of Birmingham Museum and Art Gallery, Nov. 2 – Dec. 2, 1938, no. 140 (lent by the Marquess of Crewe).
'Introducing Francis Cotes, R.A.', Nottingham University Art Gallery, Nov. 5–27, 1971, no. 36 (lent by the present owner).

276. **Sir Edward Astley, 4th Bt.** The Lord Hastings, Swanton House, Melton Constable, Norfolk. Oil on canvas, 39½ × 29 in. Signed and dated at the lower right: FCotes R.A. / px[t] 1769. Inscribed on the back: Sir Edward Astley, Bart., taken in his 39th year. Condition: Excellent.
Sir Edward Astley, 4th Bt., 1729–1802; from 1751 to 1757 he was married to Rhoda, daughter of Sir Francis Blake Delaval. His second marriage, from 1759 to 1792, was with Anne, daughter of Christopher Milles of Nackington, Kent. His third wife was Elizabeth Bullen, whom he married in 1793.
H.L., head to the left, shoulders to the right, wearing a Van Dyck costume composed of a black doublet with a lace collar and cuffs; over his right shoulder is a rose cloak, which he holds with his left hand; between his left arm and his chest he supports a sword; a background of sky.

PROVENANCE: By family descent from the sitter to the present owner.

REFERENCES: *PN.*, Vol. II, p. 5, no. 18.

A miniature after this portrait was recorded in 1927 in the collection of Major Astley Cubitt, Thorpe Hall, Norfolk (cf. *PN.*, Vol. II, p. 349, no. 2).
Supplement no. 15 is of the sitter's daughter by Anne Milles. Nos. 221 and 244 are of members of the Milles family.

277. **Midshipman George Cranfield Berkeley** (fig. 71). R. J. G. Berkeley, Esq., Berkeley Castle, Berkeley, Gloucestershire. Oil on canvas, 30 × 25 in. Signed and dated at the lower right: FCotes R.A. / px[t] 1769. F and C in monogram. Condition: Excellent.
Midshipman Berkeley, 1753–1818, later Admiral Sir George Cranfield Berkeley; he was the son of the 5th Earl of Berkeley.
H.L., head to the left, shoulders to the right, wearing the blue and white uniform of a midshipman; he leans his right arm against a ship's cannon and holds a three-cornered hat in his right hand; the background consists of sea and sky with a shoreline in the distance.

PROVENANCE: By family descent from the sitter to the present owner.

EXHIBITIONS: The portrait is on exhibit at Berkeley Castle, which is open to the public at certain times of the year.

278. **Frederick Irby, 2nd Baron Boston** (fig. 59). Private Collection, U.K. Oil on canvas, 30 × 25 in. Signed and dated at the lower right FCotes R.A. px[t] / 1769. F and C in monogram. Condition: Excellent.
The 2nd Baron Boston, 1749–1825.
H.S., to the right, in a painted oval, wearing the blue and gold academic robes of a Fellow-Commoner of St. John's College, Cambridge; a plain background.

PROVENANCE: By family descent from the sitter to the present owner.

REFERENCES: *PW.*, Vol. I, p. 16, no. 21.

For another portrait by Cotes of a sitter in the robes of a Fellow-Commoner of St. John's College, Cambridge, cf. Supplement no. 14.

279. **Sir Griffith Boynton, 6th Bt.** (fig. 64). Dr. and Mrs. Henry Clay Frick, Alpine, New Jersey. Oil on canvas, 94½ × 58 in. Signed and dated at the lower left: FCotes R.A. pxt 1769. F and C in monogram.
Condition: Excellent.
Sir Griffith Boynton, d. 1778; in 1762 he married Charlotte, daughter of Francis Topham of York; she died in 1767, and in 1768 he married Mary, daughter of James Heblethwayte (no. 253). F.L., head to the right, shoulders to the front, wearing a buff coat, leaning his right arm on the back of a green chair and holding a book in his right hand; his left hand rests on his hip; to the right is an open window and a desk, on which there are a book, an inkstand, a candle, and some letters; on one of the letters is written: 'To Sir Griffith Boynton, Bt.'.
Pendant to no. 253.

PROVENANCE: By family descent from the sitter to Capt. T. L. Wickham Boynton, Burton Agnes Hall, Driffield, Yorkshire; E. Trevelyn Turner, Esq., U.K.; Thomas Agnew and Sons, London, purchased the portrait from Mr. Turner in 1911, and in the same year sold it to M. Knoedler and Co., London. It was purchased from Knoedler's, New York, in 1915, by Mr. Henry Clay Frick, Eagle Rock, Pride's Crossing, Massachusetts; Miss Helen Clay Frick; the present owners received the portrait from Miss Frick in 1959.

EXHIBITIONS: 'Exhibition of English Masters', M. Knoedler and Co., London, 1911, no. 10 (lent by the gallery).
'The Inaugural Exhibition', The Minneapolis Institute of Arts, 1915, no. 71 (lent by M. Knoedler and Co., New York).

280. **A Girl.** The Marquess of Salisbury, Hatfield House, Hatfield, Hertfordshire. Oil on canvas, 24½ × 19½ in. Signed and dated at the middle right: FCotes R.A. pxt / 1769. F and C in monogram.
Condition: Good.
In the Hatfield House Catalogue of 1891 the sitter was incorrectly identified as Mary Amelia Hill, 1st Marchioness of Salisbury (1750–1835), who would have been nineteen years old when the picture was painted. The child in the portrait is about three to seven years old. At the present time a new identification has not been established.
H.S., to the left, in an oval, wearing a low-necked dress with a flower pattern; a plain background.

PROVENANCE: The portrait was recorded at Hatfield House in 1891; cf. below.

EXHIBITIONS: The portrait is on exhibit at Hatfield House, which is open to the public at certain times of the year.

REFERENCES: Gifford Laurence Holland, *A Descriptive and Historical Catalogue of the Collection of Pictures at Hatfield House and 20 Arlington Street*, privately printed, 1891.

281. **Captain John Jervis** (fig. 68). National Portrait Gallery, London. Oil on canvas, 50 × 40 in. Signed and dated at the middle right: FCotes R.A. pxt / 1769. F and C in monogram. Inscribed bottom right: John, Earl of St. Vincent. Condition: Excellent.
Capt. John Jervis, 1734–1823; he became Admiral in 1799; in 1801 he became First Lord of the Admiralty and 1st Earl of St. Vincent. T.Q.L., head to the left, shoulders to the right, wearing a blue and white naval uniform; in the middleground is a mound of rock and earth, in the far background a seascape with a ship.

PROVENANCE: By family descent from the sitter to the Earl of Northesk, who loaned the picture to the National Portrait Gallery in 1924. It was purchased by the Gallery in 1948.

EXHIBITIONS: 'Introducing Francis Cotes, R.A.', Nottingham University Art Gallery, Nottingham, Nov. 5–27, 1971, no. 37 (lent by the National Portrait Gallery); illus. in cat. (Pl. XV).

REFERENCES: Anon., *Catalogue of the National Portrait Gallery, 1856–1947*, London, National Portrait Gallery, 1949, no. 2026; *CWO.*, pp. 245 (fig. no. II), 251.

282. **Sir William Jones, Bt.** Private Collection, England. Oil on canvas, 49¾ × 39¼ in. Signed and dated at the lower left: FCotes R.A. pxt / 1769. F and C in monogram. Condition: Unknown.
Sir William Jones, d. 1791; he married Elizabeth, daughter of William Jones of Ramsbury; she was the sister of Mary Eleanor Jones, who married Francis Burdett.

T.Q.L., seated, to the right, wearing a green coat, and leaning on what appears to be a fence; in his right hand he holds a walking stick, and in his left hand, a hat; a post, a tree, foliage, and sky are in the background.
Pendant to no. 283.

PROVENANCE: By family descent from the sitter to Sir Francis Burdett, 7th Bt., Ramsbury Manor, Ramsbury, Wiltshire; Sir Francis Burdett Sale, Sotheby's, Dec. 2, 1953 (lot 49), bought by Leggatt Brothers, London; the present owner.

283. **Lady Jones.** National Gallery of South Australia, Adelaide. Oil on canvas, 49½ × 39¼ in. Signed and dated 1769. Condition: Good.
Lady Jones, Elizabeth, daughter of William Jones of Ramsbury, and wife of Sir William Jones, Bt.
T.Q.L., to the right, wearing a pink and white dress and a bonnet, holding her train over her right arm and with her left hand pointing to the landscape in the background.
Pendant to no. 282.

PROVENANCE: By family descent from the sitter to Sir Francis Burdett, 7th Bt., Ramsbury Manor, Ramsbury, Wiltshire; Sir Francis Burdett Sale, Sotheby's, Dec. 2, 1953 (lot 54), as Elizabeth, wife of William Jones, bought by Spiller; Mr. Walter P. Chrysler, Jr., Provincetown, Massachusetts; Walter P. Chrysler Sale, Sotheby's, Jul. 15, 1959 (lot 87), illus., bought by the Leger Galleries, London, from whom the picture was purchased in 1961 by the National Gallery of South Australia.

REFERENCES: Anon., *Bulletin of the National Gallery of South Australia*, Vol. 23, no. 2, Oct. 1961, p. 1 and cover (illus.).

284. **A Lady and a Gentleman** (figs. 92, 93). The Museum of Fine Arts, Boston, has half of this portrait (fig. 93). The figure of the gentleman was cut off and is lost. This cutting down took place in the late 1920's or in 1930. By 1931 only the portrait of the lady was known to be in existence. Oil on canvas, 53 × 60 in. (original double portrait); 48 × 33⅛ in. (the surviving part, now at Boston). The double portrait was signed and dated at the middle right:

FCotes px[t] / 1769. F and C in monogram. This signature and date were cut away. Condition: Half of the portrait has been lost, as stated. The remaining portion has been badly overcleaned, damaging the colours of the lady's costume. The pedestal, on which she leans her left arm, has been painted out.

The sitters have been called Joah Bates (1740–99) and his wife, Sarah Harrop (d. 1811). He was the conductor of the Concerts of Ancient Music, and of the Handel Commemoration of 1784. His portrait by George Dance, done in 1794, was engraved by W. Daniell in 1809. Even allowing for the difference of age, the elderly Mr. Bates in the engraving looks nothing like the sitter in Cotes's portrait, nor does the lady look like Sarah Bates, who was painted by Angelica Kauffman and Ozias Humphrey. Finally, Joah and Sarah Bates were not married until 1780, after this portrait was painted. As Philip James has pointed out, the books which appear in the portrait probably tell us something of the gentleman's career. They are *Seldeni Opera* and Petyt's *Power of Parliaments*, which would indicate a legal or political vocation rather than a musical one.

T.Q.L.; the lady is facing to the right and is standing; the gentleman is seated and facing to the left. She wears a seventeenth century pink and gold costume. In her right hand she holds a scroll. She leans her left arm on a wooden pedestal and rests her head on her left hand. He wears a suit with the coat open. He turns to the lady and presents to her a biscuit statuette of a Cupid, seated, with one hand raised to the lips. This is a copy of Étienne Maurice Falconet's famous marble statuette called 'L'Amour Menaçant', made for Madame de Pompadour, exhibited at the Salon of 1757, and now in the Louvre. On the right, next to the gentleman, is a table with the books already mentioned. The background in the double portrait was plain, except for red drapery behind the lady, which is still visible on the Boston canvas.

PROVENANCE: Sacred Harmonic Society, London (as early as 1868); Sacred Harmonic Society Sale, Christie's, Mar. 3, 1883 (lot 83), the gentleman being identified as Joah Bates, conductor in 1784, bought by Parkington; A. H. Littleton, Esq., London; A. H. Littleton Sale, Elliot and Son, and Boynton, London, Mar. 13, 1915 (lot 344d), as Mr. and Mrs. Bates; the Ehrich Galleries, New York, 1920; when exhibited in San Francisco by the Ehrich Galleries the picture was still in its original state; the Vose Galleries, Boston. It is not known exactly when the Vose Galleries acquired the picture, but while in their possession, or shortly before, it was cut down, and the figure of the gentleman was evidently discarded. The remaining portion was called a portrait of Mrs. Bates. It was published by Keyes (cf. References, *RSC*) in 1931, while at the Vose Galleries. The Vose Galleries lent it to the Carnegie Institute, Pittsburgh, in 1938, and sold it in 1943 to Mr. Walter J. Noonan, U.S.A., who gave it to the Museum of Fine Arts in 1954.

EXHIBITIONS: 'The Third and Concluding Exhibition of National Portraits Commencing with the Fortieth Year of the Reign of George The Third and Ending with the Year 1868', South Kensington Museum, London, Apr. 13, 1868, no. 780, as Mr. and Mrs. Bates (lent by the Sacred Harmonic Society).

'Exhibition of Paintings by Old Masters', Palace of Fine Arts, San Francisco, 1920, no. 112, as Mr. and Mrs. Bates (lent by the Ehrich Galleries, New York).

'Survey of British Painting', Carnegie Institute, Pittsburgh, May 10 – Je. 12, 1938, no. 21, as Mrs. Bates (lent by the Vose Galleries, Boston).

REFERENCES: Anon., *Bulletin of the Museum of Fine Arts, Boston*, Vol. 53, Summer 1955, pp. 32, 35; *CWO.*, p. 250; Emilia Lady Dilke, *French Architects and Sculptors of the Eighteenth Century*, London, George Bell and Sons, 1900, pp. 106, 107 (illus., Falconet's 'L'Amour Menaçant'); Philip James, 'A Cotes Enigma', *The Connoisseur*, Vol. 90, no. 372, August 1932, pp. 98 (illus., the original double portrait), 99; *O'D.*, Vol. 1, p. 135, no. 2, Daniell's engraving of G. Dance's portrait of Joah Bates; *RSC.*, p. 218, fig. 3, the portrait after it was cut down.

285. **Frances Lee** (fig. 69). Milwaukee Art Center Collection, Milwaukee, Wisconsin; Gift of Mr. and Mrs. William D. Vogel. Oil on canvas, 36 × 28¼ in. Signed and dated at the lower right: FCotes R.A. px[t] / 1769. F and C in monogram. Condition: Unknown.

Frances Lee, 1758–1839, the daughter of Robert Cooper Lee of London and Roxhall, Jamica.

T.Q.L., to the left, wearing a pink dress and cap, and resting both hands on the back of a chair; in her right hand she holds a handkerchief tied into a knot to look like a rabbit; the background is plain, except for a green curtain on the left.

PROVENANCE: By family descent from the sitter to Percival Bosanquet, Esq., Ponfield, Little Berkhamstead, Hertfordshire; Percival Bosanquet Sale at Ponfield, Norris and Duval, Oct. 12–13, 1915 (lot 450); R. W. Partridge, Esq., London (1915); M. Knoedler and Co., London (1916); purchased in 1922 from Knoedler's by the Fearon Gallery, New York, who exhibited the picture in 1923; John Levy Galleries, New York; purchased from the Levy Galleries by M. Knoedler and Co., New York, in 1937; Mr. and Mrs. Ralph Booth, Detroit; by family descent to Mrs. William D. Vogel, Milwaukee, who gave the picture to the Milwaukee Art Center in 1964.

EXHIBITIONS: 'Old English Furniture and Paintings', New York City Colony Club, New York, Jan. 14–17, 1923, no. 12 (lent by the Fearon Gallery). The portrait is on exhibit at the Milwaukee Art Center.

REFERENCES: Anon., 'Accessions of American Museums', *The Art Quarterly*, Vol. 27, no. 2, 1964, p. 210, fig. 2, bottom; Tracy Atkinson, 'The Milwaukee Art Center', *Antiques*, Vol. 90, no. 5, Nov. 1966, pp. 662–667.

286. **Thomas Tracy of Sandywell and Stanway.** The Earl of Wemyss and March; the picture is on loan to Capt. Guy and Lady Violet Benson, Stanway, Gloucestershire. Oil on canvas, 29 × 24 in. Signed and dated at the lower left: FCotes R.A. / px[t] 1769. F and C in monogram. Inscribed at the upper left: Tho.[s] Tracy, Esq. / 1769. Condition: Good, but with a crease along the left side of the canvas.

Thomas Tracy, 1717–1770, the seventh son of John Tracy of Stanway; he married Mary Dodwell.

H.S., seated, head to the front, shoulders to the left; a plain background.

PROVENANCE: By family descent from the sitter to the present owner.

EXHIBITIONS: 'Elizabeth I and the Royal Houses of Tudor and Stuart, Art Treasures from Gloucestershire and the Cotswolds', Cheltenham Art Gallery and Museum, Cheltenham, May 16 – Jul. 18, 1953, no. 45 (lent by the Earl of Wemyss and March).

287. **William Earle Welby, Esq., and his First Wife Penelope** (fig. 94). The family of Sir Oliver Welby, Bt., U.K. Oil on canvas

52×59 in. Signed and dated 1769. Condition; Paint damaged in several places.
William Earle Welby, Esq., of Denton, Lincolnshire, created a baronet in 1801, died in 1815. Penelope, third daughter of Sir John Glynn, Bt., of Howarden Castle, Flintshire, died in 1771.
T.Q.L. William Welby: head to the front, shoulders to the right, wearing a blue coat, his left hand rests on a chess board. He points to his only remaining black piece, which is about to be taken by his opponent's white piece. His right hand is extended in a gesture that seems to say: 'What do I do now?'. Penelope Welby: head to the front, shoulders to the left, wearing a white and green dress. She rests her right arm on the chess board and, with a pleased expression on her face, points to her white chessman, which is about to win the victory. The background is plain, except for a red curtain on the right.

PROVENANCE: By family descent from the sitter to the present owner.

EXHIBITIONS: Royal Academy, 1769, no. 26, cf. Appendix III. The catalogue description reads: 'Ditto (an oil portrait, half-length), of a lady and a gentleman at chess'. No. 287 is the only known portrait by Cotes which answers this description. The painting is really closer to a three-quarter length than a half-length; however, such a discrepancy in terminology may be discounted.
'Exhibition of Works by the Old Masters and by Deceased Masters of the British School', R.A., London, 1881, no. 49 (lent by Sir W. E. Welby-Gregory).

288. **Sarah Whatman.** Present whereabouts unknown. Oil on canvas, 30×25 in. Signed and dated 1769. Condition: Unknown.
Engraved in mezzotint by James Watson in the latter half of the eighteenth century with the following inscription: F. Cotes, R.A. pinx[t] 1769. James Watson fecit. Mrs. Whatman.
Sarah Whatman, d. 1775, daughter of Edward Stanley; in 1769 she married James Whatman of Vintners, Maidstone, Kent.
H.L., head to the left, shoulders to the front, wearing a low-necked dress and a cloak edged with fur; a plain background.

PROVENANCE: Anon. Sale, Robinson and Fisher, London, Feb. 7, 1907 (lot 95), bought by Thomas Agnew and Sons, London, and sold in the same year to George Whatman, Esq., Vintners, Maidstone, Kent; Miss Whatman, Vintners, Maidstone, Kent (1933).

REFERENCES: *CS.*, p. 1545, no. 153.

289. **William Humphrey Wykeham of Swalcliffe.** Present whereabouts unknown. Oil on canvas, 30×25 in. Signed and dated at the lower right: FCotes, R.A. px[t] 1769. F and C in monogram. Condition: Unknown.
William Humphrey Wykeham, 1734–1783.
H.L., to the right, in a painted oval, wearing a purple coat; a plain background.

PROVENANCE: By family descent from the sitter to A. A. H. Wykeham, Esq., Tythrop House, Thame, Oxfordshire; A. A. H. Wykeham Sale, at Tythrop House, Sotheby's, Aug. 21, 1933 (lot 408), illus., bought by Brownlow.

Exhibited in 1769: A lost portrait in pastel, no. 290.

290. **A Lady as Hebe.** Present whereabouts unknown. Pastel on paper, measurements unknown. Possibly signed and dated. Condition: Unknown.

PROVENANCE: Unknown.

EXHIBITIONS: R.A., 1769, no. 28, cf. Appendix III. The catalogue description reads: 'A young lady ditto (in crayons) in the character of Hebe'.

Exhibited in 1769: A lost portrait in oils, no. 291.

291. **Mrs. Bouverie.** Present whereabouts unknown. Oil on canvas, measurements unknown. Possibly signed and dated. Condition: Unknown.

PROVENANCE: Unknown.

EXHIBITIONS: R.A., 1769, no. 24, cf. Appendix III. The catalogue description reads: 'Ditto (oil portrait) of a lady, half length'. Walpole added: 'Mrs. Bouverie'.

NB. At the B. Courceau Sale, 1910, Thomas Agnew and Sons purchased a half-length oil portrait, said to be by Cotes, in which the sitter was called the Hon. Mrs. Bouverie. The portrait was sold to Mrs. Bayard Thayer, U.S.A., in 1913, and was again in Agnew's possession in 1921. Its present whereabouts are unknown. The only existing photographs of the portrait were made c. 1921 when the picture was very dirty. The photographs themselves are poor, so that it is impossible to discern the style of the painting or to decide whether this might be the lost portrait exhibited by Cotes in 1769.

c. 1769: Portraits in oils, neither signed nor dated, nos. 292 and 293.

292. **Lady Brownlow Bertie** (fig. 106). Private Collection, U.K. Oil on canvas, 48×38 in. Neither signed nor dated. Condition: Excellent.
Lady Brownlow Bertie, 1743–1804; Mary Anne, the daughter of Peter Layard, Esq.; in 1769 she married, as his second wife, Lord Brownlow Bertie, later 5th Duke of Ancaster.
T.Q.L., seated to the left, wearing a pink dress embroidered with flower sprigs; with her right hand she turns the pages of a music book that rests on her lap; a column and a green curtain in the background.

DATE: This picture is typical of Cotes's best work in the last years of his career, 1767–70. The sitter married Lord Brownlow Bertie in 1769, and the portrait was probably painted at that time.

PROVENANCE: By family descent from the sitter to the present owner.

EXHIBITIONS: 'British Portraits', R.A., London, Winter 1955–56, no. 227 (lent by the present owner).
'Introducing Francis Cotes, R.A.', Nottingham University Art Gallery, Nov. 5–27, 1971, no. 16, as Harriott Morton Pitt (1745–1763), who married Lord Brownlow Bertie in 1762 (lent by the present owner); illus. in cat. (Pl. XI). This identification was based on an inventory of Grimsthorpe Castle compiled c. 1900; it was recognized as Mary Anne Layard, the second Lady Brownlow Bertie. The style of the picture definitely favours the R.A. identification. It would be difficult to conceive of Cotes painting so beautiful and accomplished a portrait as early as 1762/63, when Harriott Morton Pitt was Lady Brownlow Bertie. On the other hand, it is natural to see the portrait in company with later pictures like nos. 205, 206, 215, 220, and 227, which partake of the same air

of casual, domestic grandeur, and are done with an equal delicacy and finesse.

REFERENCES: *CAN.*, pp. 50 (fig. 46), 51.

293. **Elizabeth Crewe.** National Gallery of Art, Washington, D.C. Oil on canvas, $30\frac{5}{8} \times 24\frac{3}{4}$ in. Neither signed nor dated. Condition: Excellent.
Elizabeth Crewe of Haddon Hall, Northamptonshire; she married Thomas Horne, Esq.; her dates are unknown.
H.S., to the left, in a painted oval, wearing a rose dress and a black lace shawl; a plain background.

DATE: The style of the portrait indicates that it could have been painted at any time between c. 1765 and 1770. The hair style was popular very late in the 1760's; consequently, a date of c. 1769 is suggested.

PROVENANCE: By family descent from the sitter to General Lord Horne, U.K.; John Levy Galleries, New York (c. 1920); purchased from the Levy Galleries by Mr. and Mrs. B. F. Jones, Sewickley Heights, Pa.; Mrs. B. F. Jones Sale, Parke-Bernet, New York, Dec. 4, 1941 (lot 34), illus., bought by Mr. W. R. Coe, U.S.A.; W. R. Coe Foundation, U.S.A.; loaned by the Coe Foundation to the American Embassy, London, in 1959. Presented by the Coe Foundation to the National Gallery of Art in 1961. The painting remained at the American Embassy from 1959 to 1969 and was then sent to the National Gallery of Art.

EXHIBITIONS:, Exhibition of Paintings by Old Masters from Pittsburgh Collections', Carnegie Institute, Pittsburgh, Apr. 30 – Je. 5, 1925, no. 8 (lent by Mrs. B. F. Jones).

REFERENCES: *PFC.*, pp. 2 (fig. 5), 6; W. Roberts, *Miss Crewe by Francis Cotes, R.A.*, London, The Chiswick Press, 1920, pp. 1–8; *Summary Catalogue of European Paintings and Sculpture, National Gallery of Art*, Washington, D.C., 1965, p. 32, no. 1646.

1770: Portraits in oils, signed and dated, nos. 294 and 295.

294. **Henry Somerset, 5th Duke of Beaufort.** The Duke of Beaufort, Badminton House, Badminton, Gloucestershire. Oil on canvas, 30 × 24 in. Signed and dated at the lower right: FCotes R.A. / px[t] 1770. F and C in monogram. Condition: Good.
The 5th Duke of Beaufort, 1744–1803; in 1766 he married Elizabeth Boscawen (no. 295).
H.S., to the right, wearing a blue coat; a plain background.
Pendant to no. 295.

PROVENANCE: By family descent from the sitter to the present owner.

EXHIBITIONS: 'Introducing Francis Cotes, R.A.', Nottingham University Art Gallery, Nov. 5–27, 1971, no. 38 (lent by the present owner). The portrait is on exhibit at Badminton House, which is open to the public at certain times of the year.

REFERENCES: *CWO.*, p. 251.

295. **The Duchess of Beaufort.** The Duke of Beaufort, Badminton House, Badminton, Gloucestershire. Oil on canvas, 30 × 24 in. Signed and dated at the middle right: FCotes R.A. px[t] / 1770. F and C in monogram. Inscribed at the top left: Eliz[th] wife of / Henry 5th D. of Beaufort / and daughter of the R[t]. Hon. / Adm[l]. Boscawen. Condition: Excellent.
The Duchess of Beaufort, d. 1828, Elizabeth, daughter of Admiral the Hon. Edward Boscawen; in 1766 she married Henry Somerset, 5th Duke of Beaufort (no. 294).
H.S., head to the left, shoulders to the front, wearing a low-necked dress and a cloak edged with ermine; a plain background.
Pendant to no. 294.

PROVENANCE: By family descent from the sitter to the present owner.

EXHIBITIONS: 'Introducing Francis Cotes, R.A.', Nottingham University Art Gallery, Nov. 5–27, 1971, no. 39 (lent by the present owner). The portrait is on exhibit at Badminton House, which is open to the public at certain times of the year.

1770: A portrait in oils, monogrammed and dated, no. 296.

296. **Sarah Cotes** (fig. 109). Present whereabouts unknown. Oil on canvas, 30 × 25 in. Monogrammed and dated at the lower right: FC 1770. F and C in monogram. Condition: Unknown.
For information on the sitter see no. 65.
H.L., to the left, wearing a striped dress, a lace shawl, and a cap; a dog rests its head on her right arm; a plain background except for some foliage at the bottom right.

PROVENANCE: H. Bendixson, Esq., London; purchased from Mr. Bendixson in 1917 by M. Knoedler and Co., London; purchased from M. Knoedler and Co., New York, in 1920 by a private collector, New York.

Exhibited in 1770: A portrait in pastel, no. 297.

297. **Sarah Cotes** (fig. 108). Present whereabouts unknown. Pastel on paper, 30 × 25 in. Neither signed nor dated. Condition: Unknown.
For information on the sitter see no. 65.
H.L., seated, to the left, wearing a low-necked gown, a sash, and a scarf over her left arm; she holds a small dog under her right arm; a plain background.

PROVENANCE: Charles Wertheimer, Esq., London (1908); purchased from Mr. Wertheimer in 1911 by M. Knoedler and Co., London; purchased from Knoedler's, New York, in 1912, by Mr. Walter Lewisohn, New York.

EXHIBITIONS: R.A., 1770, no. 59, cf. Appendix III. The catalogue description reads: 'Ditto (portrait) of a Lady in crayons'. Walpole added, 'His own wife with a shock dog'.
'Cent Pastels du XVIIIe Siècle', Galerie Georges Petit, Paris, May–Je., 1908, no. 10 (lent by Charles Wertheimer).

REFERENCES: *CWO.*, p. 251; *CWS.*, p. 176, 177 (fig. no. v); R. R. M. Sée, *English Pastels 1750–1830*, London, G. Bell and Sons, 1911, p. 49.

Exhibited in 1770: A lost portrait, possibly in pastel, no. 298.

298. **Henry Frederick, Duke of Cumberland.** Present whereabouts unknown. Possibly a pastel, measurements unknown. Possibly signed and dated. Condition: Unknown.
The Duke of Cumberland, 1745–1790.

PROVENANCE: Unknown.

EXHIBITIONS: R.A., 1770, no. 58, cf. Appendix III. The catalogue description reads: 'Ditto (portrait) of His Royal Highness the Duke of Cumberland, in crayons'.

REFERENCES: *CWO.*, p. 251. Winter refers to the portrait as a pastel; *CWS.*, p. 176; R. R. M. Sée, *English Pastels 1750–1830*, London, G. Bell and Sons, 1911, p. 49. Sée speaks of the portrait as a pastel, 'belonging to his (Cotes's) latest period'.

Exhibited in 1770: Lost portraits in oils, nos. 299–302.

299. **Henry Somerset, 5th Duke of Beaufort.** Present whereabouts unknown. Oil on canvas, measurements unknown, described in 1770 as a 'three-quarters', meaning a three-quarter length. Possibly signed and dated. Condition: Unknown.
The 5th Duke of Beaufort, 1744–1803; in 1766 he married Elizabeth Boscawen.

PROVENANCE: Unknown.

EXHIBITIONS: R.A., 1770, no. 56, cf. Appendix III. The catalogue description reads: 'Ditto (portrait) of a gentleman three quarters'. Walpole added, 'The Duke of Beaufort'.

At Badminton House there is a three-quarter length portrait of Henry Somerset, 5th Duke of Beaufort, in the regalia of a Knight of the Garter. It is not by Cotes, but in the Witt Library's Eighteenth Century Portrait Index it is listed as being 'after Cotes'. The original portrait, from which this copy is said to have been made, has been lost. Possibly, the original was the painting Cotes exhibited in 1770, no. 299.

300. **Captain Leister.** Present whereabouts unknown. Oil on canvas, measurements unknown. Possibly signed and dated. Condition: Unknown.
No information on the sitter is available.

PROVENANCE: Unknown.

EXHIBITIONS: R.A., 1770, no. 52, cf. Appendix III. The catalogue description reads: 'Ditto (portrait) of Captain Leister whole length'. In the early R.A. catalogues the medium is understood to be oil on canvas, unless otherwise specified.

301. **Mrs. Sawbridge.** Present whereabouts unknown. Oil on canvas, measurements unknown. Possibly signed and dated. Condition: Unknown.
Mrs. Sawbridge, probably Anne Sawbridge, daughter of Sir William Stephenson; in 1766 she married, as his second wife, John Sawbridge of Olantigh, Kent, who became Lord Mayor of London in 1775.

PROVENANCE: Unknown.

EXHIBITIONS: R.A., 1770, no. 50, cf. Appendix III. The catalogue description reads: 'The Portrait of a Lady (Mrs. Sawbridge). Walpole added, 'Mrs. Sawbridge, wife of the Alderman, with a palm branch and inscription "Templum felicitatis".' In the early R.A. catalogues the medium is understood to be oil on canvas, unless otherwise specified.

For Cotes's portrait of Anne Sawbridge, dated c. 1767–1770, cf. no. 247.

302. **Mr. Watman.** Present whereabouts unknown. Oil on canvas, measurements unknown. Possibly signed and dated. Condition: Unknown.
Mr. Watman, possibly related to Mrs. Whatman, who was painted by Cotes in 1769; cf. no. 288.

PROVENANCE: Unknown.

EXHIBITIONS: R.A., 1770, no. 55, cf. Appendix III. The catalogue description reads: 'Ditto (portrait) Mr. Watman'.

Without an assigned date: A lost portrait in pastel, no. 303.

303. **Miss Wilton as a Young Girl.** Present whereabouts unknown. Pastel on paper, measurements unknown. Possibly signed and dated. Condition: Unknown.
Miss Wilton, daughter of Joseph Wilton, R.A.; in 1774 she was sixteen; at approximately this time she married Sir Robert Chambers, cf. References.

PROVENANCE: Unknown.

REFERENCES: Francis Cotes, notes on crayon painting, *The European Magazine*, Feb. 1797, pp. 84–85, cf. Appendix IV; William Sandby, *The History of the Royal Academy*, Vol. I, London, Longman, Green, Longman, Roberts, and Green, 1862, p. 96; John Thomas Smith, *Nollekens and His Times*, Vol. II, London, Henry Colburn, 1828, p. 174. Smith cites a letter from Dr. Johnson to Boswell dated March 5, 1774:

> Chambers is either married, or almost married, to Miss Wilton, a girl of sixteen, exquisitely beautiful, whom he has, with his lawyer's tongue, persuaded to take her chance with him in the East.

Smith goes on to note:

> They (Miss Wilton and Chambers) were married, and Mr. Chambers, afterwards Sir Robert, dying, Lady Chambers returned to England and is now residing in Putney.

WA., p. iii.

Without an assigned date: Two lost portraits, known only through engravings, nos. 304 and 305.

304. **Lady Harriet Grosvenor.** Present whereabouts unknown. Medium and measurements unknown. Possibly signed and dated. Condition: Unknown.
Engraved in mezzotint by Benjamin Wilson and published in 1770 with the following inscription: FCotes pinx[t]. B. Wilson fecit. / Lady Harriet Gxxxxxx / If to her share some female errors fall / Look on her face and you'll forget them all. / Engraved from the original in the Possession of H.R.H. the Duke of C. (Cumberland). H.L., to the left, in an oval, wearing a low-necked dress, a robe across her shoulders, and a turban with a plume; her right hand is at the bodice of her dress; a plain background.

PROVENANCE: The Duke of Cumberland (1770).

REFERENCES: *CS.*, Vol. IV, p. 1613, no. 1.

305. **Rachel Hamilton.** Present whereabouts unknown. Medium and measurements unknown. Possibly signed and dated. Condition: Unknown.
Engraved in mezzotint by James Watson in the latter half of the

eighteenth century. It bore the following inscription: F Cotes Pinx[t]. Jas. Watson fecit.
The sitter's genealogy is unknown.
Challoner Smith describes the engraving as a H.L., in an oval, head to the front, shoulders to the left. The sitter is said to be wearing a low-necked dress and a cape. In her right hand she holds a miniature of a clergyman set into a pearl bracelet.

PROVENANCE: Unknown.

REFERENCES: *CS.*, Vol. IV, p. 1513, no. 71.

Without an assigned date: Nine miscellaneous works, now lost, which were sold from Cotes's private collection after his death, no. 306.

306.
Appendix II, p. 6, lot 16, 'One ditto (fruit piece) by F. Cotes'.
Appendix II, p. 12, lot, 32, 'A dog's head, framed and glaz'd, by Cotes'.
Appendix II, p. 12, lot 33, 'A view in the Isle of Wight by ditto (Cotes)'.
Appendix II, p. 12, lot 48, 'Two views in water colours by F. Cotes'.
Appendix II, p. 12, lot 55, 'A view of Netley Abbey by F. Cotes'.
Appendix II, p. 12, lot 56, 'The west view of ditto (Netley Abbey) by ditto (F. Cotes)'.
Appendix II, p. 13, lot 67, 'Cupids in crayons by Cotes'.
Appendix II, p. 13, lot 68, 'A Venus and Cupid by ditto (Cotes)'.
Present whereabouts unknown. Measurements unknown.

CONDITION: Unknown.

PROVENANCE: Francis Cotes, R.A., London; Francis Cotes Sale, Langford and Son, London, Feb. 21–23, 25, 1771, lots mentioned above. The catalogue is reproduced in Appendix II.

CATALOGUE SUPPLEMENT

Pictures discovered after the main catalogue was completed.

1748–1750: A lost portrait, known only through the correspondence of Samuel Richardson, no. 1.

Supplement 1. **A Lady, as Clarissa.** Present whereabouts unknown. Pastel on paper, measurements unknown. Possibly signed and dated. Condition: Unknown.

PROVENANCE: Dr. Charles Chauncey (or Chauncy) (1749/50).

REFERENCES: Anna Laetitia Barbauld (ed.), *The Correspondence of Samuel Richardson*, Vol. IV, London, Richard Phillips, 1804, pp. 256, 336.
Letter from Samuel Richardson to Dr. Charles Chauncey in MS., 1749/50, The Henry E. Huntington Library, San Marino, California, HM 6893, reproduced by permission of the Library. The sequence of the pertinent correspondence is as follows:
Samuel Richardson to Mrs. Balfour, 1749 (Barbauld, p. 256):

> Dr. Chancey, a physician in Austin Friars, a man of learning and politeness, has also a head of Clarissa in crayons; a piece that wants neither spirit nor dignity, nor such an innocence in the aspect, as made me ready, as much as I was on seeing Mr. Highmore's, to curse the Lovelace I had drawn.

Samuel Richardson to Mrs. Balfour, Feb. 2, 1749/50 (Barbauld, p. 336).

> P.S. I mentioned in a former letter that Dr. Chancy had a picture drawn of Clarissa. He had been so kind as to lend it to me. Perhaps he will send for it in a few days. You will possibly chuse to send some lady or gentleman of your acquaintance to look at it.

Samuel Richardson to Dr. Charles Chauncey, 1749/50 (HM. 6893).

> Dear Sir,
> I am extremely obliged to you for the Loan of your Clarissa. I have had many Persons to look at it, and so many Admirers of it, as Visiters. On Friday I had Mrs. Delaney, whose Pensil is greatly and justly admired, and Mrs. Talbot her mother, to see it. Very highly did they commend it, and wanted to know where to find Mr. Cotes, which I could not tell them, and was sorry I could not. Mrs. Delaney said, She should have been glad to have copy'd the Head and Neck. I was in hopes my Lancashire Lady would have had an opportunity to see it; but she plays fast and loose with me so idly, that I have some Pleasure in considering the Opportunity she has lost, as a Punishment to her.
> I hope soon, to have an Opportunity to return my personal Acknowledgements to you, Sir, for this and all other Favors, and am
> Your faithful and most obliged humble Serv[t]
> Monday Morn S. Richardson
> I hope you will find it as Safe and unhurt as I received it.

NB. Richardson wrote his small 'l' and small 't' in exactly the same way; consequently, one might be tempted to read Cotes's name as 'Coles' instead of 'Cotes'; however, a crayon painter by the name of Coles is unknown.

DATE: Richardson's *Clarissa* was published in 1748. The correspondence concerning Cotes's portrait of Clarissa took place in 1749/50; consequently, a date of 1748–1750 is suggested.
For Cotes's pastel portrait of Dr. Chauncey, cf. no. 11, dated 1750, and for his pastel portrait of a Miss Talbot, cf. Appendix V, no. 4, dated 1751.
I am indebted to Alison Shepherd Lewis for drawing my attention to the Huntington Library's letter from Richardson to Dr. Chauncy, and for relating it to the correspondence between Richardson and Mrs. Balfour.

1751: A portrait in pastel, signed and dated, no. 2.

Supplement 2. **A Gentleman.** Present whereabouts unknown. Pastel on paper, 23 × 17 in. Signed and dated at the middle left: FCotes px[t]: / 1751. F and C in monogram. Condition: Unknown. H.S.

Pendant to no. 21 in the catalogue.

PROVENANCE: Jules Féral, Paris (1928).

c. 1751 – c. 1754: A portrait in pastel, signed and probably dated, no. 3.

Supplement 3. **A Gentleman.** Private Collection, U.K. Pastel on paper, 24½ × 19½ in. Signed at the lower right: FCotes . . . F and C in monogram. The rest of the signature, and probably the date, are hidden behind the frame.

Condition: Good.

H.S., to the right, in an oval, wearing a blue coat; a plain background.

DATE: The portrait is typical of Cotes's work of the early 1750's. Three other signed and dated portraits are quite similar, no. 24 (1751), no. 39 (1752), and no. 48 (1754). A date, therefore, of c. 1751 – c. 1754 is suggested.

PROVENANCE: The portrait is known to have been in the owner's family for at least fifty years. Its earlier history is unknown.

1754: A portrait in pastel, signed and dated, no. 4.

Supplement 4. **A Girl.** Private Collection, London. Pastel on paper, approximately 23 × 17 in. Signed and dated at the lower right: FCotes px[t] 1754. F and C in monogram. Condition: Excellent.

H.L., to the left, wearing a pink dress and blue shawl; a plain background.

PROVENANCE: Unknown.

1757: Portraits in pastel, signed and dated, nos. 5 and 6.

Supplement 5. **Anne Byng.** Private Collection, U.K. Pastel on paper, approximately 30 × 25 in. Signed and dated at the lower left: FCotes px[t] 1757. F and C. in monogram. Condition: Good.

Anne Byng, d. 1806, daughter of the Rt. Hon. William Conolly; in 1761 she married George Byng of Wrotham Park, Middlesex.

H.L., head slightly to the right, shoulders to the left, wearing a low-necked dress with lace trim and slashed sleeves; a plain background.

Pendant to Supplement no. 6.

PROVENANCE: By family descent from the sitter to the present owner.

Supplement 6. **The Rt. Hon. William Conolly.** Private Collection, U.K. Pastel on paper, approximately 23 × 17 in. Signed and dated at the middle left: FCotes px[t] / 1757. F and C in monogram.

Condition: Good, minor damage in spots.

William Conolly, dates unknown, father of Anne Byng.

H.S., to the right, wearing a jacket; a plain background.

Pendant to Supplement no. 5.

PROVENANCE: By family descent from the sitter to the present owner.

1758: A portrait in pastel, signed and dated, no. 7

Supplement 7. **Catherine Gunning.** Thos. Agnew and Sons, London. Pastel on paper, 25½ × 17½ in. Signed and dated: FCotes px[t] 1758. F and C in monogram. Condition: Good.

Catherine Gunning, 1735–1773, the youngest daughter of John and Bridget Gunning; in 1769 she married Robert Travis (or Travers).

H.S., head slightly to the right, shoulders to the left, wearing a low-cut dress with a scarf and pearls; a landscape background.

PROVENANCE: By family descent from the sitter to Marjorie, Lady Russell, Little Struan, Pangbourne, Berkshire; Anon. Sale (Property of a Lady), Christie's, Je. 6, 1972, lot 107, bought by Agnew.

EXHIBITIONS: 'A Century of British Art, 1737–1837', Grosvenor Gallery, London, Summer, 1889, no. 229, lent by Sir George Russell. Here the date is noted, 1758.

Catalogue entry no. 15 may refer to a similar portrait or to the same portrait. It is important to note that no. 15 and not Supplement no. 7 was engraved. Houston's engraving of no. 15 was published in 1755; Supplement no. 7 is signed and dated 1758.

1758–1762: A portrait in pastel, signed, no. 8.

Supplement 8. **Sir William St. Quentin, 5th Bt.** The Lady Legard, Scampston Hall, Malton, Yorkshire. Pastel on paper, approximately 25 × 17 in. Signed at the lower left. Condition: Excellent.

Sir William St. Quentin, 5th Bt., 1722–1795.

H.S., to the left, wearing a jacket; a plain background.

DATE: Probably painted between 1758 and 1762. The pendant (Supplement no. 9) is of Lady St. Quentin, who married Sir William in 1758 and died in 1762. The style is of this period.

PROVENANCE: By family descent from the sitter to the present owner.

1758–1762: A portrait in pastel, neither signed nor dated, no. 9.

Supplement 9. **Lady St. Quentin.** The Lady Legard, Scampston Hall, Malton, Yorkshire. Pastel on paper, approximately 25 × 17 in. Neither signed nor dated. Condition: Excellent.

Lady St. Quentin, born Charlotte Fane, married Sir William St. Quentin in 1758, d. 1762.

H.L., to the front, wearing a dress with bows down the front; a plain background.

DATE: Probably painted between 1758 and 1762, when she was married to Sir William St. Quentin. The style is of this period.

PROVENANCE: By family descent from the sitter to the present owner.

1762: Portraits in oils, signed and dated, nos. 10 and 11.

Supplement 10. **Mrs. Hamilton of Raploch.** Present whereabouts unknown. Oil on canvas, 29½ × 24½ in. Signed and dated 1762. Condition: Unknown.

No information is available on the sitter.

H.S., to the right, wearing a gold dress and a lace bonnet; a plain background.

PROVENANCE: Lewis and Simmons, London, Chicago, and New York (1929). Anon. Sale, Sotheby's, Feb. 5, 1964 (lot 76), bought by Knill.

REFERENCES: *Gaulois Artistique*, Vol. III, Je. 1929, p. 35.

Supplement 11. **General James Sinclair.** The Countess of Sutherland, Dunrobin Castle, Golspie, Sutherland. Oil on canvas, 30 × 24½ in. Signed and dated at the lower left: FCotes pxt / 1762. F and C in monogram. Condition: Discolouration and cracking of the paint.

Gen. James Sinclair, d. 1762, son of Henry Sinclair, 10th Lord Sinclair; he married Janet, daughter of Sir David Dalrymple of Hailes.

H.S., to the right, wearing a blue-grey jacket, and resting his right hand in the front of his waistcoat; a plain background.

PROVENANCE: By family descent from the sitter to the present owner.

EXHIBITIONS: 'Introducing Francis Cotes, R.A.', Nottingham University Art Gallery, Nov. 5–27, 1971, no. 15 (lent by the present owner).

REFERENCES: *Catalogue of Pictures at Dunrobin Castle*, privately printed, 1908, no. 177, incorrectly attributed to Allan Ramsay, the sitter identified as Sir James Sinclair; *Catalogue of Pictures in Dunrobin Castle*, privately printed, 1921, stated as in the 1908 catalogue.

Exhibited in 1763: A lost portrait in oils, no. 12.

Supplement 12. **A Spaniel.** Present whereabouts unknown. Oil on canvas, measurements unknown. Possibly signed and dated. Condition: Unknown.

PROVENANCE: Unknown.

EXHIBITIONS: Society of Artists, 1763, no. 27, cf. Appendix III. The catalogue description reads: 'A spaniel in oil'.

c. 1764–1766: A portrait in oils, neither signed nor dated, no. 13.

Supplement 13. **Archibald, 9th Duke of Hamilton.** The Duke of Hamilton, Lennoxlove, East Lothian. Oil on canvas, 50 × 40 in. Neither signed nor dated. Condition: Good.

The 9th Duke of Hamilton, 1740–1819.

T.Q.L., to the right, head to the front, wearing a frock coat, and holding a walking stick and hat in his right hand; a landscape background.

DATE: The style of the picture indicates c. 1764–1766. It is similar to the Burdett portraits of the same period, nos. 147–149, 156.

PROVENANCE: By family descent from the sitter to the present owner.

c. 1765: A portrait in oils, signed and dated, no. 14.

Supplement 14. **Luke Gardiner.** Roy Miles, Esq., London. Oil on canvas, 35½ × 28 in. Signed and dated at the top left: FCotes pxt (176(?). F and C in monogram. The last digit is indecipherable. Condition: Excellent.

Luke Gardiner, 1745–1798, married Elizabeth, eldest daughter of Sir William Montgomery, in 1773, created Baron Mountjoy in 1789 and Viscount Mountjoy in 1795.

H.L., to the right, dressed as a Fellow-Commoner of St. John's College, Cambridge, wearing his gown and holding his cap in his right hand; a view of St. John's College Chapel in the background.

DATE: The style indicates a date of c. 1765.

PROVENANCE: Anon. Sale (Property of a Gentleman of Title), Sotheby's, Apr. 4, 1973 (lot 67), bought by R. Miles.

For another portrait by Cotes of a sitter wearing the robes of a Fellow-Commoner of St. John's, cf. no. 278.

c. 1766–1768: A portrait in oils, neither signed nor dated, no. 15.

Supplement 15. **Anna Maria Astley.** The Lord Hastings, Swanton House, Melton Constable, Norfolk. Oil on canvas, 30 × 25 in. Neither signed nor dated. Condition: Good.

Anna Maria Astley, daughter of Sir Edward Astley, 4th Bt. (no. 276), and Anne, daughter of Christopher Milles of Nackington, Kent.

H.L., to the left, wearing a grey dress and bonnet, and holding her skirt with both hands; a background of trees and sky.

DATE: The picture is quite similar to no. 196, signed and dated 1766. The sitter died in 1768. A date of c. 1766–1768 is suggested.

PROVENANCE: By family descent from the sitter to the present owner.

EXHIBITIONS: Exhibited at Ipswich in 1927, no. 86 (lent by the Lord Hastings).

REFERENCES: *PN.*, Vol. II, p. 2, no. 7.

1767–1770: A lost portrait in pastel, no. 16.

Supplement 16. **Prince Edward.** Present whereabouts unknown. Pastel on paper, measurements unknown. Possibly signed and dated. Condition: Unknown.

Prince Edward, 1767–1820, later Edward, Duke of Kent, son of George III and Queen Charlotte, and father of Queen Victoria.

DATE: The portrait would have been done between the sitter's birth in 1767 and Cotes's death in 1770.

PROVENANCE: A portrait of Prince Edward by 'Coates' was recorded in the Queen's Bedroom at Kew in the time of George III. It was said to be 'in crayons'.

REFERENCES: *OML.*, Vol. I, p. 23, under no. 721.

1769: Portraits in oils, signed and dated, nos. 17–19.

Supplement 17. **Elizabeth Allpress.** John Colville, Esq., The Old Rectory, Stratfield Saye, Reading, Berkshire. Oil on canvas, 30 × 25 in. Signed and dated 1769. Condition: Good.

Elizabeth Allpress, daughter of Mr. and Mrs. Samuel Allpress (nos. 274 and 275).

H.L., in an oval, wearing a blue dress; a plain background.

PROVENANCE: By family descent from the sitter to the present owner.

Supplement 18. **A Lady.** Private Collection, U.K. Oil on canvas, approximately 29 × 24 in. Signed and dated at the middle right:

FCotes R.A. px[t] / 1769. F and C in monogram. Condition: Unknown.
H.L., to the front, head slightly to the left, dressed in blue with scarf over her head.

PROVENANCE: Unknown.

EXHIBITIONS: On loan to the City of Birmingham Museum and Art Gallery, 1962.

Supplement 19. **Sir John H. Thursby.** Present whereabouts unknown. Oil on canvas, 50 × 40 in. Signed and dated at the lower right: FCotes px[t] 1769. F and C in monogram. Condition: Unknown.
Sir John H. Thursby of Abington Abbey, dates unknown.
T.Q.L., head to the left, shoulders to the right, wearing a coat, holding a hat in his right hand and a shotgun in his left hand, and leaning his left arm on a fence post; a background of trees and sky.

PROVENANCE: G. S. Sedgwick; purchased from Mr. Sedgwick in 1906 by Thomas Agnew and Sons, London; purchased from Agnew's in 1907 by Sir John D. Thursby.

Without an assigned date: Lost portraits in pastel, nos. 20–22.

Supplement 20. In W. H. Pyne's *The History of the Royal Residences*, London, Vol. I, A. Dry, 1819, p. 20, it was noted that in the State Bedroom at Frogmore House there was a 'Portrait of the Duchess of Ancaster—Portrait of Lady Holderness; painted in crayons by Francis Coates'. It is not clear from the reference whether Pyne is referring to a double portrait or to two portraits. In any case, the present whereabouts of this picture or pictures are unknown.

REFERENCES: *OML.*, Vol. I, p. 21; Pyne, as cited above.

Supplement 21. **The Prince of Wales and the Bishop of Osnabourgh.** Present whereabouts unknown. Pastel on paper, 32 × 26½ in. Possibly signed and dated. Condition: Unknown.

PROVENANCE: The royal collection. In the inventory of Buckingham House (c. 1790–95) the picture is recorded in the Blue Closet.

REFERENCES: *OML.*, Vol. I, p. 21.

Supplement 22. **The Virgin and Child after Guido Reni.** Present whereabouts unknown. Pastel on paper, measurements unknown. Possibly signed and dated. Condition: Unknown.

PROVENANCE: Francis Cotes, R.A. The last will and testament of Francis Cotes, R.A., dated Je. 16, 1769, proved Jul. 30, 1770. Cotes gives to his father, Robert Cotes, 'the picture of the Virgin and Child in crayons from Guido painted by myself'.

REFERENCES: The will cited above, kept at Somerset House, London.

An additional portrait in oils, neither signed nor dated, no. 23.

Supplement 23. **Lady Sarah March.** Present whereabouts unknown. Oil on canvas, 35 × 28¼ in., neither signed nor dated. Condition: Good, but paint slightly damaged in the background.
H.L., seated at a table, to the right, wearing a red dress and a black lace shawl, and resting her head on her left hand; a green curtain in the background. The sitter's ruffled sleeve is reflected in the table.

DATE: The portrait is similar to no. 160 and typical of Cotes's work from about 1764 to 1770.

PROVENANCE: Anon. Sale, Sotheby's, Dec. 13, 1972 (101), bought by Douglas.

EXHIBITIONS: Possibly Society of Artists, 1764, no. 22; cf. no. 160.

1 George Knapton: *John Spencer, later 1st Earl Spencer, and an unknown Child.* Pastel, c.1740. The Earl Spencer, Althorp, Northamptonshire

2 George Knapton: *The Hon. John Spencer and his Son, John, later 1st Earl Spencer, with their Servant, Caesar Shaw.* Oil, 1749. The Earl Spencer, Althorp, Northamptonshire

3 Rosalba Carriera: *Lady Sophia Fermor.* Pastel, 1714. The Earl of Shelburne, Bowood, Calne, Wiltshire

4 A *Gentleman* (No. 1). Pastel, 1747. Leicestershire Museums and Art Galleries, Leicester

5 *Catherine Wilson* (No. 2). Pastel, 1747. Captain John Litchfield, R,N., U.K.

6 *Maria Gunning* (No. 19). Pastel, 1751. The Duke of Argyll, Inveraray Castle, Inveraray, Argyllshire

7 *Charlotte Tulliedeph* (No. 42). Pastel, 1752.
Sir David Ogilvy, Bt., Winton House, Pencaitland, East Lothian

8 *Sir John Ripton* (No. 39). Pastel, 1752.
Mr. and Mrs. Rockwell Gardiner, Stamford, Connecticut

9 Hubert Gravelot: *The Good Mother*. Engraving for an early edition of Samuel Richardson's *Pamela*, n.d.
Victoria and Albert Museum, London

10 Francis Hayman: *Lovers in a Landscape*. Oil, c.1740–50. Mr. and Mrs. Paul Mellon Collection, U.S.A.

11 Joseph Highmore: *Pamela Asks Sir Jacob Swinford's Blessing*. Oil, 1743–4. Tate Gallery, London

12 *A Lady* (No. 47). Oil, 1753. Croome Estate Trustees, U.K.

13 *A Lady* (No. 46). Pastel, 1753. Ralph Edwards, Esq., London

14 *Elizabeth Hulse* (No. 56). Pastel, 1755. Ralph B. Verney, Esq., Claydon House, Bletchley, Buckinghamshire

15 Jean-Étienne Liotard: *Lady Mary Fawkener*. Pastel, c.1754. The Hon. P. M. Samuel, Farley Hall, Farley Hill, Berkshire

16 Anton Raphael Mengs: *Louis de Silvestre*. Pastel, c.1750. Staatliche Kunstsammlungen, Dresden

17 *Robert Cotes* (No. 75). Pastel, 1757. Royal Academy of Arts, London

18 *Sir Edward Hulse, 1st Bt.* (No. 77). Pastel, 1757. Sir Westrow Hulse, Bt., Breamore House, Breamore, Hampshire

19 Maurice-Quentin de La Tour: *Claude Dupouch*. Pastel, c.1740. National Gallery of Art, Washington, D.C., Samuel H. Kress Collection

20 Allan Ramsay: *Margaret Lindsay*. Oil, c.1754. National Gallery of Scotland Edinburgh

21 *Sir Richard Hoare* (No. 76). Pastel, 1757. National Trust, Stourhead House, Stourton, Wiltshire

22 Sir Joshua Reynolds: *The Duchess of Hamilton as Venus.* Oil, exhibited in 1760. Lady Lever Art Gallery, Port Sunlight, Cheshire

23 Edward Fisher: *Anne Sandby as Emma, the Nut-Brown Maid.* Mezzotint, after an oil portrait by Francis Cotes of 1759 (No. 96), published in 1763. British Museum, London

24 *Joseph and John Gulston* (No. 52). Pastel, 1755. Private Collection, U.K.

25 *View of Purley Hall* (No. 71). Watercolour, 1756. Victoria and Albert Museum, London

26 Paul Sandby: *Rochester, a View of the Castle from across the Medway*. Watercolour. Whitworth Art Gallery, University of Manchester

27 Sir Joshua Reynolds: *Lady Anstruther*. Oil, 1761. Tate Gallery, London

28 *Elizabeth Adams* (No. 103). Oil, 1762. The Earl Cawdor, Golden Grove House, Broad Oak, Carmarthenshire

29 Sir Joshua Reynolds: *Rear-Admiral George Brydges Rodney, later Admiral and 1st Baron Rodney*. Oil, 1761. The Lord Egremont, Petworth House, Petworth, Sussex

30 *Henry Paulet, 6th Duke of Bolton* (No. 109). Oil, c. 1762. Metropolitan Museum of Art, New York (Bequest of Jacob Ruppert)

31 *Lieutenant-Colonel Alexander Campbell* (No. 123). Oil, 1763. The Earl Cawdor, Golden Grove House, Broad Oak, Carmarthenshire

32 Sir Joshua Reynolds: *Captain Augustus Hervey, later 3rd Earl of Bristol.* Oil, 1762. Private Collection, U.K.

33 *Lady Fortescue* (No. 113). Oil, c.1762–3. Lady Margaret Fortescue, Castle Hill, Barnstaple, Devon

34 Sir Joshua Reynolds: *Lady Elizabeth Keppel, later Marchioness of Tavistock.* Oil, 1761–2. The Marquess of Tavistock, Woburn Abbey, Woburn, Bedfordshire

35 Sir Joshua Reynolds: *Commodore Augustus Keppel, later Admiral and Viscount Keppel.* Oil, 1753–4. National Maritime Museum, Greenwich

36 Sir Joshua Reynolds: *The Ladies Elizabeth and Henrietta Montagu.* Oil, 1763. The Duke of Buccleuch and Queensberry, U.K.

37 *A Lady* (No. 22). Pastel, 1751. Henry E. Huntington Library and Art Gallery, San Marino, California

38 *A Lady* (No. 119). Pastel, 1763. Henry E. Huntington Library and Art Gallery, San Marino, California

39 Sir Joshua Reynolds: *The Hon. Harriet Bouverie, later Lady Tilney-Long.* Oil, 1764. Private Collection, U.K.

40 *Lady Alston* (No. 144). Oil, 1764. Present whereabouts unknown

41 *Maria, Dowager Countess of Waldegrave* (No. 143). Pastel, 1764. Private Collection, U.K.

42 *Lady Susan Fox-Strangeways* (No. 128). Pastel, 1763–4. Lady Teresa Agnew, Melbury House, Dorchester, Dorset

43 *Laura Keppel* (No. 155). Pastel, c.1764. Private Collection, U.K.

44 *William O'Brien* (No. 120). Pastel, 1763.
Lady Teresa Agnew, Melbury House, Dorchester, Dorset

45 *Dr. John Gregory* (No. 139). Pastel, 1764.
Sir Andrew Forbes-Leith, Bt., Fyvie Castle, Aberdeenshire

46 *William Chambers* (No. 137). Pastel, 1764.
Scottish National Portrait Gallery, Edinburgh

47 James Watson: *William Campbell Skinner*. Mezzotint, after a portrait by Francis Cotes (No. 153), c.1764. British Museum, London

48 *A Boy of the Barwell Family* (No. 146). Oil, 1764. Mrs. J. B. Campbell, New York

49 Sir Joshua Reynolds: *Edward Lascelles, later 1st Earl of Harewood* Oil, 1762–4. The Earl of Harewood, Harewood House, Yorkshire

50 *A Boy of the Barwell Family* (No. 145). Oil, 1764. Mrs Jackson Martindell, U.S.A.

51 Allan Ramsay: *Philip, 2nd Earl Stanhope*. Oil, 1749. Trustees of the Chevening Estate, Chevening, Kent

52 Pompeo Battoni: *Sir John Armytage, 2nd Bt.* Oil, 1758. Formerly Central Picture Galleries, New York

53 Sir Joshua Reynolds: *Sir John Anstruther*. Oil, 1761. Present whereabouts unknown

54 *Francis Burdett* (No. 147). Oil, 1764. Ferens Art Gallery, Hull

55 *William Jones* (No. 159). Oil, c.1764. Aitken Collection, U.S.A.

56 *Charles Colmore* (No. 157). Oil, c.1764. Present whereabouts unknown

57 *Admiral Augustus Keppel* (No. 168). Pastel, 1765. Private Collection, U.K.

58 *John Hobart, 2nd Earl of Buckinghamshire* (No. 193). Oil, 1766.
The Marquess of Lothian, Melbourne Hall, Derby

59 *Frederick Irby, 2nd Baron Boston* (No. 278). Oil, 1769. Private Collection, U.K.

60 *James Duff, 2nd Earl of Fife* (No. 173). Oil, 1765.
The North Carolina Museum of Art, Raleigh, North Carolina

61 Sir Joshua Reynolds: *James Waldegrave, 2nd Earl Waldegrave*.
Oil, 1759. The Earl Waldegrave, Chewton House,
Chewton Mendip, Bath

62 *Sir Robert Burdett, 4th Bt.* (No. 214). Oil, 1767.
G. F. Pinney, Esq., England

63 *Richard Myddelton* (No. 245). Oil, c.1767–70.
Lt.-Col. Ririd Myddelton, Chirk Castle, Chirk, Denbighshire

64 *Sir Griffith Boynton, 6th Bt.* (No. 279). Oil, 1769. Dr. and Mrs. Henry Clay Frick, Alpine, New Jersey

65 Sir Joshua Reynolds: *Captain Alexander Hood, later Vice-Admiral, 1st Viscount and Baron Bridport*. Oil, 1764. National Maritime Museum, Greenwich

66 *Dr. Connell* (No. 180). Oil, c.1765. Private Collection, U.K.

67 *Admiral Sir Edward Hawke* (No. 239). Oil, c.1767–70. National Maritime Museum, Greenwich

68 *Captain John Jervis, later Admiral and 1st Earl of St. Vincent* (No. 281). Oil, 1769. National Portrait Gallery, London

69 *Frances Lee* (No. 285). Oil, 1769. Milwaukee Art Center Collection, Milwaukee, Wisconsin; Gift of Mr. and Mrs. William D. Vogel

70 *Charles Collyer* (No. 195). Oil, 1766.
Mr. and Mrs. Paul Mellon Collection, U.S.A.

71 *Midshipman George Cranfield Berkeley* (No. 277). Oil, 1769.
R. J. G. Berkeley, Esq., Berkeley Castle, Berkeley, Gloucestershire

72 *Lewis Cage* (No. 255). Oil, 1768. Private Collection U.K.

73 Allan Ramsay: *John, Lord Mountstuart, later 4th Earl and 1st Marquess of Bute*. Oil, 1759. The Marquess of Bute, Mount Stuart, Rothesay, Isle of Bute

74 Sir Joshua Reynolds: *Thomas Lister, later 1st Lord Ribblesdale*. Oil, 1764. Earl of Swinton, U.K.

75 *Master Smith* (No. 270). Oil, c.1768–70. The Lord Burton's Trustees, U.K.

76 *Lady Cunliffe* (No. 176). Oil, 1765. Walker Art Gallery, Liverpool

77 *A Lady* (No. 259). Oil, 1768. National Gallery, London, with life interest for a private collector

78 *Sarah Child* (No. 190). Pastel, 1766. The Earl of Jersey, Radier Manor, Longueville, Jersey

79 *Lady Broughton* (No. 233). Oil, c.1767–70. National Trust, Attingham Park, Atcham, Shropshire

80 *Lady Hoare* (No. 204). Pastel, c.1766–70. National Trust, Stourhead House, Stourton, Wiltshire

81 Sir Joshua Reynolds: *Lady Sarah Bunbury Sacrificing to the Three Graces*. Oil, 1765. Art Institute, Chicago, W. W. Kimball Collection

82 *Anne Sandby as Emma, the Nut-Brown Maid* (No. 183). Oil, c.1765. Mrs. M. Smiley, Scotland

83 *The Duchess of Hamilton as Venus, Queen of Beauty*. (No. 219). Oil, 1767. The Duke of Argyll, Inveraray Castle, Inveraray, Argyllshire

84 *Mrs. William Colquhoun* (No. 256). Oil, 1768. Present whereabouts unknown

85 *Agneta Yorke* (No. 228). Oil, 1767/8. Private Collection, U.K.

86 *Lady Stanhope and Lady Effingham as Diana and her Companion* (No. 250). Oil, c.1767–70. The Earl of Mexborough, Methley Park, Leeds (on loan to Temple Newsam House, Leeds)

87 Philippe Mercier: *The Letter Writer*. Oil, probably painted in the 1740s.
Iveagh Bequest, Marble Hill, Twickenham

88 Sir Joshua Reynolds: *James Paine and his Son*. Oil, 1764.
Ashmolean Museum, Oxford

89 *Mr. and Mrs. Thomas Crathorne* (No. 216). Oil, 1767. Henry E. Huntington Library and Art Gallery, San Marino, California

90 Detail of the drapery on the figure of Thomas Crathorne in Fig. 89

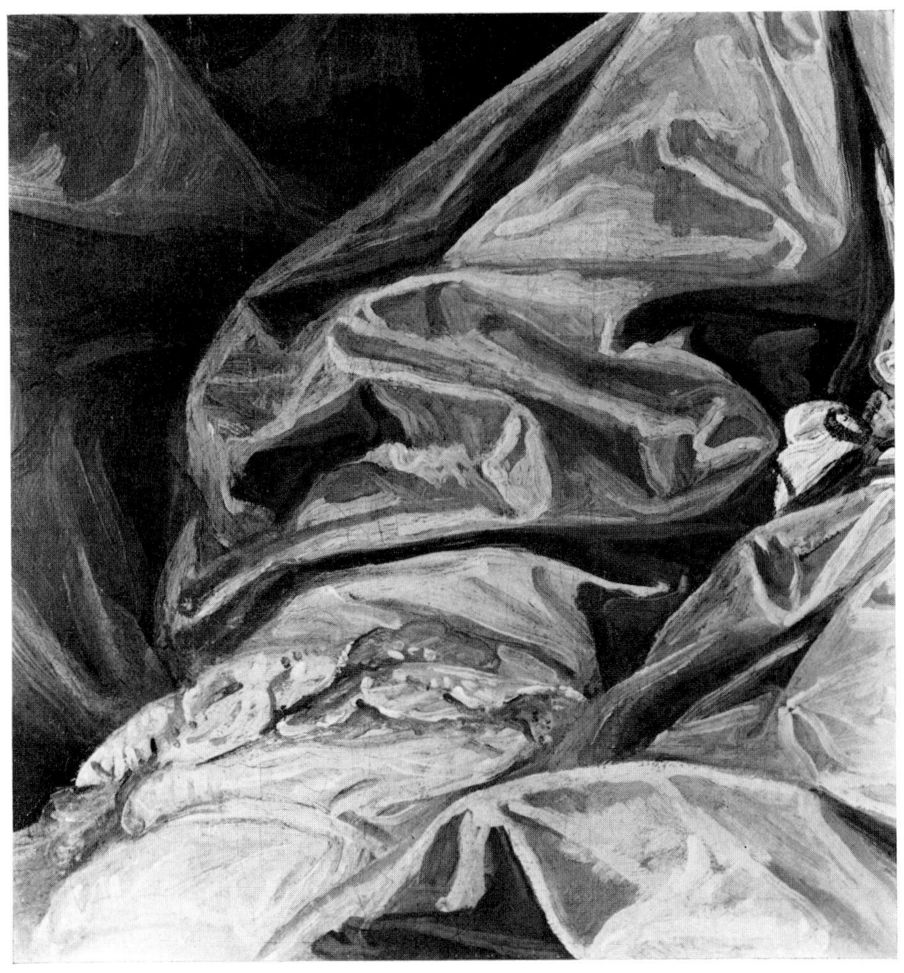

91 Detail of the drapery on the figure of Mrs. Crathorne in Fig. 89

92 *A Lady and a Gentleman* (No. 284). Oil, 1769. Around 1930 the picture was cut in two. One half is in Boston, cf. Fig. 93. The present whereabouts of the other half is unknown.

93 *A Lady* (cf. No. 284). Oil, 1769. The remaining half of No. 284, fig. 92. Museum of Fine Arts, Boston

94 *Mr. and Mrs. William Earle Welby* (No. 287). Oil, 1769. The family of Sir Oliver Welby, Bt.

95 Allan Ramsay: *Lady Susan Fox-Strangeways*. Oil, 1761.
Lady Teresa Agnew, Melbury House, Dorchester, Dorset

96 Allan Ramsay: *Queen Charlotte*. Oil, c.1761.
The Earl of Seafield, Cullen House, Cullen, Banffshire

97 Allan Ramsay: *Queen Charlotte*. Oil, 1761.
H.M. The Queen, Buckingham Palace

98 Allan Ramsay: *Queen Charlotte and Her Children*. Oil, 1763–5.
H.M. The Queen, Buckingham Palace

99 *Princess Caroline Matilda* (No. 188). Pastel, 1766.
S. K. H. der Prinz von Hannover, Herzog zu Braunschweig und Lüneburg; on loan to the Bomann-Museum, Celle, Lower Saxony

100 *Princess Louisa* (No. 227). Oil, c.1767.
H.M. Queen Elizabeth The Queen Mother, Clarence House

101 *Two Ladies at Music* (No. 225). Ink and wash, c.1767. Henry E. Huntington Library and Art Gallery, San Marino, California

102 *Princess Louisa and Queen Caroline Matilda of Denmark* (No. 220). Oil, 1767. H.M. The Queen, Buckingham Palace

103 *Queen Charlotte with Princess Charlotte* (No. 205). Pastel, 1767.
H.M. The Queen, Buckingham Palace

104 *Queen Charlotte with Princess Charlotte* (No. 206). Pastel, 1767.
The Duke of Northumberland, Syon House, Brentford, Middlesex

105 *Queen Charlotte with Princess Charlotte* (No. 215). Oil, 1767. H.M. The Queen, Windsor Castle

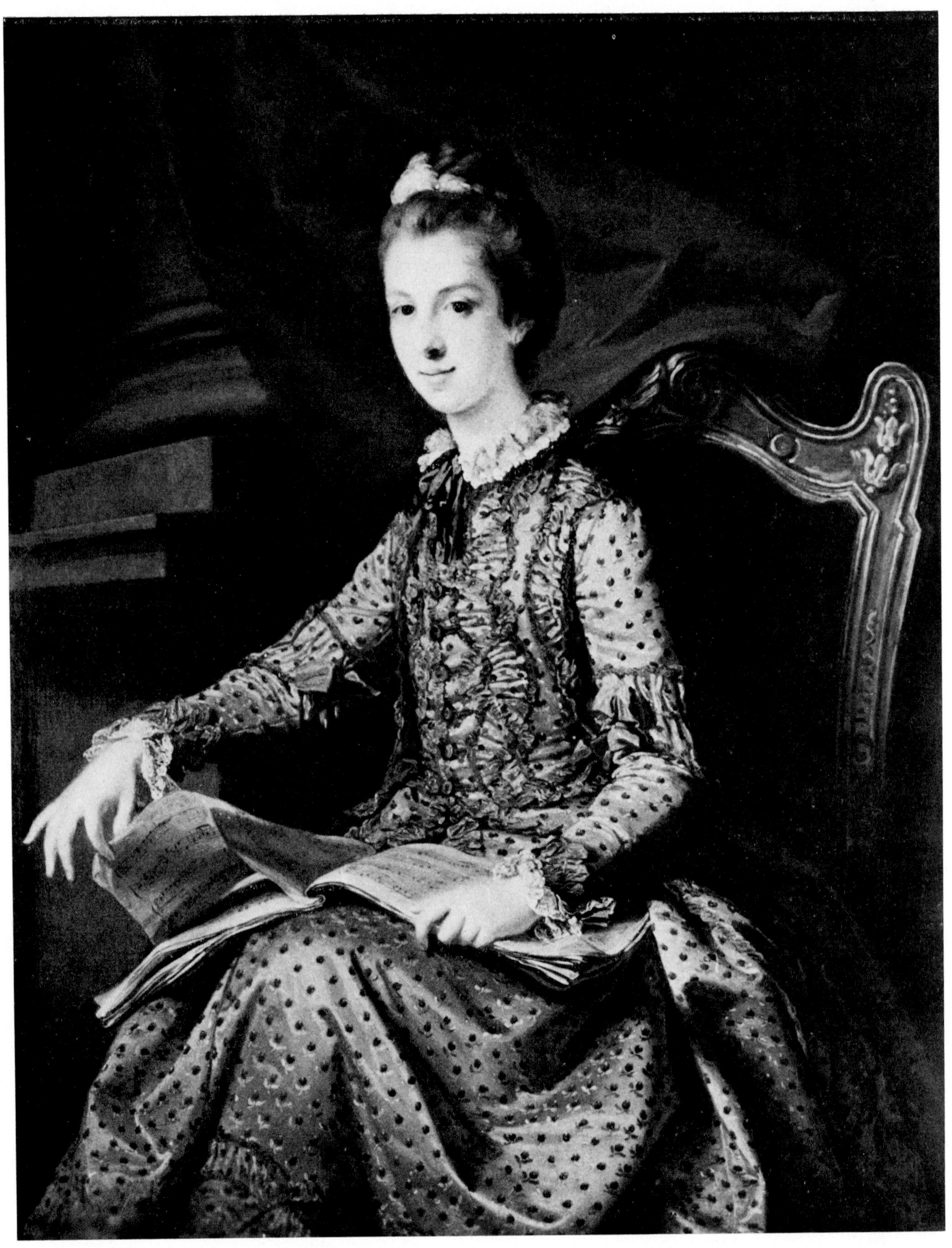

106 *Lady Brownlow Bertie* (No. 292). Oil, c.1769. Private Collection, U.K.

107 *A Lady* (No. 65). Pencil and wash, c.1755–c.1765.
Victoria and Albert Museum, London

108 *Sarah Cotes* (No. 297). Pastel, exhibited in 1770.
Present whereabouts unknown

109 *Sarah Cotes* (No. 296). Oil, 1770. Present whereabouts unknown

110 *Prince William Henry, Duke of Gloucester* (No. 273). Pastel, 1769. H.M. The Queen, Windsor Castle

APPENDIX I

The Cotes family tree. Source: Nichols, p. 35.

GUTHLAXTON.] AYLESTON. 35

PEDIGREE of COTES, of AYLESTON and BURBACH.

From the Visitations of 1619 and 1682 [1].

Arms: Argent, fretty Azure; on a canton Or, a lion rampant Sable. Crest, a cock proper, combed and wattled Or; Plate XII. fig. 13.

John Cotes, second son of John Cotes, of Cotes, co. Stafford, and Woodcote [2], co. Salop, esq.; died 1518. = Ellen second daughter of Richard Littleton, second son of Judge Littleton; died 1530.

John Cotes, of Norbury, co. Stafford, died 1544. = ...

Alexander Cotes, of Whittington, co. Stafford. = Margaret, dau. and heir of John Justinian, of Whittington.

1. Francis Cotes. = ...

2. John Cotes, of Ayleston. = Agnes, daughter of Robert Starkey, of Sutton on the Hill, co. Derby.

1. Francis Cotes, æt. 34, 1619.

1. Thomas Cotes, of Belgh Grange, co. Derby, æt. 48, 1619. = Amye, dau. of Ri. Johnson, of Callishull, c. Lanc.

1. Richard, æt. 23, 1619.

2. Alexander Cotes, of Knighton, æt. 52, 1619. = Amye, d. of J. Warde, of Knighton.

3. John Cotes, of Ayleston, æt. 46, 1619. = Anne, da. of . . . .

4. Roger Cotes, of the Borough of Leicester, mayor there 1629. = Ellen, da. of Robert Gillot, mayor of Leicester 1600.

Eleanor, dau. and coheir of W. Yarde [3], LL.B. of Cosby; 1st wife. = 1. John Cotes, æt. 26, 1619, of Callow Hall, co. Staff. 1652. = Elizabeth, dau. of Francis Aspinal, by Katherine his wife, daughter and coheir of Thomas Rugeley, of Hawkestead, co. Staff. esq.

2. Robert, æt. 10.
3. Thomas, æt. 13, 1619.

Alexander, æt. 6 months 1619; d. young.

1. John.
2. William.

1. Katharine, wife of Wm. Ironmonger, of Burton.
2. Anne, d. s. p.
3. Grace, wife of T. Herryman.
4. Elizabeth.
5. Dorothy, d. s. p.
6. Eleanor.

1. Elizabeth, married, 1st, Thomas Lingfield, of Houghton; 2dly, Fabian Andrews, of Stretton.
2. Katherine, married, 1st, Robert Roe, of Alport, co. Derby; 2dly, Nicholas Foxley, of Basset House.
3. Ann, married Richard Swinfen, of Sutton Cheyney.

1. John Cotes, of Ayleston, or Markfield, lived upon his estate; but, being ruined in the rebellious wars by Cromwell, sold his estate, and went to a place called Lorpora, and lived there for some time before he went to Ireland. = ...

2. Alexander Cotes, mayor of Leicester the same year Henry Cromwell was lord-lieutenant of Ireland.

3. Robert, æt. 4, 1619.

Anne, æt. 5, 1619.

Robert Cotes, of the Borough of Leicester, bapt. Sept. 2, 1610; living 1682, then æt. 73. = Margaret, d. of Henry Astley, of the town of Leicester.

1. William Cotes, of Roscommon in Ireland. = ... daughter of . . . . . Rous, of Elphin in Ireland.

2. . . . . . Cotes, ma. Thomas Hancock, of Ireland.
3. . . . . . . mar. . . . Pennock.

Grace, dau. of John Farmer, of Barwell; bur. June 25, 1677; first wife. = 1. Robert Cotes, bapt. Sept. 9, 1649; M. A. and rector of Aston cum Burbach 1679; bu. Nov. 12, 1717. = Mary . . . . d. May 23, 1719; second wife.

1. Eleanor, mar. to Walter Hudd, of Leicester.
2. Catharine, born 1636; died young.
3. Elizabeth, marr. 1639, Tho. Somerfeild, of Hinckley.
4. Margaret, b. 1642.
5. Abigail, bapt. Ap. 28, 1664; living, unmarried, 1682.
6. Hannah, b. 1646; unmarried 1682.
7. Mary, mar. 1682.

Anne, dau. to Nathaniel Fowler, of Prescot-street, London; died Dec. 11, 1722; first wife. = Robert Cotes, of St. Mary le Strand, in Middlesex; di. 1774. = Elizabeth, dau. of Francis Lynn, esq. secretary to the African Company; second wife.

1. Anthony Cotes, born May 8, bapt. June 1, 1681; buried Feb. 18, 1688.
2. Roger Cotes [4], the celebrated Mathematician; one of the greatest men this county has produced; born at Burbach July 10, bapt. July 25, 1682; died June 5, 1716.

Susanna, bapt. Aug. 14, 1683.

Robert Cotes, born Nov. 12, 1722; di. in March following.

1. Francis Cotes, esq. R. A. the celebrated painter, died July 19, 1770.
2. Robert Cotes, died young.
3. Samuel Cotes, esq. living 1804.
4. Frances-Maria, died an infant.

APPENDIX II

The sale of Francis Cotes's personal possessions.
Source: Francis Cotes Sale Catalogue,
Langford and Son, London, February 21–23, 25, 1771;
now kept at the Victoria and Albert Museum Library, London.

A
CATALOGUE
OF THE
L E A S E
OF THE
Large and commodious HOUSE,
With an elegant SUITE of Five Rooms on the First Floor, and Coach-Houſes and Stabling,
OF
FRANCIS COTES, Eſq;
Deceas'd;
Situate on the South-Side of *Cavendiſh-Square*;
As likewiſe of all
The genteel HOUSEHOLD FURNITURE, PICTURES; a large Collection of CASTS; Library of BOOKS; in which are the firſt Impreſſions of the MUSEI FLORENTINI, and the TRAJAN and ANTONINE COLUMNS; high finiſhed DRAWINGS; elegant wrought and chaſed PLATE; ornamental and uſeful CHINA; LINEN,
And other EFFECTS;

Which (by ORDER of the EXECUTORS)
Will be ſold by AUCTION,
By Mr. LANGFORD and Son,
On the PREMISES,
On *Thurſday* the 21ſt of this Inſtant *February* 1771,
and the Three following Days (*Sundays* excepted).

The ſame may be viewed on *Tueſday* the 19th, and till the Time of Sale, which will begin each Day punctually at Twelve o'Clock.

Printed Particulars of the Houſe, and Catalogues of the Effects, may be then had at the Place of Sale; and at Meſſ. LANGFORD's in *Covent Garden*.

Conditions of SALE,
For the GOODS.

1ſt, THAT the *higheſt Bidder* is to be the *Buyer*; and if *any Diſpute* ſhall ariſe between any *two* or *more Bidders*, the LOT ſo *diſputed* ſhall be *immediately put up again*, and *reſold*.

2dly, That no *Perſon* advance *leſs* than 6*d. under* a *Pound*; *above* a *Pound* 1*s. above* Five Pounds 2*s.* 6*d.* and ſo on *in Proportion*.

3dly, That the *Purchaſers* give in their *Names* and *Places of Abode*, and pay down *Five Shillings in the Pound (if required)* in Part of Payment of the *Purchaſe Money*; in Default of which, the LOT or LOTS *ſo purchaſed*, ſhall be *immediately put up again, and reſold*.

4thly, That the LOTS ſhall be *taken down and fetched away* with all Faults, at the *Buyer's Expence*, within One Day after the SALE; and the *Remainder* of the *Purchaſe Money* be ABSOLUTELY paid ON or BEFORE the *Delivery*.

Laſtly, That upon *Failure of complying* with the *above Conditions*, the Money ſo *depoſited* in *Part* of *Payment*, ſhall be *forfeited*; the LOTS *uncleared* within *the* Time abovementioned, ſhall be *reſold*, by *public* or *private Sale*, and the *Deficiency* (if any) *together with the Charges attending ſuch Reſale*, ſhall be *made good* by the *Defaulters* at this Sale.

[3]

Firſt Day's Sale, *Thurſday*, *Feb.* 21.

Numb. I. *The Upper Story backwards.*

LOT
1 A Four-poſt bedſtead on caſtors, with green ſerge furniture
2 A feather bed, bolſter, and pillow
3 Three blankets and a quilt
4 A table bedſtead, a feather bed, bolſter and pillow
5 Three blankets, and a printed linen quilt
6 A low wainſcot cheſt with drawers
7 Four chair ſeats covered with leather, braſs nailed, and a ſwing dreſſing glaſs
8 Four large prints of *Alexander*'s battles, fram'd, and 11 others fram'd
9 Three heads in crayons, and a drawing framed and glazed
10 Three paintings
11 A ſide lanthorn in a mahogany frame, with a looking glaſs back, 2 ſtools, and a pair of linſey curtains

The LEASE of the DWELLING HOUSE, OFFICES, &c.

THE Premiſes conſiſt of three large and lofty rooms on a Floor 3 ſtories high. and 5 good bedchambers on the 4th, with two large and well proportioned rooms with ſky-light and dome cielings added to the FIRST FLOOR, forming an ELEGANT SUITE; all of which are fitted up at a great expence, and finiſhed with rich marble chimney pieces, neat wainſcotting, and ſilk and other flock paper hangings.—In the *Dining Parlour*, there is an elegant receſs for the ſideboard, with fluted pilaſters, and enriched capitals and freeze.

Below Stairs, the offices are uſeful and convenient.—The *Garden* is *large*, and at the end is a lofty room with a portland chimney piece, &c. there is alſo ſtabling for 5 horſes, a coach houſe, coachman's room, and haylofts.

A 2 All

[4]

All the ſaid premiſes are in the moſt perfect repair, a very large ſum having been very lately expended in compleating the ſame. They are held for a term of 34 years from *Midſummer laſt paſt*, with an exception to the uſual trades, and ſubject to the payment of £105. *per Annum*; and together with all the valuable fixtures and appurtenances, will be put up at—*whatever Sum the Company ſhall approve.*

N.B. The purchaſer of the Houſe is to pay the ſum o £ . over and above the purchaſe money for the ſaid Leaſe for ſundry fixtures not ſcheduled to the premiſes, and a ſchedule of which will be produced at the time of ſale.

Numb. II. *The party-coloured Bed Chamber, two pair of Stairs*

1 A four-poſt ſacking bottom double ſcrew bedſtead, wit party-coloured feet poſt, on caſtors, with red copper plat furniture lin'd and fring'd, and a feſtoon window curtai ditto, compleat
2 A feather bed in a border'd tick, a bolſter, and 2 dow pillows
3 A white Holland mattraſs, and a check ditto
4 Three large blankets
5 A large white Holland quilt
6 Eight neat bamboo chairs, with ſtuft ſeats covered with th ſame as the bed furniture
7 A party-coloured japan'd night table and ſtool
8 A ditto low cheſt with drawers
9 A ditto baſon ſtand, with baſon and bottle
10 An oval ſconce 24 inch. by 17 inch. in a party-coloure frame
11 A dreſſing glaſs in a japan frame
12 An open work fender, ſhovel, tongs and poker, and 2 bed ſide carpets

Numb. III. *The Drawing Room.*

1 A very neat ſweep fronted ſteel ſtove on obeliſk feet wi pierced border and ſweep fender, ſhovel, tongs, ar poker
2 A mahogany pole fire ſkreen
3 Six mahogany ſtool back chairs covered with crimſon mi damaſk, braſs nailed, fluted feet, on caſtors, and crimſ ſerge caſes

4 Tw

(5)

4 Two mahogany elbow stool back chairs, covered with ditto
5 Two mahogany card tables on fluted feet, lin'd
6 An oval pier glass 32 inch. by 21 inch. in a carved and gilt frame, with a ribband top
7 A ditto
8 A beautiful green and white carpet, 19 feet 4 inch. by 16 feet 4 inch.
9 *Apollo* and *Daphne* in plaister bronz'd, on an ebony stand
10 Three crimson festoon mixt damask window curtains, compleat

PLATE, &c.

1 Four bottle tickets, and 4 salt spoons
2 Two ragoo spoons, and a scuer
3 A scollopt soup ladle
4 An embossed and fluted cream ewer, with a twisted handle
5 A neat open work sugar basket
6 Three neat large castors with handles, and pine apple tops
7 A small square waiter on feet, with a gadroon edge
8 A pair of round scollopt ditto
9 A large ditto
10 An elegant open work bread basket on feet
11 A very neat scollopt coffee pot
12 A ditto open work ink stand, with a gadroon edge
13 A pair of elegant fluted pillar candlesticks
14 A ditto
15 A neat snuffer pan, with a gadroon edge
16 A shagreen case, with 12 green ivory hafted knives and 12 forks, silver mounted
17 Six table spoons, and a marrow ditto
18 A shagreen case with 12 green ivory hafted desert knives and 12 forks, silver mounted
19 Twelve desert spoons
20 A large salver
21 Two small ditto
22 A pair of plated candlesticks, and a dish stand and lamp

Numb. IV. *The Breakfasting Parlour.*

1 Six mahogany chairs with horsehair seats
2 A mahogany fly leg table
3 A painted chimney blind, a tin fender, shovel, tongs, and poker

PRINTS.

[6]

PRINTS and DRAWINGS, *framed and glazed.*

4 A drawing by *Albano* in a *Carlo Marrat frame, glaz'd*
5 Six prints of marriage alamode, by *Hogarth*
6 Three mezzotintos after *Cotes*
7 Four ditto
8 Four ditto
9 Two ditto
10 One large ditto of *Miss Lascelles*
11 Two drawings after *Guercino* and *Bouchardon*
12 Two ditto, General *Wolfe*, &c.
13 Three ditto in water colours
14 Three portraits in crayons of *Erasmus, Locke* and *Newton*
15 Two fruit pieces in ditto
16 One ditto by *F. Cotes*
17 Six small prints by *Callot*
18 Four anatomical figures
19 A pair of horse pistols, holster and sumpter cloth
20 A model of the *Dreadnought* privateer
21 A glass globe lamp, shade, and brass bracket (*on the Stairs*)
22 A passage oil cloth, a long broom, and a dry rubber (*in the Passage*)

Second Day's Sale, *Friday, Feb.* 22.

Numb. V. *The Upper Story forwards.*

LOT
1 A Four post bedstead on castors, with green serge furniture
2 A feather bed bolster and pillow
3 Three blankets, and a printed linen quilt
4 A low wainscot chest with drawers
5 A field bedstead on castors with red check furniture, a counterpane, and 2 pair of window curtains and rods
6 A feather bed, bolster, and 3 blankets
7 A mahogany night table and stool
8 An high mahogany chest with drawers

9 A

[7]

9 A square mahogany bason stand, a bason and ewer, and a bedside carpet
10 A deal toilet table, with a crimson coat stript muslin veil, dimity cover, and a swing dressing glass in a mahogany frame with drawers

CHINA and GLASS.

1 A blue and white tea pot, 5 breakfast cups, 5 saucers, a sugar dish, cover and plate, a cream ewer, a bread and butter plate, (*of the Nankeen china*), 8 small cups, 10 saucers, and 2 basons
2 Three blue and white dishes, 3 odd table plates, and 4 scollopt tart plates
3 Two blue and white bowls, and 2 basons
4 Two enamell'd image mugs
5 Four blue and white sallad dishes
6 A blue and white tea pot, 12 handle tea cups, 12 saucers, 6 coffee cups, a sugar dish and cover (*of the Nankeen china*), 3 odd cups, 2 saucers, and a bason
7 Three enamelled and painted basons, and 4 plates
8 A blue and white tureen and cover, and 12 plates (*different patterns*)
9 Sixteen ditto soup plates, and 4 scollopt shells
10 Two dozen of table plates
11 Eight blue and white scollopt oblong dishes
12 Eight ditto
13 Five large ditto
14 A white jug, 5 blue and white mugs, 2 sauce boats, a potting pot, a bason, 3 butter cups, and a jar and cover
15 Two blue and white slippers and covers
16 Five wine decanters, 2 water ditto, and 12 wine glasses
17 Six cut water decanters, 2 dozen and a half of cut wine glasses, 2 salts, and 11 sweetmeat, and other glasses
18 One dozen of water glasses, 2 wine and water ditto, and 2 beer ditto
19 Two cut glass cruets, 4 salts with a mahogany stand, and 4 green cruets for soy, &c.

Numb.

(8)

Numb. VI. *The printed Cotton Bed Chamber, two-pair of Stairs forwards.*

1 An elegant lath bottom double screw canopy bedstead, with neat mahogany feet posts and board, chintz pattern printed cotton furniture, lin'd and fring'd
2 Three festoon window curtains of the same cotton as the bed, lin'd and fring'd, compleat
3 A feather bed in a bordered tick, in a check case, a bolster, and 2 down pillows
4 An hair mattrass
5 Three large blankets, and a printed linen quilt
6 A large white callico quilt
7 A fender, shovel, tongs, poker, bellows, 3 bedside carpets, and a dressing glass in a mahogany frame
8 Six stained matted bottom elbow chairs, with hair cushions, and printed cotton cases fring'd
9 A mahogany Pembroke table on castors
10 A mahogany night table and stool, with a slide
11 A low mahogany chest with drawers on castors
12 A ditto with a shaving stand top, and 6 green ivory handle rasors, &c.
13 An high mahogany cloaths press, with 4 drawers
14 Two oval pier glasses, in carved and painted frames
15 A deal toilet table, with crimson coat and gauze cover, a dressing glass in a japan frame, with a gauze veil, and 10 japan dressing boxes
16 Two plaister vases, and 2 boys
17 A low deal chest of drawers

Numb. VII. *The Dining Parlour.*

1 Six mahogany chairs, with horse hair seats, and brass nailed
2 Two elbow ditto
3 A neat mahogany sideboard, with fluted front and feet
4 Two square mahogany flap dining tables, to join occasionally
5 An oval pier glass, the plate 32 inch. by 22 inch. in a carved and gilt frame
6 Two worsted damask festoon window curtains fring'd, compleat

7 A

(9)

7 Two pair of canvas window blinds in mahogany frames, and an open work fender, shovel, tongs and poker
8 A *Turkey* carpet 11 feet by 10 feet, and a small *India* mat
9 Two brown enamell'd basons
10 Two enamell'd scarlet jars, and 2 bottles
11 Two enamell'd paned jars and covers
12 Two beautiful enamell'd image jars and covers, and 2 beakers ditto

Numb. VIII. *The Painting Room, and Room adjoining.*

1 Six mahogany stool back chairs, covered with crimson mixt damask, brass nailed, on castors, and crimson serge covers
2 Two elbow ditto
3 A large mahogany commode, with a desk top, variety of drawers, and mask and fluted corners
4 A mahogany writing table on a pillar and claw, and 2 mahogany stools
5 A *Wilton* carpet 19 feet 6 inches by 18 feet
6 A stage covered with carpetting, with a mahogany machine chair cover'd with mixt damask, and crimson serge case
7 A mahogany box for colours, mounted with brass, on a stand, with a drawer
8 A wainscot tool chest with tools
9 An high pair of steps, and a serge window curtain, with a brass rod
10 A mahogany nest of drawers with folding doors

The Shew Room.

11 A *Turkey* carpet 9 feet by 7 feet 7 inch. a shovel, tongs, poker, bellows and brush
12 A brazier, and an high pair of steps
13 Nine canvas spring window blinds
14 An *India* floor mat, 22 feet 6 inches, by 14 feet 6 inches

B Numb.

(10)

Numb. IX. *The Pupil's Room.*

MODELS *in* CASTS *and* PLAISTER.

1 Sundry parts of figures, boys, gladiators, &c.
2 Ten arms moulded from nature
3 Eight feet ditto, from *Bernini*
4 Eight ditto
5 Fifteen boys from *Fiamingo*, &c.
6 A colossal foot, and 2 others, from the antique
7 A boy from *Fiamingo*, and 2 trunks from *Bernini*, and the antique
8 Four masks from the antique
9 Five ditto from nature, a fine boys head by *Fiamingo*, and a trunk of *Daphne*, &c.
10 Two trunks from *Bernini*, and a satyr's mask
11 A crouching *Venus*, an original cast from the antique
12 The *Gladiator* and the *Antinous*
13 Three heads of *Niobe*'s mother, &c.
14 Three ditto, *Bernini's Proserpine*, the *Apollo* of the *Belvidere*, and 1 of *Niobe*
15 Three antique heads of *Jupiter*, *Seneca*, and another
16 Three ditto from the antique
17 Two heads of *Homer* and *Minerva*, and two of *Niobe*'s family
18 Three figures, *Germanicus*, *a fine cast*, *Roubilliac*'s anatomy, and another from *Bernini*
19 Three, a fine head of *Augustus Cæsar*, 1 of *Attalanta*, a mask from *Fiamingo*, and a ditto from the antique
20 Ten pieces, boys from *Fiamingo*, arms and heads from ditto, &c.
21 Nine ditto
22 Nine ditto, and a greyhound
23 Eight heads from *Fiamingo* and the antique
24 Three busts, *Plautilla*, *Niobe*'s daughter, and *Milo*

N. B. *The remaining Lots of this Number will be sold To-morrow*; *see Page* 13.

Third

Third Day's Sale, *Saturday*, *Feb.* 23.

Numb. X. *The Butler's Room.*

LOT

1 A Painted press bedstead
2 A feather bed, bolster, and 1 pillow
3 Three blankets, and 2 quilts
4 A napkin press, and a wainscot flap table
5 Five iron bound casks, a runlet, 2 coolers, and 1 pail *(in the back airy)*
6 A parcel of glass bottles

Numb. XI. PAINTINGS *in the Painting Room, and shew Room.*

1 Twelve various
2 Eight basso relievos, &c.
3 Seven small sketches
4 Eleven various
5 Eight unfinished
6 Six half lengths and kit cats
7 Five half lengths
8 Three of various sketches
9 Four half lengths, &c.
10 Five 3 quarters
11 An unfinished whole length
12 An half length
13 A landscape and figures
14 A piece of ruins and figures
15 A *Dutch* family
16 Three various in crayons
17 Five unfinished heads in crayons
18 Five ditto
19 Four ditto of ladies
20 Two ditto finished
21 Two ditto
22 Three ladies, in ditto
23 Two ditto, the Queen of *Denmark* and Miss *Lassels*
24 A man's head fram'd and glaz'd

B 2 25 One

25 One ditto of Miss *Jones*, fram'd and glaz'd
26 One ditto of a lady, fram'd and glaz'd
27 Two ditto of the Dutchess of *Hamilton* and lady *Coventry*
28 Two heads, fram'd and glaz'd
29 Two ditto
30 A small whole length of *Emma*
31 A fryar's head, and 1 other
32 A dog's head, *framed and glaz'd*, by *Cotes*
33 A view in the Isle of *Wight* by *ditto*
34 A woman with a lamp by *Giuseppe Chiari*
35 A man's head on a pannel. *Flemish*
36 A small half length on copper
37 *Vandycke's* portrait, copied by Mr. *Dahl*
38 A sea piece by *Seres*
39 A ditto by *Cuyp*
40 A landscape by *Gainsborough*
41 A ditto by *Wilson*
42 A storm by *Vandevelde*
43 A boy asleep, a sketch by *Vandyck*
44 Two heads by *Dobson*

PRINTS and DRAWINGS, *framed and glazed.*

In the Dining Parlour.

45 Two prints after *Salvator Rosa* by *Pond*
46 One, ruins and figures
47 Two round views in red chalk
48 Two views in water colours by *F. Cotes*
49 Two ruins and figures in bister by *Panini*
50 Two ditto
51 Two ditto
52 Two ditto in colours by *Panini*
53 Two ditto by *ditto*
54 Two ditto by *ditto*
55 A view of *Netly Abbey* by *F. Cotes*
56 The west view of ditto by *ditto*

In the Drawing Room.

57 The discovery of *Calista* by *Veugles*
58 The deluge by *ditto*
59 A landscape and figures by *Horizonti*
60 Ditto, its companion
61 A landscape and figures by *Zuccarelli*

62 A

62 A man and a woman by *Metzu*
63 Two landscapes in water colours by *Marco Rice*
64 Two ditto
65 A large view by Mr. *P. Sandby*
66 A ditto
67 *Cupid* in crayons by *Cotes*
68 A *Venus* and *Cupid* by *ditto*

Numb. IX. *The Pupil's Room; continued from Page* 10.

25 Three figures *Antinous*, 2 from *John de Bologna*, and a bust of *Venus*
26 A very fine terra cota model by *John de Bologna*
27 A bust of the *Venus de Medicis*
28 A terra cota model of history by *Rysbrack*
29 A fine cast of the infant *Hercules*
30 A bust of *Carracalla*
31 A ditto of *Lucius Papyrius's* mother
32 The trunk of Mr. *Lock's Venus*, 2 legs from *Fiamingo*, a head and a feet
33 The group of wrestlers, a fine cast
34 King [illegible] on horseback by *Rysbrack (bronzed)*
35 Three fine casts from *Rysbrack* of *Fiamingo*, *Inigo Jones*, and *Palladio*
36 A fine cast of *Venus* from Mr. *Pigalle's* model
37 A ditto of *Mercury* from *ditto*.
N. B. These are are original casts from the model
38 A marble statue of *Diana*, from the antique
39 A skelleton of a lay man
40 A large lay woman
41 Three eazells
42 A mahogany, and a painted ditto
43 A porphyry stone to grind colours, and a muller
44 A box of very fine lake
45 Thirteen glass jars with variety of colours, 5 empty glass jars, and [illegible] boxes with variety of colours
46 A marble stone for mixing of colours, several boxes with crayons, and a shagreen case with instruments
47 A colour box, a crayon ditto, a ditto for drawings, 3 pallets, and a parcel of pencil brushes
48 A *German* stove and pipe
49 A wainscot table with drawers, a chair, and a stool

Fourth

Fourth Day's Sale, *Monday*, *Feb.* 25.

Numb. XII. *The Kitchen.*

LOT

1 A Large fender, shovel, tongs, poker, bellows, 2 meat spits, a lark ditto, a pig iron, a salamander, a pair of hanging spit racks, 2 hanging irons, 4 trevets, and a frying pan
2 A gridiron, a cinder shovel, a pair of heater tongs, a dripping pan stand, a trevet, a cleaver, a chopping knife, a sugar hatchet, a pair of steak tongs, a meat fork, 4 scuers, 2 japan'd candlesticks, 1 iron ditto, 3 pair of snuffers, an extinguisher, 2 flat irons, 1 box ditto, and a stand
3 A large boiling pot and cover
4 A ditto less
5 A copper fish pan plate and cover
6 A copper stewing pan and cover, and a large sauce pan and cover
7 Four copper sauce pans with 2 covers, and a tea kettle
8 A small copper frying pan, a chocolate pot, 3 skimmers, and 2 ladles
9 A copper coal skuttle, and a warming pan
10 A large copper coal skuttle
11 A japan capuchin plate warmer
12 Twelve pewter table plates
13 Three scolloped hard metal pewter dishes, and 12 plates ditto
14 A pair of princes metal pillar candlesticks
15 A bell metal skillet, a pair of brass scales with 5 weights, a brass tinder box, a drudger, and a pepper box
16 A brass pail and cover
17 A large marble mortar and wood pestle
18 A dinner bell, 3 window bells, six wooden chairs, a wainscot table, and a spice cup-board
19 An eight day clock with an astronomical dial by *Wady*, in a japan case

20 Nine

20 Nine dishes, 24 plates, 4 sauce boats, 4 bleaumenge cups, 2 sugar dishes and covers *(of the Queen's ware)*
21 A parcel of tin, stone, earthen and wooden ware
22 Two dozen of horn hafted knives, and 2 dozen of forks, a green ivory hafted carving knife and fork in a mahogany tray, a wainscot box, and 3 calf skin bottle stands

LINNEN.

1 Two pair of *Russia* sheets
2 Two pair of ditto
3 Two pair of ditto
4 Two pair of ditto, and 2 pair of pillow cases
5 Two pair of fine ditto, and 2 pair of pillow cases
6 A pair of *Holland* sheets, 1 large callico sheet, and 2 pair of pillow cases
7 Four huckaback table cloths
8 Four ditto
9 Three damask ditto
10 Three ditto
11 Two large fine ditto, and 6 napkins
12 Six diaper breakfast napkins, and 6 huckaback towels
13 Four jack towels, 12 glass cloths, and 6 knife ditto

BOOKS.

OCTAVO & DUODECIMO.

1 About 40 odd volumes
2 Three, Terentii Comœdiæ, and 2 others
3 The State of cork, and 12 others
4 Dying Speeches, 2 vol. and 3 others
5 Roman Antiquities, and 5 others
6 Collier's View of the Stage—Drake against Collier, and 2 others
7 History of standing Armies—— Davenant's Essays, and 4 others
8 Montaigne's Essays, 3 vol.
9 Swift's Miscellanies, 2 vol. and 2 other odd volumes
10 Temple's Letters, 2 vol.—Pope's Letters—Lord Arlington's Letters
11 Shaftsbury's Characteristicks, 3 vol.
12 Collier's Essays—Huet on Human Understanding, and 2 others

13 History

13 History of Europe, 2 vol.——History of England
14 Tacitus, 3 vol.
15 Sublime and Beautiful——The Love of Fame
16 Geographical Grammar —— Experimental History of Colours
17 Roman History, 5 vol.
18 Historical Register, 10 vol.
19 Monthly Register, 4 vol.
20 Art of English Poetry—Prior's Poems
21 Poetical Miscellanies, 3d, 4th and 6th parts — Dryden's Juvenal
22 Mist's Miscellany Letters, 2 vol.
23 Tracts about the Spanish Succession, and 2 others
24 State Tryals, 6 vol.
25 The Lives of eminent Painters—A Treatise on Painting by Leonardo da Vinci
26 Webb on Painting——Algarotti on Painting—Dryden's Art of Painting, and 2 others
27 Polygraphice——Woodward's Natural History —— The Pantheon
28 Fugitive Pieces—Webb on Poetry
29 Every Man his own Broker— A short Account of Geneva
30 Hoole's Tasso, 2 vol.
31 Metastasio's Works, 2 vol.
32 Francis's Horace, 4 vol.
33 The Works of Shakespear, 10 vol.
34 Yorick's Sermons, 4 vol.
35 Clarke's Sermons, 10 vol.
*35 Dodsley's Poems, 6 vol.

QUARTO.

36 Bacon's Advance of Learning—Sylva Sylvarum
37 Locke's Essay on Understanding
38 Burnet's Theory
39 British Apollo, 3 vol.
40 Mr. Walpole's Anecdotes on Painting, 3 vol.
41 Painter's Dictionary
42 London and Westminster improved
43 Robertson's History, 3 vol. —— 1769
44 Boyer's Dictionaire, 2 vol.

FOLIO.

APPENDIX III

Catalogues of the Society of Artists (1760–1768)
Catalogues of the Royal Academy (1769–1770)
Marginal Notes by Horace Walpole

Sources

The John [Bowyer] Nicholls Collection of original Society of Artists catalogues, 1760–1790, now kept at the Print Room, the British Museum, London.

The J. R. Anderdon collection of original Royal Academy Catalogues, Vol. I, 1769–1775, now kept at the Print Room, the British Museum, London.

Hugh Gatty (ed.), 'Notes by Horace Walpole, Fourth Earl of Orford, on the Exhibitions of the Society of Artists and the Free Society of Artists, 1760–1791', (Walpole's catalogues from the collection of W. S. Lewis, Farmington, Connecticut). *The Walpole Society*, Vol. XVII, Oxford, The Walpole Society, 1939, p. 63.

Algernon Graves, *The Society of Artists of Great Britain, 1760–1791; The Free Society of Artists, 1761–1783, A Complete Dictionary of Contributors and Their Work from the Foundation of the Societies to 1791*, London, George Bell and Sons, 1907, p. 65.

Algernon Graves, *The Royal Academy of Arts, A Complete Dictionary of Contributors and Their Work from Its Foundation in 1769 to 1904*, London, Henry Graves and Co., and George Bell and Sons, 1905, p. 175.

The catalogue entries are taken from the original catalogues in the Bowyer and Anderdon collections. The marginal comments by Horace Walpole are taken from Hugh Gatty and Algernon Graves (cf. above), and are designated accordingly. While it is known that Gatty consulted Walpole's catalogues from the Lewis collection, it is not known what set of Walpole's catalogues Graves used. Occasionally the comments differ; all comments are recorded in the Appendix.

Catalogues of Society of Artists Exhibitions

1760. Opening day, April 21

Mr. Francis Cotes

10. A Lady in Crayons.
11. A Man's Head.
12. The Late Sir Edward Hulse.
13. Half Length in Oil of a Young Lady in the Character of Emma, or the Nut-brown Maid.

1761. Opening day, May 9

Mr. Francis Cotes

17. A portrait of a lady in crayons.
18. Ditto of a gentleman, ditto.
19. Two children, ditto.
20. Whole length of a young gentleman, in oil.
21. Half length of Mr. Paul Sandby, ditto.
22. Ditto of a lady.

1762. Opening day, May 7

Mr. Francis Cotes

12. A lady, half length.
13. A sea officer, ditto.
14. A lady, kit cat.
15. Ditto, three quarters.
16. A head of a young gentleman.
17. A lady's head, crayons.
18. A ditto, in ditto.
19. A gentleman, ditto.

1763. Opening day, May 14

Mr. Francis Cotes

23. A countess in her coronation robes, whole length.
    Walpole's comment: 'very good. Countess of Macclesfield, with a view of Westminster Abbey'. (Gatty)
24. A lady, half length.
25. A lady, in crayons.
26. Mr. Obrien, ditto.
    Walpole's comment: 'the comedian. the best picture in the exhibition'. (Gatty)
27. A spaniel in oil.

1764. Opening day, April 9

Mr. Francis Cotes

20. A gentleman's head in crayons.
    Walpole's comment: 'good'. (Gatty)
21. Ditto.
    Walpole's comment: 'good. General Keppel'. (Gatty)
22. A lady in oil, kit cat.
    Walpole's comment: 'Leaning on a table, which reflects her ruffles'. (Graves)
23. A gentleman ditto, half length.
    Identified by Graves as 'John Gregory.'

1765. Opening day, April 23

Mr. Francis Cotes, Cavendish Square

16. Emma, a whole length.
 Walpole's comment: 'The figure very pretty'. (Gatty)
17. A nobleman, ditto.
 Walpole's comment: 'Earl of Fife'. (Gatty)
18. A gentleman ditto.
 Walpole's comment: 'part of it, good. Mr. Milner, an old gentleman'. (Gatty)
 According to Graves, Walpole's comment was: 'Mr. Mills, Engineer to New River Company'.
19. A lady, in crayons.
20. A child playing with a greyhound, ditto.
 Walpole's comment: 'very pretty'. (Gatty)
21. Portrait of a gentleman, ditto.
 Walpole's comment: 'Admiral Keppel, good'. (Gatty)

1766. Opening day, April 21

Mr. Francis Cotes, Cavendish Square

25. Portrait of an officer, half length.
26. Ditto of ditto.
 Walpole's comment: 'Colonel Philips'. (Gatty)
27. Ditto of a lady, ditto.
28. Ditto of a young lady in an oval.
29. Ditto of a lady in crayons.
 Walpole's comment: 'very good. Oval'. (Gatty)
 According to Graves, Walpole's remark was: 'Mrs. Child'.
30. Ditto ditto.

1767. Opening day, April 22

Mr. Francis Cotes, Cavendish Square

32. Portrait from the life of her Majesty, with the Princess Royal, in crayons.
 Walpole's comment: 'The Queen fine; the Child, incomparable. The Duchess of Northumberland has the Original, given to her by the Queen. There is a whole length of the same (This is oval) at the Queen's house in the Park and has been engraved. The sleeping Child is equal to Guido. Cotes succeeded much better in crayons than in oils'. (Gatty)
 According to Graves, Walpole's comment was: 'A handsome likeness'.
33. Portrait of a gentleman in ditto.
 Walpole's comment: 'Knapton the Painter'. (Gatty)
34. A child's head ditto.
35. A lady, whole length.
 Walpole's comment: 'Eliz. Gunning Duchess of Hamilton; awkward'. (Gatty)
 According to Graves, Walpole's comment was: 'Duchess of Hamilton, Not like'.
36. A gentleman, kitcat.
37 A young lady, three quarters.

1768. Opening day. April 28

Mr. F. Cotes, Cavendish Square

30. A lady, whole length.
31. A conversation.
32. A lady's head in crayons.
 Walpole's comment: 'Polly Jones'. (Gatty)

1768 (second exhibition). Opening day, September 30

Mr. Francis Cotes

22. A lady, whole length.
23. A gentleman in crayons.

Catalogues of Royal Academy Exhibitions

(Catalogue entries are from Anderdon; Walpole's remarks are from Graves.)

1769. Opening day, April 26

Francis Cotes, R.A., Cavendish Square

22. A portrait of a lady, whole length.
23. Ditto of a young gentleman.
 Walpole's comment: 'Very pretty'.
24. Ditto of a lady, half length.
 Walpole's comment: 'Mrs. Bouverie'.
25. Ditto of a gentleman.
26. Ditto, of a lady and gentleman at chess.
27. A portrait in crayons of his Royal Highness the Duke of Gloucester.
 Walpole's comment: 'Exceedingly like'.
28. A young lady ditto in the character of Hebe.
 Walpole's comment: 'Very Pretty'.

1770

Francis Cotes, R.A., Cavendish Square

50. The Portrait of a Lady (Mrs. Sawbridge).
 Walpole's comment: 'Mrs. Sawbridge, wife of the Alderman, with a palm branch and inscription "Templum felicitatis" '.
51. Ditto of a gentleman } whole lengths.
52. Ditto Captain Leister } whole lengths.
53. Ditto of a lady, whole length.
54. Ditto an Oval.
55. Ditto Mr. Watman.
56. Ditto a gentleman } three quarters.
 Walpole's comment: 'Duke of Beaufort'. } three quarters.
57. Ditto.
58. Ditto of His Royal Highness the Duke of Cumberland.
 According to Graves, the catalogue description was: 'A portrait of His Royal Highness the Duke of Cumberland, in crayons'.
59. Ditto of a lady in crayons.
 Walpole's comment: 'His own wife with a shock dog'.
60. Ditto.

APPENDIX IV

Notes on crayon painting by Francis Cotes, found among his papers after his death.
Source: *The European Magazine*, February 1797, pp. 84, 85.

The following is the Copy of a Manuscript found among the Papers of the late Francis Cotes, Esq. the celebrated Crayon Painter. It cannot fail to afford pleasure to such of your Readers as amuse themselves in the study and practice of this elegant branch of the Fine Arts.

CRAYON PAINTING

Crayon Pictures are in their nature more delicate, and consequently more liable to injury, than almost every other kind of painting: they are usually executed upon a paper ground, pasted over the finest linen, and are often painted upon blue, but most commonly upon paper prepared with a size ground, rendered of a middle teint for the sake of expedition, and sometimes upon paper perfectly white. It must not be concluded that because Crayon pictures are easily injured, that they cannot with care be preserved a great length of time; nay, for many centuries; but it will always be necessary to keep them with attention, and above all things to take care that they are not left in damp rooms, or in moist places, for the paste which is used in preparing the grounds will inevitably produce a mildew, and blacks and the darkest colours be covered with spots.

All the light teints of English Crayons are perfectly safe and durable, and pictures of this description are to be seen that have been painted more than forty years, and which have been exposed to the climates of the East and West Indies; and are, notwithstanding, in no respect decayed. It must always be remembered, that as Crayon pictures are dry, and have of course a powdery surface, they never should be left uncovered with a glass; because whatever dust settles upon them cannot be blown off or removed in any other manner. Crayon pictures, when finely painted, are superlatively beautiful, and decorative in a very high degree in apartments that are not too large; for, having their surface dry, they partake in appearance of the effect of Fresco, and by candle light are luminous and beautiful beyond all other pictures.

The finest examples that are known in this branch of painting are the pictures by the Caval. Mengs in the gallery at Dresden, the Seasons and other beautiful paintings by Rosalba, and certain portraits of Liotard, which are dispersed and to be found all over Europe, as he painted in almost every country; perhaps to these may be added a few of my late master's portraits; and finally, if it will not be deemed too much presumption, my father's portrait and Mr. Knapton's, her Majesty with the Princess Royal sleeping, Mrs. Child, Miss Jones, Miss Wilton, and a few other portraits by myself.

Whatever spots appear in the blacks and darkest colours are easily removed with care by the point of a penknife; and if any spots should arise upon the light parts of the flesh, or other places, they should in like manner be scraped off and repainted in, a spot at a time, exactly corresponding with the surrounding teints, till all the decayed parts are restored, which has often been done with admirable effect.

APPENDIX V

Unverified attributions

All the portraits in this appendix have been attributed to Cotes. Most of them were never photographed and are now lost or damaged beyond recognition. Several, however, are known to be in private collections which the author has not had the opportunity to visit. In the future, it is hoped that enough evidence will be assembled on these portraits so that one will be in a position to judge whether they are or are not by Cotes. No such judgement is made at the present time. For the reader's convenience these portraits are listed briefly. If a more detailed description of a portrait is desired, consult the sources mentioned in the entry.

1745–1750

1. **Hannah Chamber,** presumably oil on canvas, 30 × 24 in., neither signed nor dated. P. Berney Ficklin, Esq., Tasburgh Hall, Norfolk (1908). Present whereabouts unknown. Cf. *PN.*, Vol. II, p. 337, no. 17, dated by Duleep Singh, 1745–1750. NB. An oil portrait at this date would be highly unusual in Cotes's oeuvre.

1750

2. **Jane Morgan,** oil on canvas, 36 × 28 in., neither signed nor dated. Formerly in the collection of the Lord Tredegar, Tredegar Park, Newport, Monmouthshire. Present whereabouts unknown. Exhibited at the National Museum of Wales, 1934. Cf. *PW.*, Vol. II, p. 164, dated by Steegman, 1750.

1750–1760

3. **Mary Elizabeth, Marchioness of Buckingham,** presumably oil on canvas, neither signed nor dated. Sir Maurice Boileau, Ketteringham Hall, Ketteringham, Norfolk (1912). Present whereabouts unknown. *PN.*, Vol. I, p. 363, no. 87, dated by Duleep Singh, 1750–1760.

1751

4. **Elizabeth Talbot,** pastel on paper, $23\frac{1}{2} \times 17\frac{1}{2}$ in., possibly signed and dated 1751. Cf. Anon. Sale, Christie's, March 14, 1903 (lot 83). In the sale catalogue the date 1751 is assigned to the picture, but a signature and date are not mentioned. Present whereabouts unknown. This may be the Mrs Talbot referred to by Samuel Richardson, cf. Supplement no. 1.

1752

5. **A Gentleman,** pastel on paper, $23\frac{1}{8} \times 17\frac{1}{2}$ in., signed and dated 1752. The Marquess of Normanby. Cf. The Rev. Canon the Marquess of Normanby Sale, Christie's, May 8, 1897 (lot 92), bought by West.

6. **A Lady,** pastel on paper, $22 \times 16\frac{1}{2}$ in., signed and dated 1752. Cf. Anon. Sale, Christie's, May 10, 1912 (lot 67), bought by P. and D. Colnaghi, London. Present whereabouts unknown.

7. **A Lady,** pastel on paper, 23 × 18 in., signed and dated 1752. Cf. Anon. Sale, Christie's, July 25, 1919 (lot 47), bought by Shoebridge. Present whereabouts unknown.

1753

8. **Charles Dillon, Later 12th Viscount Dillon,** pastel on paper, 24 × 18 in., signed and dated 1753. Cf. The Viscount Dillon Sale, Sotheby's, May 24, 1933 (lot 5), bought by Neville. Present whereabouts unknown.

1755

9. **A Lady,** pastel on paper, signed and dated 1755. Cf. Seymour Robert Delmé Sale, Christie's, July 7, 1894 (lot 65), bought by Rutley. Present whereabouts unknown.

1756

10. **A Lady,** pastel on paper, $24\frac{1}{2} \times 20\frac{1}{2}$ in., signed and dated 1756. Cf. Jeffrey Whitehead Sale, Christie's, August 6, 1915 (lot 52), bought by Stettiner. Present whereabouts unknown.

1757

11 [Erratum]. **A Lady of the Conolly Family,** pastel on paper, signed and dated 1757. Now catalogued as Supplement no. 5.

12 [Erratum]. **A Gentleman,** pastel on paper, signed and dated 1757. Now catalogued as Supplement no. 6.

c. 1757(?)

13. **A Gentleman,** pastel on paper, a companion picture to nos. 11 and 12 in this Appendix; presumably no. 13 was done at approximately the same time. The Earl of Strafford (1937). Present whereabouts unknown. Cf. Records of Professor E. K. Waterhouse.

1758

14 [Erratum]. **Catherine Gunning,** pastel on paper, $25\frac{1}{2} \times 17\frac{1}{2}$ in., signed and dated 1758. Now catalogued as Supplement no. 7.

1760

15. **Lady Anne Fitzpatrick, as a Child,** pastel on paper, 23½ × 17½ in., signed and dated 1760. Present whereabouts unknown. The Lord Ravensworth Sale, Eslington Park, No. 6, 1951 (lot 439), as by 'artist unknown'. Also cf. Records of Professor E. K. Waterhouse.

16. **Lady Mary Forbes, Countess of Granard,** oil on canvas, 30 × 24½ in., signed and dated 1760. Cf. Henry Weigall Sale, Christie's, July 6, 1925 (lot 153), bought by Clements. Present whereabouts unknown.

c. 1760

17. **Richard Edwards of Nanhoran,** 1696–1770, oil on canvas, neither signed nor dated. Mrs. Alan Gough, Nanhoran, Pwllheli, Caernarvonshire (1957). Present whereabouts unknown. Cf. *PW.*, Vol. I, p. 55, no. 11, dated by Steegman, c. 1760.

18. **Mary Anne Jullian,** pastel on paper, 23 × 18½ in., neither signed nor dated. Major Herbert Charles Goodeve Allen, Cwm Wenol, Saundersfoot, Pembrokeshire (1962). Present whereabouts unknown. Cf. *PW.*, Vol. II, p. 182, no. 5, dated by Steegman, c. 1760.

19. **William Mason,** presumably oil on canvas, neither signed nor dated. R. Harvey Mason, Esq., Necton Hall, Necton, Norfolk (1908). Present whereabouts unknown. Cf. *PN.*, Vol. II, p. 93, no. 18, dated by Duleep Singh, c. 1760.

1763

20. **Mary Coleby,** oil on canvas, 50 × 40 in., neither signed nor dated by Cotes. According to Steegman, in the nineteenth century there was an inscription on the back with the name of the sitter and the date, 1763. Harpton Court, Harpton, Radnorshire (1962). Present whereabouts unknown. Cf. *PW.*, Vol. II, p. 212, no. 7.

1764

21. **Dorothea Tucker,** pastel on paper, 23½ × 17½ in., signed and dated 1764. Cf. Anon. Sale, Christie's, Mar. 14, 1952 (lot 53), bought by Mears. Present whereabouts unknown.

22. **Admiral John Forbes, R.N.,** oil on canvas, 29 × 24 in., signed and dated 1764. Cf. Henry Weigall Sale, Christie's, July 6, 1925 (lot 154), bought by Clements. Present whereabouts unknown.

23. **Lieutenant Colonel Francis Smith,** oil on canvas, dated 1764 in the Witt Library's Eighteenth Century Portrait Index. No further information is presently available.

1764 (exhibited)

24. **John Gregory,** oil on canvas, kitcat (36 × 28 in.). Exhibited with the Society of Artists, 1764, no. 23 (cf. Appendix III). Present whereabouts unknown. According to Graves, the sitter is John Gregory, presumably Dr. John Gregory (cf. no. 139). Graves's source for the identification is not stated. The sitter is neither identified in the unmarked exhibition catalogue, nor in Walpole's marked catalogue published by Gatty; consequently, the information presently available is too slight to warrant the inclusion of the picture in the catalogue.

1765

25. **Esther Thompson,** later Mrs. Arthur Maister, oil on canvas, 50 × 40 in., signed and dated 1765. Col. R. A. Alec-Smith, Winestead, Hull, Yorkshire. In the early twentieth century the portrait was damaged by fire. The whole figure of the sitter was 'restored'. Not a trace of Cotes's style remains. A photograph of the portrait before it was damaged has not been located; consequently, very little can be determined about its original nature. Cf. Rev. A. G. Maister Sale, July 13, 1938 (lot 118), bought by Col. R. A. Alec-Smith (the present owner).

c. 1765

26. **A Lady,** presumably oil on canvas, measurements unknown, neither signed nor dated. The Lord Cranworth, Letton Hall, Norfolk (1907). Cf. *PN.*, Vol. I, p. 402, no. 75, dated by Duleep Singh, c. 1765. Some pictures from Letton Hall are in storage and inaccessible. They are the property of the Lord Cranworth, Grundisburgh Hall, Woodbridge, Suffolk. The portrait cited here may be among these pictures.

1767

27. **Jacob, 2nd Earl of Radnor,** medium unrecorded, 30 × 25 in., signed and dated 1767. Mrs. Pleydell-Bouverie, Coleshill House, Coleshill, Berkshire (1950). Present whereabouts unknown. Cf. Records of Professor E. K. Waterhouse.

c. 1767

28. **The Duchess of Hamilton** (Elizabeth Gunning), oil on canvas, measurements unknown. Marjorie, Lady Russell, Little Struan, Pangbourne, Berkshire. The picture has not been examined; it is in storage and inaccessible. It may be either a copy of part of no. 219 or a genuine portrait by Cotes. At present, there is no way of telling. If it is genuine, it would have been painted around the same time as no. 219, 1767. Cf. *RTG.*, p. 133 (illus. opposite).

c. 1767–1770

29. **Mary Charleton,** pastel on paper, measurements unknown. Present whereabouts unknown. Cf. R. R. M. Sée, *English Pastels 1750–1830*, London, G. Bell and Sons, 1911, p. 49. Sée spoke of this pastel as typical of Cotes's 'latest period', which was from c. 1767 to 1770.

30. **Mrs. Greenaway,** medium and measurements unknown. Mr. Lawrence P. Fisher, Detroit (1931). Present whereabouts unknown. Cf. *PFC.*, p. 6. Heil said that the portrait was from Cotes's 'last and most mature period', which was from c. 1767 to 1770.

31. **Rhoda, Lady Huband,** pastel on paper, measurements unknown. Present whereabouts unknown. Cf. R. R. M. Sée, *English Pastels 1750–1830*, London, G. Bell and Sons, 1911, p. 49. Sée spoke of the pastel as typical of Cotes's 'latest period', which was from c. 1767 to 1770.

1768

32. **The Daughter of Dr. Blomberg, Court Physician to George I,** oil on canvas 29½ × 24 in., signed and dated 1768. Cf. Mrs. H. C. B. Lethbridge Sale, Christie's, Nov. 17, 1967 (lot 109), bought by Barker. Present whereabouts unknown.

33. **A Lady in a Green Dress and Lace Bonnet,** and **A Lady with a Muff,** a pair, oil on canvas, 29½ × 24 in., signed and dated 1768. Cf. Sotheby's Sale, June 22, 1949 (lot 57). Present whereabouts unknown.

1769

34. **John Crawley,** oil on canvas, 29½ × 24½ in., signed and dated 1769. Cf. Sir Henry C. Hawley Sale, Christie's, March 8, 1920 (lot 16), bought by Buttery. Present whereabouts unknown. The pendant is no. 37 in this Appendix.

35. **A Lady,** oil on canvas, 30 × 25 in., in a painted oval, signed and dated 1769. The Trustees of the Stoneleigh Settlement, Stoneleigh Abbey, Kenilworth, Warwickshire. The author has not had the opportunity to examine this picture.

36. **A Lady Caressing a Spaniel,** pastel on paper, 23 × 17½ in., signed and dated 1769. Cf. Captain Eric Noble Sale, Christie's, October 5, 1945 (lot 55), bought by Lumley. Present whereabouts unknown. The lady is wearing a pink dress and a white lace cap. No. 297, exhibited in 1770, is somewhat similar to this portrait, but the sitter's costume and the type of dog portrayed are different.

1769(?)

37. **Mrs. John Crawley,** born Elizabeth Hawley, oil on canvas, 29½ × 24½ in., neither signed nor dated. Cf. Sir Henry C. Hawley Sale, Christie's, March 8, 1920 (lot 16), bought by Buttery. This picture is the pendant to no. 34 in this Appendix, signed and dated 1769. Possibly, both pictures were done at the same time.

c. 1770

38. **Brampton Gurdon-Dillingham,** presumably oil on canvas, measurements unknown. The Lord Cranworth, Letton Hall, Norfolk (1907). Cf. *PN.*, Vol. I, p. 392, no. 24, dated c. 1770 by Duleep Singh. Some pictures from Letton Hall are in storage and inaccessible. They are the property of the Lord Cranworth, Grundisburgh Hall, Woodbridge, Suffolk. The portrait of Brampton Gurdon-Dillingham may be among these pictures.

Without an assigned date, miscellaneous works, nos. 39–57.

39. **Harriet Mary Amyand,** aged 9, later 1st Countess of Malmsbury, medium and measurements unknown. Exhibited in 'Fair Children', The Grafton Galleries, 1895, no. 232 (lent by the Countess of Minto); the portrait is no longer in the Minto collection and is believed to have been destroyed by fire.

40. **George Anne Bellamy,** the actress, medium and measurements unknown. An engraving after part of the portrait was made by Francesco Bartolozzi in 1785. The engraving shows George Anne Bellamy as a comic muse. There is the following inscription: George Anne Bellamy / late of Covent Garden Theatre / The face copied after a picture by Coates / in the Possession of Sir George Metham / The figure modernized by Ramberg / and the whole engraved by Bartolozzi. The 'Coates' referred to could be either Francis or Samuel Cotes. The present whereabouts of the original portrait is unknown. Cf. *O'D.*, Vol. I, p. 163, no. 1; A. de Vesme and A. Calabi, *Francesco Bartolozzi, Catalogue des Estampes*, Milan, Guido Modiano, 1928, p. 270, no. 1042; George Anne Bellamy, *An Apology for the Life of George Anne Bellamy, Late of Covent-Garden Theatre*, Vol. I, London, J. Bell, 1786, frontispiece.

41. **Eleanor, Lady Bunbury,** pastel on paper, approximately 28 × 24 in., neither signed nor dated. Sir Henry Bunbury, Bt., Barton Hall, Suffolk (1904). Cf. *PSW.*, p. 15, no. 5. Barton Hall was burned to the ground in 1912, and this picture is believed to have perished.

42. **Henry William Bunbury,** pastel on paper, approximately 16 × 10 in., neither signed nor dated. Sir Henry Bunbury, Bt., Barton Hall, Suffolk (1904). Cf. *PSW.*, p. 17, no. 11. Barton Hall burned to the ground in 1912, and this picture is believed to have perished.

43. **Caroline Burdett,** pastel on paper, 23¼ × 17½ in., neither signed nor dated. Sir Francis Burdett Sale, Sotheby's, Dec. 2, 1953 (lot 42), bought by Lord Wilton. At present, the portrait is with Mr. H. J. Hyams, Ramsbury Manor, Ramsbury, Wiltshire. The author has not had the opportunity to examine the picture.

44. **Francis Cotes,** possibly a self-portrait, pastel on paper, measurements unknown. In his will Francis Cotes bequeathed to his father, Robert Cotes, 'the crayon picture of myself'. Cf. The last will and testament of Francis Cotes, R.A., dated June 16, 1769, proved July 30, 1770, now kept at Somerset House, London.

45. **The Duchess of Hamilton,** Elizabeth Gunning, pastel on paper, 23½ × 17¼ in. The National Trust for Scotland, Brodick Castle, Isle of Arran. The author has not had the opportunity to examine this picture.

46. **Sir Thomas Hanmer, 4th Bt.,** oil on canvas, approximately 30 × 24 in., neither signed nor dated. Sir Henry Bunbury, Bt. (1904), Barton Hall, Suffolk. Cf. *PSW.*, p. 23, no. 31. Barton Hall burned to the ground in 1912, and this picture is believed to have perished.

47. **Catherine Jones,** oil on canvas, 50 × 40 in., signed but not dated. Walter Roch, Esq., Llanarth Court, Monmouthshire. Llanarth Court was sold in 1948, and the pictures were dispersed. The present whereabouts of this portrait is unknown. Cf. *PW.*, Vol. II, p. 139, no. 24.

48. **A Lady,** oil on canvas, 26 × 22 in., neither signed nor dated. Edward Brooke, Esq., Ufford Place, Suffolk (1918). Present whereabouts unknown. Cf. *PS.*, Vol. III, pp. 151–152, no. 73.

49. **A Lady and Two Children,** oil on canvas, measurements unknown, neither signed nor dated. The Lord Sondes, North Elmham Hall, Norfolk (1909). Present whereabouts unknown. Cf. *PN.*, Vol. I, p. 145, no. 13.

50. **Mrs. William Locke of Norbury Park,** pastel on paper, 30 × 25 in., signed but not dated. Exhibited in 'Expositions des Pastellistes Anglais du XVIIIe Siècle', Galeries Brunner, Paris, Apr. 8 – Je. 15, 1911, no. 24 (lent by the Lord Wallscourt). Present whereabouts unknown.

51. **Mary, Duchess of Norfolk,** medium and measurements unknown. The Duke of Norfolk, Arundel Castle, Arundel, Sussex (1931). Present whereabouts unknown. Cf. *CWO.*, p. 250.

52. **William Onslow,** husband of Charlotte Ryves, pastel on paper, 23¼ × 17¼ in., signed but not dated. Exhibited in 'Expositions des Pastellistes Anglais du XVIIIe Siècle', Galeries Brunner, Paris, Apr. 8 – Je. 15, 1911, no. 6 (lent by Colonel R. Malthus). Colonel R. Malthus Sale, Christie's, Dec. 16, 1938 (lot 15), bought by Peel. Present whereabouts unknown. The pendant is no. 53 in this Appendix.

53. **Charlotte Onslow,** born Ryves, the wife of William Onslow, pastel on paper, 23¼ × 17¼ in., signed but not dated. Exhibited in 'Expositions des Pastellistes Anglais du XVIIIe Siècle', Galeries Brunner, Paris, Apr. 8 – Je. 15, 1911, no. 17 (lent by Colonel R. Malthus). Colonel R. Malthus Sale, Christie's, Dec. 16, 1938 (lot 15), bought by Peel. Present whereabouts unknown. The pendant is no. 52 in this Appendix.

54. **John Russell,** a miniature, medium and measurements unknown. Present whereabouts unknown. Cf. G. C. Williamson, *John Russell*, London, 1894, p. 8 (illus.). The illustration is inadequate. It is impossible to judge whether this miniature is by Francis Cotes. He is not known to have painted miniatures.

55. **Master John Ryves,** pastel on paper, 14½ × 11⅓ in., neither signed nor dated.
Master Thomas Ryves, pastel on paper, 13 × 11⅓ in., neither signed nor dated.
Miss Charlotte Ryves, pastel on paper, 13¾ × 11¼ in., neither signed nor dated.
Miss Elizabeth Ryves, pastel on paper, 13¾ × 11¼ in., neither signed nor dated.
The portraits of John and Thomas Ryves were exhibited in 'Expositions des Pastellistes Anglais du XVIIIe Siècle', Galeries Brunner, Paris, Apr. 8 – Je. 15, 1911, nos. 20 and 21, respectively (both lent by Colonel R. Malthus). All four portraits were sold together at the Colonel R. Malthus Sale, Christie's, Dec. 16, 1938 (lot 19), bought by Aubrey. Present whereabouts unknown.

56. **Percy Wyndham, Earl of Thomond,** pastel on paper, approximately 30 × 24 in., neither signed nor dated. Brigadier H. Bulwer-Long, Heydon, Norwich. The author has not had the opportunity to examine the picture. Cf. *PN.*, Vol. II, p. 144, no. 43.

APPENDIX VI

The most important of the pictures erroneously attributed to Cotes

Portraits in public collections, erroneously attributed to Cotes at one time: nos. 1 and 2.

1. **Mrs. Cadoux,** oil on canvas, 83¾ × 55½ in., neither signed nor dated. Tate Gallery, London. The portrait is now listed under 'British School'; it was formerly attributed to Cotes. Cf. *CC18.*, p. 273 (illus.); *CWS.*, p. 172 (illus.); *CWO.*, p. 250.

2. **Lady Carlingford,** oil on canvas, 31 1/16 × 26 in., neither signed nor dated. Worcester Art Museum, Worcester, Massachusetts. The portrait is not given to Cotes now, but it was formerly attributed to him. Cf. *Worcester Art Museum Annual*, Vol. IV, 1941, p. 40, and Daniel Catton Rich, note on the portrait of Lady Carlingford, *Worcester Art Museum News Bulletin and Calendar*, Vol. XXVIII, no. 1, Oct. 1962, pp, 1, 2.

Portraits erroneously attributed to Cotes in the collections of museums and public institutions: nos. 3–25.

3. **Miss Adney,** oil on canvas, approximately 30 × 25 in. (sight), neither signed nor dated. The Leicester Museum and Art Gallery, Leicester.

4. **Admiral Lord Anson,** pastel on paper, 23½ × 17½ in., neither signed nor dated. National Trust, Shugborough, Gray Haywood, Staffordshire. Cf. *NTA.*, p. 253.

5. **Sir William Chambers,** pastel on paper, approximately 23½ × 17½ in., neither signed nor dated. Royal Institute of British Architects, London. The portrait came from the collection of Thomas Hardwick, Chambers's assistant. It is a copy of the Scottish National Portrait Gallery's pastel of Chambers, no. 137, signed and dated 1764. The hand is not that of Francis Cotes, but the portrait may have been done in the eighteenth century at Chambers's instigation. A number of old copies of the Scottish picture are in existence, cf. nos. 6 and 33 in this Appendix. Also cf. John Harris, *Sir William Chambers, Knight of the Polar Star*, London, A. Zwemmer, 1970, p. 173; R. A. Riches, 'Sir William Chambers and Francis Cotes', *The Connoisseur*, Vol. 94, no. 397, Sept. 1934, pp. 143, 144.

6. **Sir William Chambers,** oil on canvas, 27½ × 22¼ in., neither signed nor dated. Ministry of Public Building and Works, London. The picture is on loan to Somerset House, London. This is a copy of the Scottish pastel, no. 137; for other copies see nos. 5 and 33 in this Appendix. Cf. R. A. Riches, 'Sir William Chambers and Francis Cotes', *The Connoisseur*, Vol. 94, no. 397, Sept. 1934, p. 143, 144.

7. **Mary Coleby,** oil on canvas, 36½ × 28½ in., neither signed nor dated. The Carnegie Institute, Pittsburgh, Pennsylvania. Exhibited in 'Paintings by Old Masters from Pittsburgh Collections', Carnegie Institute, Pittsburgh, no. 9 (lent by Mrs. J. Willis Dalzell), who gave the portrait to the Institute in 1925.

8. **Mary Coleby,** oil on canvas, 36 × 24 in., neither signed nor dated. Cheltenham Art Gallery and Museum, Cheltenham, Gloucestershire. Exhibited in 'The Whinyates Collection', Cheltenham Art Gallery and Museum, Jan., 1969, unnumbered entry.

9. **The Countess of Coventry,** Maria Gunning, oil on canvas, 29½ × 24⅝ in., in a painted oval, neither signed nor dated. This is a copy of no. 19, signed and dated 1751. National Gallery of Ireland, Dublin. Cf. Anon., *Concise Catalogue of the Oil Paintings, National Gallery of Ireland*, Dublin, The Stationery Office, 1963, p. 23, no. 14; Ellen Duncan, 'The Irish National Portrait Collection', *The Burlington Magazine*, Vol. 12, Oct. 1907, pp. 13, 15 (illus.).

10. **Miss Cruttenden,** oil on canvas, 50 × 40 in., neither signed nor dated. William Rockhill Nelson Gallery of Art, Kansas City. Exhibited at the R.A., 1857, no. 1, as by Gainsborough (lent by Arthur Purvis, Esq.). Cf. *The Art Digest*, Dec. 1, 1933, Vol. 8, p. 21; *The Art News*, Dec. 9, 1933, Vol. 32, p. 28.

11. **Miss Dennison and a Small Boy,** oil on canvas, 59½ × 37½ in., neither signed nor dated. Fogg Art Museum, Harvard University, Cambridge, Massachusetts. Cf. Frank Pemberton 'Mysteries in Art', *Harvard Today*, Spring, 1965, pp. 23–24.

12. **Lady Gertrude Fitzpatrick,** oil on canvas, 30 × 25 in., neither signed nor dated. Carnegie Institute, Pittsburgh, Pennsylvania. Exhibited in 'Exhibition of Paintings from the Collection of Howard A. Noble', Carnegie Institute, Pittsburgh, [Apr.] 13 – May 21, 1944, no. 3. Cf. *The Art Quarterly*, Vol. XXVII, no. 3, 1964, p. 383. The portrait is a copy after Reynolds's *Lady Charlotte Fitzwilliam.*

13. **Samuel Foote,** in the character of Mrs. Cole in 'The Minor', pastel on paper, 15¼ × 10½ in., neither signed nor dated. British Museum, London. Exhibited in 'British Portraits', R.A., London, Winter, 1956–1957, no. 656 (lent by the British Museum); 'Introducing Francis Cotes, R.A.', Nottingham University Art Gallery, Nov. 5–27, 1971, no. 41 (lent by the British Museum). Cf. *LB.*, p. 257, no. 2; *CAN.*, p. 51.

14. **Admiral Sir Francis Geary,** oil on canvas, 36 × 28 in., neither signed nor dated. National Maritime Museum, Greenwich. Cf. Anon., *Concise Catalogue of Paintings, National Maritime Museum, Greenwich*, London, Her Majesty's Stationery Office, 1958, p. 9.

15. **A Girl,** oil on canvas, 30⅝ × 25¼ in., neither signed nor dated. Corcoran Gallery of Art, Washington, D.C. Cf. *Checklist of the Edward C. and Mary Walker Collection*, Corcoran Gallery of Art, Washington, D.C., no. 6.

16. **Miss Hargreaves,** oil on canvas, 49½ × 38½ in., neither signed nor dated. Birmingham Museum and Art Gallery. Exhibited in 'Art Treasures of the Midlands', Birmingham Museum and Art Gallery, 1934, no. 443A. Cf. *City of Birmingham Museum and Art Gallery, Supplement to the Catalogue of the Permanent Collection of Paintings*, Birmingham, n.d., p. 12, no. 87.

17 [Erratum]. **William Hoare, R.A.,** pastel on paper, 20 × 15½ in., neither signed nor dated. Royal Academy of Arts, London. This is, in fact, a self-portrait by William Hoare, now recognized as such. Exhibited in 'Introducing Francis Cotes, R.A.', Nottingham University Art Gallery, Nov. 5–27, 1971, no. 1 (lent by the R.A.). Cf. Anon., *Catalogue of the Diploma and Gibson Galleries*, London, William Clowes and Sons, 1939, p. 21, no. 205; Council Minutes of the Royal Academy, in MS., now kept at the Academy, for March 9, 1835; the minutes include an excerpt from Prince Hoare's will in which he gives to the Academy 'the portrait of my father (William Hoare) painted by himself in crayon....' Also cf. William Sandby, *The History of the Royal Academy of Arts*, London, Longman, Green, Longman, Roberts, and Green, Vol. II, 1862, p. 409; *CAN.*, p. 51.

18. **A Lady, A Flower Painter,** oil on canvas, 30 × 25⅝ in., neither signed nor dated. National Gallery of Victoria, Melbourne, Australia. Cf. Ursula Hoff, *European Paintings Before Eighteen Hundred*, Melbourne, National Gallery of Victoria, 1967, p. 30, illustration no. 50.

19. **A Lady,** oil on canvas, 7⅞ × 6¼ in., in an oval, neither signed nor dated. Also **Portrait of a Lady,** oil on canvas, 7⅞ × 6¼ in., in an oval, neither signed nor dated. A pair. Both pictures are in the collection of the National Gallery of Art, Washington, D.C. Cf. Anon., *National Gallery of Art, Summary Catalogue of European Paintings and Sculpture*, Washington, D.C., nos. 1558 and 1559. These are probably early copies after lost portraits by Cotes.

20. **A Lady,** oil on canvas, 30 × 25 in., neither signed nor dated. Evansville Museum of Arts and Sciences, Evansville, Indiana. A photograph of the portrait before it was damaged and subsequently restored reveals that it was never by Francis Cotes.

21. **A Lady,** oil on canvas, 29 × 24 in., neither signed nor dated. Hove Museum, Hove, Sussex.

22. **A Lady,** oil on canvas, 90 × 64 in., neither signed nor dated. Ministry of Public Buildings and Works, London. The portrait is on loan to the British Consulate in Istanbul.

23. **A Lady of the Vaux Family,** pastel on paper, 25½ × 19 in., neither signed nor dated. Victoria and Albert Museum, London.

24. **Mrs. Richard Plowden,** pastel on paper, 23 × 18 in., signed at the lower right: F. Cotes fecit. The handwriting and the form of the signature are unlike Cotes's, and the style of the portrait is foreign to him. John Herron Art Institute, Indianapolis, Indiana. Cf. Wayne Craven, 'An Eighteenth-Century Portrait', *The Bulletin of the Art Association of Indianapolis, John Herron Art Institute*, Vol. XLII, no. 2, Oct. 1955, cover (illus.) and pp. 26–27.

25. **Mrs. Wells,** oil on canvas, approximately 30 × 25 in. (sight), in a painted oval, neither signed nor dated. Lady Lever Art Gallery, Port Sunlight, Cheshire. Cf. C. Reginald Grundy and Sydney L. Davidson, *Illustrated Guide to the Lady Lever Collection*, Port Sunlight, Cheshire: Lady Lever Gallery, Published by the Trustees, 1956, p. 23, Pl. 24.

Two figure studies, erroneously attributed to Cotes: nos. 26 and 27.

26. **Study of a Girl Asleep,** pastel on paper, 26 × 17 in., neither signed nor dated, bequeathed to the Royal Academy in 1835 by Prince Hoare. Cf. Council Minutes of the Royal Academy of Arts, in MS., kept at the Academy, Mar. 17, 1835, containing an excerpt of Prince Hoare's will. He speaks of the pastel as 'the picture of the Sleeping Venus'; he does not attribute it to Cotes, yet it is listed as by Cotes in the Academy's inventory. It is probably by a member of the Hoare family.

27. **Preparing for the Bath,** pastel on paper, 29 × 24 in., neither signed nor dated, bequeathed to the Royal Academy by Prince Hoare in 1835. Cf. Council Minutes of the Royal Academy of Arts, in MS., kept at the Academy, March 17, 1835. Prince Hoare speaks of the pastel as 'the picture of a female coming from a bath'. He does not attribute it to Cotes, yet it is listed as by Cotes in the Academy's inventory. It is probably by a member of the Hoare family.

Other important portraits erroneously attributed to Cotes in art, literature or at exhibitions: nos. 28–61.

28. **George Keppel, 3rd Earl of Albemarle,** pastel on paper, 23¾ × 17½ in. Private Collection, U.K. Cf. *PN.*, Vol. II, p. 152, no. 29.

29. **The Duchess of Ancaster** (Mary Panton), pastel on paper, 29½ × 23¼ in., neither signed nor dated. Marjorie Lady Russell, Little Struan, Pangbourne, Berkshire. Exhibited in 'A Century of Art from 1737 to 1837', Grosvenor Gallery, London, Summer 1889, no. 220. *RTG.*, p. 119, illus. opposite p. 120.

30. **Lady Astley** (Anne Milles), second wife of Sir Edward Astley, 4th Bt., oil on canvas, 49 × 39 in., neither signed nor dated. The Lord Hastings, Swanton House, Melton Constable, Norfolk. Cf. *PN.*, Vol. II, p. 2, no. 5.

31. **Rachel Baillie-Hamilton,** oil on canvas, approximately 30 × 25 in., neither signed nor dated, present whereabouts unknown. Cf. Frank Rutter, 'Fame Returns to Francis Cotes', *The Antique Collector*, Vol. VI, no. 2, July 18, 1931, p. 169 (illus.).

32. **Hugh Barron,** oil on canvas, 29 × 24½ in., neither signed nor dated. Mr. and Mrs. Paul Mellon, U.S.A. Exhibited in 'Exhibition of Old Masters of the English School', Thomas Agnew and Sons, London, Nov.–Dec. 1920, no. 4; 'Four Georges Exhibition', Royal Northern Hospital, London, 1931, no. 35, lent by W. M. de Zoete; 'Exhibition of British Art, c. 1000–1860', R.A., London, 1934, no. 308, lent by W. M. de Zoete; 'Music in Painting', University of Illinois, Urbana, Feb. 26 – April 2, 1950, no. 6; 'Exhibition of Music and Art', Milwaukee Art Institute, Milwaukee, Sept. 10 – Oct. 24, 1954, no. 33. Cf. *CWO.*, p. 250.

33. **Sir William Chambers,** oil on canvas, approximately 30 × 25 in. (sight), neither signed nor dated. Dr. J. G. Salter, Bromley House, Abbots Bromley, Rugeley, Staffordshire. The picture came to Dr. Salter via a family ancestor, Thomas Collins, who was

Chambers's executor. It is a copy of Cotes's signed and dated pastel portrait of Chambers, no. 137. Cf. John Harris, *Sir William Chambers, Knight of the Polar Star*, London, A. Zwemmer, 1970, p. 173. For other copies cf. nos. 5 and 6 in this Appendix.

34. **The Countess of Dysart** (Charlotte Tollemache), pastel on paper, 23½ × 17½ in., neither signed nor dated. Private Collection, U.K. Cf. *PN.*, Vol. II, p. 161, no. 61.

35. **The Countess of Erroll** (Isabella Carr), pastel on paper, approximately 29 × 22 in., neither signed nor dated. This portrait is probably by Catherine Read. Exhibited in 'Expositions des Pastellistes Anglais du XVIIIe Siècle', Galeries Brunner, Paris, [Apr.] 8 – [Je.] 11, 1911, no. 23 (lent by Messrs. Wallis), London. Cf. R. R. M. Sée, *English Pastels 1750–1830*, London, G. Bell and Sons, 1911, p. 59.

36. **Sir Matthew Fetherstonhaugh,** pastel on paper, 23½ × 17¼ in., neither signed nor dated. Mrs. Richard Meade-Fetherstonhaugh, Uppark, South Harting, Sussex. Cf. *NTH.*, p. 256. The pendant is no. 37 in this Appendix.

37. **Sarah Fetherstonhaugh,** pastel on paper, 23½ × 17¼ in., neither signed nor dated. Mrs. Richard Meade-Fetherstonhaugh, Uppark, South Harting, Sussex. Cf. *NTH.*, p. 256. The pendant is no. 36 in this Appendix.

38. **A Young Girl in a Lace Cap,** oil on canvas, 13¾ × 11¼ in., neither signed nor dated. Formerly at the Leonard Koetser Gallery, London. Exhibited in the Leonard Koetser Gallery, Autumn Exhibition, 1963, no. 46a. The pendant, no. 46b in the catalogue, was never photographed; therefore, no decision can be made concerning it. Cf. *The Burlington Magazine*, Vol. 105, no. 728, Nov. 1963, p. 520, fig. 55.

39. **The Duchess of Gloucester** (Maria Walpole), pastel on paper, approximately 17 × 13½ in., neither signed nor dated. Formerly in the collection of R. R. M. Sée, London; present whereabouts unknown. Exhibited in 'Expositions des Pastellistes Anglais du XVIIIe Siècle', Galeries Brunner, Paris, 1911, no. 22 (lent by R. R. M. Sée). Cf. *CWS.*, p. 176; R. R. M. Sée, *English Pastels, 1750–1830*, London, G. Bell and Sons, 1911, pp. 49, 65.

40. **Thomas Grosvenor,** later Field-Marshal Thomas Grosvenor, pastel on paper, 17 × 16 in., neither signed nor dated. The Duke of Westminster, London. This portrait and its pendant, also in the collection of the Duke of Westminster, are probably by Cotes's pupil, John Russell. Exhibited in 'Introducing Francis Cotes, R.A.', Nottingham University Art Gallery, Nottingham, Nov. 5–27, 1971, no. 25 (lent by the present owner). Cf. *CAN.*, p. 51.

41. **Bridget Gunning,** present whereabouts unknown. Cf. *RTG.*, illustrated opposite p. 100.

42. **Katherine Jervis,** oil on canvas, 50 × 40 in., neither signed nor dated. R. St. Vincent Parker-Jervis, Esq., United Kingdom (1938); present whereabouts unknown. Exhibited in 'An Exhibition of Treasures from Midland Homes', City of Birmingham Museum and Art Gallery, Nov. 2 – Dec. 2, 1938, no. 138 (lent by R. St. Vincent Parker-Jervis, Esq.).

43. **Polly Jones,** pastel on paper, 29½ × 23½ in., neither signed nor dated. This portrait is probably by Catherine Read. Sabin Galleries, London. Exhibited in 'English Portraits, 1500–1830', Sabin Galleries, London, Nov. 18 – Dec. 19, 1970, no. 6.

44. **A Lady,** oil on canvas, 30 × 25 in., neither signed nor dated. Dr. D. M. McDonald. Exhibited in 'An Exhibition of Paintings from the Collection of Dr. D. M. McDonald', Leggatt Brothers, London, Oct. 16 – Nov. 6, 1970, no. 3 (lent by the present owner). Cf. Theodore Crombie, 'Friends, Romans, and Countrymen', *Apollo*, Vol. XCII, no. 105, Nov. 1970, pp. 379, 380 (fig. 4).

45. **A Lady,** pastel on paper, 24 × 18 in., neither signed nor dated. Mrs. H. Protheroe-Beynon, Hurst House, Langharne, Carmarthenshire. Cf. *PW.*, Vol. II, p. 68, no. 7.

46. **Lady Milford** (Mary Philipps), pastel on paper, 22½ × 16 in., said to be signed and dated 1772. The Lady Dunsany, Manorbier Castle, Manorbier, Pembrokeshire. Cf. *PW.*, Vol. II, p. 192, no. 27. A copy of the portrait was catalogued at Penty Park, cf. *PW.*, Vol. II, p. 187, no. 23.

47. **A Young Man of the Molyneux Family,** pastel on paper, 21 × 17½ in., neither signed nor dated. Mrs. C. C. Molyneux, Trewyn, near Abergavenny, Monmouthshire. Cf. *PW.*, Vol. II, p. 170, no. 19.

48 [Erratum]. **The Duchess of Montagu** (Mary Montagu), oil on canvas, approximately 30 × 25 in., neither signed nor dated. The Duke of Buccleuch and Queensberry, United Kingdom. Cf. C. H. Collins Baker, *British Painting*, London, The Medici Society, 1933, Pl. 61. This portrait is now accepted as by Cotes, but it should be noted that at some time before 1933 the shoulders, arms and visible hand of the figure were badly restored and in a style unlike that of Cotes.

49. **Robert Nugent, Earl Nugent,** pastel on paper, approximately 25 × 17 in., neither signed nor dated. Formerly in the collection of Sir Maurice Boileau, Ketteringham Hall, Norfolk (1912). Cf. *PN.*, Vol. I, p. 367, no. 104.

50. **Lady Northington** (Jane Huband), pastel on paper, 24 × 18 in., neither signed nor dated. The Lord Henley, Scaleby Castle, Carlisle, Cumberland. Cf. R. R. M. Sée, *English Pastels 1750–1830*, London, G. Bell and Sons, 1911, p. 49.

51. **An Officer,** oil on canvas, 35 × 27½ in., neither signed nor dated. Anon. Sale, Sotheby's, July 26, 1961 (lot 81), bought by P. Pollack; present whereabouts unknown. This portrait is probably by Tilly Kettle. Exhibited in 'Famous Paintings', Joseph Sartor Galleries, Dallas, Texas, Apr. 9–23, 1939, no. 10. Cf. *CWO.*, p. 246 (fig. no. III).

52. **The Misses Prosser** (Lucretia Hamilton and Elizabeth Plowden), oil on canvas, 51 × 41 in., neither signed nor dated. John Levy Galleries, New York (1919); present whereabouts unknown. Cf. W. Roberts, *The Misses Prosser by Francis Cotes, R.A.*, London, The Chiswick Press, 1920, pp. 1–8.

53. **Lady Ranelagh and her Daughter,** oil on canvas, measurements unknown, neither signed nor dated. Sir F. Hervey Bathurst, United Kingdom (1938). Exhibited at Winchester, 1938, no. 1 (lent by Sir F. Hervey Bathurst).

54. **Lady St. Aubyn** (Elizabeth Wingfield), oil on canvas, 37½ × 29½ in., neither signed nor dated. This portrait is probably by Allan Ramsay. The Lord St. Levan, St. Michael's Mount, Marazion, Cornwall. Exhibited in 'Fair Women', The Grafton Galleries, London, Summer 1894, no. 106 (lent by M. de Falbe). Cf. De Falbe Sale, Christie's, May 19, 1900 (lot 12), bought by Lord St. Levan.

55. **Sir Harvey and Lady Smith and their Son,** oil on canvas, 81½ × 49 in., neither signed nor dated. Present whereabouts unknown. Cf. *PFC.*, pp, 5, 11.

56. **Charles Townshend,** oil on canvas, 24 × 20 in., neither signed nor dated. W. A. Twiston Davies, Esq., The Mynde, Much Dewchurch, Herefordshire. Exhibited in 'Introducing Francis Cotes, R.A.', Nottingham University Art Gallery, Nov. 5–27, 1971, no. 28 (lent by the present owner). Cf. *CAN.*, p. 51; *PW.*, Vol. II, p. 148, no. 8.

57. **George, 2nd Marquess Townshend, and Lord John Townshend,** pastel on paper, 23½ × 27½ in., neither signed nor dated. This portrait is probably by Catherine Read. Mrs. Edith de Kosinsky, Maplewood, New Jersey. Cf. *PN.*, Vol. II, p. 238, no. 18.

58. **Charlotte Walpole, Laura Walpole, Maria Walpole,** all pastel on paper, 18½ × 14½ in., neither signed nor dated. Bertram Keppel Sale, Christie's, June 19, 1911 (lot 4). The portraits of Charlotte and Laura were in the Reid Sale, American Art Association—Anderson Galleries, New York, May 14–18, 1935 (lots 1146 and 1147), respectively. The present whereabouts of all three portraits is unknown. Cf. *PN.*, Vol. I, p. 405 (no. 7), p. 406 (no. 11), p. 407 (no. 15).

59. **Charlotte Walpole, Laura Walpole,** medium and measurements unknown, neither signed nor dated. These are different portraits from the ones cited in no. 58 of this Appendix. In the photographs available at the Witt Library, the medium appears to be pastel on paper. O. Gutekunst, Esq., London. Exhibited in 'Retrospective Exhibition of British Paintings', Grand Central Art Galleries, New York, Jan. 10 – Feb. 28, 1925, nos. 8 and 9.

60. **Miss West,** oil on canvas, 20½ × 16¼ in., in a painted oval, neither signed nor dated. Captain W. R. West, United Kingdom (1938); present whereabouts unknown. Exhibited in 'An Exhibition of Treasures from Midland Homes', City of Birmingham Museum and Art Gallery, Nov. 2 – Dec. 2, 1938, no. 86 (lent by Captain W. R. West).

61. **Miss West,** oil on canvas, 28¾ × 25¼ in., neither signed nor dated. Captain W. R. West, United Kingdom (1938), present whereabouts unknown. Exhibited in 'An Exhibition of Treasures from Midland Homes', City of Birmingham Museum and Art Gallery, Nov. 2 – Dec. 2, 1938, no. 147 (lent by Captain W. R. West).

A portrait erroneously recorded as a self-portrait by Cotes: no. 62.

62. **Nathaniel Hone,** by himself, oil on canvas, approximately 30 × 25 in., neither signed nor dated. Anon. Sale, Robinson and Fisher, London, London, June 16, 1932, as a self-portrait by Cotes; present whereabouts unknown. The inscription on Edward Fisher's engraving after the portrait reads: Se ipse Pinxit, Edwardus Fisher Sculpsit. Nathnl Hone, Pictor et Acadae Florae Socs. Cf. *CS.*, Vol. II, p. 496, no. 30.

BIBLIOGRAPHY

EIGHTEENTH-CENTURY SOURCES

Diaries, Notes, and Journals

Bellamy, George Anne. *An Apology for the Life of George Anne Bellamy, Late of Covent Garden Theatre.* Vol. I. London: Printed for the author and sold by J. Bell, 1786.
Bellamy discovers the Gunnings in Ireland. Bartolozzi's engraving after a portrait of Bellamy, possibly by Francis Cotes, is the frontispiece; cf. Appendix v, no. 40.

Cotes, Francis. Notes on crayon painting. *The European Magazine*, Feb. 1797, and *The Universal Magazine of Knowledge and Pleasure*, Feb. 1797.
Cotes lists himself among the leading pastellists of the eighteenth century and cites some of his best portraits as examples of his work. These notes, as they appeared in *The European Magazine*, are reproduced in Appendix IV.

Farington, Joseph. *The Farington Diary.* Edited by James Greig. 8 vols. London: Hutchinson and Co., 1922ff.
Useful information on Peter Toms.

Russell, John. *Diary.* 8 vols., in MS., 1766–1789, 1801–1802, now kept at the Victoria and Albert Museum Library, London.
A first-hand account of Cotes's illness and death.

Thrale, Hester Lynch. *Thraliana, the Diary of Hester Lynch Thrale (later Mrs. Piozzi).* Edited by Katherine C. Balderston. 2 vols. Oxford: Clarendon Press, 1951.
An amusing account of a dinner party at Cotes's house in which Mrs. Thrale reveals the date of Cotes's marriage.

Vertue, George. *Notebooks. The Walpole Society.* Vol. XXII. Oxford: University Press, 1934.
Vertue notes the popularity of crayon painting in England.

Walpole, Horace (Earl of Orford). *Journal of Visits to Country Seats. The Walpole Society.* Vol. XVI. Oxford: University Press, 1928.
Walpole's confusing remarks on the relationship between nos. 205 and 206.

Essays and Discourses

Ramsay, Allan. *Dialogue on Taste.* London. 1762.
Ramsay's praise of the 'natural' art of La Tour; cf. Footnote 44.

Russell, John. *Elements of Painting with Crayons.* London: J. Wilkie and J. Walter, 1772.
Russell expounds Cotes's methods of making and working with crayons.

Walpole, Horace. *Anecdotes of Painting in England.* Original edition, 1765–71; edition used in the text throughout is by the Rev. James Dallaway. 5 vols. London: John Major and Robert Jennings, 1828.
Walpole considered Cotes to be more important as a pastellist than as an oil painter. This is an important critical judgment. He also mentioned some of Cotes's principal pastels.

Exhibition Catalogues

The J. R. Anderdon collection of original Royal Academy catalogues. MS. vols. now kept in the Print Room of the British Museum, London, dating from the first exhibition in 1769 to 1849.
Cf. Appendix III.

The John Bowyer Nicholls collection of original Society of Artists catalogues, 1760–1790, now kept in the Print Room of the British Museum, London.
Cf. Appendix III.

Exhibition Catalogues with Marginal Notes

Gatty, Hugh (editor). 'Notes by Horace Walpole, Fourth Earl of Orford, on the Exhibitions of the Society of Artists and the Free Society of Artists, 1760–1791' (Walpole's catalogues are from the collection of W. S. Lewis, Farmington, Connecticut), *The Walpole Society.* Vol. XVII. Oxford: The Walpole Society, 1939.
Cf. Appendix III. Walpole's notes are extremely helpful in identifying pictures exhibited by Cotes with the Society of Artists.

General Works

Mariette, P. J. *Abécédario de P. J. Mariette.* Edited by P. De Chennevières and A. De Montaiglon. 6 vols. Paris: J.-B. Dumoulin, 1851–1860.
Very good on Maurice-Quentin de la Tour.

Letters

Barbauld, Laetitia (editor). *The Correspondence of Samuel Richardson.* 6 vols. London: Richard Phillips, 1804.
Cotes's portrait of 'Clarissa' is mentioned in two letters from Samuel Richardson to Mrs. Balfour; cf. Supplement no. 1.

Ilchester, Countess of, and Stavordale, Lord (editors). *The Life and Letters of Lady Sarah Lennox, 1745–1826.* 2 vols. London: John Murray, 1901.
Cf. nos. 120 and 128.

Lewis, W. S.; Smith, Warren Hunting; Lam, George L. (editors). *Horace Walpole's Correspondence.* 34 vols. New Haven: Yale University Press, 1937–1965.
Walpole's correspondence with Sir Horace Mann is one of the best sources of information on the Gunning sisters and Cotes's portraits of the Gunning sisters.

Letter from Samuel Richardson to Dr. Charles Chauncy, in MS., written in 1749 or 1750, now kept at the Henry E. Huntington Library, San Marino, California, HM. 6893.
Richardson discusses Cotes's portrait of 'Clarissa'; cf. Supplement no. 1, where the letter is reproduced with the permission of the Henry E. Huntington Library.

Smith, John Thomas. *Nollekens and His Times.* London: Richard Bentley and Son, 1895.
Smith reproduces an interesting letter from Mary Moser to Henry Fuseli, written several days after Cotes's death; cf. Footnote 84.

Wool, Rev. John (editor). *Biographical Memoirs of the Late Rev*[d]

Joseph Warton, D.D. London: T. Cadell and W. Davies, 1806. Letter of James Harris to Dr. Warton, concerning Cotes's pastel portrait of Queen Charlotte and Princess Charlotte; cf. no. 205.

Magazines

The Gentleman's Magazine, July 1770.
A notice of Cotes's death.

The London Chronicle, May 5–7, 1767.
A review of the Society of Artists' exhibition of 1767.

Also cf. Francis Cotes's notes on crayon painting, published in two magazines cited under *Diaries, Notes, and Journals.*

Newspapers

The Daily Advertiser, Jan. 30, 1771.
The advertisement by Langford and Sons for the sale of Cotes's house and personal effects appears on p. 3.

The Gazetteer and New Daily Advertiser, July 25, 1770.
Cotes's obituary.

The Gazeteer and Daily Advertiser, Feb. 14, 1771.
Another advertisement by Langford and Sons for the sale of Cotes's house and personal effects.

The London Advertiser, Apr. 6, 1752.
An advertisement for McArdell's mezzotints after Cotes's portraits of the Countess of Coventry and the Duchess of Hamilton. These mezzotints could only be obtained from Cotes's residence in Cork Street. The most important aspect of the advertisement is that it reveals Cotes's address in 1752. The original protraits McArdell engraved are nos. 16 and 19.

The Public Advertiser, May 2, 1764.
A review of the Society of Artists' exhibition of 1764.

The Public Advertiser, May 20, 1765.
A review of the Society of Artists' exhibition of 1765 appears on p. 2.

Pamphlets

Anon. *The Conduct of the Royal Academicians.* London, 1771.
The conflict over the hanging of Cotes's pictures at the Society of Artists' exhibition of 1767.

Sale Catalogues

Francis Cotes Sale Catalogue, Langford and Sons, London, Feb. 21–23, 25, 1771; now kept at the Victoria and Albert Museum Library, London.
The sale of Cotes's house and personal effects, including pictures, sculptures, casts, and the artist's library. The catalogue is reproduced in Appendix II.

Strawberry Hill Sale Catalogue, George Robbins, Strawberry Hill, May 9, 1842.
The pastels by Rosalba Carriera, collected by Walpole and his family, were among the items sold.

Miscellaneous Documents

A Copy of the Royal Charter and Statutes of the Society of Artists of Great Britain. London: By Order of the Society, 1769; now kept in the Print Room of the British Museum, London.
Cotes is listed as one of the artists who petitioned George III to grant the Society a royal charter; he is also listed as a director of the Society.

The Case of Robert Cotes, Esq., Mayor, and John Staunton, Esq., Recorder of Gallway. On Behalf of Themselves, and the Majority of the Corporation of Gallway. In Answer to a Petition Preferr'd to the Honourable House of Commons by Thomas Simcocks and Edward Barrett, Aldermen. Dublin, 1717; now kept at the British Museum, London.
A prime source of information on Robert Cotes, the artist's father.

Council Minutes of the Royal Academy of Arts. MS. vols., now kept at the Academy, London. Continuously from 1768 onwards.
Especially important for the bequests of Prince Hoare to the Royal Academy; cf. Appendix VI, nos. 17, 26, and 27.

General Court Minutes of the Foundling Hospital. MS. vols., now kept at the Thomas Coram Foundation for Children, London. Continuously from the first meeting on Nov. 20, 1739.
Cotes's portrait of Taylor White is recorded as being donated to the Foundling Hospital; cf. no. 86.

The Last Will and Testament of Francis Cotes, R.A., dated June 16, 1769, proved July 30, 1770; now kept at Somerset House, London.
A primary source of information on Cotes's estate. Two lost portraits are also mentioned; cf. Appendix V, no. 44, and Supplement no. 22.

Royal Academy of Arts, General Assembly Minute Books. MS. vols., now kept at the Royal Academy of Arts, London.
The minutes for Dec. 14, 1768 and Jan. 2, 1769, are some of the best sources of information on the founding of the Academy. Cotes was appointed a member of the governing Council.

St. Mary-le-Strand Parish Register, in MS., now kept at the Westminster Public Library, London.
Cotes's date of birth and date of christening are recorded on May 29, 1726.

GENERAL REFERENCE WORKS

Collectors' Marks

Lugt, Frits. *Les Marques de Collections de Dessins et d'Estampes.* Amsterdam: Vereenigde Drukkerijen, 1921.
Cf. no. 230.

County History

Nichols, John. *The History and Antiquities of the County of Leicester.* 4 vols., each with 2 parts. London: John Nichols and Son, 1795–1815.

The principal source of information on the genealogy of Cotes and his family. The family tree is reproduced in Appendix I.

Exhibitions

Graves, Algernon. *A Century of Loan Exhibitions, 1813–1912.* 5 vols. London: Algernon Graves, 1913.

Graves, Algernon. *The Royal Academy of Arts, A Complete Dictionary of Contributors and their Work from its Foundation in 1769 to 1904.* 8 vols. London: Henry Graves and Co. and George Bell and Sons, 1905.
Cf. Appendix III.

Graves. Algernon. *The Society of Artists of Great Britain, 1760–1791; The Free Society of Artists 1761–1783, A Complete Dictionary of Contributors and their Work from the Foundation of the Societies to 1791.* London: George Bell and Sons, 1907.
Cf. Appendix III.

Genealogy

Burke's Landed Gentry and *Burke's Peerage* have been especially helpful. The editions used are cited below.

Townend, Peter (editor). *Burke's Landed Gentry.* London: Burke's Peerage, Ltd. Vol. I, 1965; Vol. II, 1969.

Townend, Peter (editor). *Burke's Peerage, Baronetage, and Knightage.* London: Burke's Peerage, Ltd., 1970.

Sales

Graves, Algernon. *Art Sales from Early in the Eighteenth Century to Early in the Twentieth.* 3 vols. London: Batsford, 1918–1921.

Redford, George. *A History of Sales of Pictures and Other Works of Art.* 2 vols. London: Bradbury, Agnew and Co., and Whitefriars Press, 1888.

ARTICLES ON COTES

Heil, Walter. 'Portraits by Francis Cotes', *Art in America.* Vol. XX, no. 1, Dec. 1931, pp. 2–12.

Johnson, Edward. 'Cotes at Nottingham', *The Burlington Magazine.* Vol. CXIV, no. 826. Jan. 1972, pp. 51–52.

Keyes, Homer Eaton. 'The Rising Star of Francis Cotes', *Antiques.* Vol. 19, Mar. 1931, pp. 217–220.

Rutter, Frank. 'Fame Returns to Francis Cotes', *The Antique Collector.* Vol. VI, no. 2, Jul. 18, 1931, pp. 169–171.

Winter, Carl. 'Francis Cotes, R.A.', *The Connoisseur.* Vol. 88, no. 361, Sept. 1931, pp. 170–177; Vol. 88, no. 362, Oct. 1931, pp. 244–252.
The most comprehensive of the articles and one frequently cited.

ARTICLES ON THE ROCOCO IN ENGLAND

(which provide helpful background information)

Girouard, Mark. 'Coffee at Slaughter's—English Art and the Rococo, Part I', *Country Life.* Vol. 139, no. 3593, Jan. 13, 1966, pp. 58–61; 'Hogarth and His Friends—English Art and the Rococo, Part II', Vol. 139, no. 3595, Jan. 27, 1966, pp. 188–190; 'The Two Worlds of St. Martin's Lane—English Art and the Rococo, Part III', Vol. 139, no. 3596, Feb. 3, 1966, pp. 224–255.

Hayes, John. 'English Painting and the Rococo', *Apollo.* Vol. XC, no. 90, Aug. 1969, pp. 114–125.

SURVEYS AND LECTURES

Surveys

Baker, C. H. Collins, and James, M. R. *British Painting.* London: The Medici Society, 1933.

Borenius, Tancred. *La Peinture Anglaise Au XVIIIme Siècle.* Paris: Hyperion, 1938.

Edwards, Edward. *Anecdotes of Painters.* London: Leigh and Sotheby, W. J. and J. Richardson, R. Faulder, T. Payne and J. White, 1808.
An important source of information on Cotes's employment of Peter Toms, and on Cotes's prices; cf. Footnotes 48 and 51.

Gosse, Edmond. *British Portrait Painters and Engravers of the Eighteenth Century, Kneller to Reynolds.* London: Goupil and Co., 1906.
Cotes is viewed against the background of art in England in the 1740's.

Grundy, C. Reginald. *English Art in the Eighteenth Century.* London: The Studio, 1928.

Hutchinson, Sidney C. *The History of the Royal Academy, 1768–1968.* London: Chapman and Hall, 1968.

Noble, Mark. *A History of the College of Arms.* London: J. Debrett, 1804.
Information on Cotes's use of Peter Toms.

Redgrave, R. and S. *A Century of Painters of the English School,* first edition, London, 1886; second edition, London: Phaidon Press, 1949.

Sandby, William. *The History of the Royal Academy.* 2 vols. London: Longman, Green, Longman, Roberts, and Green, 1862.

Sée, R. R. M. *English Pastels, 1750–1830.* London. G. Bell and Sons, 1911.

Schönberger, Arno and Soehner, Halldor. *The Rococo Age.* London: McGraw-Hill, 1960.
Themes in rococo art; cf. Footnote 45.

Spielman, M. H. *British Portrait Painting to the Opening of the Nineteenth Century.* 2 vols. London: The Berlin Photographic Co., 1910.
Gainsborough is said to have been one of the pallbearers at Cotes's funeral. The source of this information is unknown; cf. Vol. I, p. 73 of Spielman.

Waterhouse, E. K. *Painting in Britain 1530–1790.* London and Baltimore: Penguin Books, 1953.
A brief critical appraisal of Cotes.

Whitley, William T. *Artists and their Friends in England.* 2 vols. London: The Medici Society, 1928.
A very helpful reference. The sources used by Whitley in his discussion of Cotes have been indexed in *The Whitley Papers,* now kept in the Print Room of the British Museum.

Lecture

Waterhouse, E. K. *Three Decades of British Art, 1740–1770.* Jayne Lectures for 1964. Philadelphia: American Philosophical Society, 1965.

CATALOGUES

Museums and Institutions

Allen, Josephine L. and Gardner, Elizabeth E. *A Concise Catalogue of the European Paintings in the Metropolitan Museum of Art.* New York: The Metropolitan Museum, 1954.
Cf. no. 109.

Andrup, O. *Det Nationalhistoriske Museum pi Frederiksborg. Et udvalg af Museets Erhvervelsen, 1913–1925.* Frederiksborg: National historiske Museum, 1925.
Cf. no. 189.

Andrup, O. *Katalog over de udstillende Portraeeter og Genstande paa Frederiksborg.* Frederiksborg: Nationalhistoriske Museum, 1943.
Cf. no. 189.

Anon. *Catalogue of the Diploma and Gibson Galleries* (Royal Academy of Arts). London: William Clowes and Sons, 1939.
Cf. Appendix VI, no. 17.

Anon. *Catalogue of the National Portrait Gallery, 1856–1947.* London: National Portrait Gallery, 1949.
Cf. nos. 87 and 281.

Anon. *Catalogue of the New York Historical Society.* New York: The New York Historical Society.
Cf. no. 68.

Anon. *Concise Catalogue of Oil Paintings, National Gallery of Ireland.* Dublin: The Stationery Office, 1963.
Cf. no. 197 and Appendix VI, no. 9.

Anon. *Concise Catalogue of Paintings, National Maritime Museum, Greenwich.* London: Her Majesty's Stationery Office, 1958.
Cf. no. 239 and Appendix VI, no. 14.

Anon. *National Gallery Catalogue.* London: Printed for the Trustees, 1912.
Cf. no. 95.

Anon. *Scottish National Portrait Gallery.* Edinburgh: By Order of the Trustees, 1951.
Cf. no. 137.

Anon. *Summary Catalogue of European Paintings and Sculpture, National Gallery of Art.* Washington, D.C. National Gallery of Art, 1965.
Cf. no. 293 and Appendix VI, no. 19.

Anon. *The Dyce Collection. A Catalogue of Paintings, Miniatures, Drawings, Engravings, and Miscellaneous Objects Bequeathed by the Reverend Alexander Dyce, South Kensington Museum.* London: Her Majesty's Stationery Office, 1874.
Cf. no. 65.

Anon. *The Foundling Hospital, Catalogue of Pictures, Relics, and Works of Art.* London: The Foundling Hospital (now called the Thomas Coram Foundation for Children), 1946.
Cf. no. 86.

Anon. *The Frick Collection, An Illustrated Catalogue.* New York: The Frick Collection, 1968.
Cf. no. 79.

Baker, C. H. Collins. *Catalogue of British Paintings in the Henry E. Huntington Library and Art Gallery.* San Marino, California: Published by the Library, 1936.
Cf. nos. 22 and 119.

Binyon, Laurence. *Catalogue of Drawings by British Artists and Artists of Foreign Origins Working in Great Britain, Preserved in the Department of Prints and Drawings in the British Museum.* London: The British Museum, 1898.
Cf. nos. 80, 224, 230, and Appendix VI, no. 13.

Chamot, Mary. *The Tate Gallery, British School.* London: Printed for the Trustees, 1953.
Cf. nos. 95, 174, 232, and Appendix VI, no. 1.

Davies, Martin. *British School.* National Gallery Catalogue. London: Printed for the Trustees, 1946.
This is an interesting catalogue because it lists the pictures by Cotes formerly at the National Gallery and now at the Tate, nos. 174, 232, and Appendix VI, no. 1. There is also information on no. 259.

Hoff, Ursula. *European Paintings before Eighteen Hundred.* Melbourne: National Gallery of Victoria, 1967.
Cf. Appendix VI, no. 18.

O'Donoghue, Freeman and Hake, Sir Henry M. *Catalogue of Engraved British Portraits . . . in the British Museum.* 6 vols. London: The British Museum, 1908–1925.
Most of the engravings after portraits by Cotes are listed here. It should be noted, however, that not all the entries in this catalogue refer to engravings; occasionally the reference is to a photograph or illustration in the British Museum's collection.

Shaw, J. Byam. *Paintings by Old Masters at Christ Church, Oxford.* London: Phaidon Press, 1967.
Cf. no. 269.

Valentiner, W. R. *Catalogue of Paintings, North Carolina Museum of Art.* Raleigh: By Order of the Trustees, 1956.
Cf. no. 173.

Other Collections

Adams, C. K. A. *A Catalogue of the Pictures in the Garrick Club.* London: Published by the Club, 1936.
Cf. no. 184.

Anon. *Catalogue of Pictures of Dunrobin Castle.* Dunrobin Castle, Sutherland: Privately Printed, 1908.
Cf. Supplement no. 11.

Anon. *Catalogue of Pictures at Dunrobin Castle.* Dunrobin Castle, Sutherland: Privately Printed, 1921.
Cf. Supplement no. 11.

Borenius, Tancred and Hodgson, J. V. *A Catalogue of the Pictures at Elton Hall in Huntingdonshire in the Possession of Colonel Douglas James Proby.* London: The Medici Society, 1924.
Cf. nos. 25, 26, 27, and 29.

Duleep Singh, Prince Frederick. *Portraits in Norfolk Houses.* 2 vols. Norwich: Jarrold and Sons, 1928.

A valuable source of information used frequently throughout the catalogue.

Farrer, Rev. Edmund. *Portraits in Suffolk Houses* (*West*). London: Bernard Quaritch, 1908.

Farrer, Rev. Edmund. *Portraits in Suffolk Houses* (*East*). 5 vols. in MS., deposited at the Ipswich Public Library, n.d.
A valuable source of information used frequently throughout the catalogue.

Goulding, Richard W. *Catalogue of the Pictures Belonging to His Grace The Duke of Portland, K.G. At Welbeck Abbey, 17 Hill Street, London, and Langwell House*. Cambridge: The University Press, 1936.
Cf. nos. 208, 211, and 212. This catalogue is particularly valuable because the author has reproduced the bill from Cotes for the three pictures mentioned above.

Holland, Gifford Laurence. *A Descriptive and Historical Catalogue of the Collection of Pictures at Hatfield House and 20 Arlington Street*. Privately Printed, 1891.

Millar, Oliver. *The Later Georgian Pictures in the Collection of Her Majesty The Queen*. 2 vols. London: Phaidon Press, 1969.
For pictures by Cotes in the collection cf. nos. 205, 215, 220, 267, and 273; Millar also discusses nos. 188, 189, 206, and 272.

Steegman, John. *A Survey of Portraits in Welsh Houses*. 2 vols. Cardiff: National Museum of Wales, Vol. I, 1957; Vol. II, 1962.

Prints

De Vesme, A. and Calabi, A. *Francesco Bartolozzi, Catalogue des Estampes*. Milan: Guido Modiano, 1928.
Cf. nos. 251, 252, and Appendix V, no. 40.

Smith, John Chaloner. *British Mezzotinto Portraits*. 5 vols., and a portfolio of plates. London: Henry Sotheran and Co., 1878–1883.

Also cf. O'Donoghue and Hake, *Catalogue of Engraved British Portraits . . . in the British Museum*, listed under *Museums and Institutions*.

Exhibitions

Cummings, Frederick and Staley, Allen. *Romantic Art in Britain, Paintings and Drawings, 1760–1860*. Philadelphia: Philadelphia Museum of Arts, 1968.
Cf. Footnotes 60 and 61.

Other exhibition catalogues are fully documented in the Catalogue of Cotes's works; cf. Index of Exhibited Pictures. One of these is of particular importance:

Smart, Alastair. 'Introducing Francis Cotes, R.A.', Nottingham University Art Gallery, Nottingham, Nov. 5–27, 1971.
This was the first exhibition ever devoted exclusively to Cotes's work; cf. *CAN.*, pp. 51–52.

Sales Catalogues After 1800

These are fully documented in the Catalogue of Cotes's works.

HAND LISTS

Anon. *Check List of the Edward C. and Mary Walker Collection*. Washington, D.C.: Corcoran Gallery of Art, n.d.
Cf. Appendix VI, no. 15.

Hoare, Sir Richard Colt. *A List of the Contents of Stourhead*, in MS. Stourhead House, Stourton, Wiltshire, c. 1818.
Cf. nos. 72 and 76.

St. John Gore, Robert. 'Pictures in National Trust Houses', *The Burlington Magazine*. Vol. CXI, no. 793, April 1969, pp. 237–262.
Cf. nos. 32, 72, 76, 110, 204, and Appendix VI, nos. 36 and 37.

GUIDES AND MUSEUM PAMPHLETS

Anon. *Gorhambury*. A Guide with an Inventory of Pictures. Privately Printed, 1938.
Cf. no. 175.

Anon. *Victoria and Albert Museum, Portrait Drawings*. London: Her Majesty's Stationery Office, 1948.
Cf. no. 65.

Grundy, C. Reginald and Davidson, Sydney L. *Illustrated Guide to the Lady Lever Collection*. Port Sunlight, Cheshire: Lady Lever Gallery, Published by the Trustees, 1956.
Cf. Appendix VI, no. 25.

WORKS ON OTHER ARTISTS CITED

Anon. 'Samuel Cotes, Esq.', *The Gentleman's Magazine*, Mar. 1814, p. 403.
This obituary of Francis Cotes's brother contains some valuable information on their father, Robert Cotes.

Dilke, Emilia Lady. *French Architects and Sculptors of the Eighteenth Century*. London: George Bell and Sons, 1900.
Cf. no. 284.

Esdaile, Katherine Ada. *The Life and Works of Louis François Roubiliac*. Oxford: University Press, 1928.
Cf. no. 82, Cotes's portrait of Roubiliac.

Gunnis, Rupert. *Dictionary of British Sculptors, 1600–1851*. London: The Abbey Library, 1969.
Cf. no. 71.

Graves, Algernon and Cronin, William Vine. *A History of the Works of Sir Joshua Reynolds, P.R.A.* 4 vols. London: Henry Graves and Co., 1899–1901.
Cf. no. 244.

Harris, John. *Sir William Chambers, Knight of the Polar Star*. London: A. Zwemmer, 1970.
Harris mentions no. 137 and Appendix VI, nos. 5 and 33; for other portraits of Chambers and his daughters, cf. nos. 117, 136, and Appendix VI, no. 6.

Levey, Michael. *Painting in XVIII Century Venice*. London: Phaidon Press, 1959.

Milner, James D. 'Tilly Kettle', *The Walpole Society*. Vol. XVI. Oxford: The Walpole Society, 1926–1927, pp. 49–104.

Kettle's works are often confused with those of Cotes. For information on Kettle this is the best source.

Northcote, James, R. A. *The Life of Sir Joshua Reynolds.* 2 vols. London: Henry Colburn, 1819.
An interesting discussion of Cotes, but an incorrect reading of his prices.

Sandby, William. *Thomas and Paul Sandby, Royal Academicians.* London: Seeley and Co., 1892.
Cotes's portraits of members of the Sandby family are mentioned.

Ward, Humphrey and Roberts, W. *Romney.* London: Thomas Agnew and Sons, 1904.
Information on Cotes's house, which was bought by Romney.

Waterhouse, E. K. *Reynolds.* London: Kegan Paul, Trench Trubner and Co., 1941.
Reynolds and Cotes are compared.

BIOGRAPHIES OF SITTERS

Alec-Smith, Col. R. A. 'The Maisters of Hull', *Country Life.* Vol. CVII, no. 2765, Jan. 13, 1950.
Cf. no. 166.

Bleackley, Ruth M. 'The Beautiful Misses Gunning', *The Connoisseur,* Vol. 12, nos. 47 and 48, Jul. and Aug., 1905, pp. 158–164 and 227–232, respectively.

Chapman, Hester W. *Caroline Matilda, Queen of Denmark, 1751–1775.* London: Jonathan Cape, 1971.
Cf. Footnote 64.

Cope, Joan Penelope. *Bramshill, the Memoirs of Joan Penelope Cope.* Bungay: Richard Clay and Co., 1938.
Cf. no. 185.

Cripps-Day, F. H. 'Cripps and Kitchener', *The Connoisseur.* Vol. 90, no. 372, Aug. 1932, pp. 76–81, 95.
Cf. nos. 91 and 92.

Cust, Albinia Lucy (Mrs. Wherry). *The Chronicles of Erdigg on the Wyke.* London: John Lane, 1914.
Cf. no. 235.

James, Philip. 'A Cotes Enigma', *The Connoisseur.* Vol. 90, no. 372, Aug. 1932, pp. 98–99.
Cf. no. 284.

Oswald, Arthur. 'Breamore House—Hampshire, Parts II and III', *Country Life.* Vol. CXXI, nos. 3153 and 3154, Je. 20 and Je. 27, 1957, pp. 1268–1271 and 1320–1323, respectively.
Cf. nos. 77, 97, and 101.

Roberts, W. *Deborah, Lady Dering by Francis Cotes, R.A.* London: Chiswick Press, 1920, pp. 1–8.
Cf. no. 217.

Roberts, W. *The Misses Prosser by Francis Cotes, R.A.* London: Chiswick Press, 1919, pp. 1–8.
Cf. Appendix VI, no. 52.

Roberts, W. *Miss Elizabeth Crewe by Francis Cotes, R.A.* London: Chiswick Press, 1920, pp. 1–8.
Cf. no. 293.

Russell, Constance Lady. *Three Generations of Fascinating Women.* London: Longmans, Green, and Co., 1904.
One of the best sources of information on the Gunnings.

Taylor, Sir Herbert. *The Taylor Papers.* London: Longmans, Green, and Co., 1913.
Cf. no. 85.

Wildridge, T. Tindall. *Old and New Hull.* Hull: M. D. Peck and Son, 1884.
Cf. no. 166.

WORKS ON COSTUME

Books

Cunnington, C. Willet and Cunnington, Phillis. *Handbook of English Costume in the Seventeenth Century.* London: Faber and Faber, 1955.

Cunnington, C. Willet and Cunnington, Phillis. *Handbook of English Costume in the Eighteenth Century.* London: Faber and Faber, 1957.

Jarrett, Dudley. *British Naval Dress.* London: J. M. Dent and Sons, 1960.

Reynolds, P. W. *Military Costume in the 18th and 19th Centuries.* MS. vols., now kept at the Victoria and Albert Museum Library, London, n.d.

Articles

Nevinson, J. L. 'Vandyke Dress', *The Connoisseur.* Vol. 157, no. 633. Nov. 1964, pp. 166–171.

Pearce, Stella Mary. 'The Study of Costume in Paintings', *Studies in Conservation.* Vol. 4, no. 4, Nov. 1959, pp. 127–139.

Steegman, John. 'A Drapery Painter of the Eighteenth Century', *The Connoisseur.* Vol. 97, no. 418, June 1936, pp. 309–315.

LIST OF ILLUSTRATIONS OF WORKS BY OTHER ARTISTS

Plate III D. P. Pariset: *Francis Cotes*. Stipple engraving after a drawing of 1768 by Pierre Falconet, $6\frac{7}{8}\times4\frac{7}{8}$ in. British Museum, London.

Fig. 1 George Knapton: *John Spencer, later 1st Earl Spencer*, and an *Unknown Child*. Pastel on paper, $23\frac{3}{4}\times29\frac{3}{4}$ in. c. 1740. The Earl Spencer, Althorp, Northamptonshire.

Fig. 2 George Knapton: *The Hon. John Spencer and his Son, John, later 1st Earl Spencer, with their Servant Caesar Shaw*. Oil on canvas 98×60 in. Signed and dated 1749. The Earl Spencer, Althorp, Northamptonshire.

Fig. 3 Rosalba Carriera: *Lady Sophia Fermor*. Pastel on paper, 23×17 in. 1714. By permission of the Earl of Shelburne, Bowood, Calne, Wiltshire. Photograph Courtauld Institute.

Fig. 9 Hubert Gravelot: *The Good Mother*. Engraving for an early edition of Richardson's *Pamela*, text on the reverse, $4\frac{3}{4}\times3\frac{3}{4}$ in. n.d. By courtesy of the Victoria and Albert Museum, London.

Fig. 10 Francis Hayman: *Lovers in a Landscape*. Oil on canvas, $19\frac{1}{2}\times21$ in. c. 1740–50. Mr. and Mrs. Paul Mellon Collection, U.S.A.

Fig. 11 Joseph Highmore: *Pamela Asks Sir Jacob Swinford's Blessing*. Oil on canvas, 24×29 in. 1743–4. Tate Gallery, London.

Fig. 15 Jean-Etienne Liotard: *Lady Mary Fawkener*. Pastel on paper, $29\times23\frac{1}{2}$ in. c. 1754. The Hon. P. M. Samuel, Farley Hall, Farley Hill, Berkshire.

Fig. 16 Anton Raphael Mengs: *Louis de Silvestre*. Pastel on paper, approximately 23×18 in. c. 1750. Staatliche Kunstsammlungen, Dresden.

Fig. 19 Maurice-Quentin de la Tour: *Claude Dupouch*. Pastel on paper. $23\frac{3}{8}\times19\frac{5}{8}$ in. c. 1740. National Gallery of Art, Washington, D.C., Samuel H. Kress Collection.

Fig. 20 Allan Ramsay: *Margaret Lindsay* (the artist's wife). Oil on canvas, 30×25 in. c. 1754. By courtesy of the National Gallery of Scotland, Edinburgh.

Fig. 22 Sir Joshua Reynolds: *The Duchess of Hamilton as Venus*. Oil on canvas. $92\frac{7}{8}\times57\frac{1}{2}$ in. Exhibited with the Society of Artists in 1760. By courtesy of The Trustees of the Lady Lever Art Gallery, Port Sunlight, Cheshire.

Fig. 23 Edward Fisher: *Anne Sandby as Emma, the Nut-Brown Maid*. Mezzotint engraving, $13\frac{1}{2}\times11$ in. (after an oil portrait of 1759 by Francis Cotes, no. 96), published in 1763. British Museum, London.

Fig. 26 Paul Sandby: *Rochester, a View of the Castle from across the Medway*. Watercolour with ink on paper, $12\frac{5}{8}\times18\frac{3}{4}$ in. Whitworth Art Gallery, University of Manchester.

Fig. 27 Sir Joshua Reynolds: *Lady Anstruther*. Oil on canvas, $48\frac{3}{4}\times39$ in. 1761. Tate Gallery, London.

Fig. 29 Sir Joshua Reynolds: *Rear-Admiral George Brydges Rodney, later Admiral and 1st Baron Rodney*. Oil on canvas, 50×40 in. 1761. The Lord Egremont, Petworth House, Petworth, Sussex.

Fig. 32 Sir Joshua Reynolds: *Captain Augustus Hervey, later 3rd Earl of Bristol*. Oil, on canvas, $49\frac{1}{4}\times39\frac{5}{8}$ in. 1762. Private Collection, U.K.

Fig. 34 Sir Joshua Reynolds: *Lady Elizabeth Keppel, later Marchioness of Tavistock*. Oil on canvas, $94\times58\frac{1}{2}$ in. 1761–2. The Marquess of Tavistock, Woburn Abbey, Woburn, Bedfordshire.

Fig. 35 Sir Joshua Reynolds: *Commodore Augustus Keppel, later Admiral and Viscount Keppel*. Oil on canvas, 94×58 in. 1753–4. National Maritime Museum, Greenwich.

Fig. 36 Sir Joshua Reynolds: *The Ladies Elizabeth and Henrietta Montagu*. Oil on canvas, $59\frac{7}{8}\times43\frac{3}{4}$ in. 1763. The Duke of Buccleuch and Queensberry, U.K.

Fig. 39 Sir Joshua Reynolds: *The Hon. Harriet Bouverie, later Lady Tilney-Long*. Oil on canvas, $31\frac{1}{2}\times37\frac{3}{4}$ in. 1764. The Earl of Radnor, Longford Castle, Salisbury, Wiltshire.

Fig. 47 James Watson: *William Campbell Skinner*. Mezzotint engraving, $11\frac{3}{8}\times9$ in. (after a pastel portrait by Francis Cotes of c. 1764, no. 153). British Museum, London.

Fig. 49 Sir Joshua Reynolds. *Edward Lascelles, later 1st Earl of Harewood*. Oil on canvas $48\frac{3}{8}\times38\frac{5}{8}$ in. 1762–4. The Earl of Harewood, Harewood House, Harewood, Yorkshire.

Fig. 51 Allan Ramsay: *Philip, 2nd Earl Stanhope*. Oil on canvas, $49\times39\frac{1}{4}$ in. Signed and dated 1749. By permission of the Trustees of the Chevening Estate, Chevening, Kent. Photograph Courtauld Institute.

Fig. 52 Pompeo Battoni: *Sir John Armytage, 2nd Bt*. Oil on canvas, approximately 50×40 in. Inscribed and dated 1758. Formerly with Central Picture Galleries, New York.

Fig. 53 Sir Joshua Reynolds: *Sir John Anstruther*. Oil on canvas, $48\frac{3}{4}\times39$ in. 1761. Present whereabouts unknown.

Fig. 61 Sir Joshua Reynolds: *James Waldegrave, 2nd Earl Waldegrave*. Oil on canvas, $92\frac{7}{8}\times57\frac{1}{2}$ in. 1759. The Earl Waldegrave, Chewton House, Chewton Mendip, Bath.

Fig. 65 Sir Joshua Reynolds: *Captain Alexander Hood, later Vice-Admiral, 1st Viscount and Baron Bridport*. Oil on canvas, 50×40 in. 1764. National Maritime Museum, Greenwich.

Fig. 73 Allan Ramsay. *John, Lord Mountstuart, later 4th Earl and 1st Marquess of Bute*. Oil on canvas, 93 × 58 in. Signed and dated 1759. The Marquess of Bute, Mount Stuart, Rothesay, Isle of Bute.

Fig. 74 Sir Joshua Reynolds: *Thomas Lister, later 1st Lord Ribblesdale*. Oil on canvas, $90\frac{1}{2}\times55\frac{1}{8}$ in. 1764. By permission of the Earl of Swinton, U.K. Photograph Courtauld Institute.

Fig. 81 Sir Joshua Reynolds: *Lady Sarah Bunbury Sacrificing to the Three Graces*. Oil on canvas, 94×60 in. 1765. Art Institute, Chicago. W. W. Kimball Collection.

Fig. 87 Philippe Mercier: *The Letter Writer*. Oil on canvas, $49\times33\frac{3}{4}$ in. Probably painted in the 1740s. Iveagh Bequest, Marble Hill, Twickenham.

Fig. 88 Sir Joshua Reynolds: *James Paine and his Son*. Oil on canvas, $50\times44\frac{1}{4}$ in. 1764. Ashmolean Museum, Oxford.

Fig. 95 Allan Ramsay: *Lady Susan Fox-Strangeways*. Oil on canvas, $35\frac{1}{4}\times27\frac{1}{2}$ in. Signed and dated 1761. Lady Teresa Agnew, Melbury House, Dorchester, Dorset.

Fig. 96 Allan Ramsay: *Queen Charlotte*. Oil on canvas, 30×25 in. c. 1761. The Earl of Seafield, Cullen House, Cullen, Banffshire.

Fig. 97 Allan Ramsay: *Queen Charlotte*. Oil on canvas, 98×63 in. 1761. H.M. The Queen, Buckingham Palace. Reproduced by gracious permission of H.M. The Queen.

Fig. 98 Allan Ramsay: *Queen Charlotte and Her Children*. Oil on canvas, 98×64 in. 1763–1765. H.M. The Queen, Buckingham Palace. Reproduced by gracious permission of H.M. The Queen.

LIST OF OWNERS

LIST OF SITTERS